RADIANT

TONY VALENTE

CONTENTS

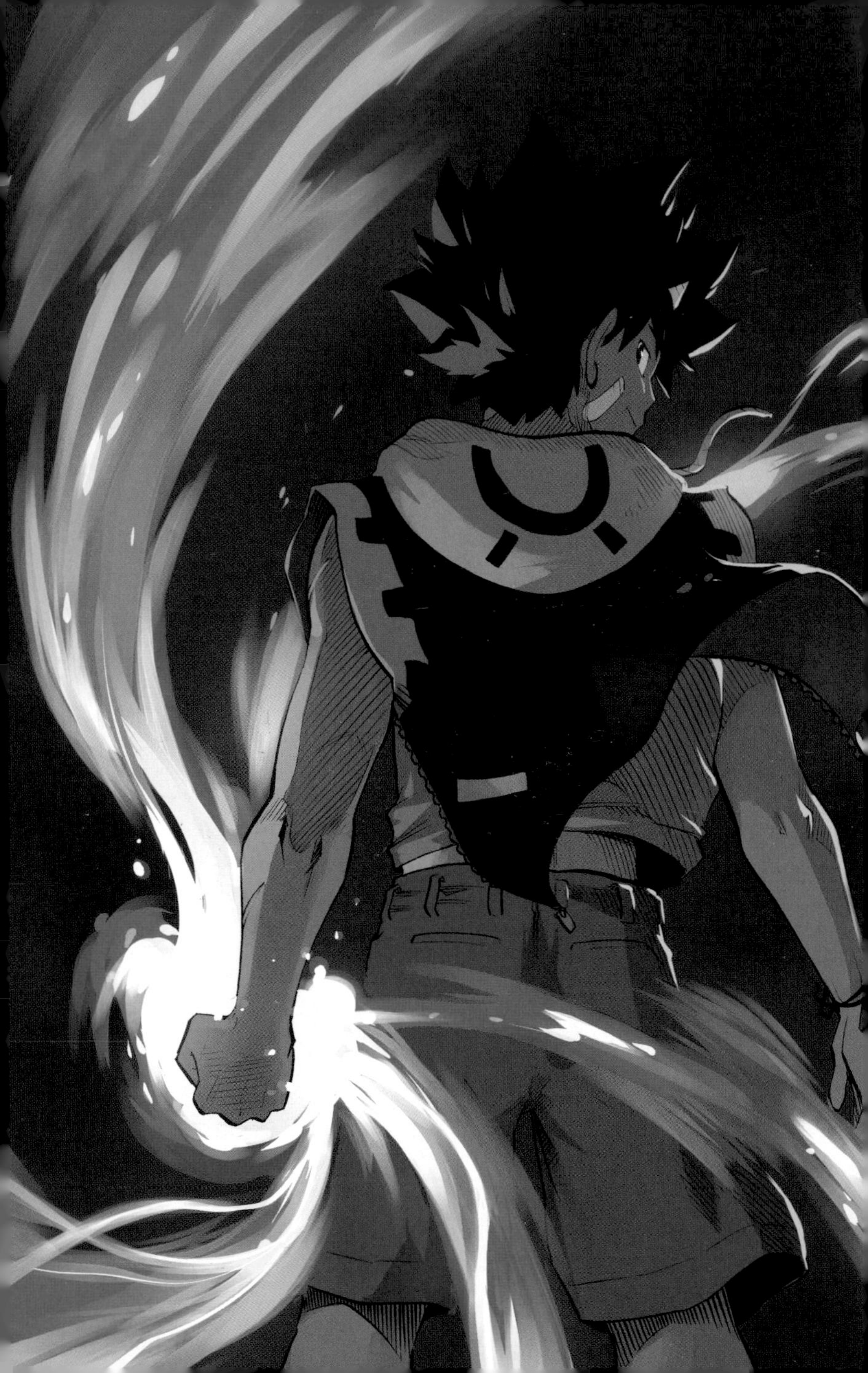

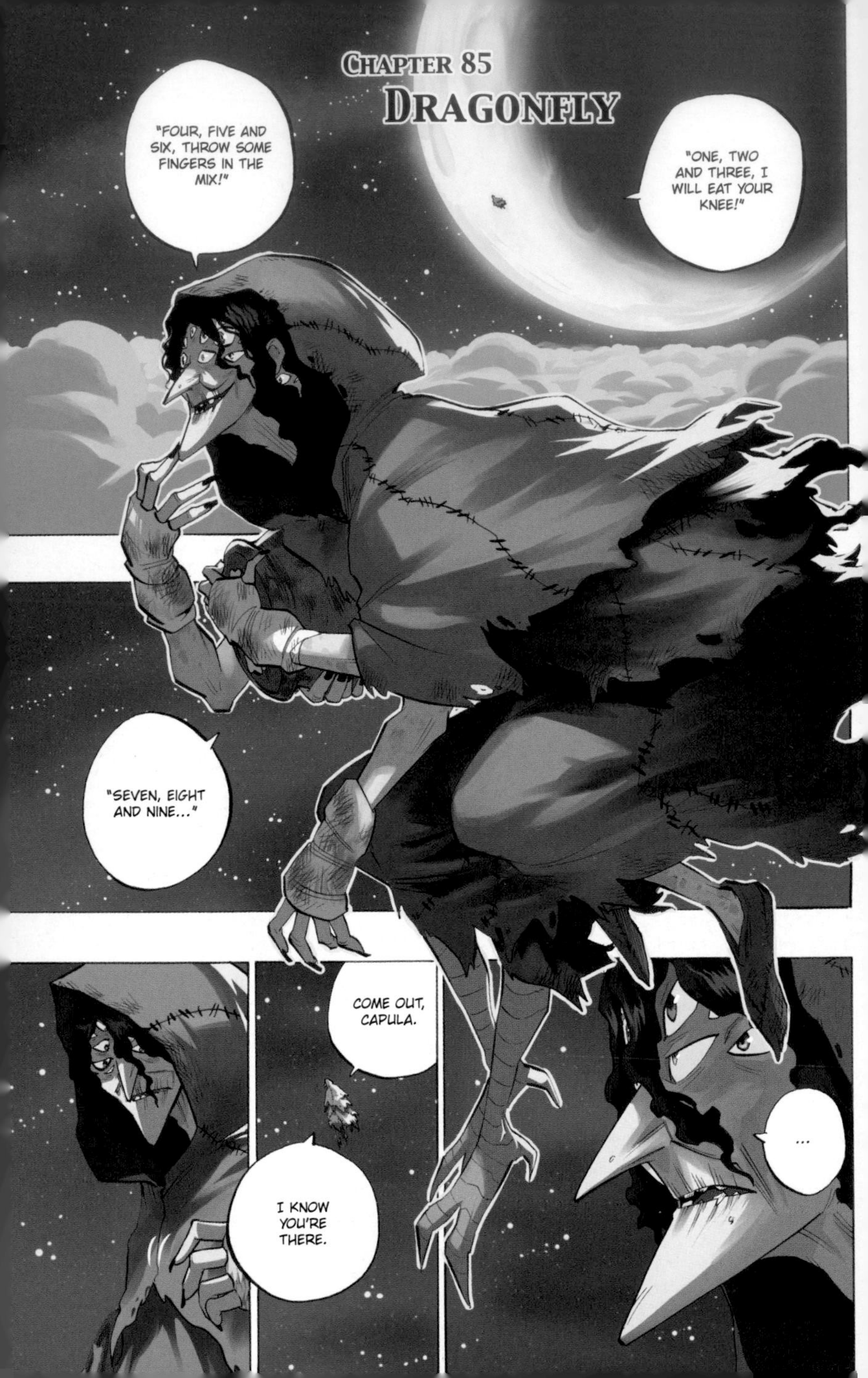
CHAPTER 85
DRAGONFLY
"ONE, TWO AND THREE, I WILL EAT YOUR KNEE!"
"FOUR, FIVE AND SIX, THROW SOME FINGERS IN THE MIX!"
"SEVEN, EIGHT AND NINE..."
...
COME OUT, CAPULA.
I KNOW YOU'RE THERE.

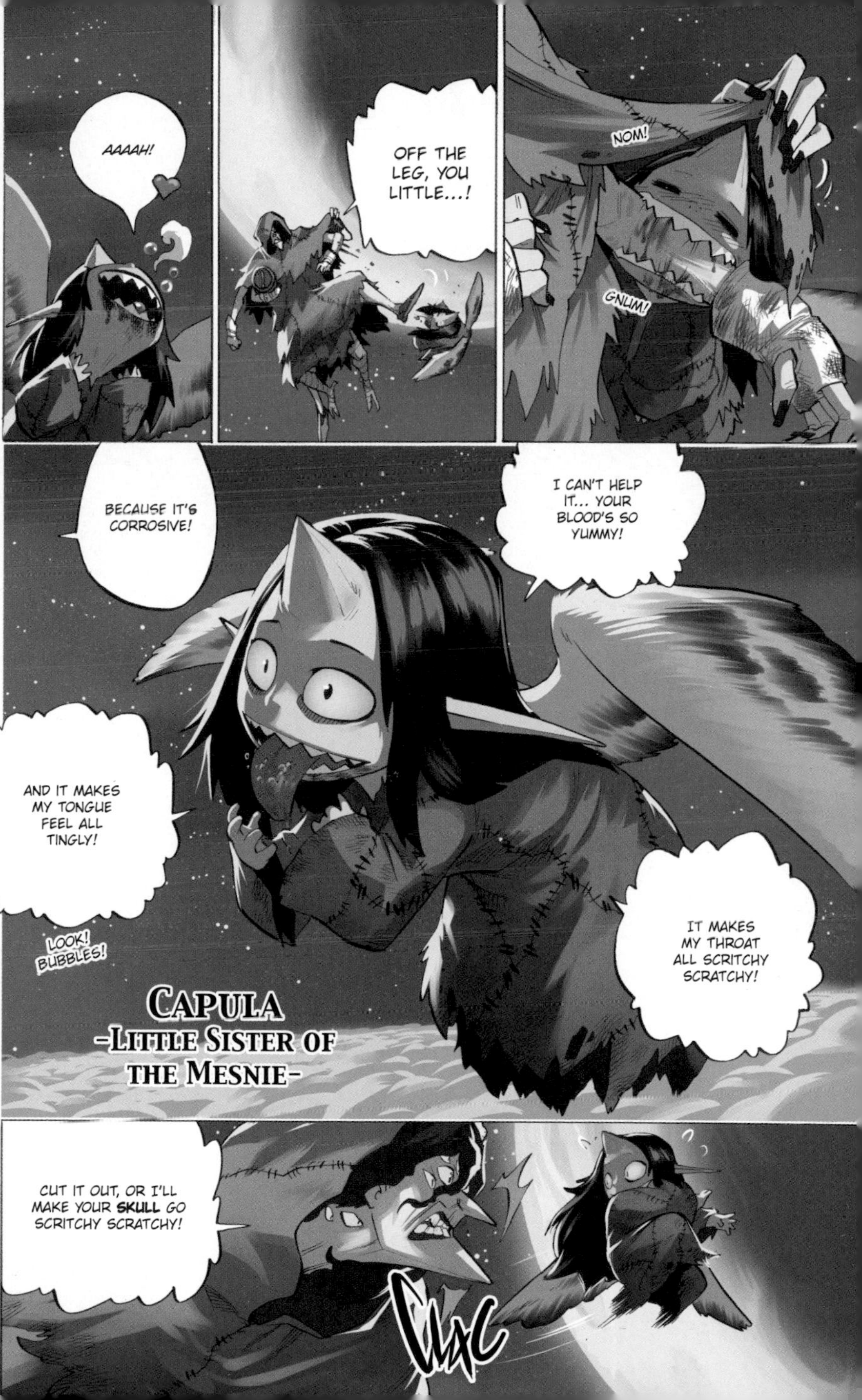
NOM!
GNUM!
OFF THE LEG, YOU LITTLE...!
AAAAH!
I CAN'T HELP IT... YOUR BLOOD'S SO YUMMY!
BECAUSE IT'S CORROSIVE!
IT MAKES MY THROAT ALL SCRITCHY SCRATCHY!
AND IT MAKES MY TONGUE FEEL ALL TINGLY!
LOOK! BUBBLES!
CAPULA
-LITTLE SISTER OF THE MESNIE-
CUT IT OUT, OR I'LL MAKE YOUR **SKULL** GO SCRITCHY SCRATCHY!
CLAC

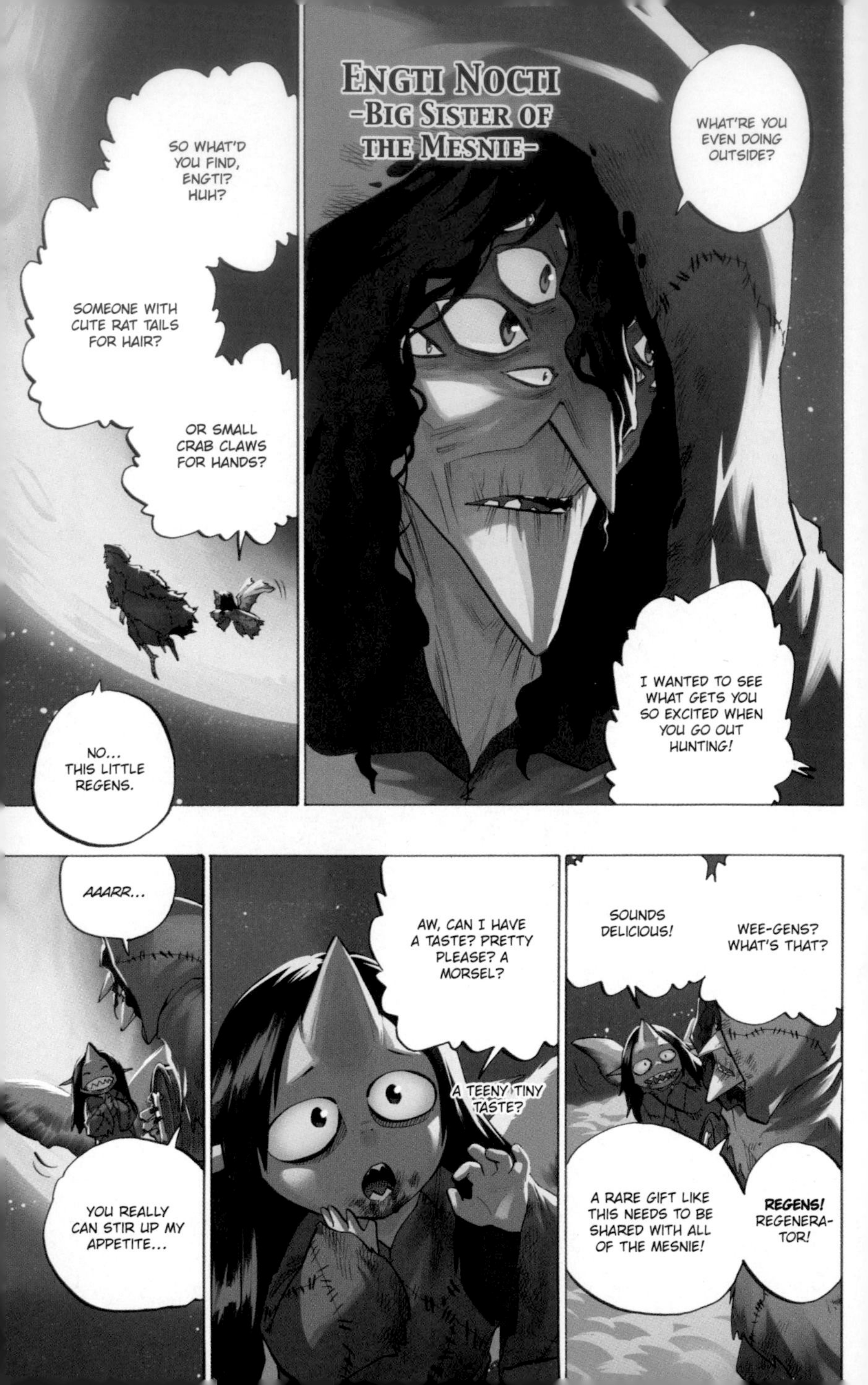
ENGTI NOCTI
-BIG SISTER OF THE MESNIE-
WHAT'RE YOU EVEN DOING OUTSIDE?
I WANTED TO SEE WHAT GETS YOU SO EXCITED WHEN YOU GO OUT HUNTING!
SO WHAT'D YOU FIND, ENGTI? HUH?
SOMEONE WITH CUTE RAT TAILS FOR HAIR?
OR SMALL CRAB CLAWS FOR HANDS?
NO... THIS LITTLE REGENS.
WEE-GENS? WHAT'S THAT?
SOUNDS DELICIOUS!
REGENS! REGENERA-TOR!
A RARE GIFT LIKE THIS NEEDS TO BE SHARED WITH ALL OF THE MESNIE!
AW, CAN I HAVE A TASTE? PRETTY PLEASE? A MORSEL?
A TEENY TINY TASTE?
AAARR...
YOU REALLY CAN STIR UP MY APPETITE...

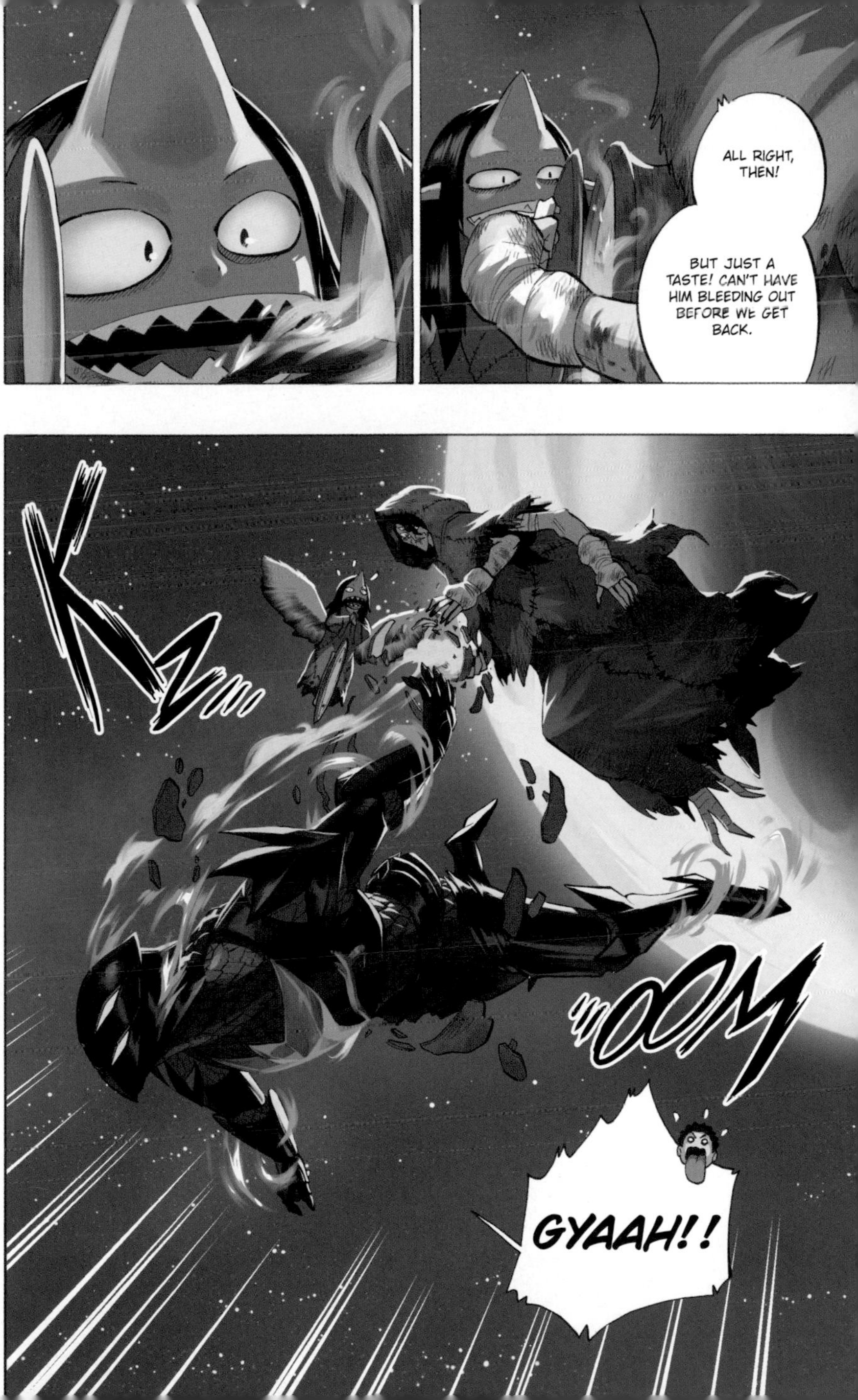
ALL RIGHT, THEN!
BUT JUST A TASTE! CAN'T HAVE HIM BLEEDING OUT BEFORE WE GET BACK.
KZ...
...OOM
GYAAH!!

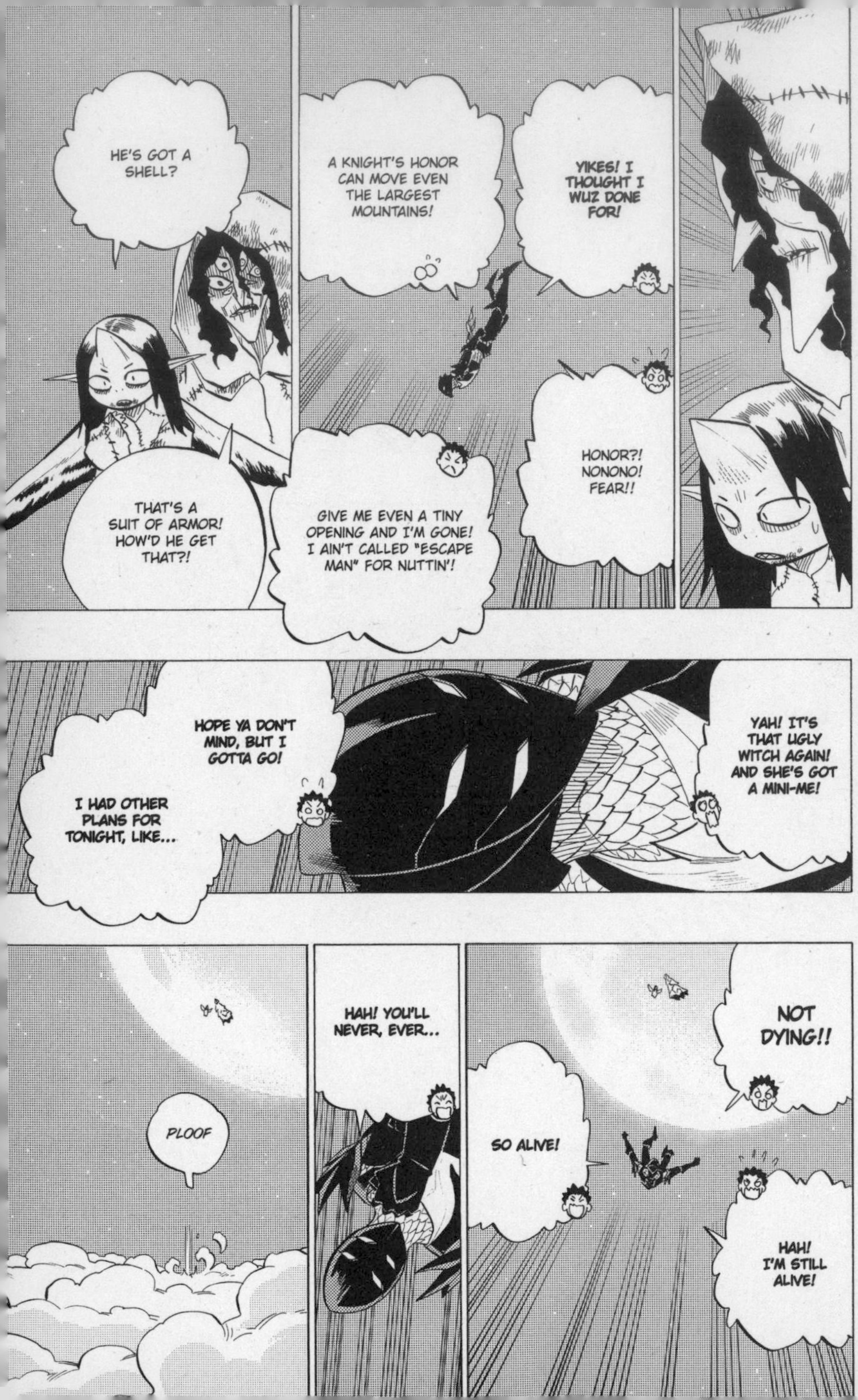
YIKES! I THOUGHT I WUZ DONE FOR!
A KNIGHT'S HONOR CAN MOVE EVEN THE LARGEST MOUNTAINS!
HONOR?! NONONO! FEAR!!
GIVE ME EVEN A TINY OPENING AND I'M GONE! I AIN'T CALLED "ESCAPE MAN" FOR NUTTIN'!
HE'S GOT A SHELL?
THAT'S A SUIT OF ARMOR! HOW'D HE GET THAT?!
YAH! IT'S THAT UGLY WITCH AGAIN! AND SHE'S GOT A MINI-ME!
HOPE YA DON'T MIND, BUT I GOTTA GO!
I HAD OTHER PLANS FOR TONIGHT, LIKE...
NOT DYING!!
SO ALIVE!
HAH! I'M STILL ALIVE!
HAH! YOU'LL NEVER, EVER...
PLOOF

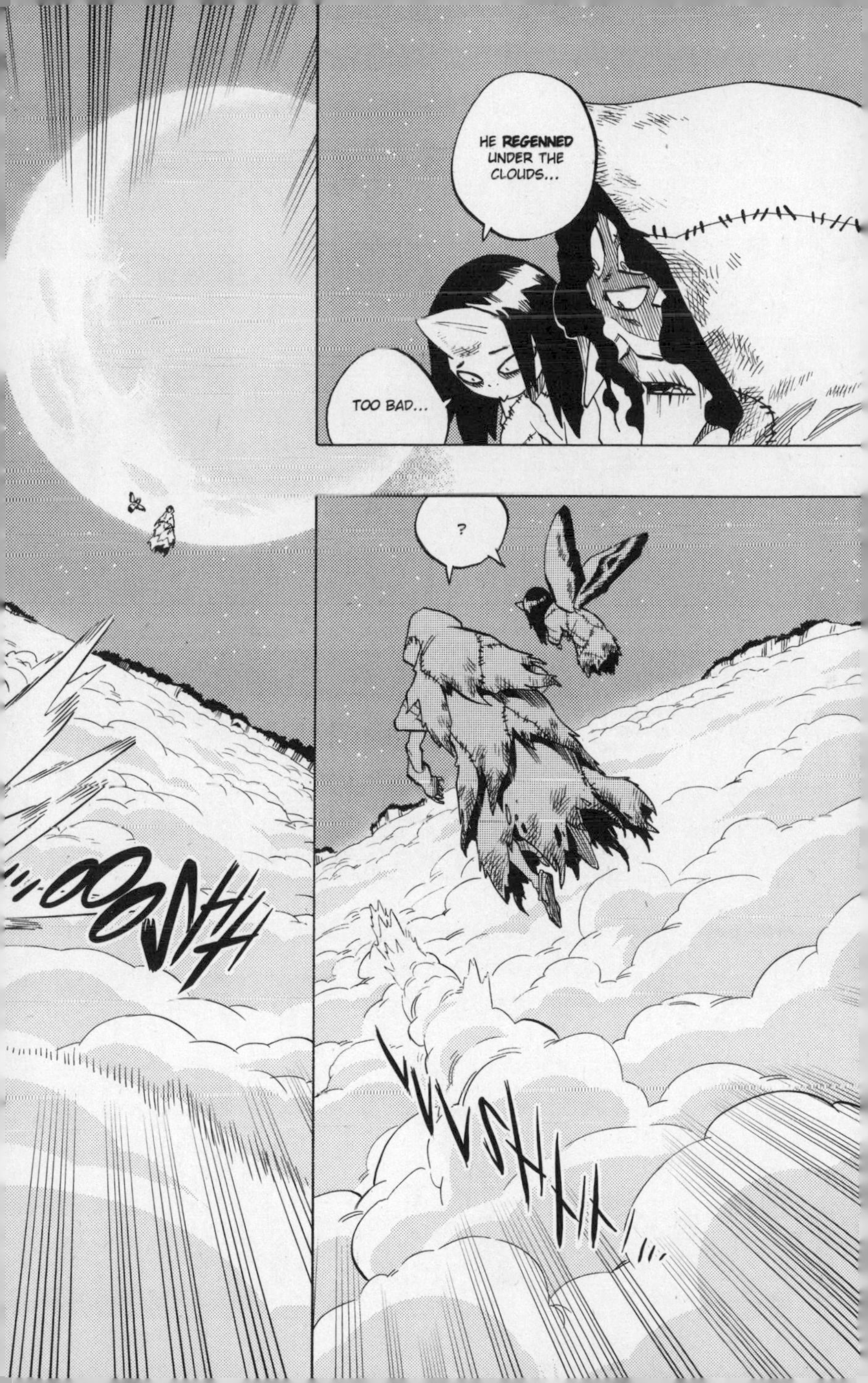
HE REGENNED UNDER THE CLOUDS...
TOO BAD...
?

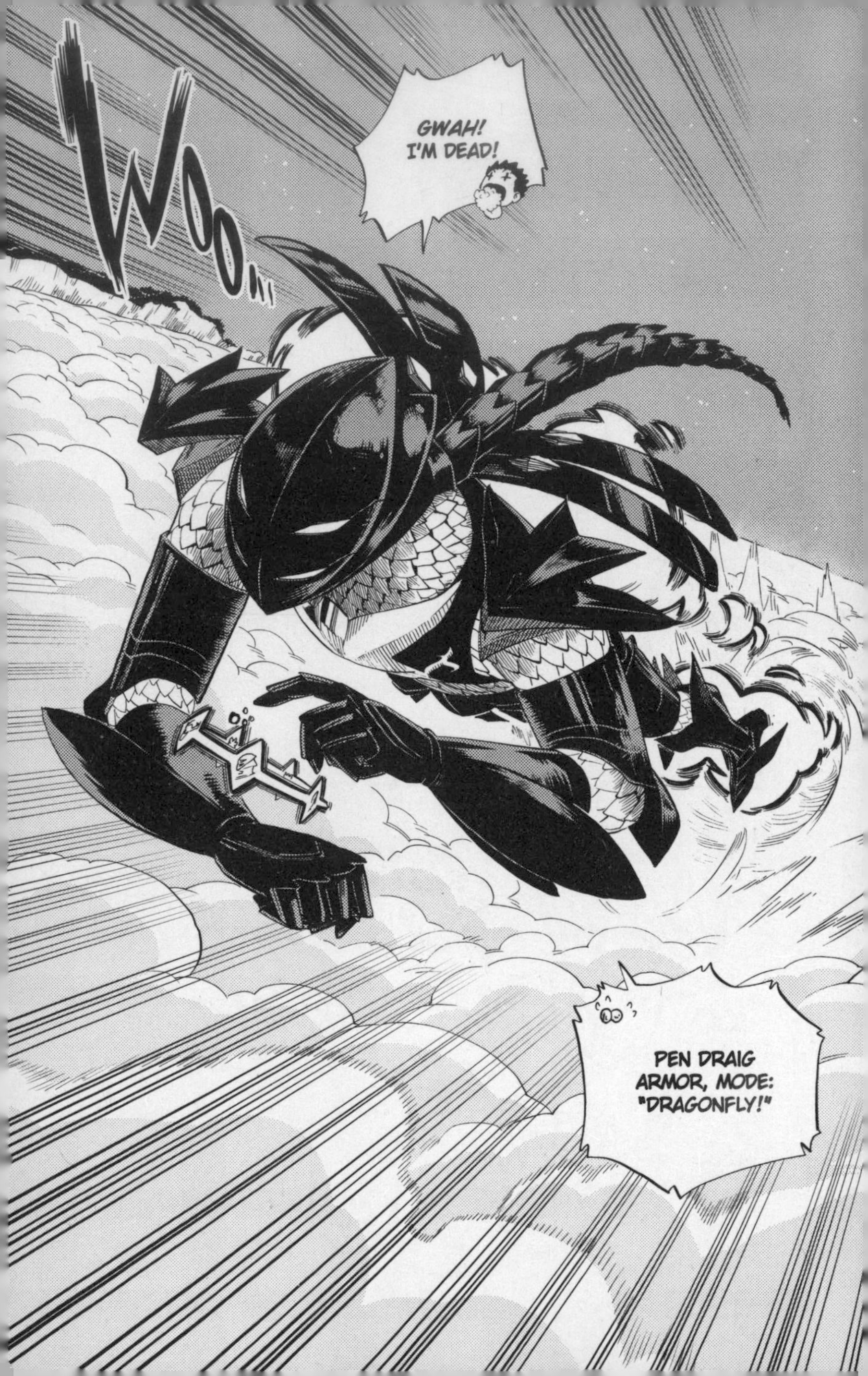
WOO...
GWAH! I'M DEAD!
PEN DRAIG ARMOR, MODE: "DRAGONFLY!"

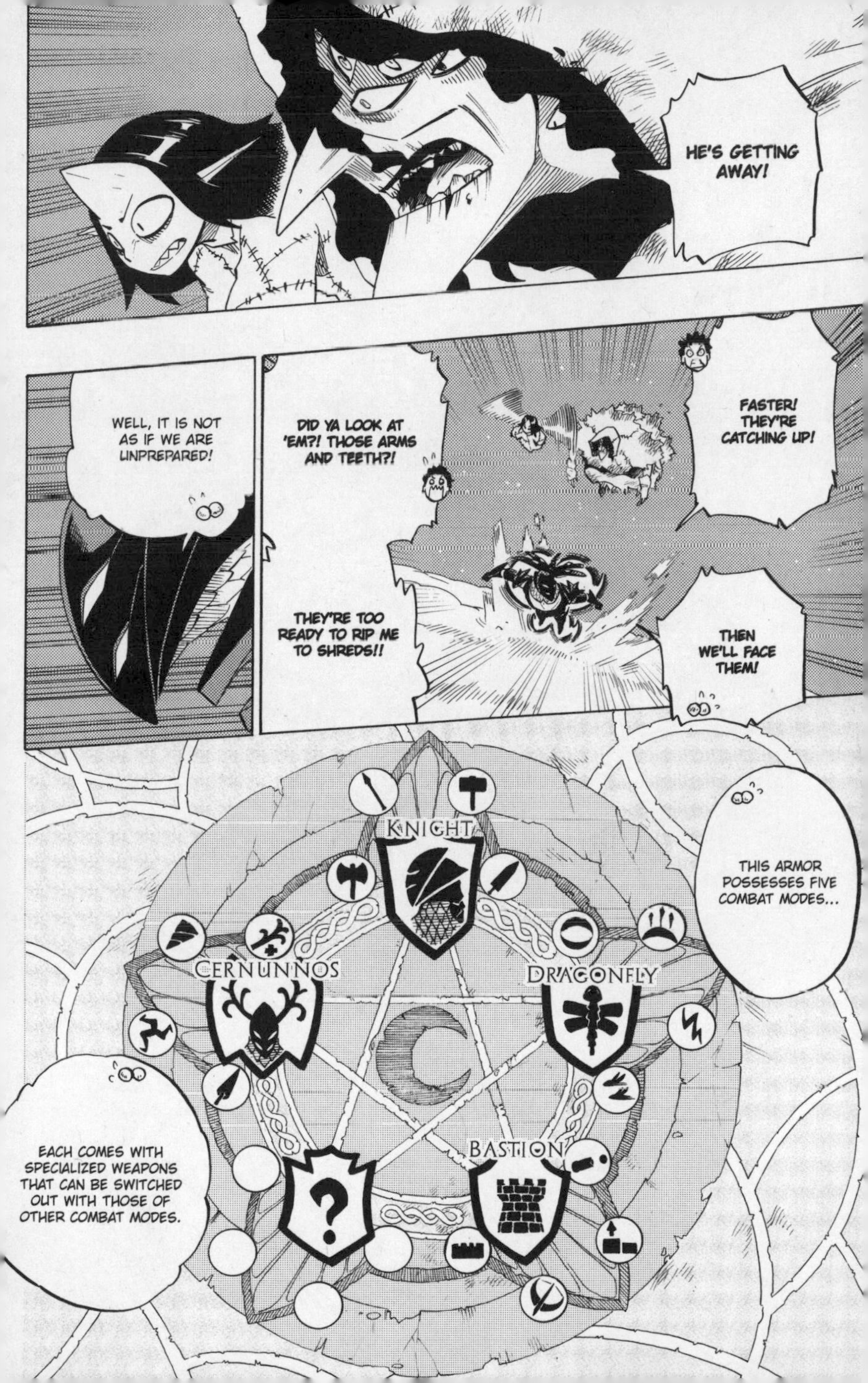
HE'S GETTING AWAY!
FASTER! THEY'RE CATCHING UP!
DID YA LOOK AT 'EM?! THOSE ARMS AND TEETH?!
THEY'RE TOO READY TO RIP ME TO SHREDS!!
THEN WE'LL FACE THEM!
WELL, IT IS NOT AS IF WE ARE UNPREPARED!
THIS ARMOR POSSESSES FIVE COMBAT MODES...
KNIGHT
DRAGONFLY
CERNUNNOS
BASTION
?
EACH COMES WITH SPECIALIZED WEAPONS THAT CAN BE SWITCHED OUT WITH THOSE OF OTHER COMBAT MODES.

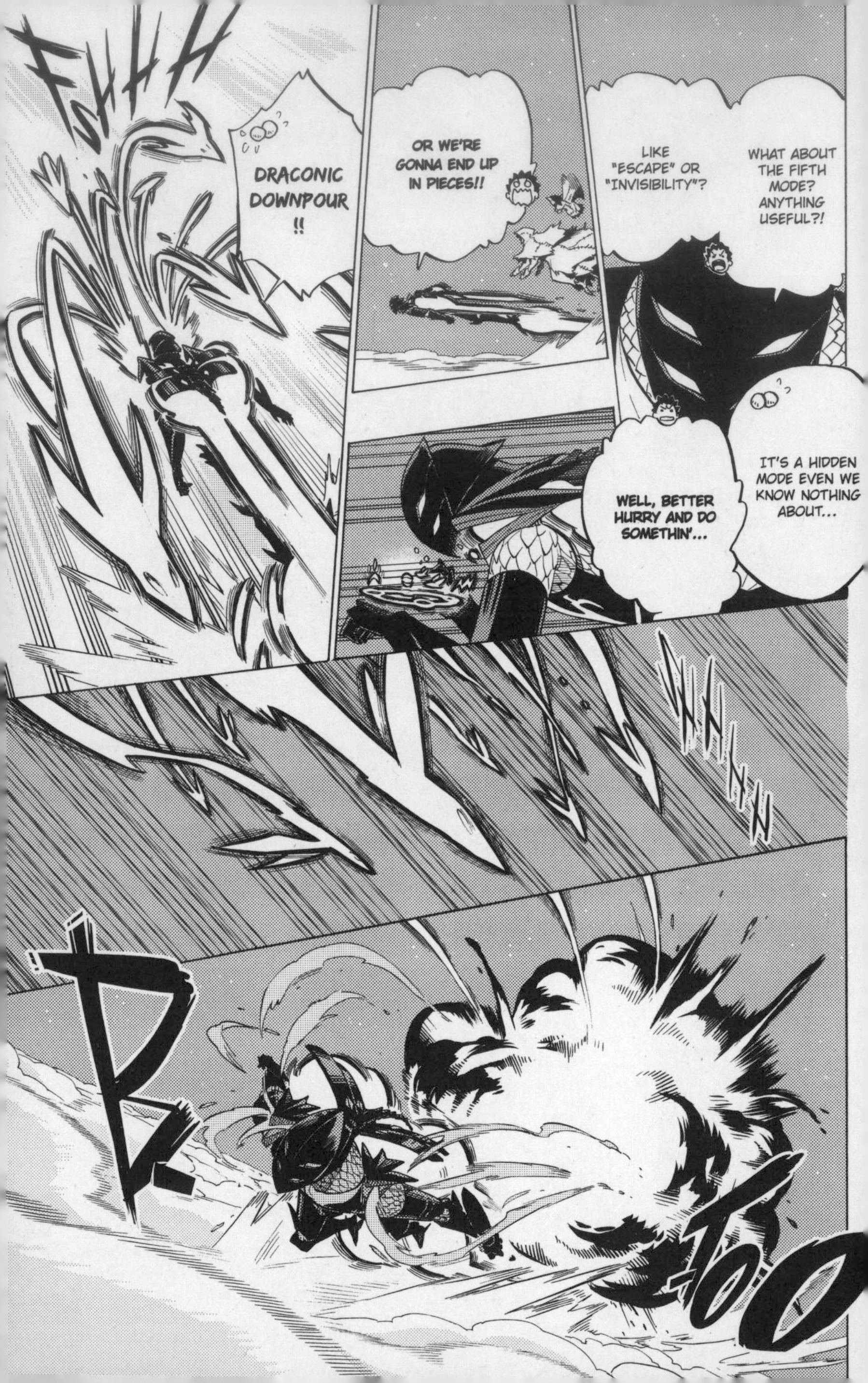
WHAT ABOUT THE FIFTH MODE? ANYTHING USEFUL?!
LIKE "ESCAPE" OR "INVISIBILITY"?
OR WE'RE GONNA END UP IN PIECES!!
IT'S A HIDDEN MODE EVEN WE KNOW NOTHING ABOUT...
WELL, BETTER HURRY AND DO SOMETHIN'...
FSHHH
DRACONIC DOWNPOUR !!
SHHHHH
B-DOO

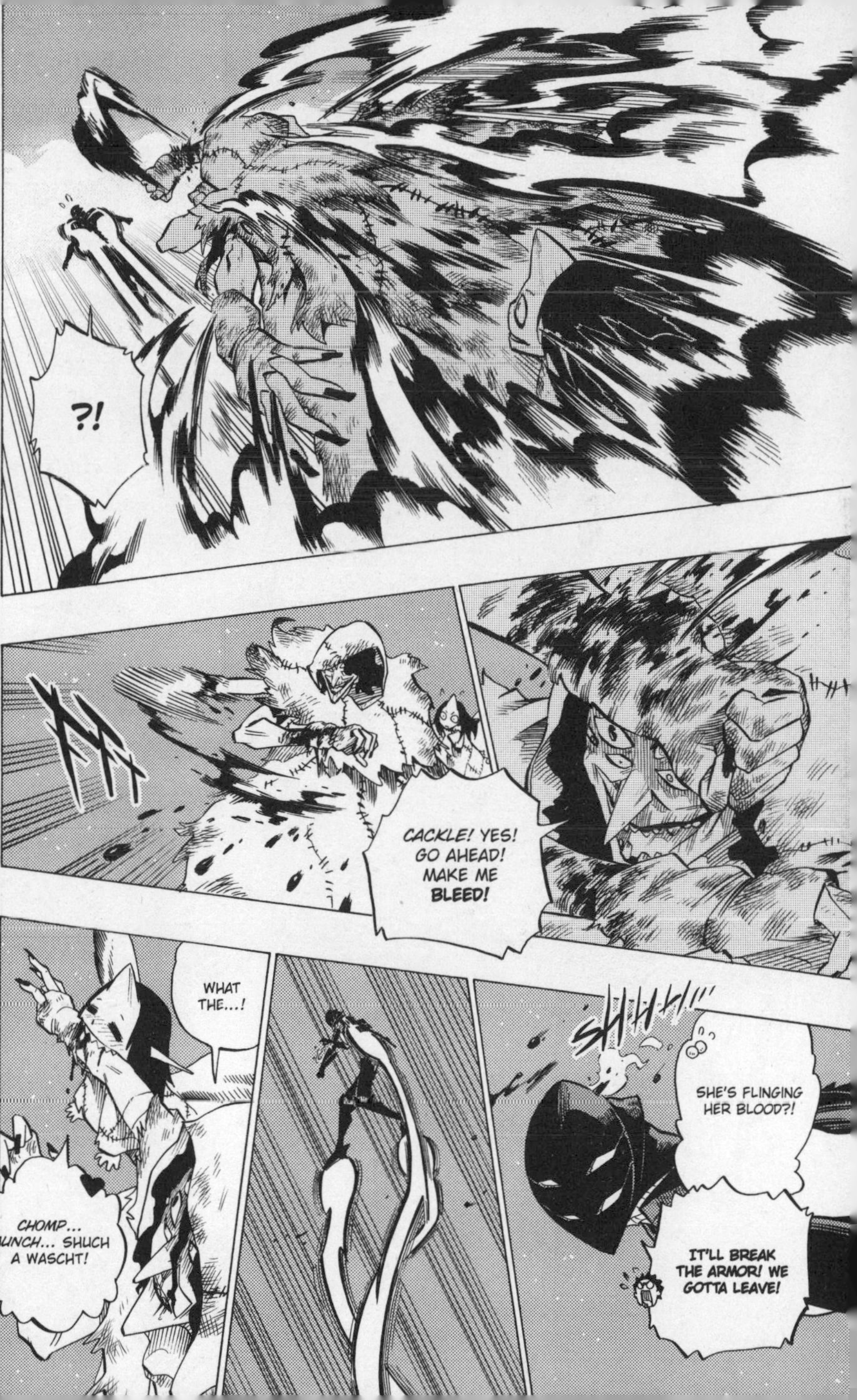
?!
CACKLE! YES! GO AHEAD! MAKE ME BLEED!
SHE'S FLINGING HER BLOOD?!
IT'LL BREAK THE ARMOR! WE GOTTA LEAVE!
WHAT THE...!
CHOMP... MUNCH... SHUCH A WASCHT!

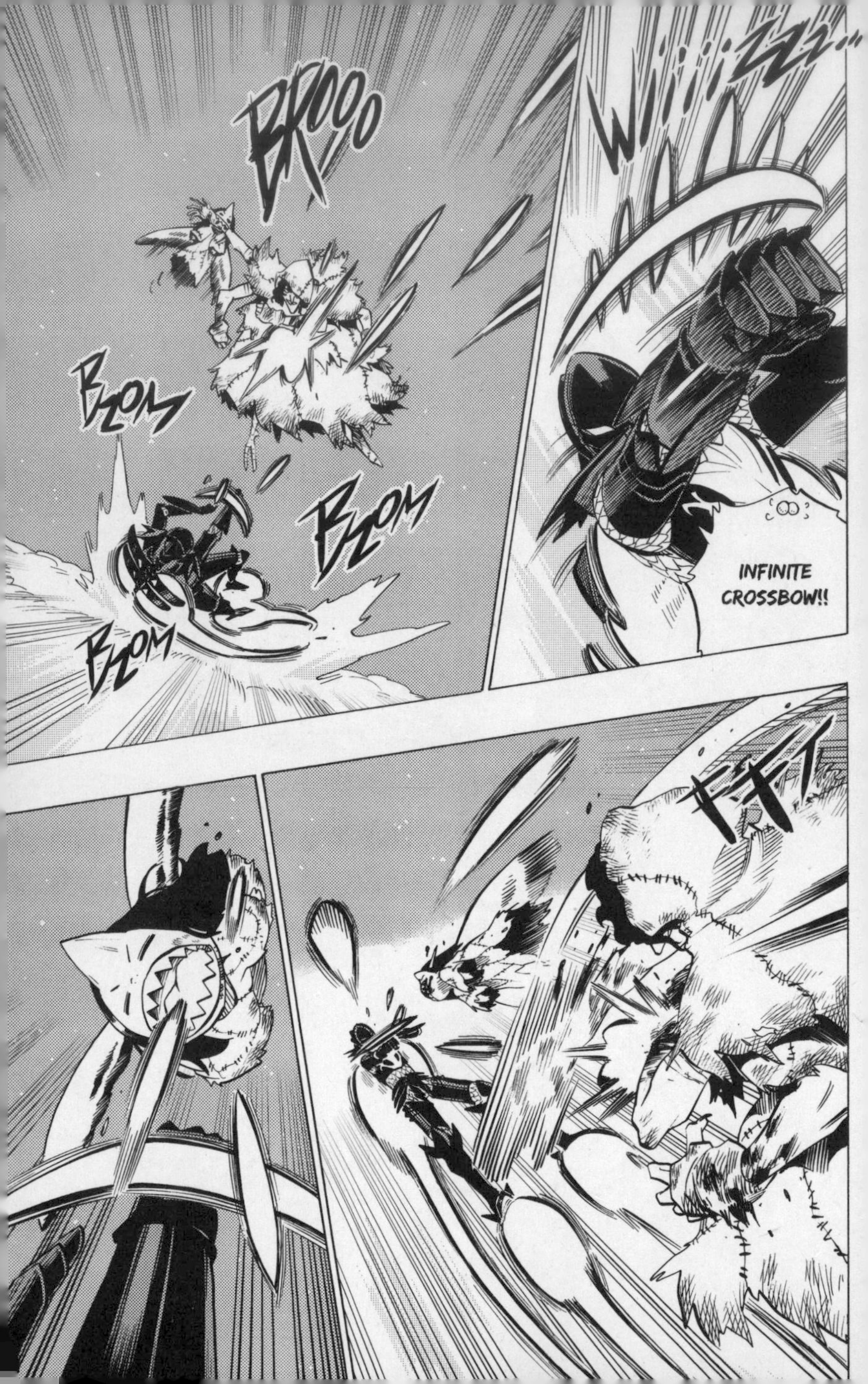
WIIIIIZZZZ...
INFINITE CROSSBOW!!
BROOOO
BZOM
BZOM
BZOM
FFFT

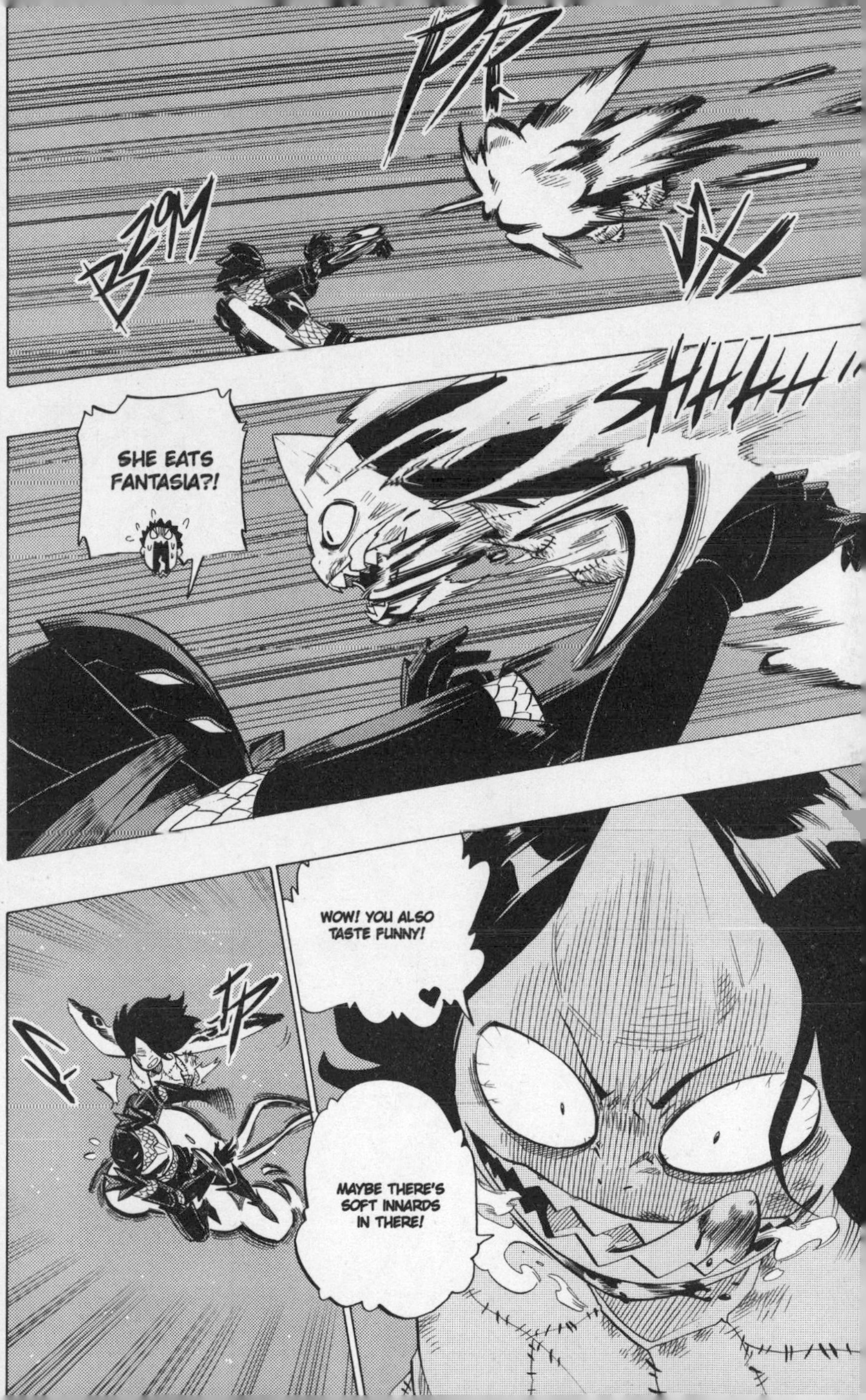
SHE EATS FANTASIA?!
WOW! YOU ALSO TASTE FUNNY!
MAYBE THERE'S SOFT INNARDS IN THERE!

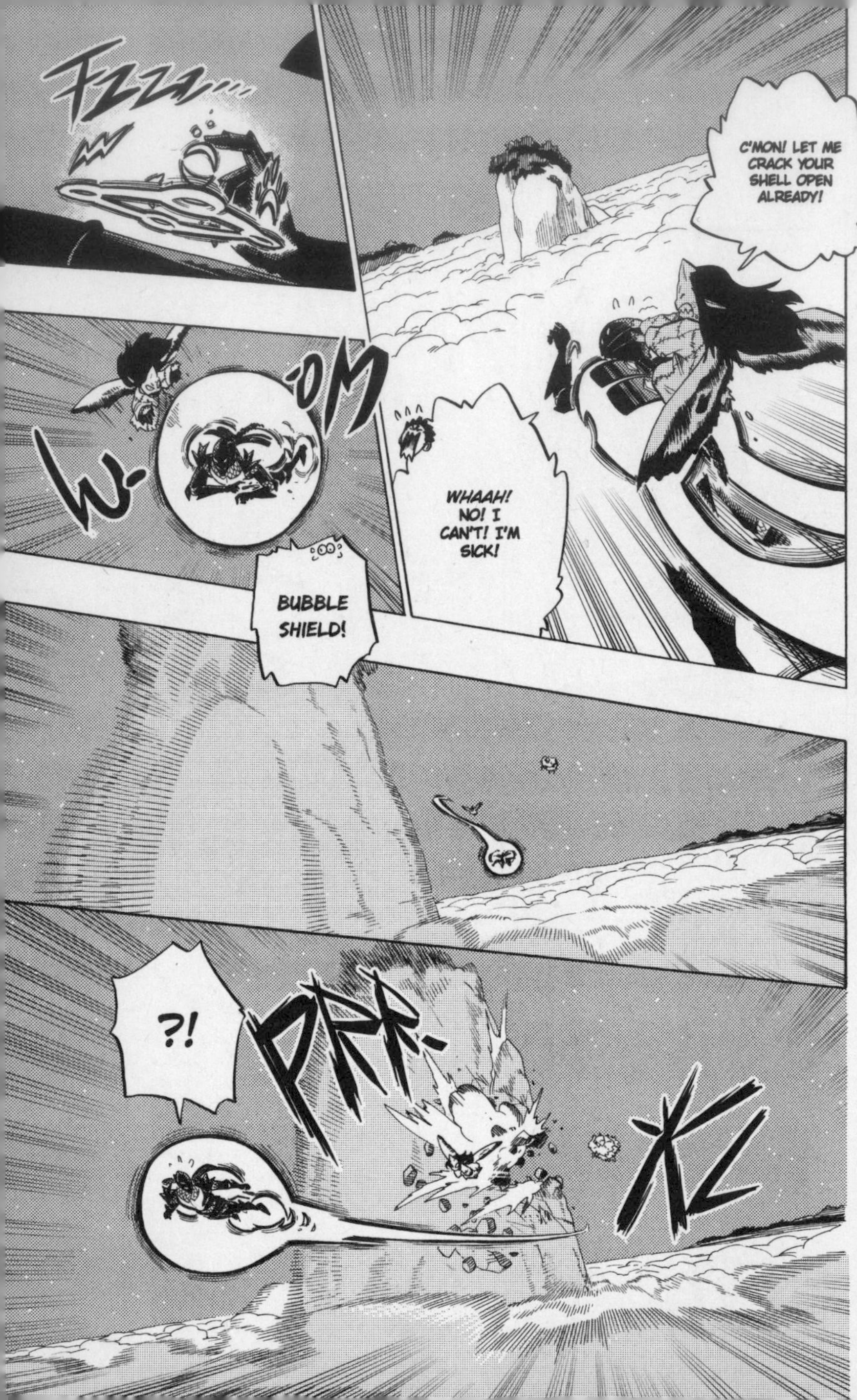
C'MON! LET ME CRACK YOUR SHELL OPEN ALREADY!
WHAAH! NO! I CAN'T! I'M SICK!
FZZZA...
W-OOM
BUBBLE SHIELD!
?!
PRR-
KL

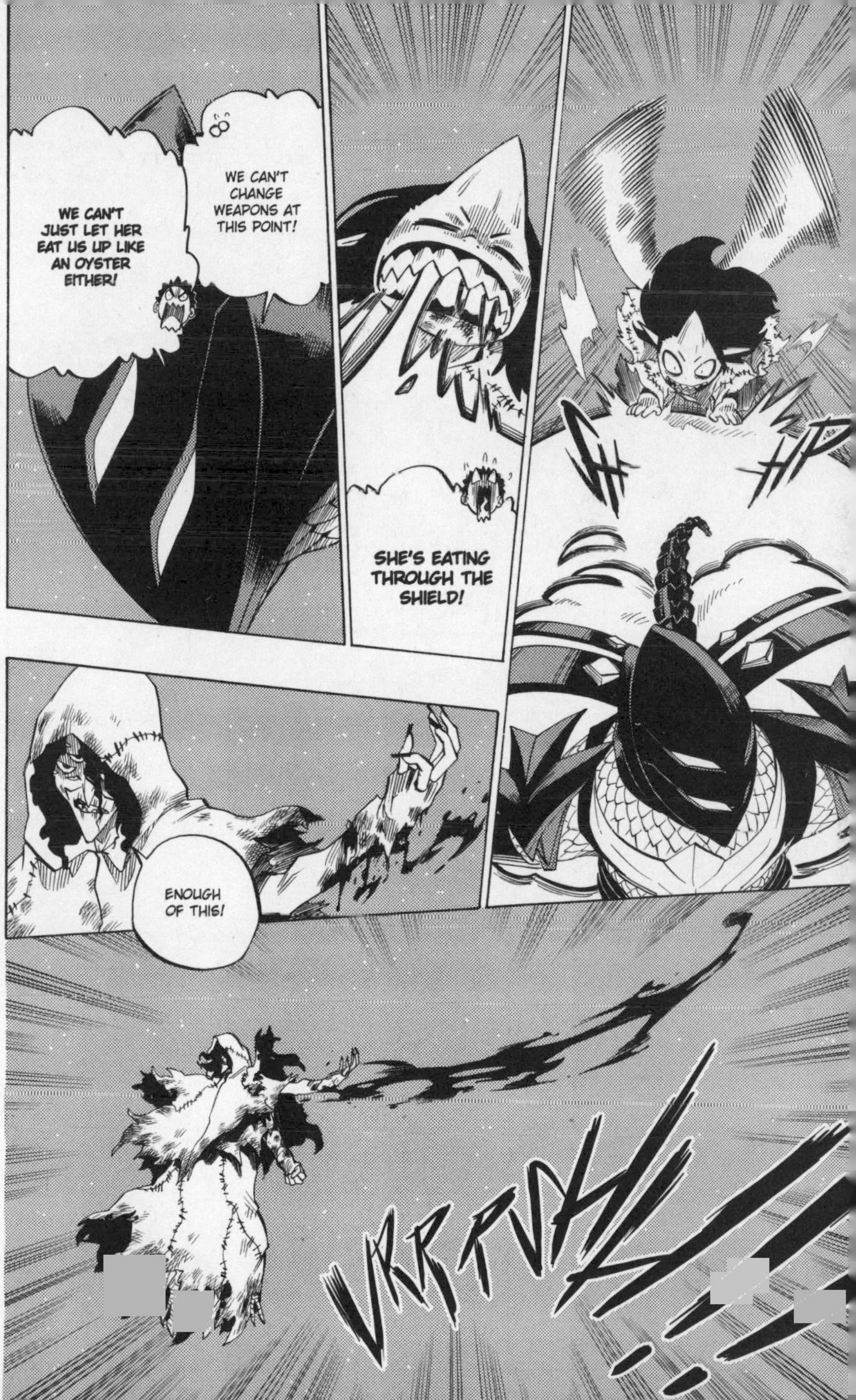

CHHP
SHE'S EATING THROUGH THE SHIELD!
WE CAN'T CHANGE WEAPONS AT THIS POINT!
WE CAN'T JUST LET HER EAT US UP LIKE AN OYSTER EITHER!
ENOUGH OF THIS!
VRRRCH!!

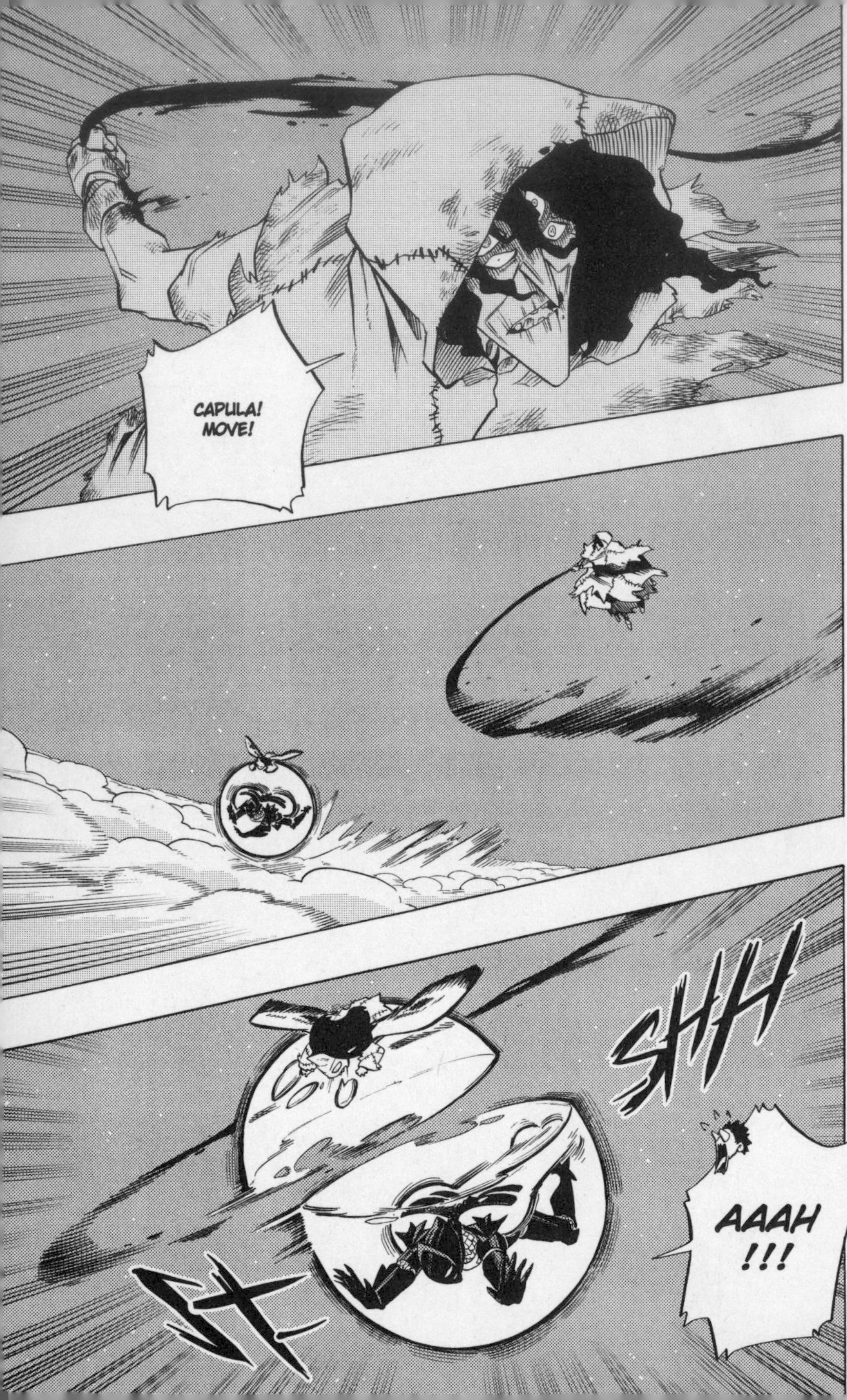
CAPULA! MOVE!
SHH
AAAH!!!
SFX

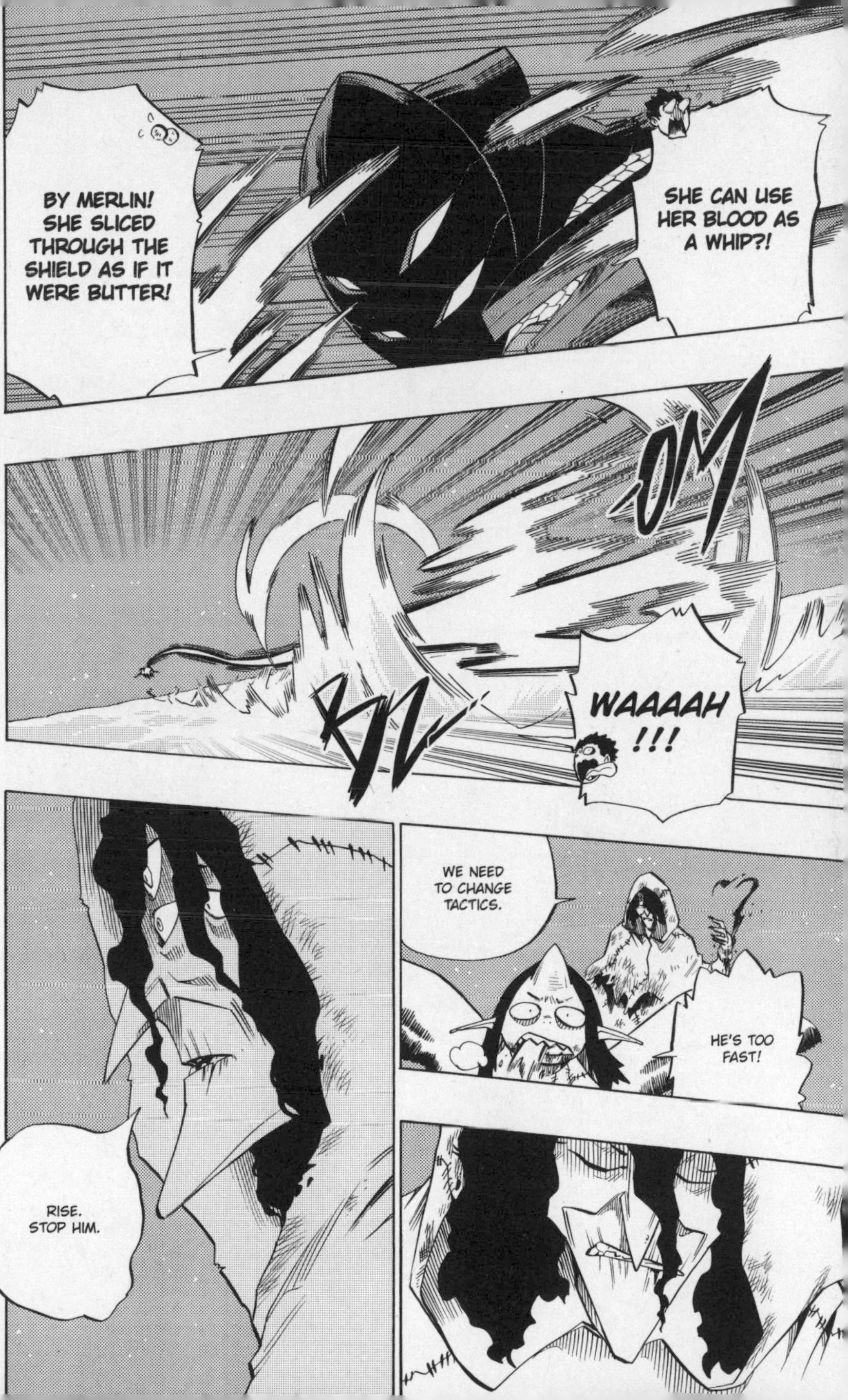
SHE CAN USE HER BLOOD AS A WHIP?!
BY MERLIN! SHE SLICED THROUGH THE SHIELD AS IF IT WERE BUTTER!
WAAAAH !!!
HE'S TOO FAST!
WE NEED TO CHANGE TACTICS.
RISE. STOP HIM.

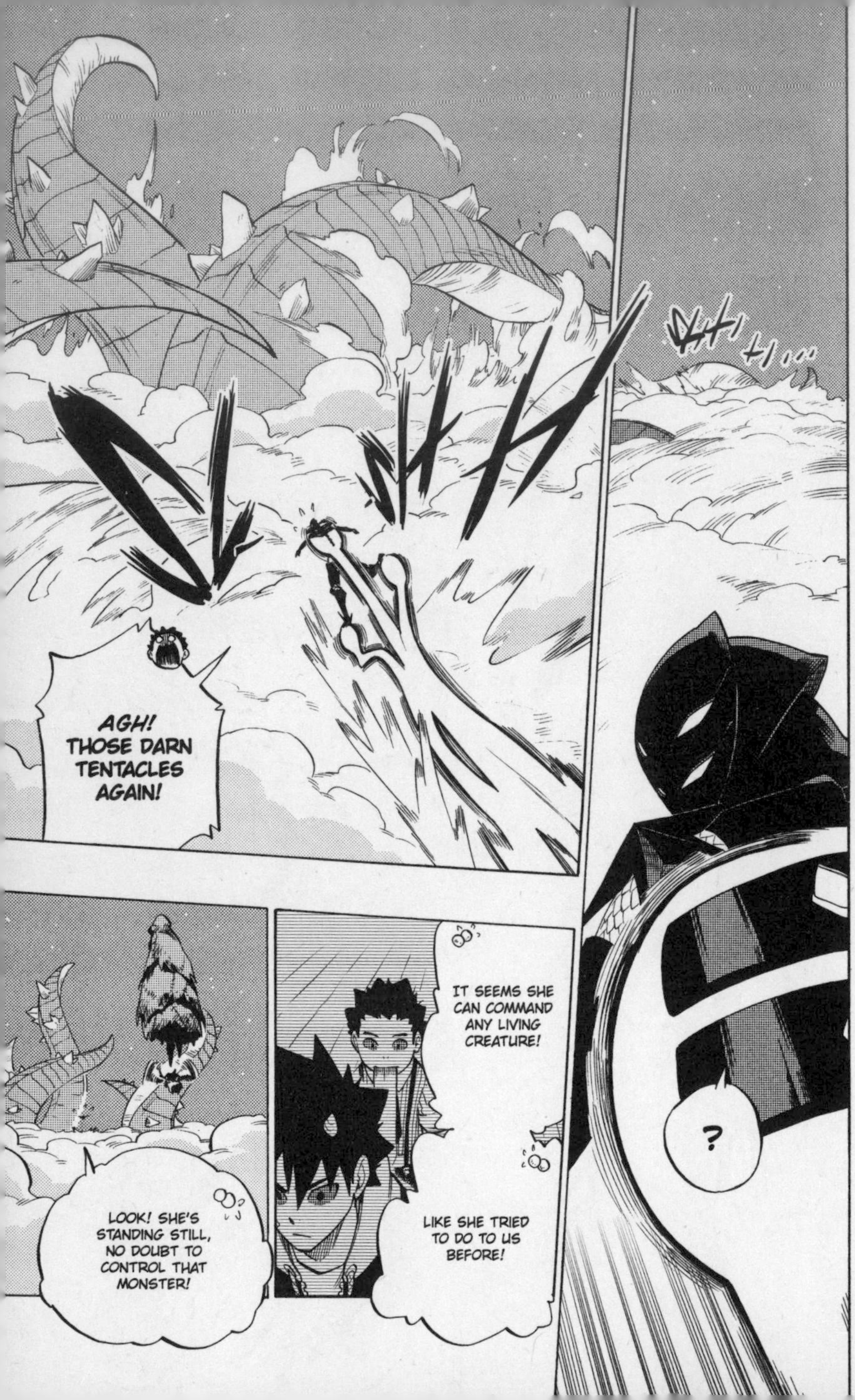
?
AGH! THOSE DARN TENTACLES AGAIN!
IT SEEMS SHE CAN COMMAND ANY LIVING CREATURE!
LIKE SHE TRIED TO DO TO US BEFORE!
LOOK! SHE'S STANDING STILL, NO DOUBT TO CONTROL THAT MONSTER!

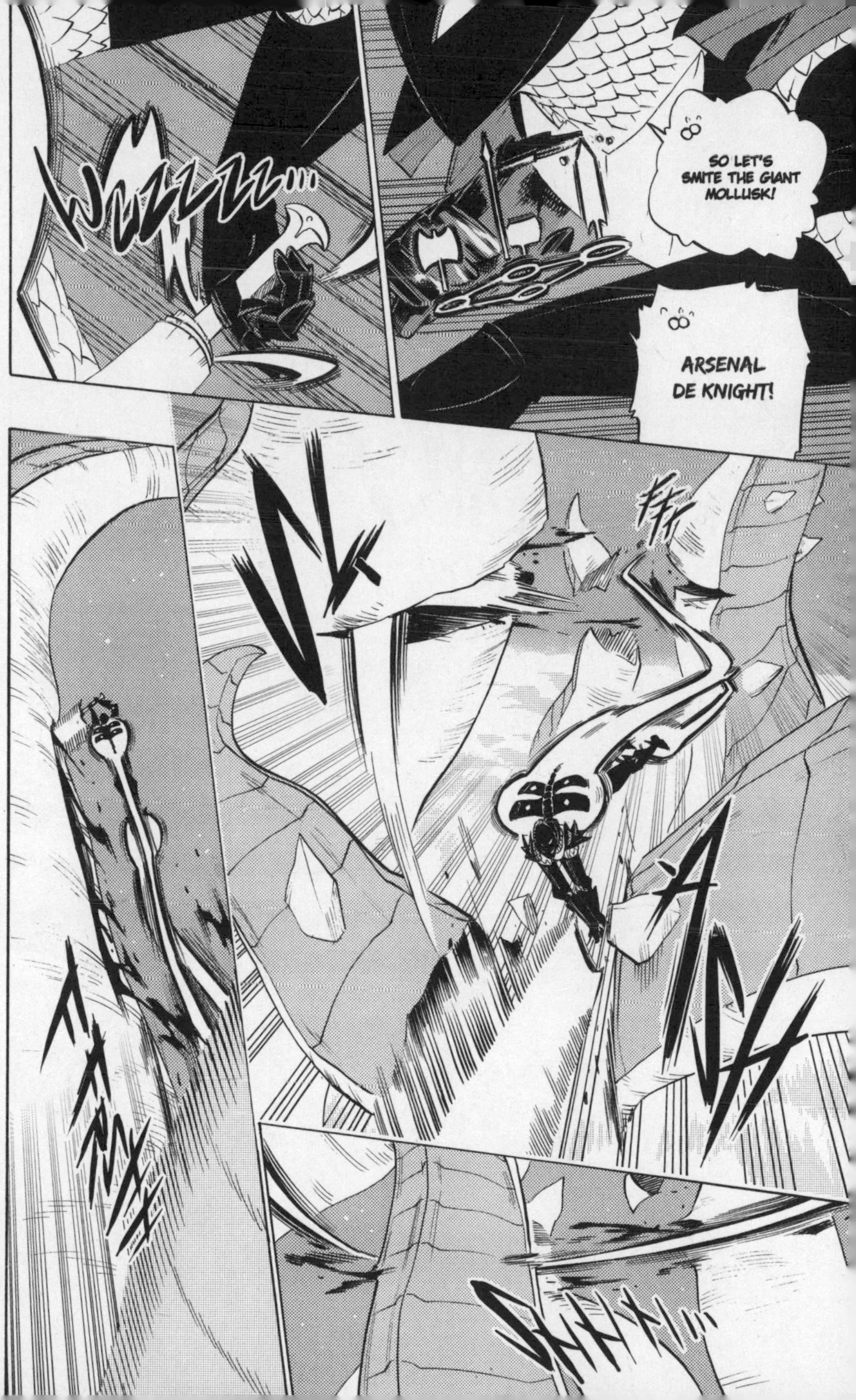
SO LET'S SMITE THE GIANT MOLLUSK!
ARSENAL DE KNIGHT!

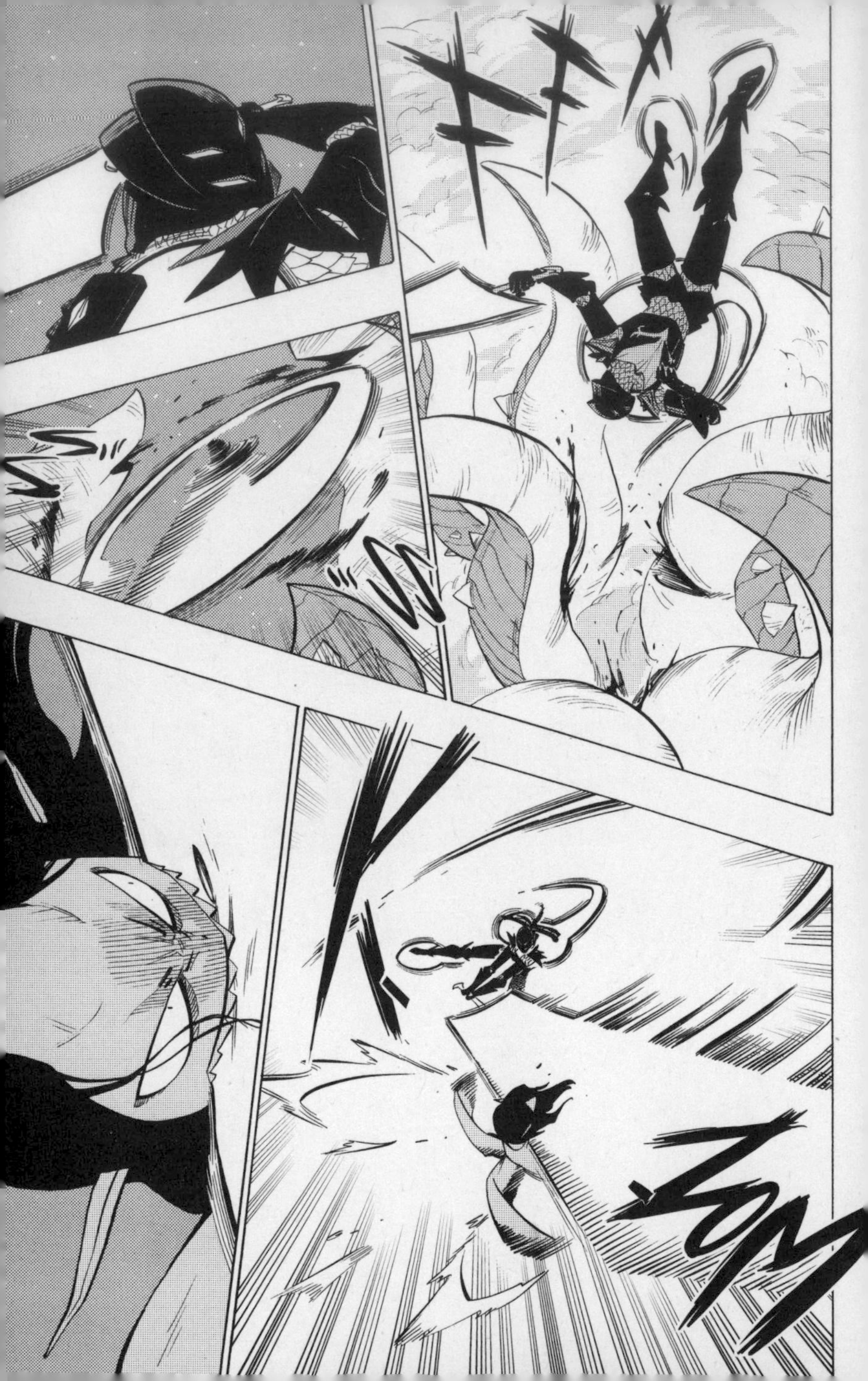

Chapter 86

Devour Him

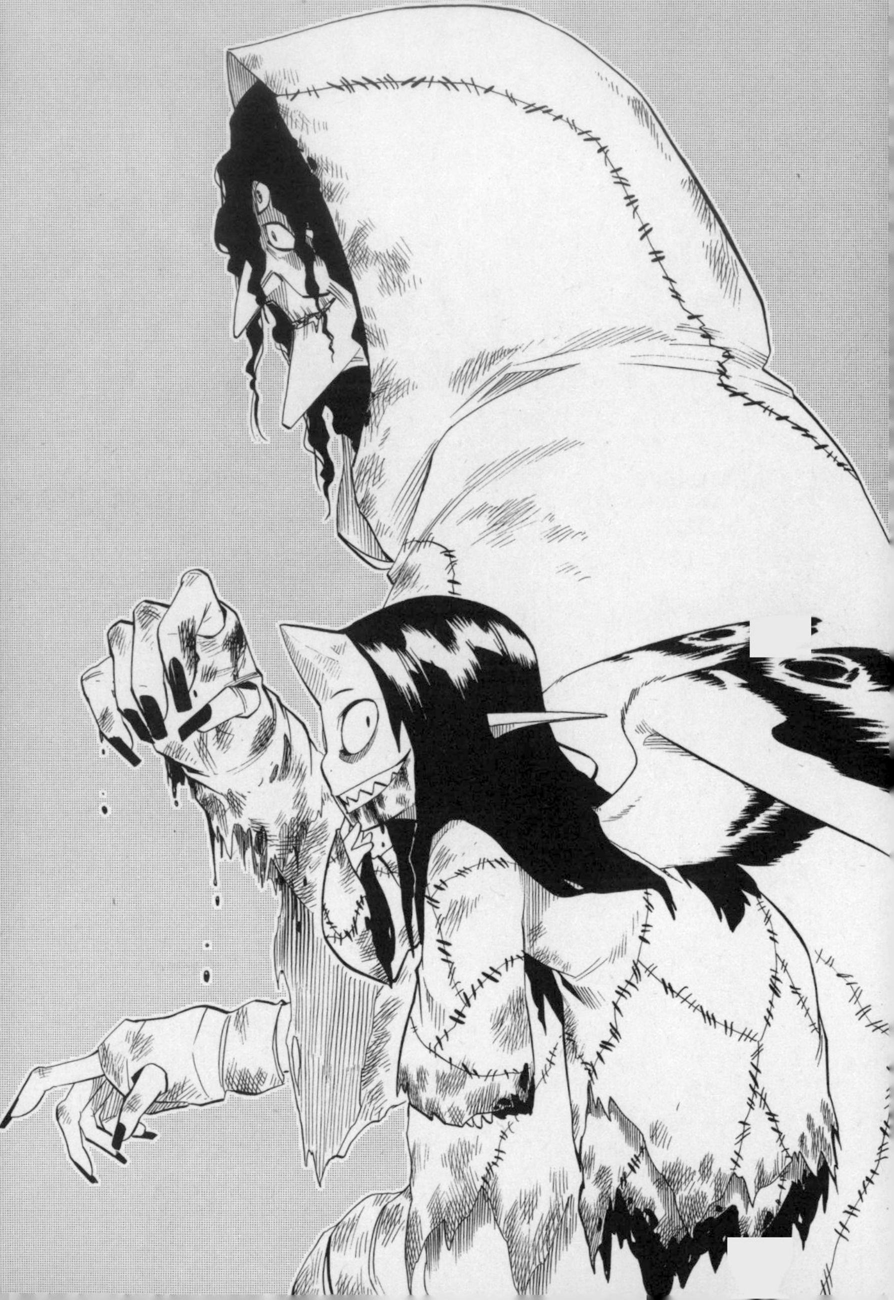

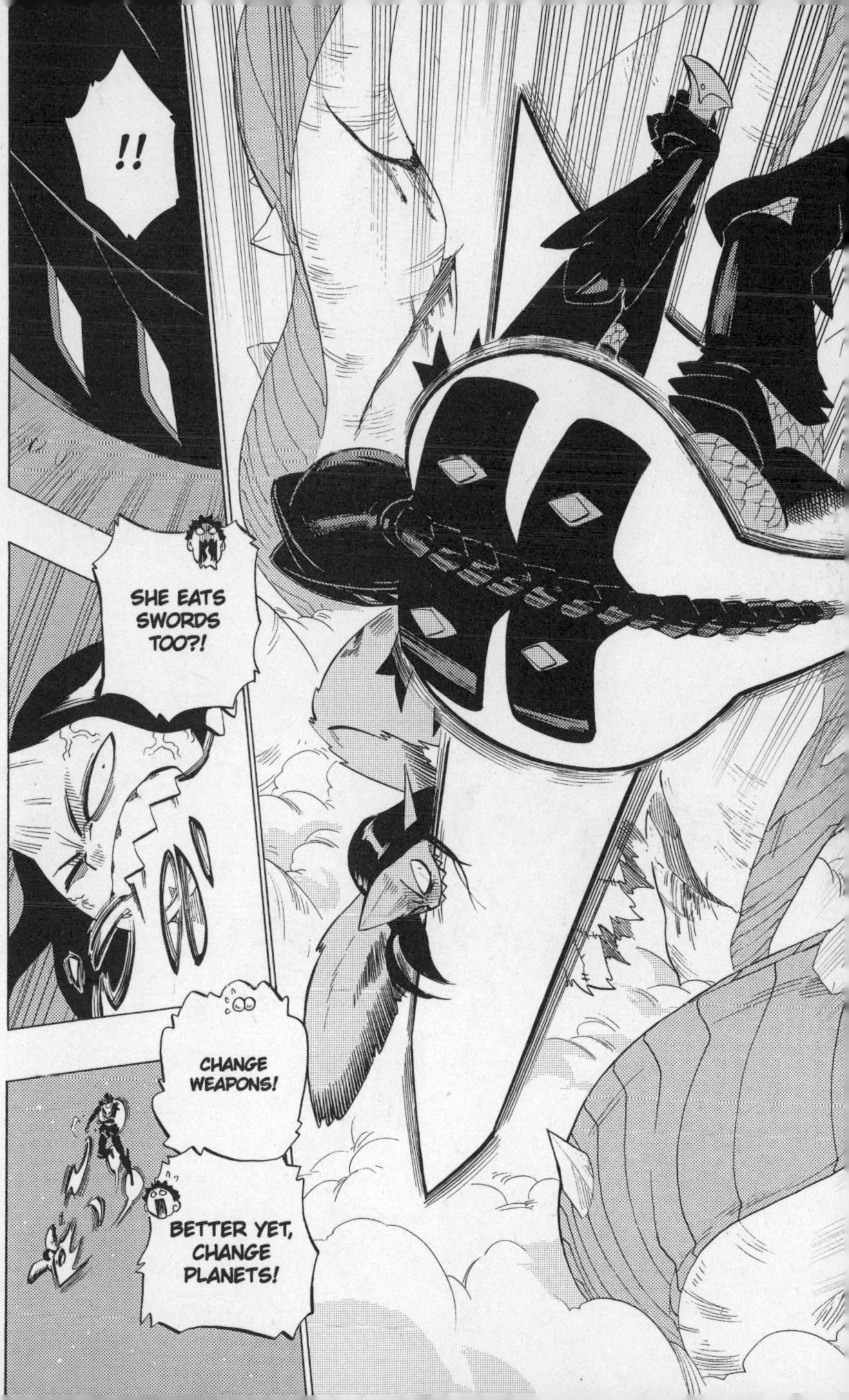
!!
SHE EATS SWORDS TOO?!
CHANGE WEAPONS!
BETTER YET, CHANGE PLANETS!

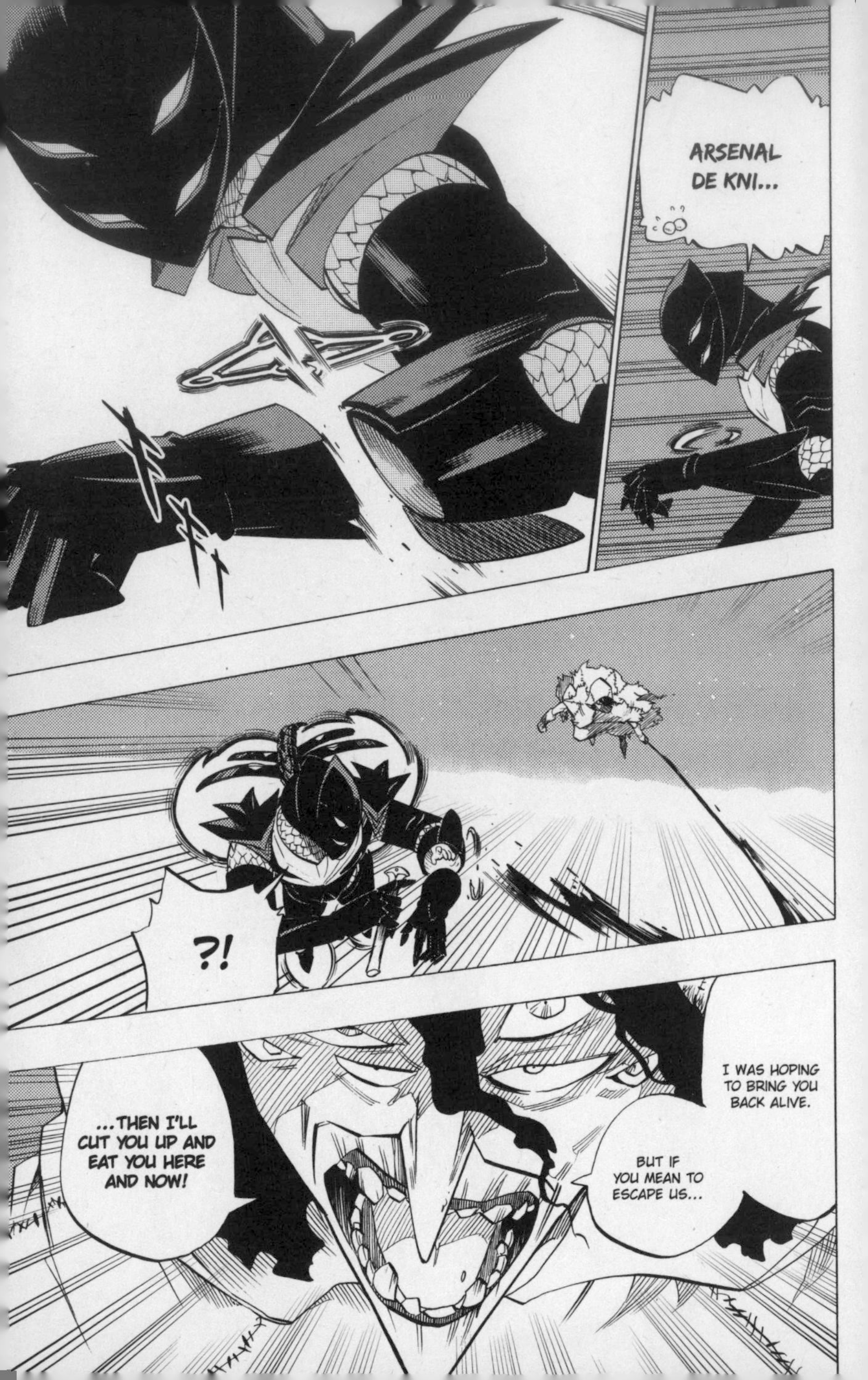
ARSENAL DE KNI...
?!
I WAS HOPING TO BRING YOU BACK ALIVE.
BUT IF YOU MEAN TO ESCAPE US...
...THEN I'LL CUT YOU UP AND EAT YOU HERE AND NOW!

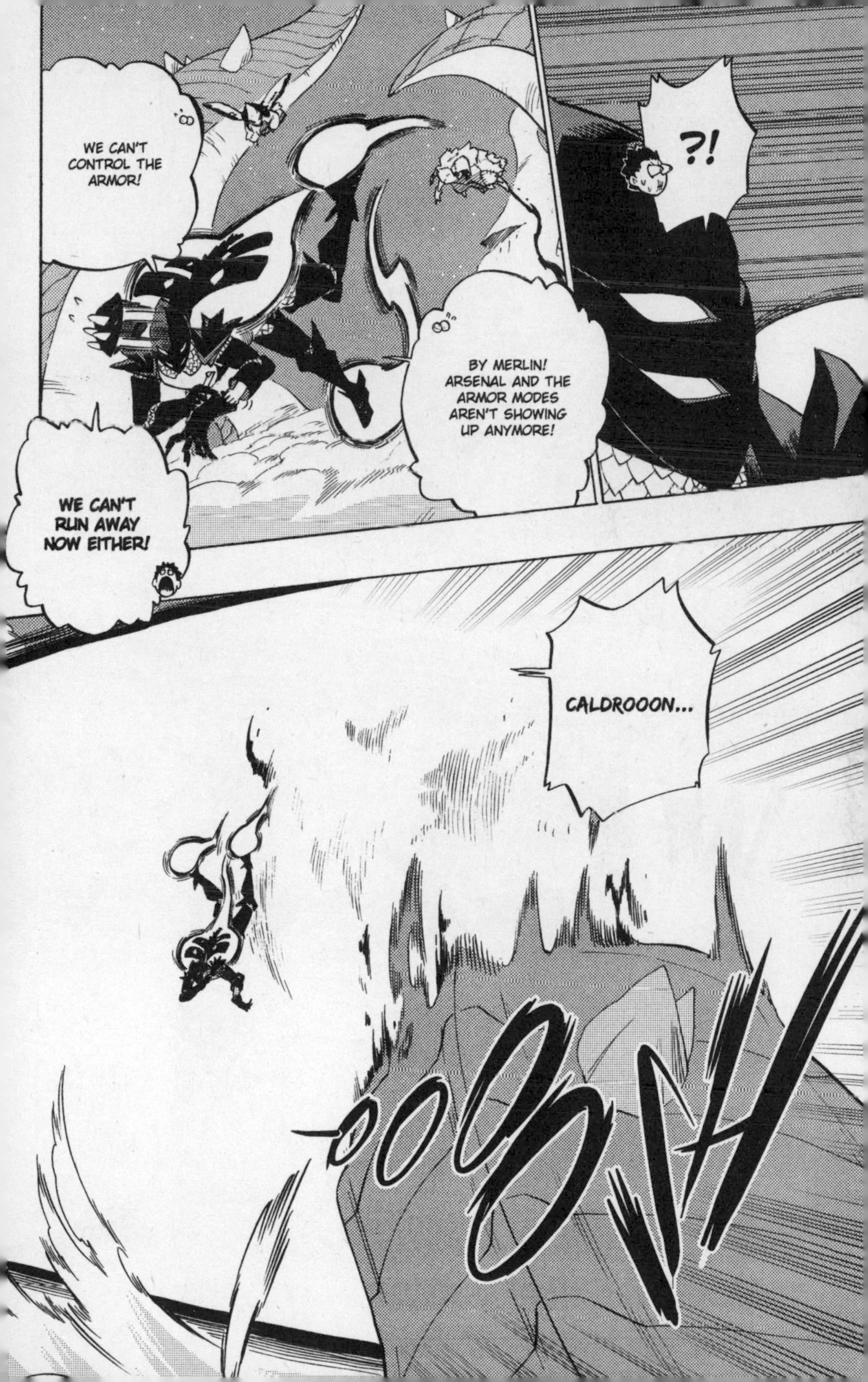
?!
BY MERLIN! ARSENAL AND THE ARMOR MODES AREN'T SHOWING UP ANYMORE!
WE CAN'T CONTROL THE ARMOR!
WE CAN'T RUN AWAY NOW EITHER!
CALDROOON...

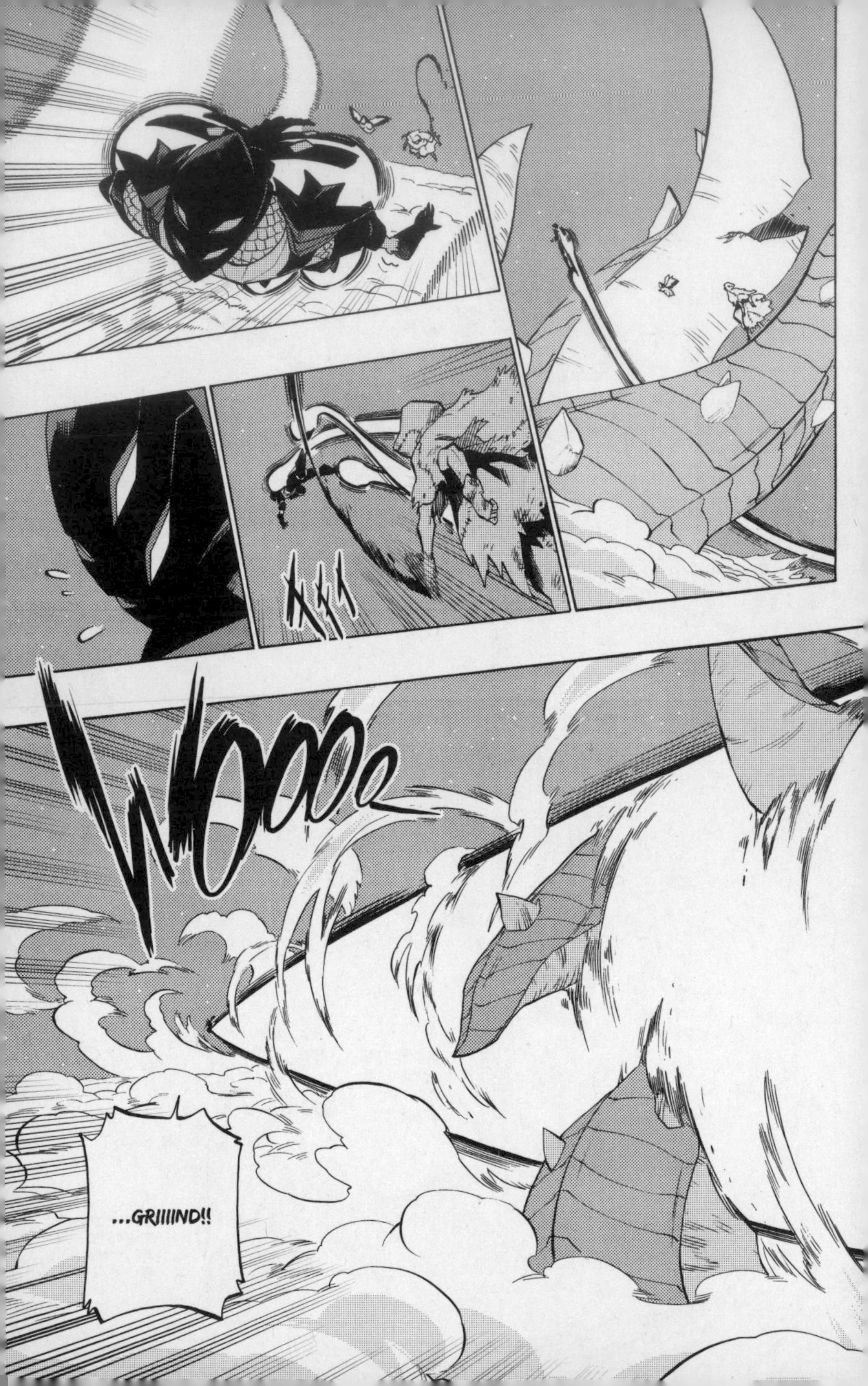
WOOO
...GRIIIIND!!

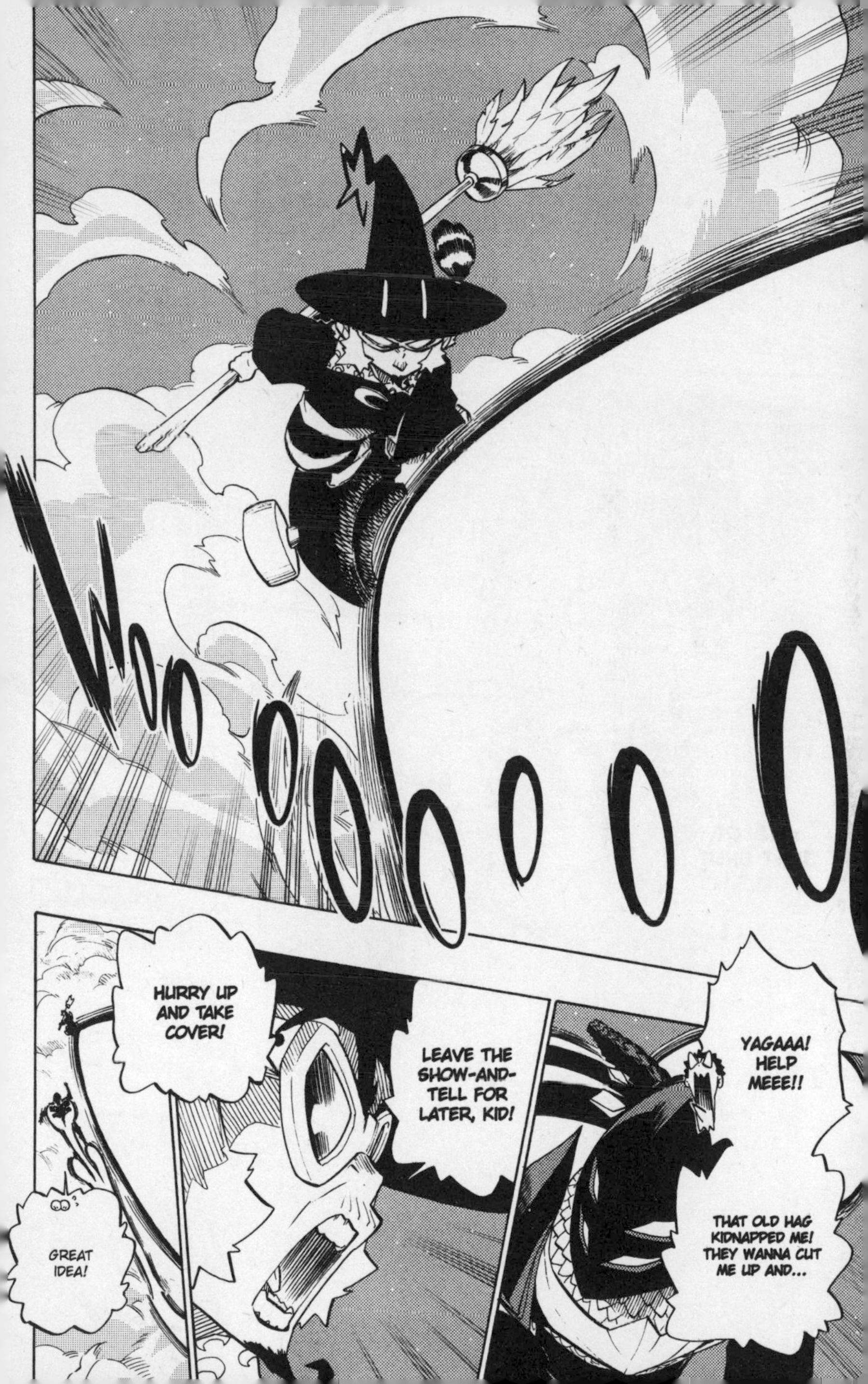
WOOOOOOOOO
YAGAAA! HELP MEEE!!
THAT OLD HAG KIDNAPPED ME! THEY WANNA CUT ME UP AND...
LEAVE THE SHOW-AND-TELL FOR LATER, KID!
HURRY UP AND TAKE COVER!
GREAT IDEA!

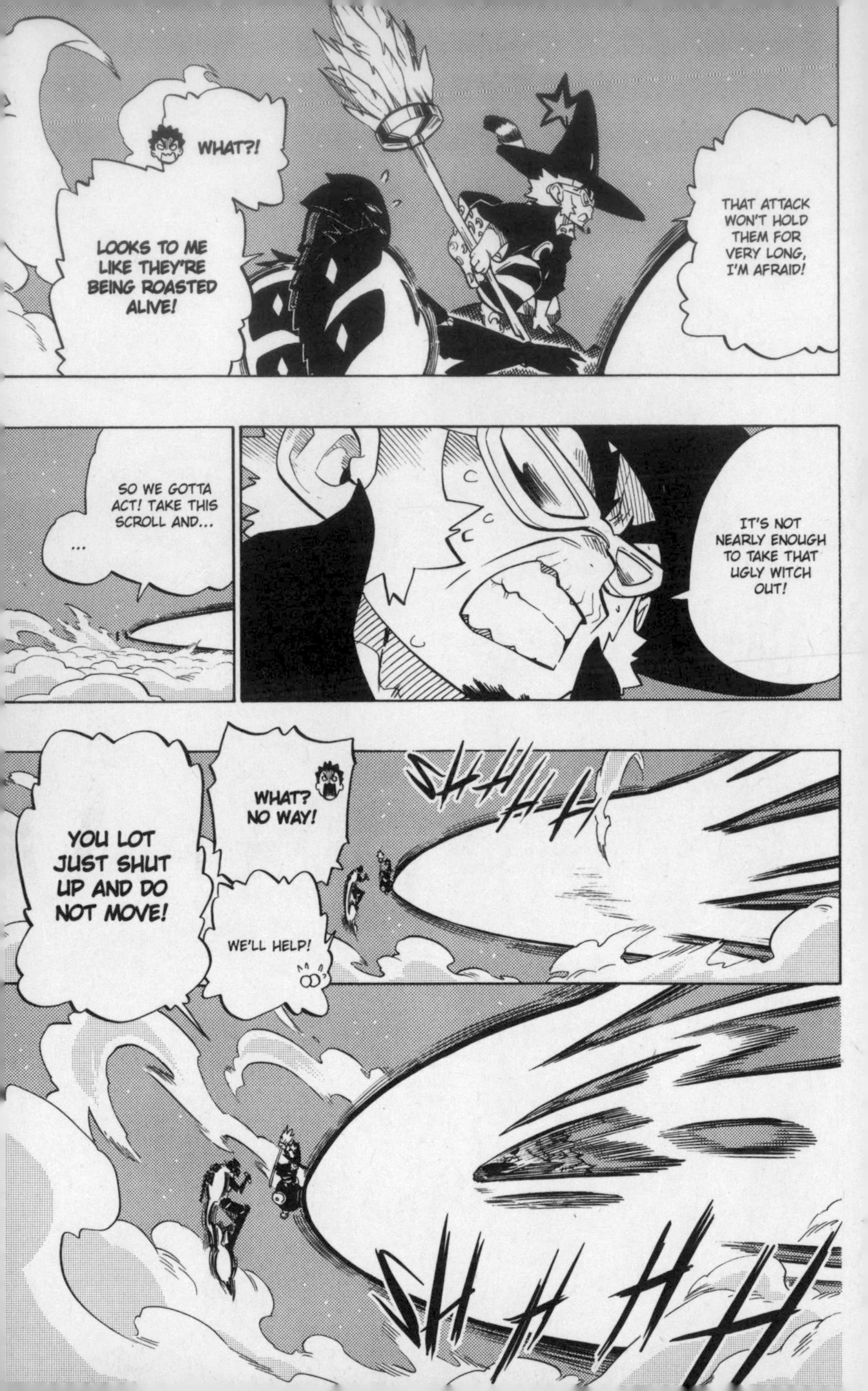
THAT ATTACK WON'T HOLD THEM FOR VERY LONG, I'M AFRAID!
LOOKS TO ME LIKE THEY'RE BEING ROASTED ALIVE!
WHAT?!
IT'S NOT NEARLY ENOUGH TO TAKE THAT UGLY WITCH OUT!
SO WE GOTTA ACT! TAKE THIS SCROLL AND...
...
SHHHH
YOU LOT JUST SHUT UP AND DO NOT MOVE!
WHAT? NO WAY!
WE'LL HELP!
SHHHHH

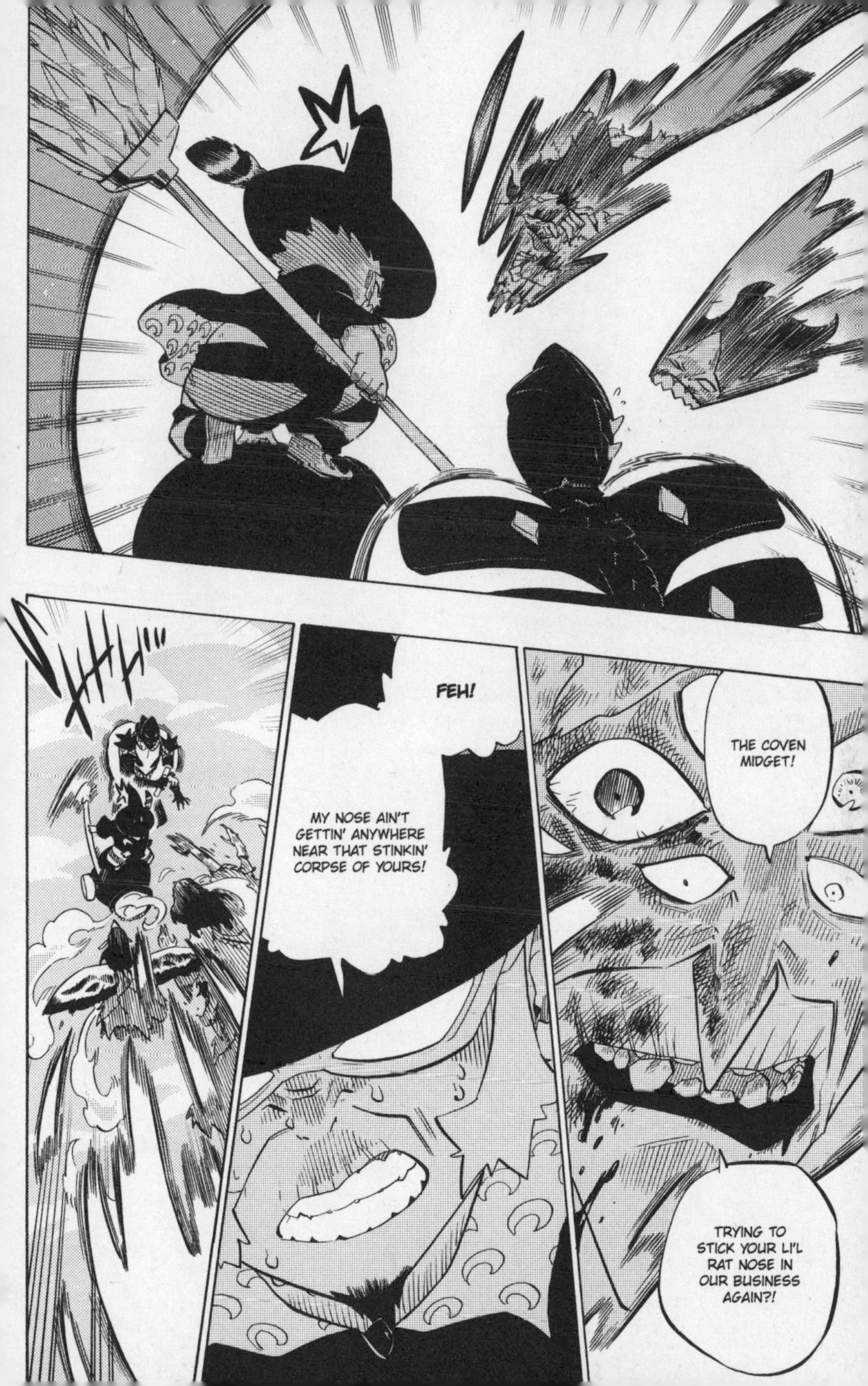
THE COVEN MIDGET!
TRYING TO STICK YOUR LI'L RAT NOSE IN OUR BUSINESS AGAIN?!
FEH!
MY NOSE AIN'T GETTIN' ANYWHERE NEAR THAT STINKIN' CORPSE OF YOURS!

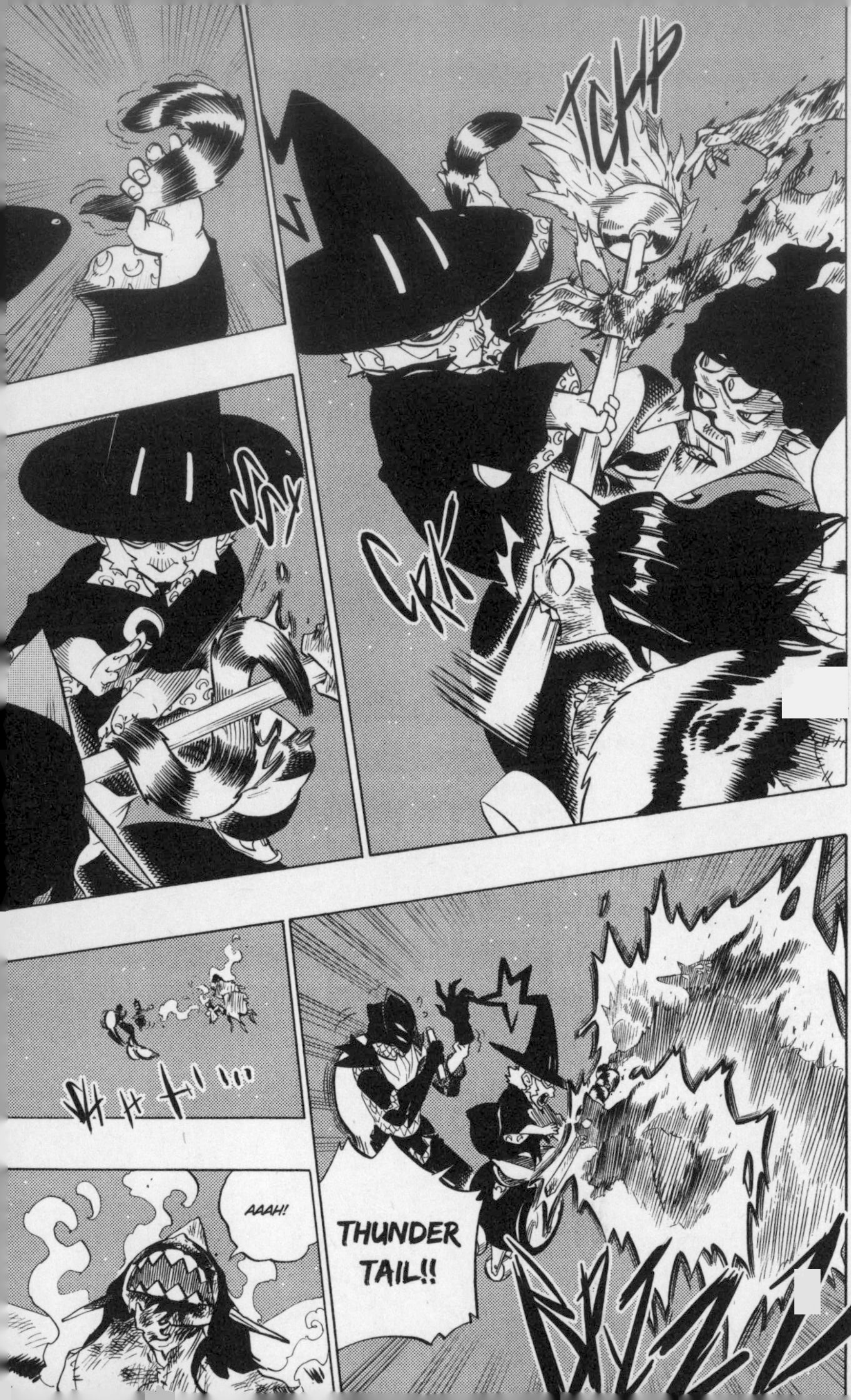
TCHP
CRK
THUNDER TAIL!!
AAAH!

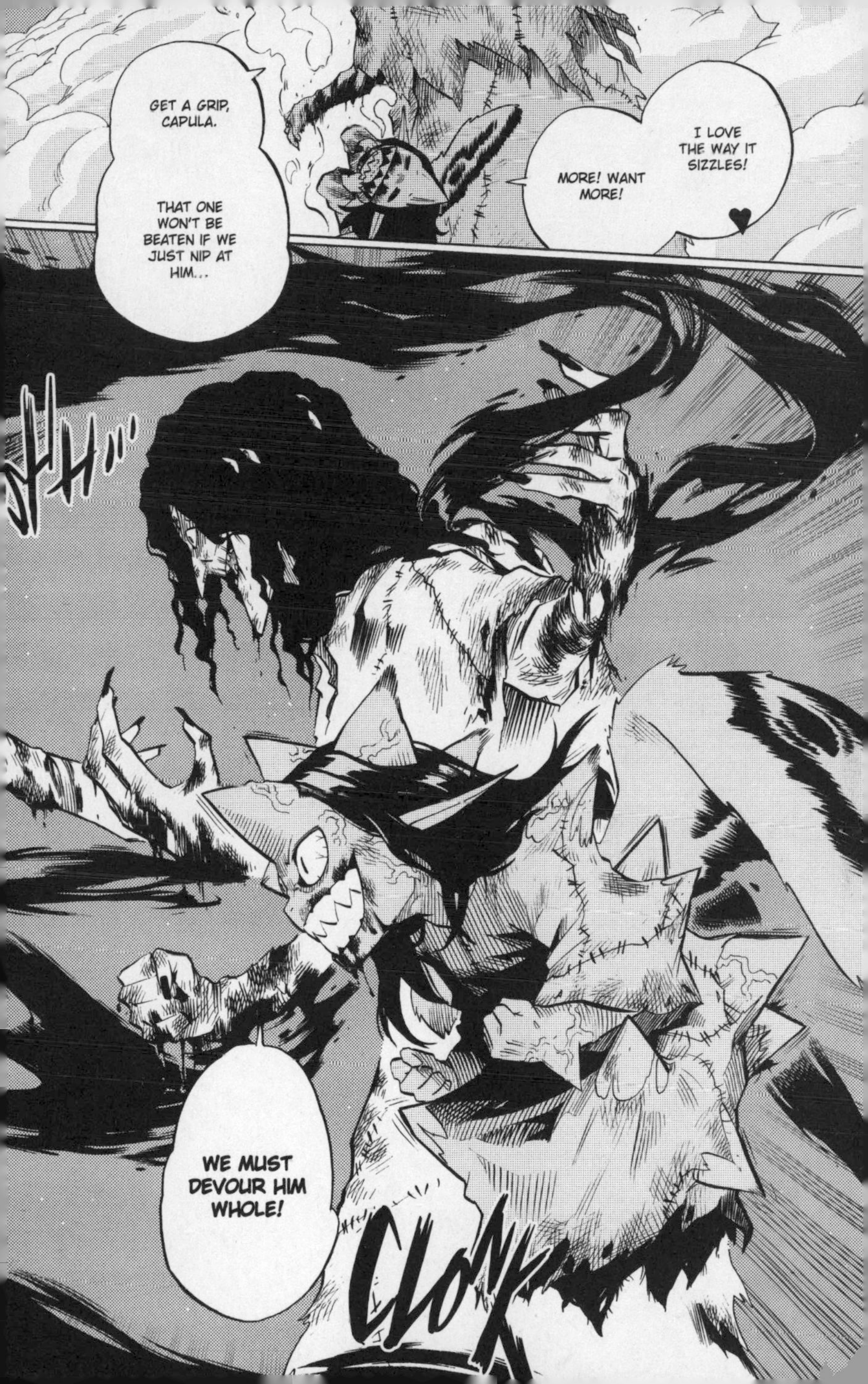
I LOVE THE WAY IT SIZZLES! ♥
MORE! WANT MORE!
GET A GRIP, CAPULA.
THAT ONE WON'T BE BEATEN IF WE JUST NIP AT HIM...
WE MUST DEVOUR HIM WHOLE!

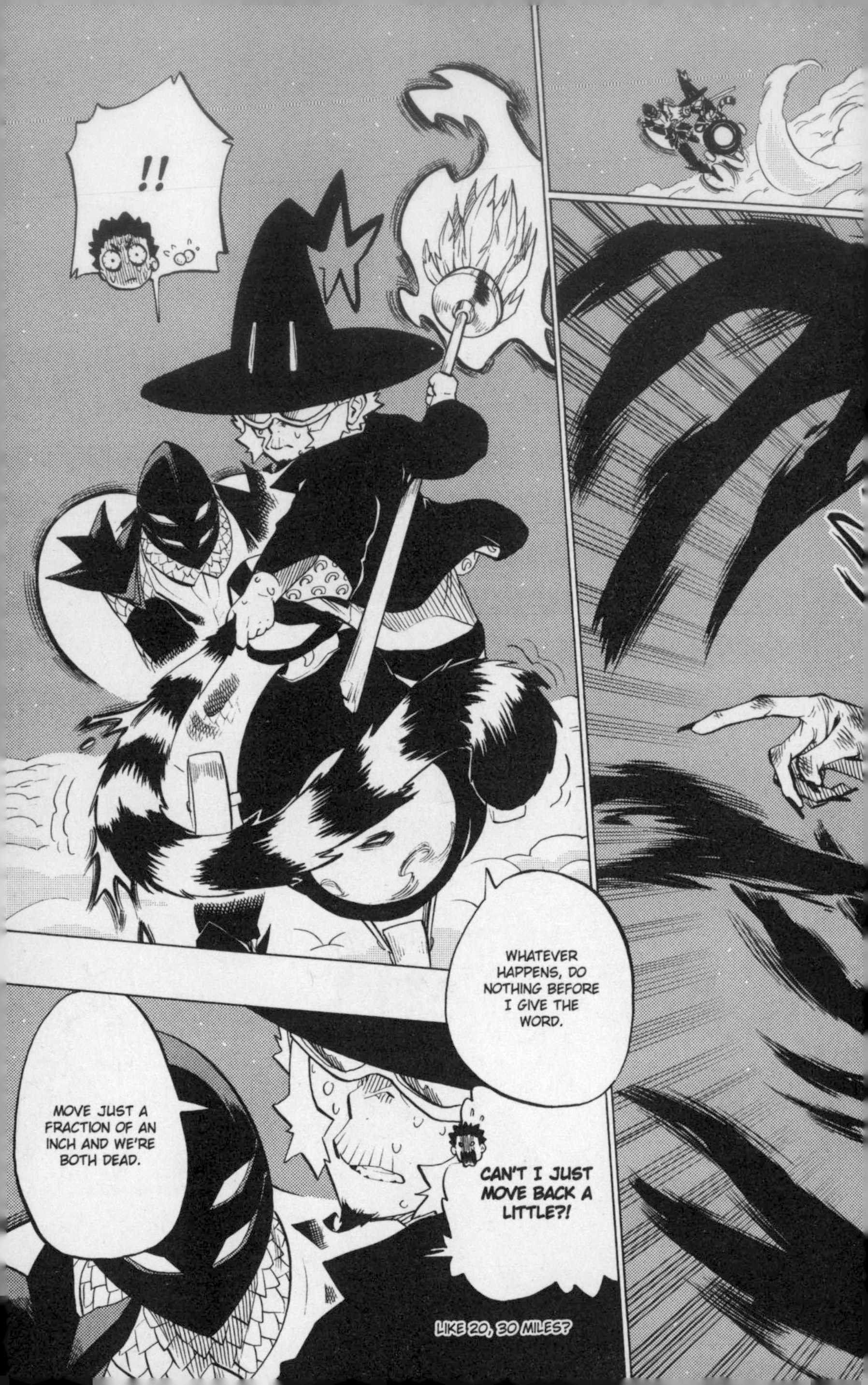
!!
WHATEVER HAPPENS, DO NOTHING BEFORE I GIVE THE WORD.
MOVE JUST A FRACTION OF AN INCH AND WE'RE BOTH DEAD.
CAN'T I JUST MOVE BACK A LITTLE?!
LIKE 20, 30 MILES?

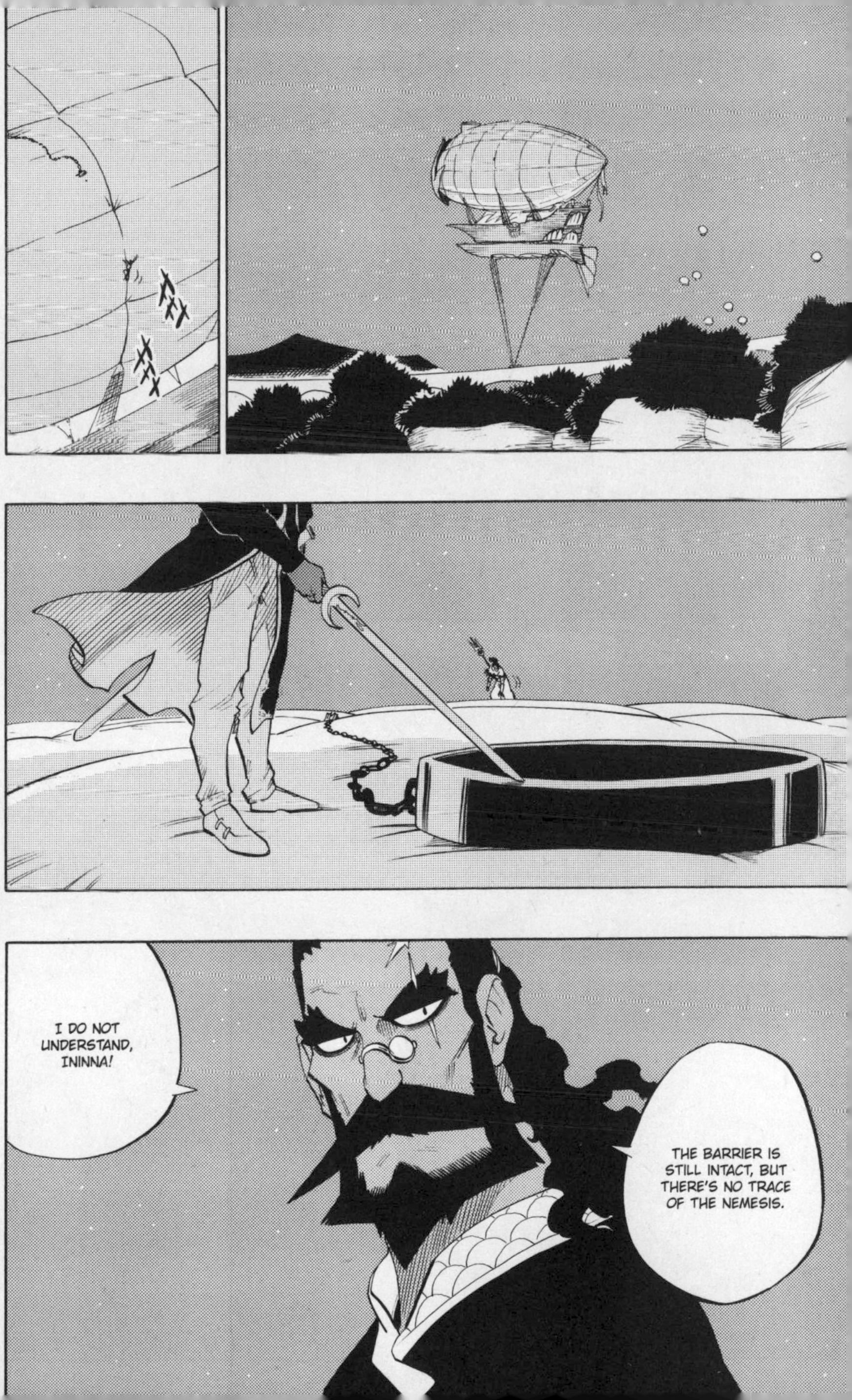
THE BARRIER IS STILL INTACT, BUT THERE'S NO TRACE OF THE NEMESIS.
I DO NOT UNDERSTAND, ININNA!

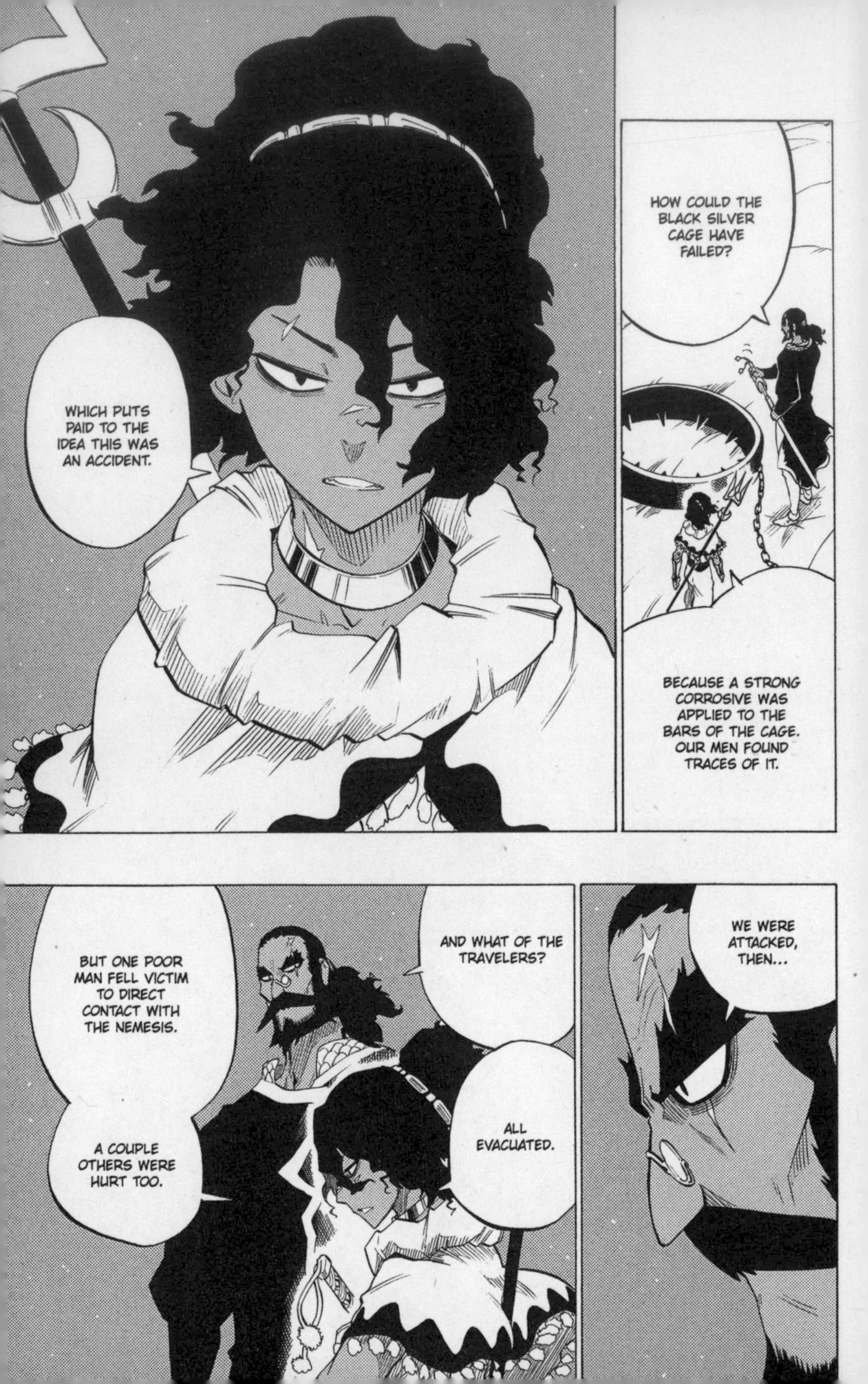
HOW COULD THE BLACK SILVER CAGE HAVE FAILED?
BECAUSE A STRONG CORROSIVE WAS APPLIED TO THE BARS OF THE CAGE. OUR MEN FOUND TRACES OF IT.
WHICH PUTS PAID TO THE IDEA THIS WAS AN ACCIDENT.
WE WERE ATTACKED, THEN...
AND WHAT OF THE TRAVELERS?
ALL EVACUATED.
BUT ONE POOR MAN FELL VICTIM TO DIRECT CONTACT WITH THE NEMESIS.
A COUPLE OTHERS WERE HURT TOO.

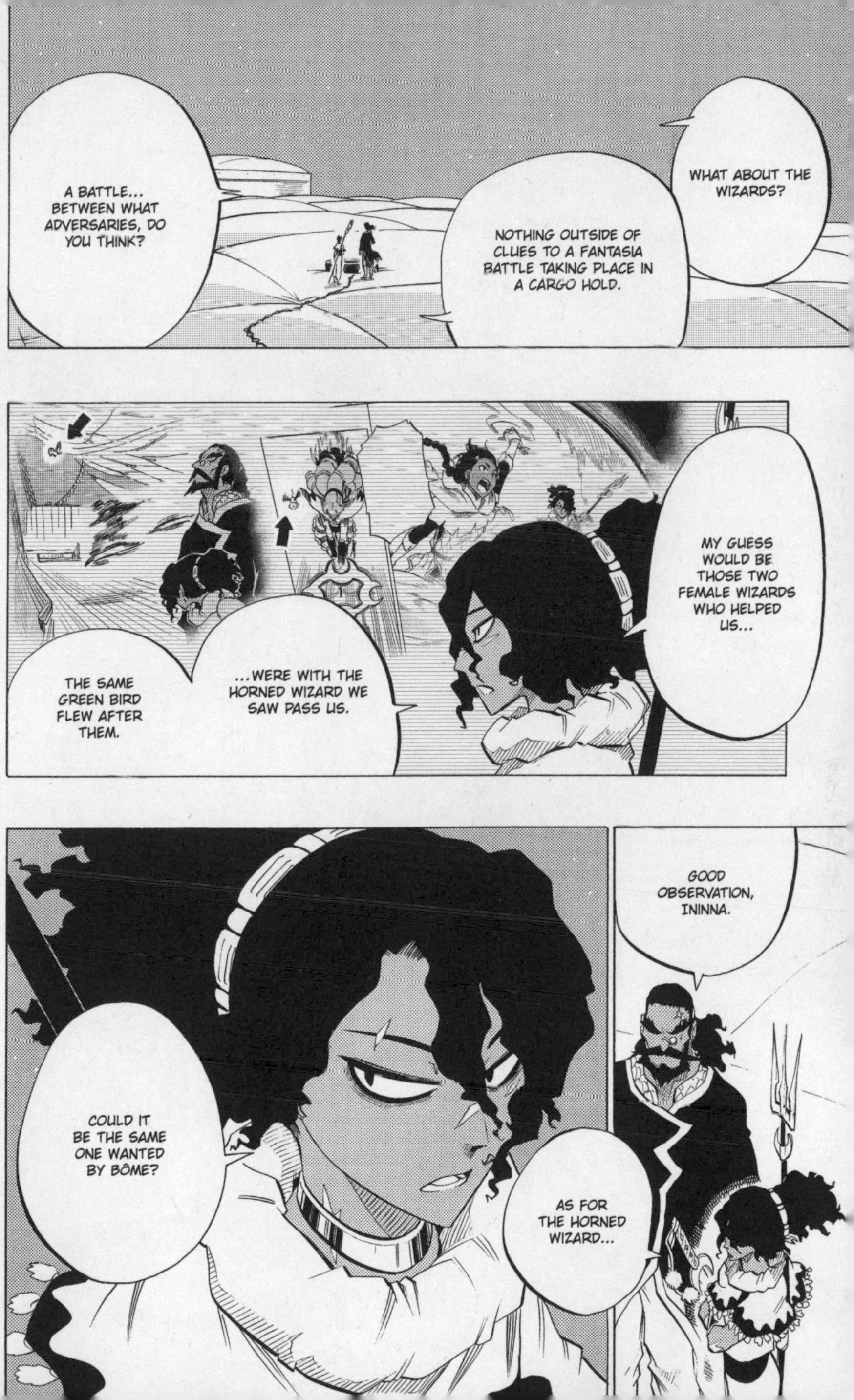
WHAT ABOUT THE WIZARDS?
NOTHING OUTSIDE OF CLUES TO A FANTASIA BATTLE TAKING PLACE IN A CARGO HOLD.
A BATTLE... BETWEEN WHAT ADVERSARIES, DO YOU THINK?
MY GUESS WOULD BE THOSE TWO FEMALE WIZARDS WHO HELPED US...
...WERE WITH THE HORNED WIZARD WE SAW PASS US.
THE SAME GREEN BIRD FLEW AFTER THEM.
GOOD OBSERVATION, ININNA.
AS FOR THE HORNED WIZARD...
COULD IT BE THE SAME ONE WANTED BY BÔME?

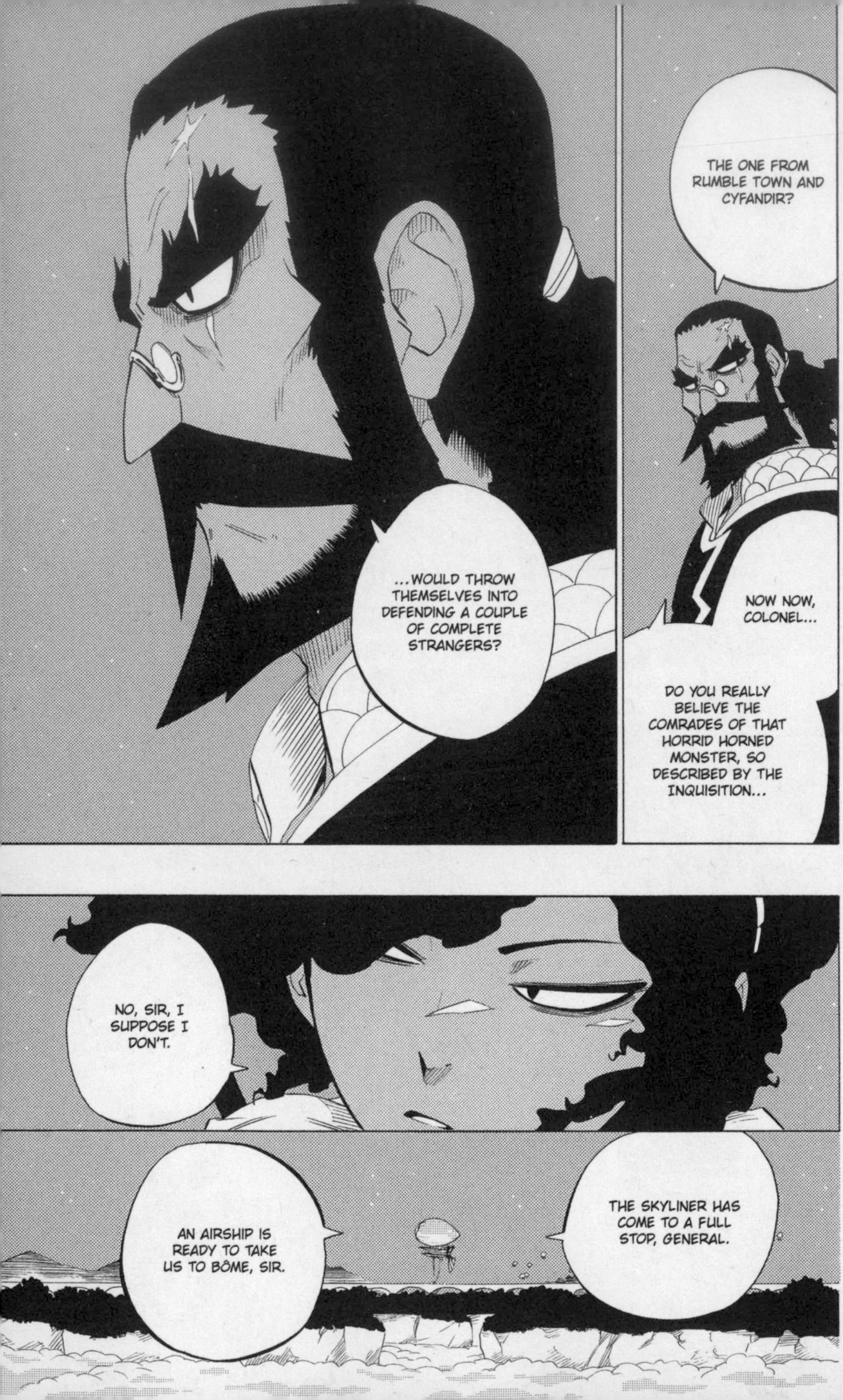
THE ONE FROM RUMBLE TOWN AND CYFANDIR?
NOW NOW, COLONEL...
DO YOU REALLY BELIEVE THE COMRADES OF THAT HORRID HORNED MONSTER, SO DESCRIBED BY THE INQUISITION...
...WOULD THROW THEMSELVES INTO DEFENDING A COUPLE OF COMPLETE STRANGERS?
NO, SIR, I SUPPOSE I DON'T.
THE SKYLINER HAS COME TO A FULL STOP, GENERAL.
AN AIRSHIP IS READY TO TAKE US TO BÔME, SIR.

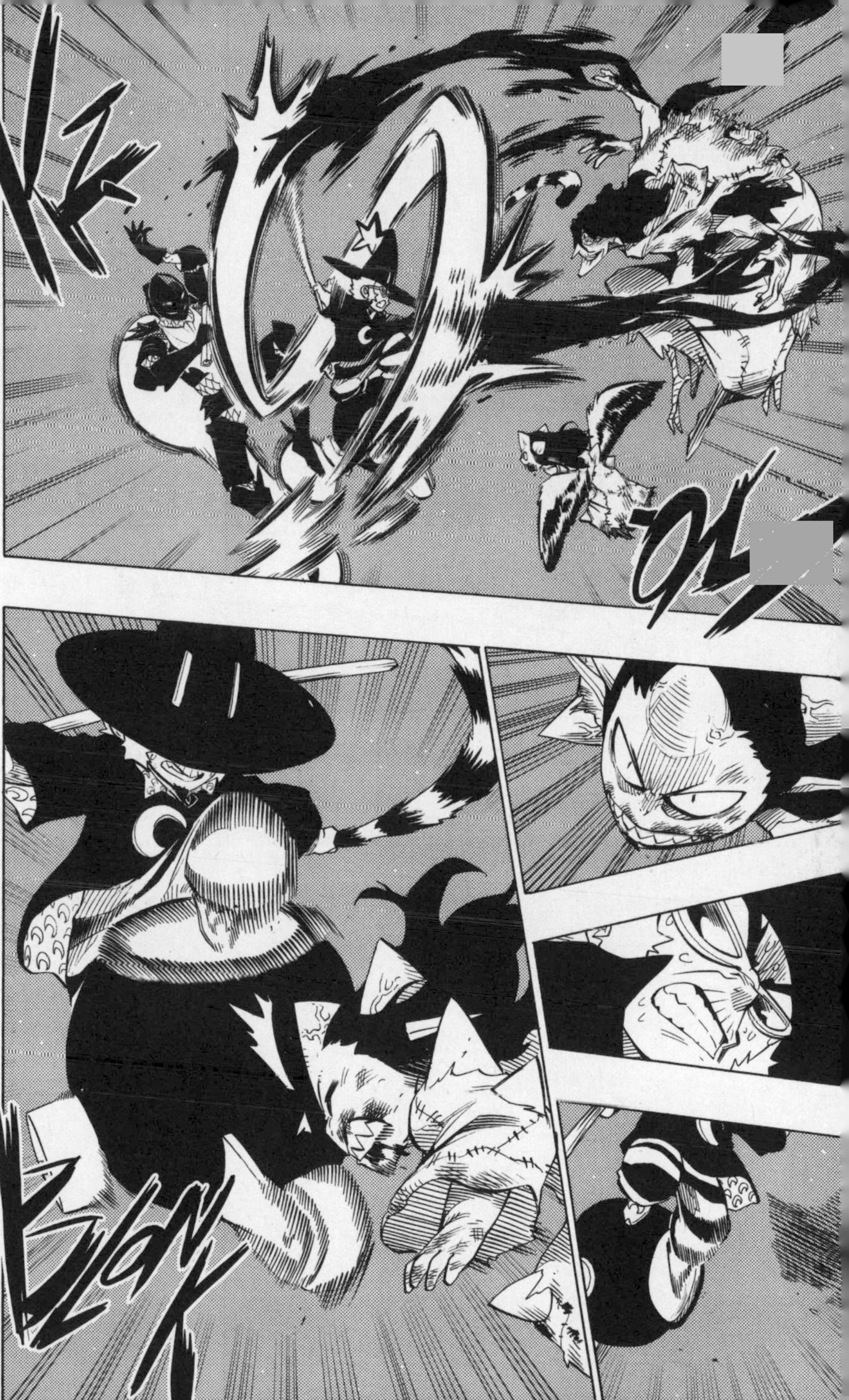

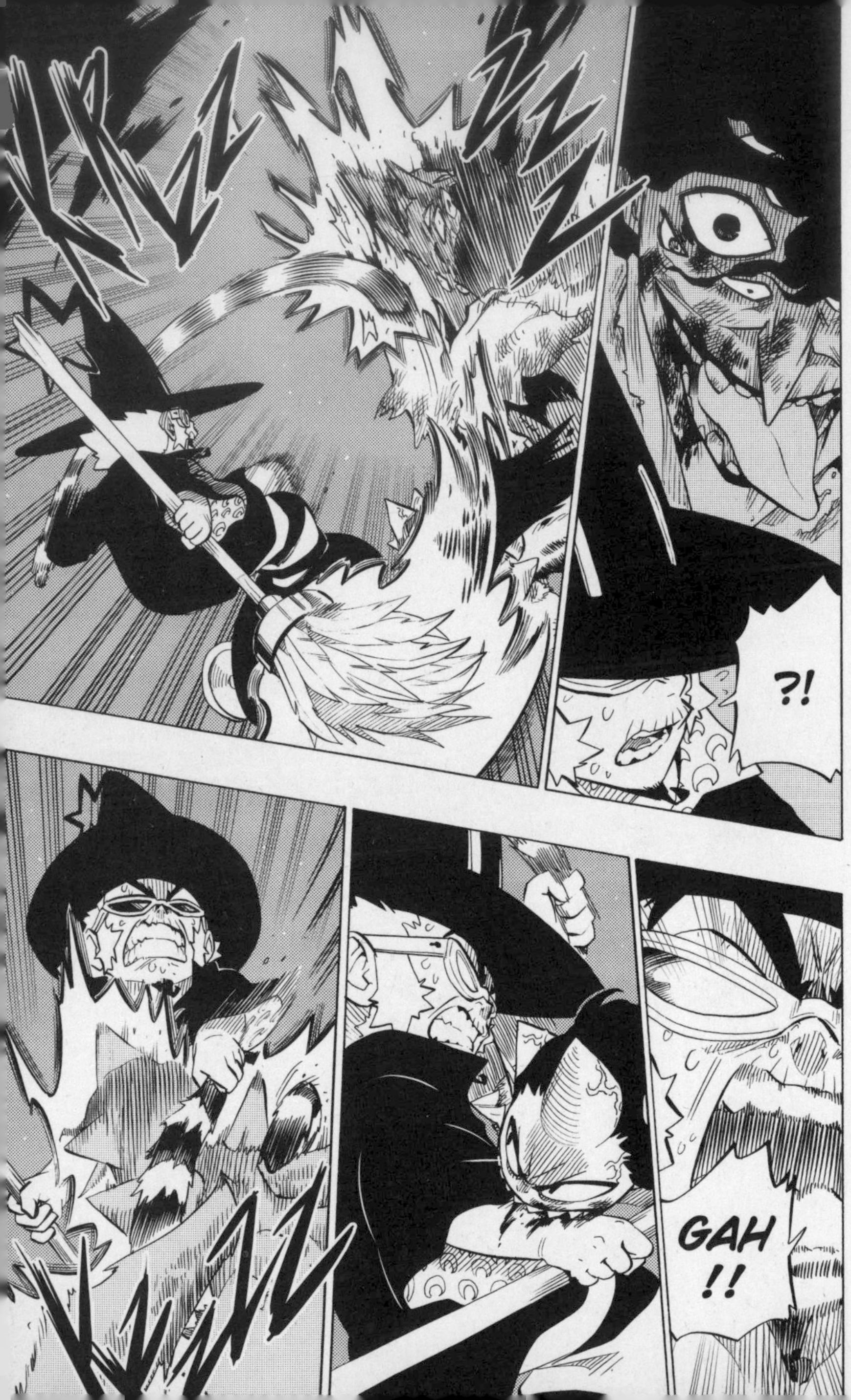
?!
GAH !!

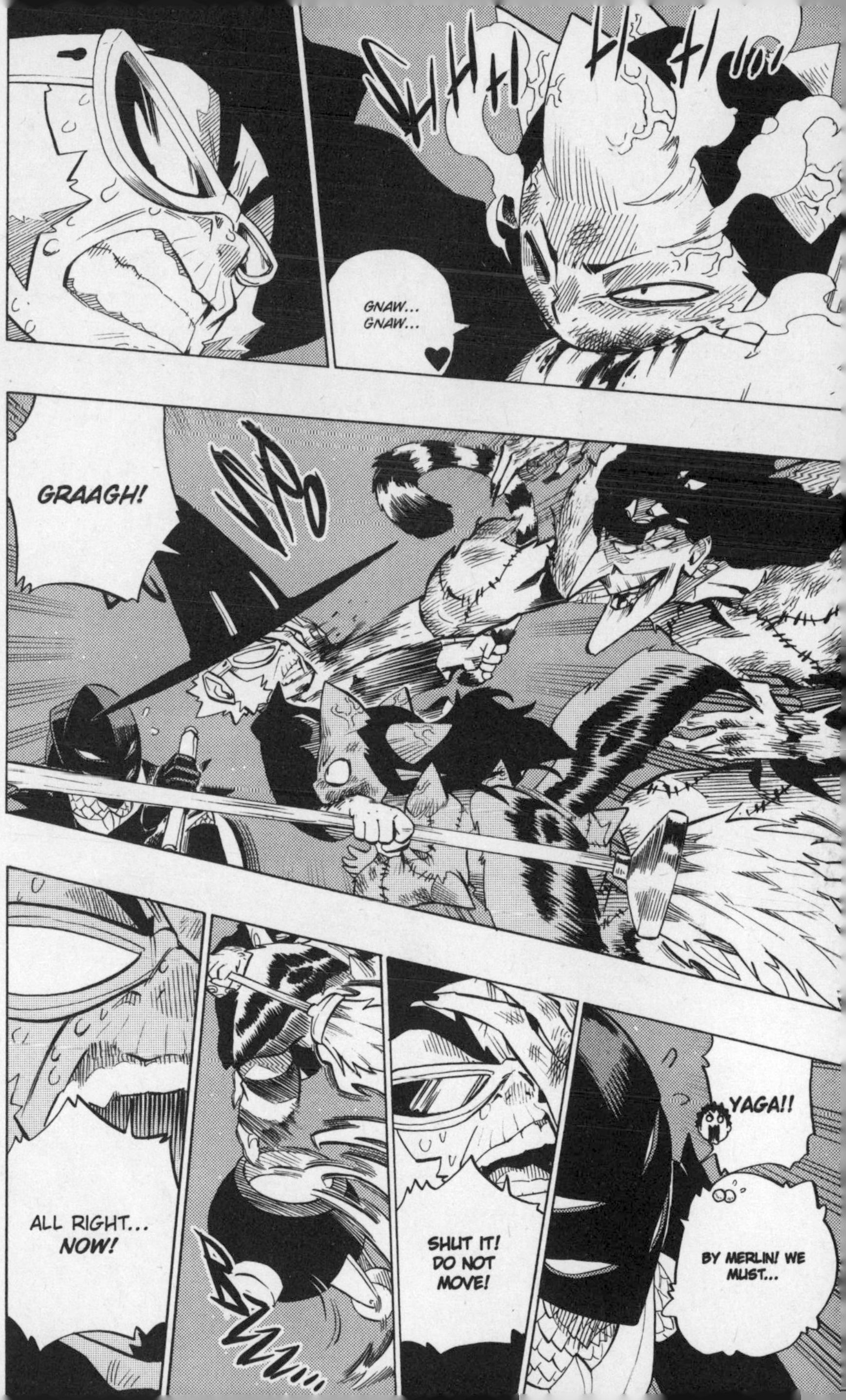
GNAW... GNAW...
GRAAGH!
YAGA!!
BY MERLIN! WE MUST...
SHUT IT! DO NOT MOVE!
ALL RIGHT... NOW!

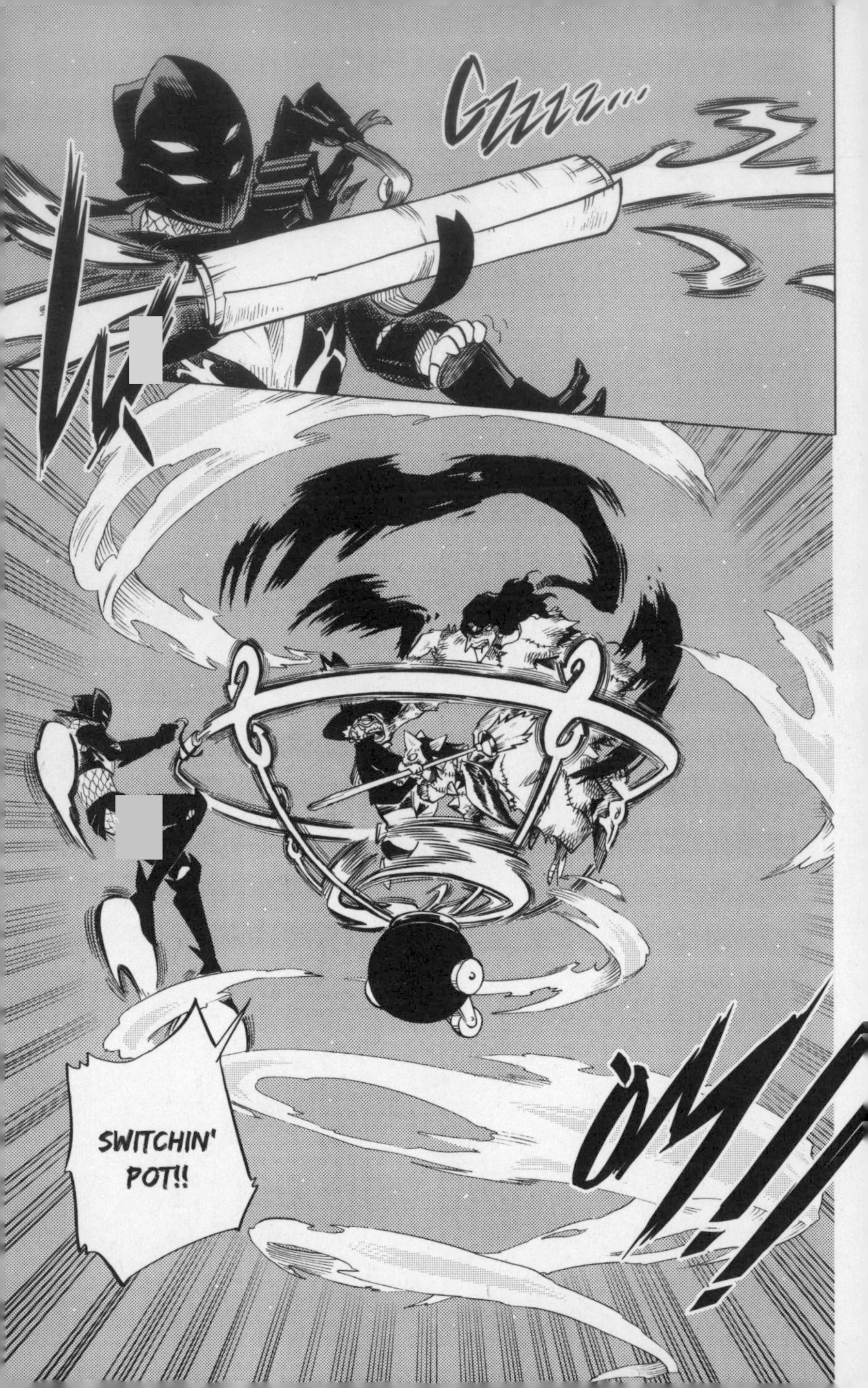
SWITCHIN' POT!!

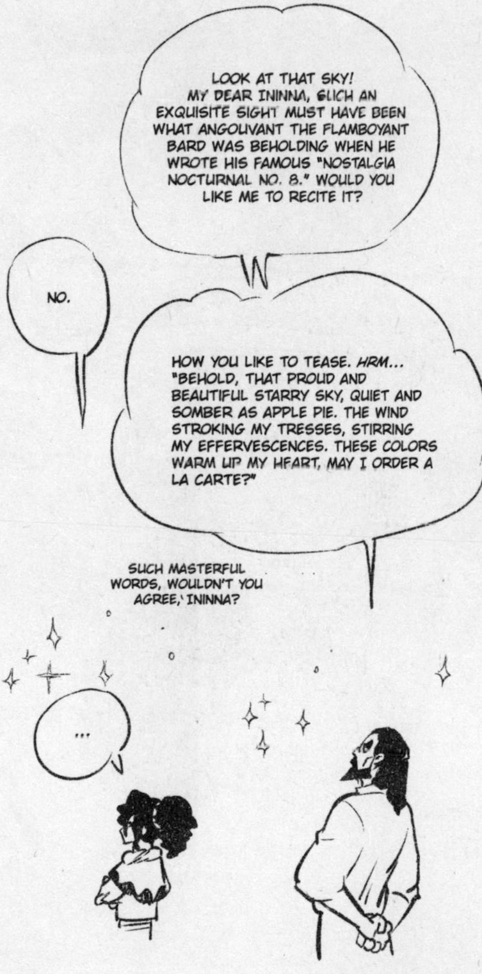
LOOK AT THAT SKY! MY DEAR ININNA, SUCH AN EXQUISITE SIGHT MUST HAVE BEEN WHAT ANGOUVANT THE FLAMBOYANT BARD WAS BEHOLDING WHEN HE WROTE HIS FAMOUS "NOSTALGIA NOCTURNAL NO. 8." WOULD YOU LIKE ME TO RECITE IT?
NO.
HOW YOU LIKE TO TEASE. *HRM*... "BEHOLD, THAT PROUD AND BEAUTIFUL STARRY SKY, QUIET AND SOMBER AS APPLE PIE. THE WIND STROKING MY TRESSES, STIRRING MY EFFERVESCENCES. THESE COLORS WARM UP MY HEART, MAY I ORDER A LA CARTE?"
SUCH MASTERFUL WORDS, WOULDN'T YOU AGREE, ININNA?
...

CHAPTER 87 SOUP

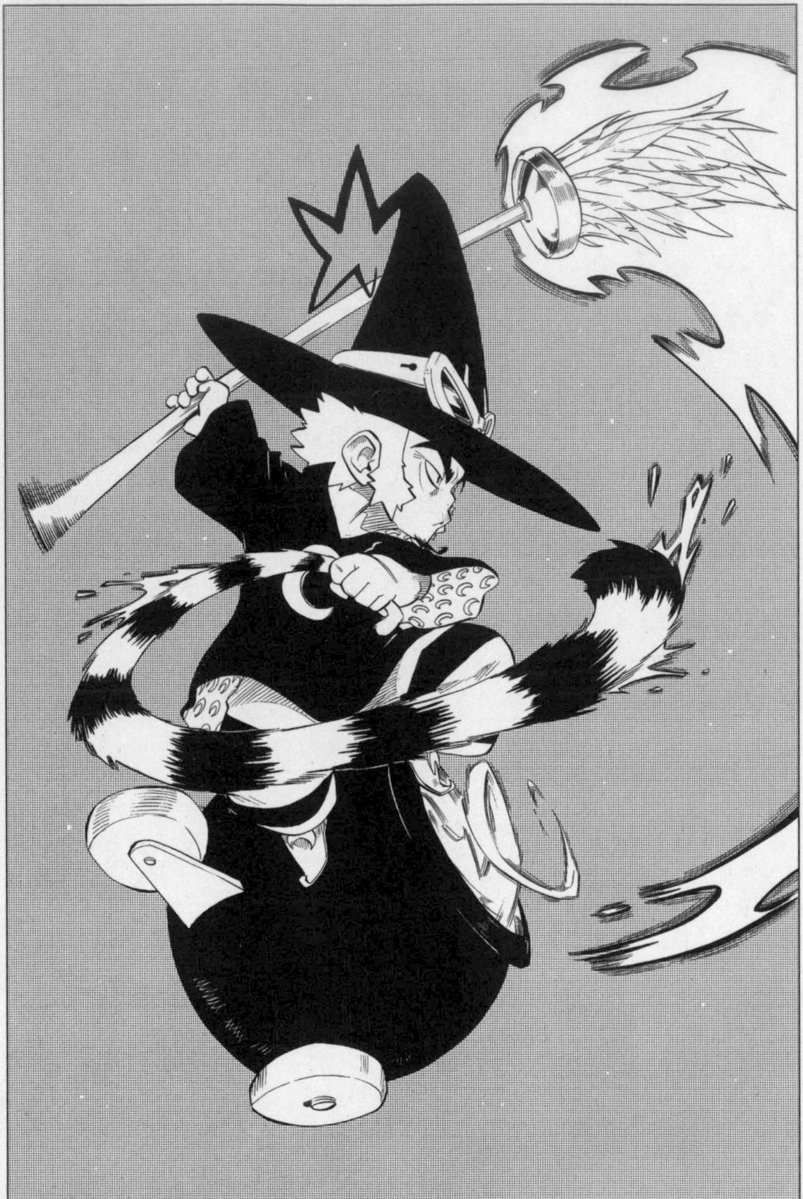

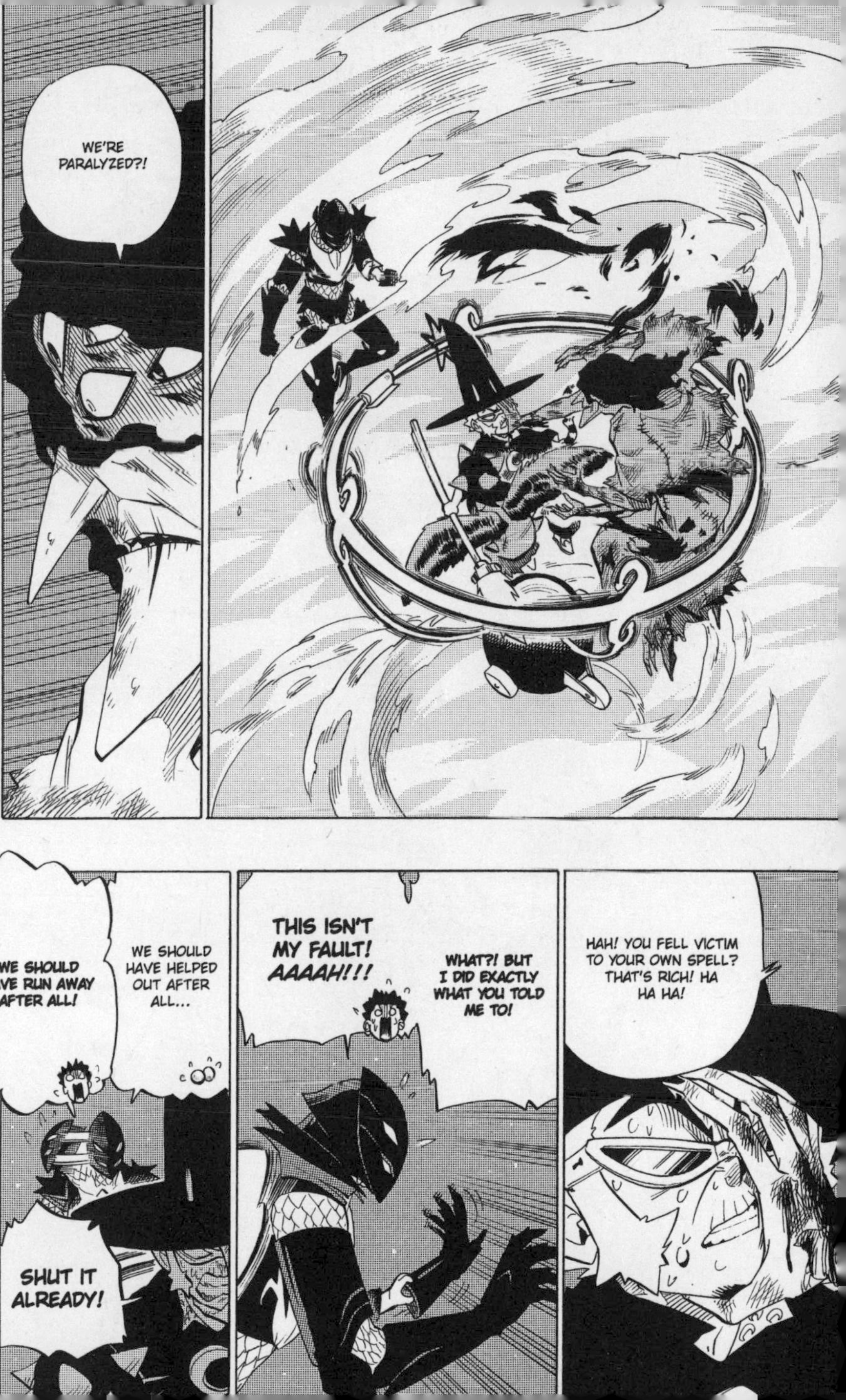
WE'RE PARALYZED?!
HAH! YOU FELL VICTIM TO YOUR OWN SPELL? THAT'S RICH! HA HA HA!
WHAT?! BUT I DID EXACTLY WHAT YOU TOLD ME TO!
THIS ISN'T MY FAULT! AAAAH!!!
WE SHOULD HAVE HELPED OUT AFTER ALL...
WE SHOULD HAVE RUN AWAY AFTER ALL!
SHUT IT ALREADY!

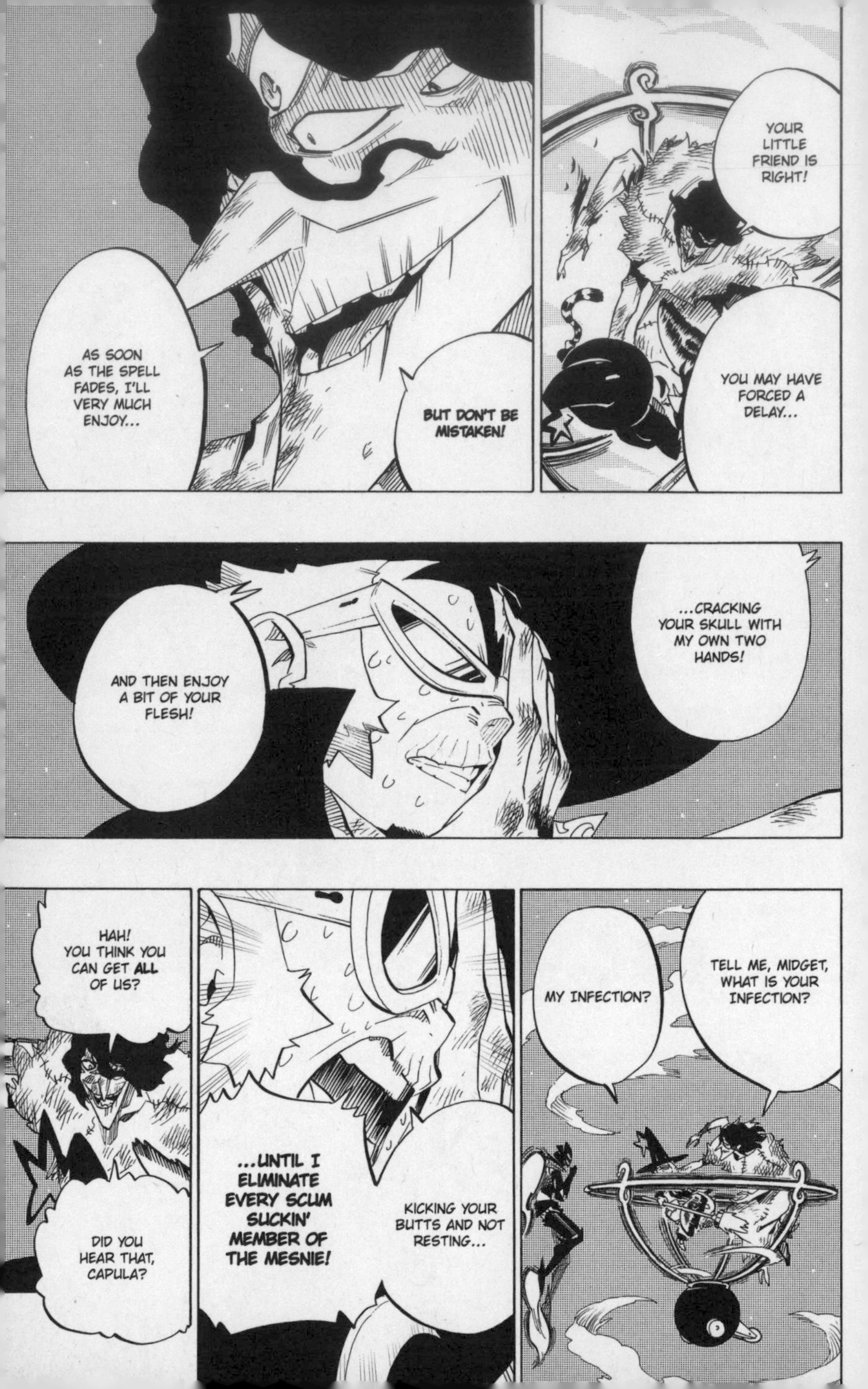
YOUR LITTLE FRIEND IS RIGHT!
YOU MAY HAVE FORCED A DELAY...
BUT DON'T BE MISTAKEN!
AS SOON AS THE SPELL FADES, I'LL VERY MUCH ENJOY...
...CRACKING YOUR SKULL WITH MY OWN TWO HANDS!
AND THEN ENJOY A BIT OF YOUR FLESH!
TELL ME, MIDGET, WHAT IS YOUR INFECTION?
MY INFECTION?
KICKING YOUR BUTTS AND NOT RESTING...
...UNTIL I ELIMINATE EVERY SCUM SUCKIN' MEMBER OF THE MESNIE!
HAH! YOU THINK YOU CAN GET ALL OF US?
DID YOU HEAR THAT, CAPULA?

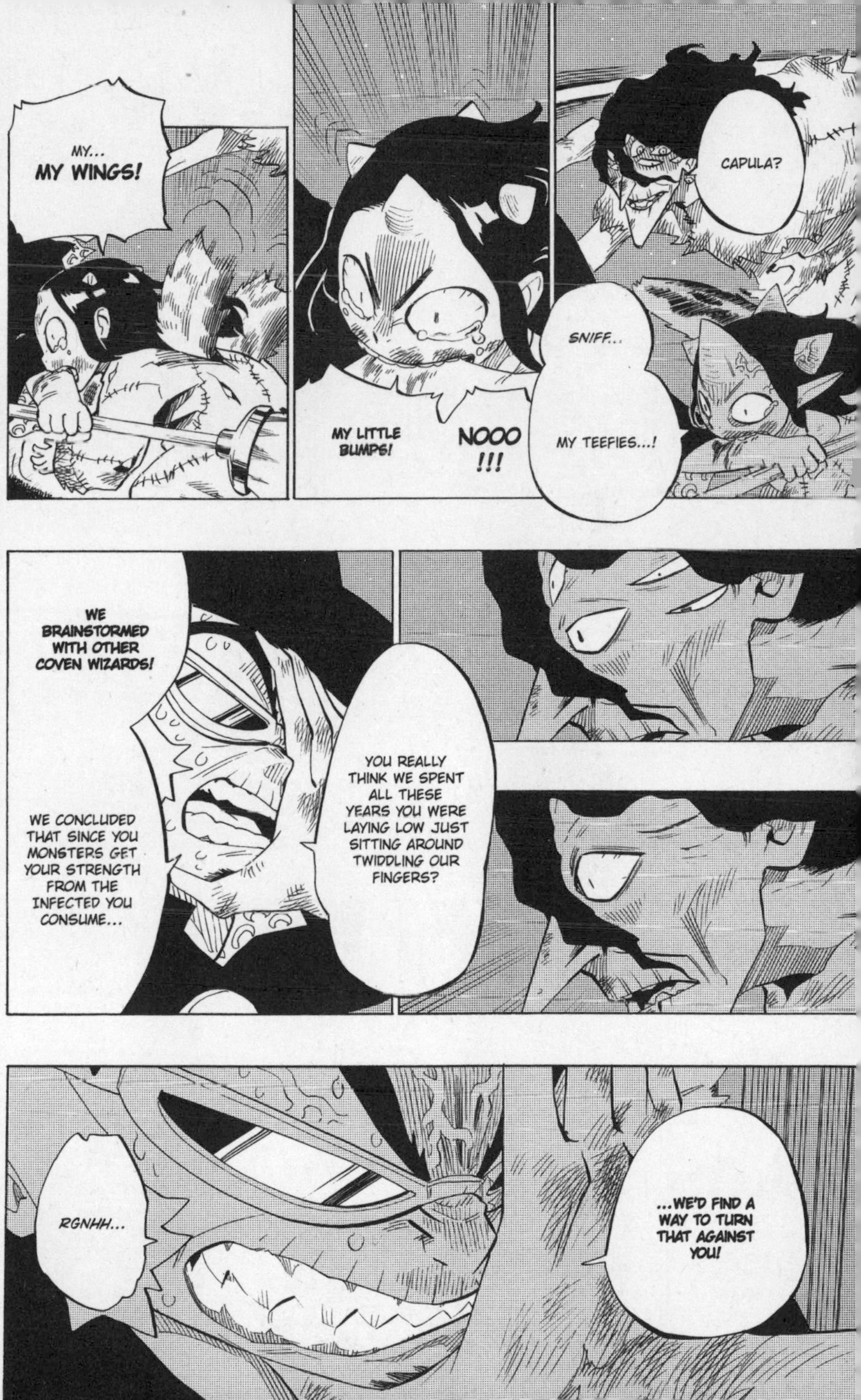
CAPULA?
SNIFF... MY TEEFIES...!
NOOO!!!
MY LITTLE BUMPS!
MY... MY WINGS!
YOU REALLY THINK WE SPENT ALL THESE YEARS YOU WERE LAYING LOW JUST SITTING AROUND TWIDDLING OUR FINGERS?
WE BRAINSTORMED WITH OTHER COVEN WIZARDS!
WE CONCLUDED THAT SINCE YOU MONSTERS GET YOUR STRENGTH FROM THE INFECTED YOU CONSUME...
...WE'D FIND A WAY TO TURN THAT AGAINST YOU!
RGNHH...

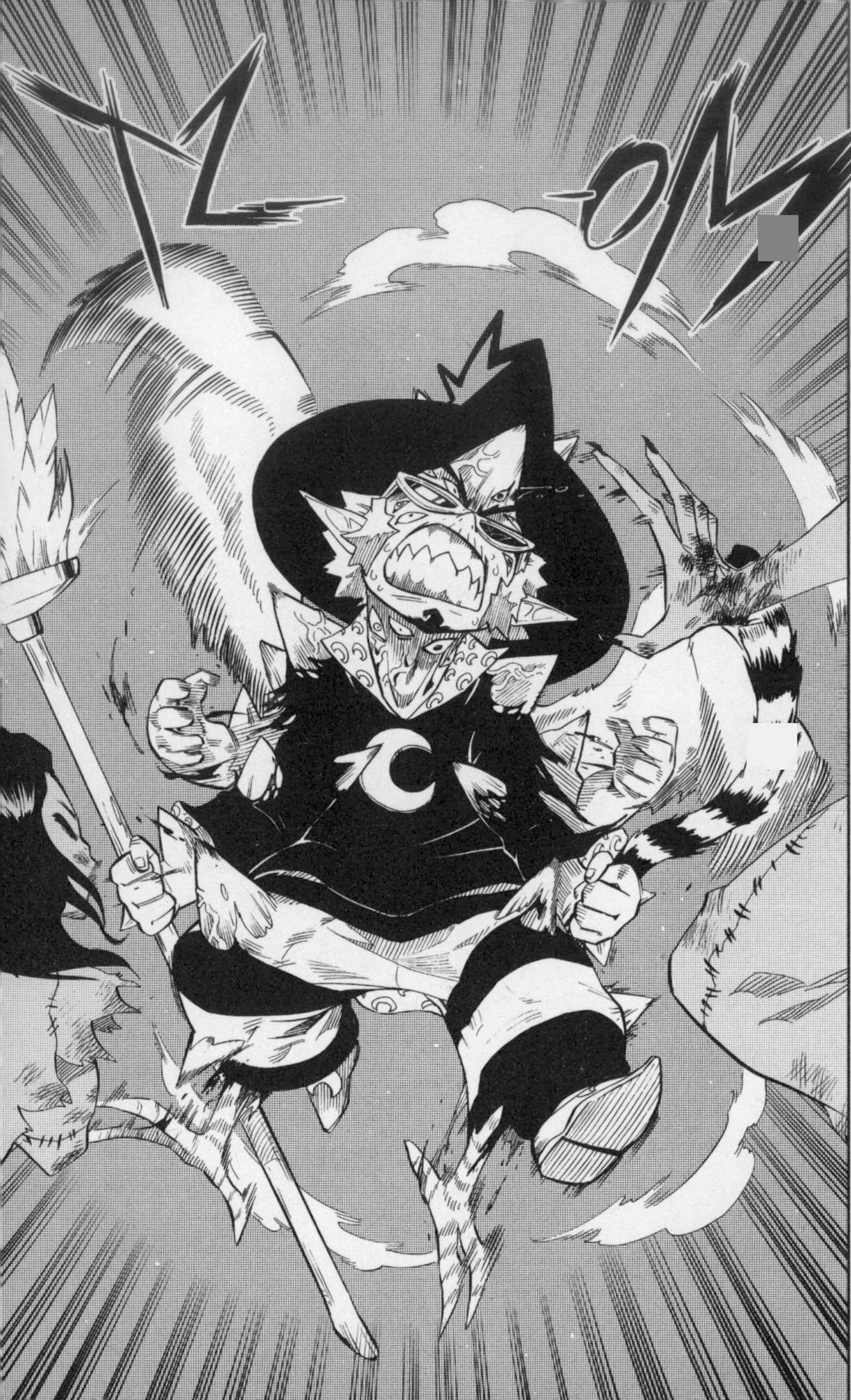

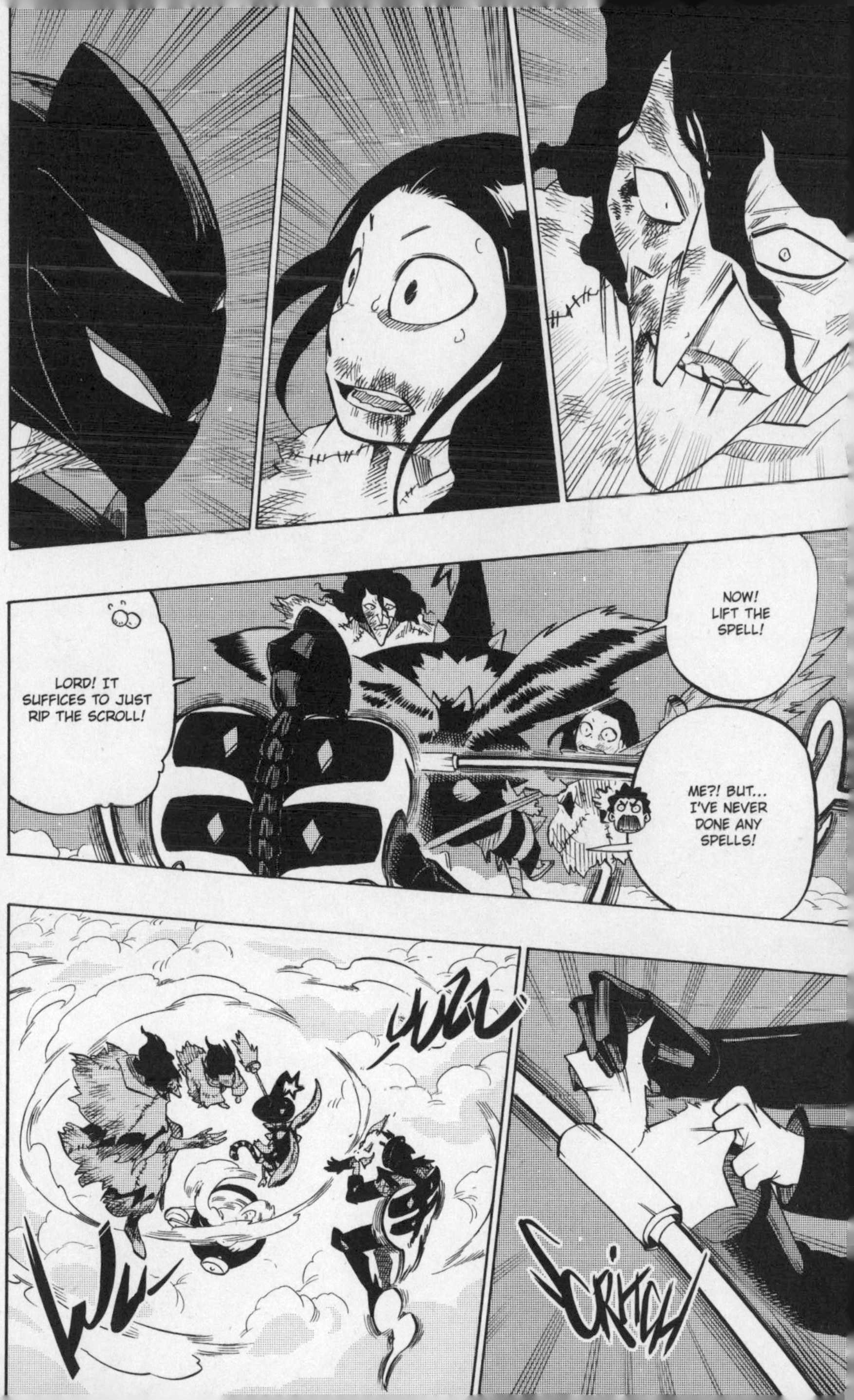
NOW! LIFT THE SPELL!
ME?! BUT... I'VE NEVER DONE ANY SPELLS!
LORD! IT SUFFICES TO JUST RIP THE SCROLL!
SCRITCH
WUZZ
WU

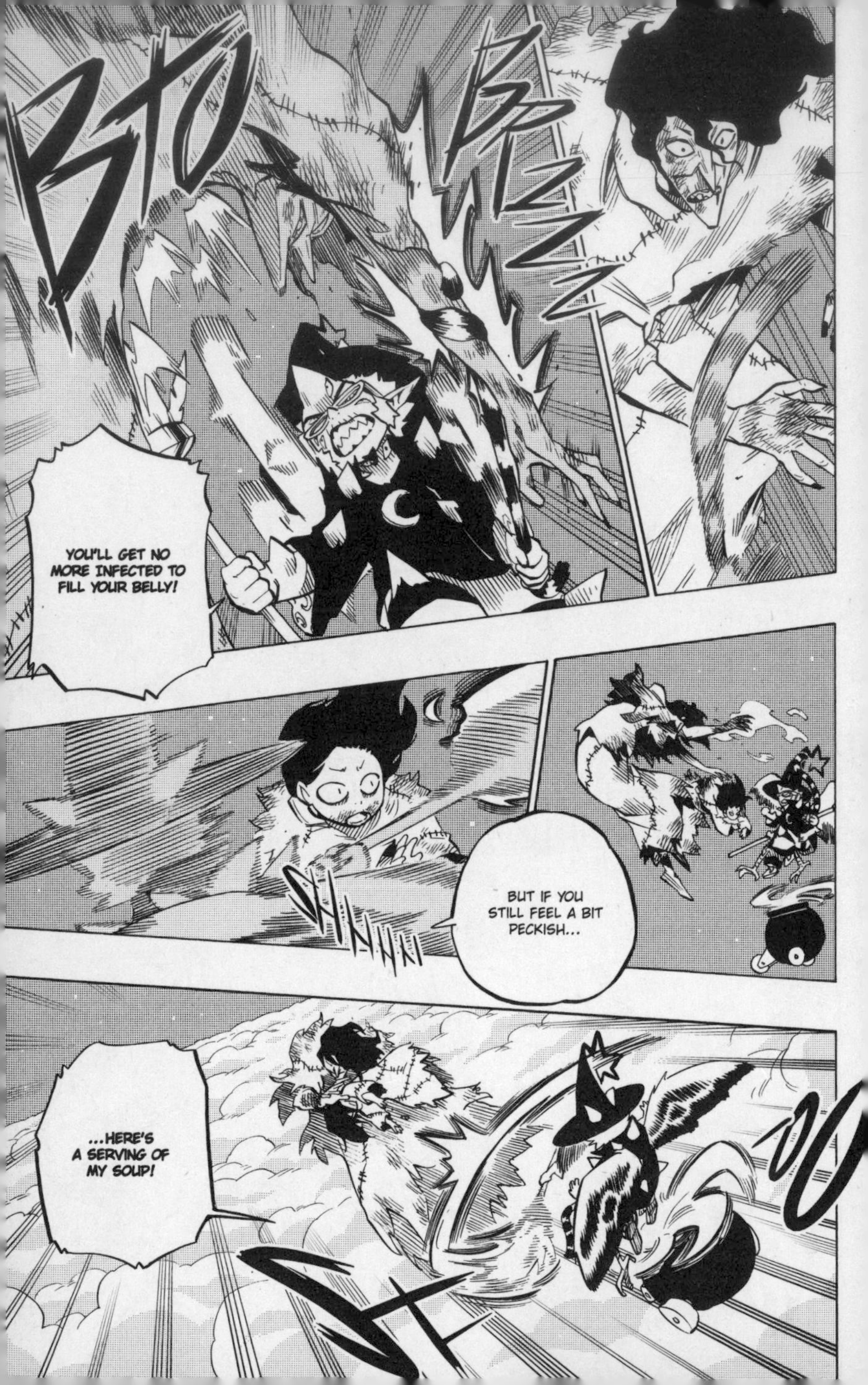
YOU'LL GET NO MORE INFECTED TO FILL YOUR BELLY!
BUT IF YOU STILL FEEL A BIT PECKISH...
...HERE'S A SERVING OF MY SOUP!

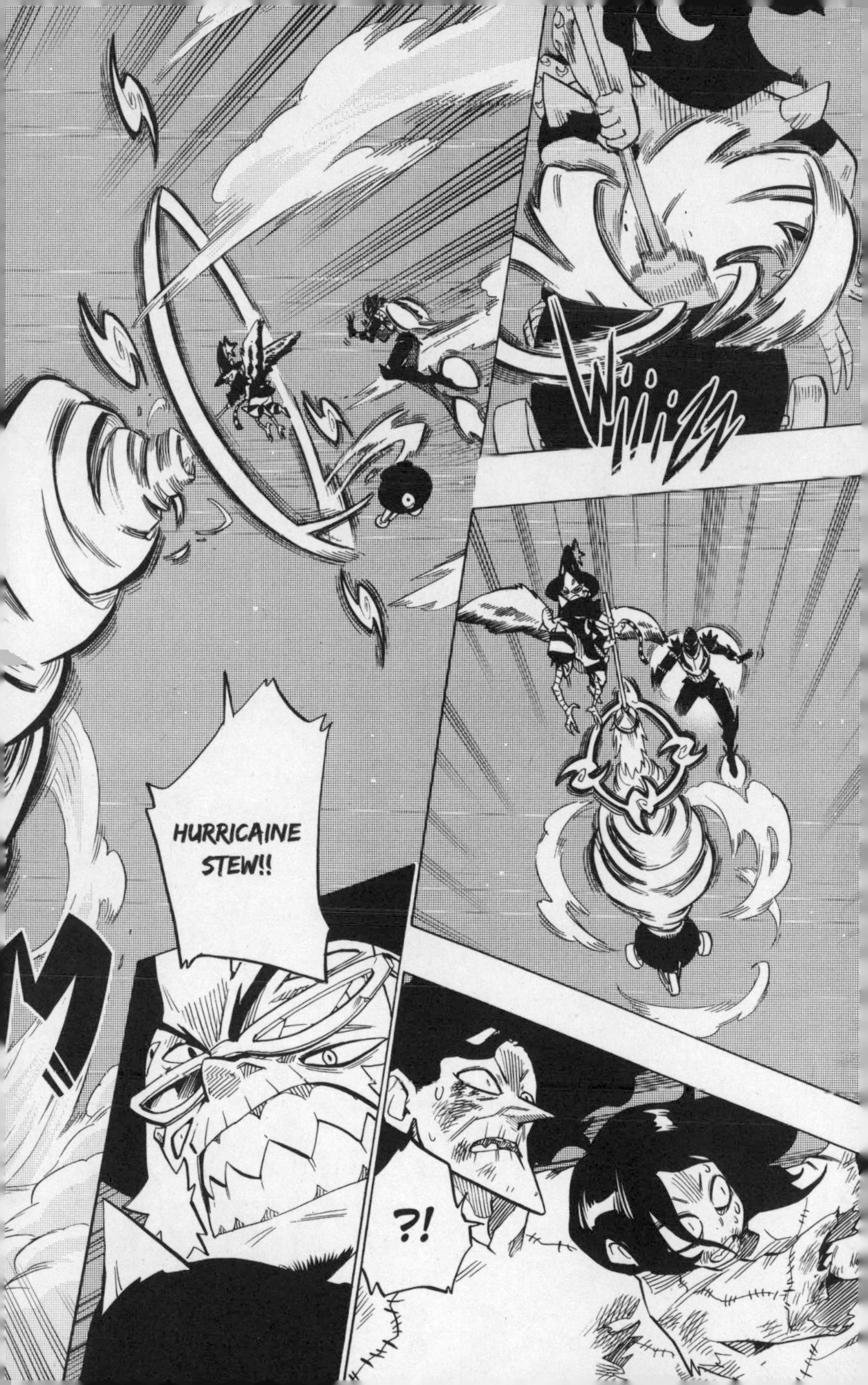
WHIZZ
HURRICAINE STEW!!
?!

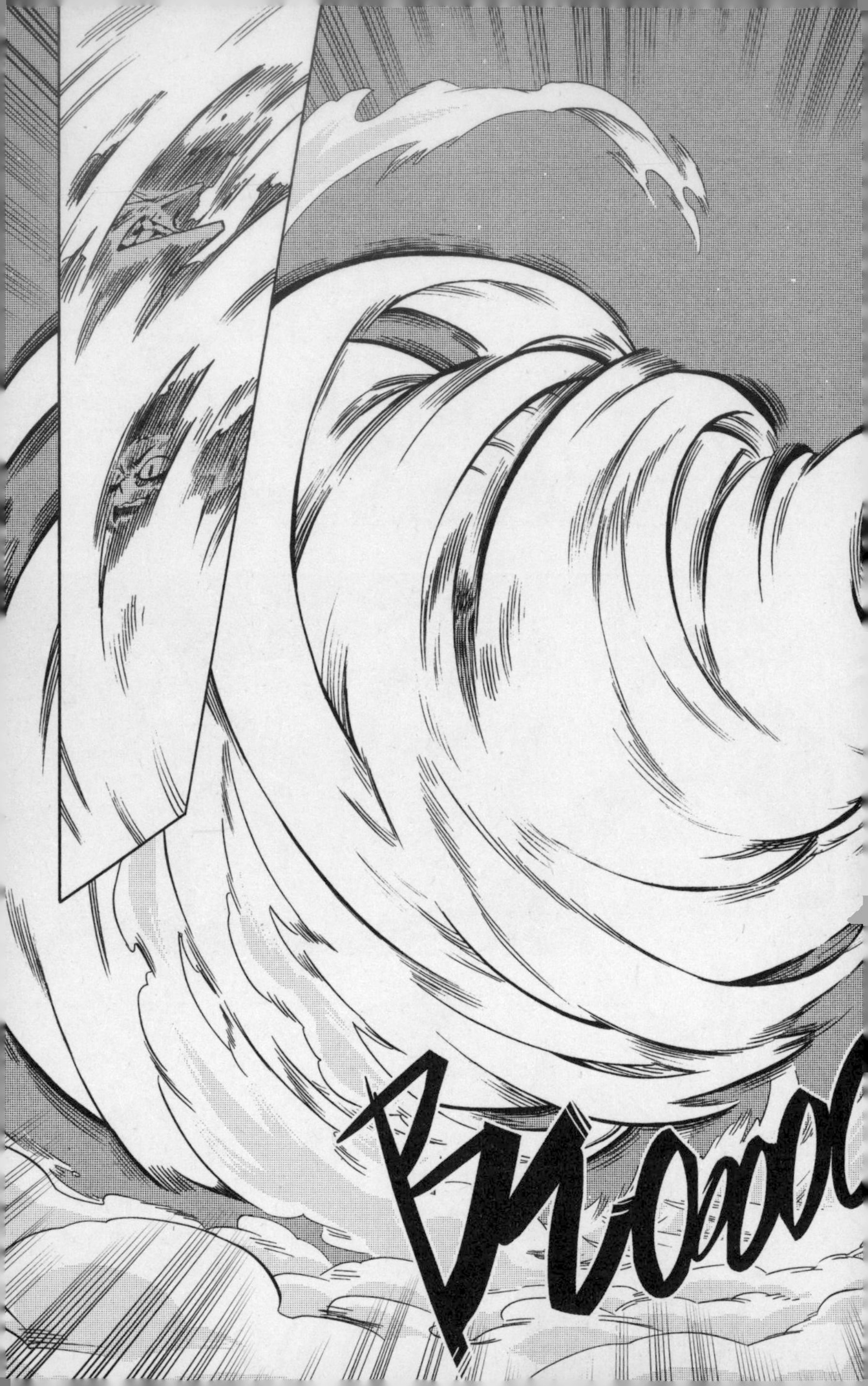
Brooo

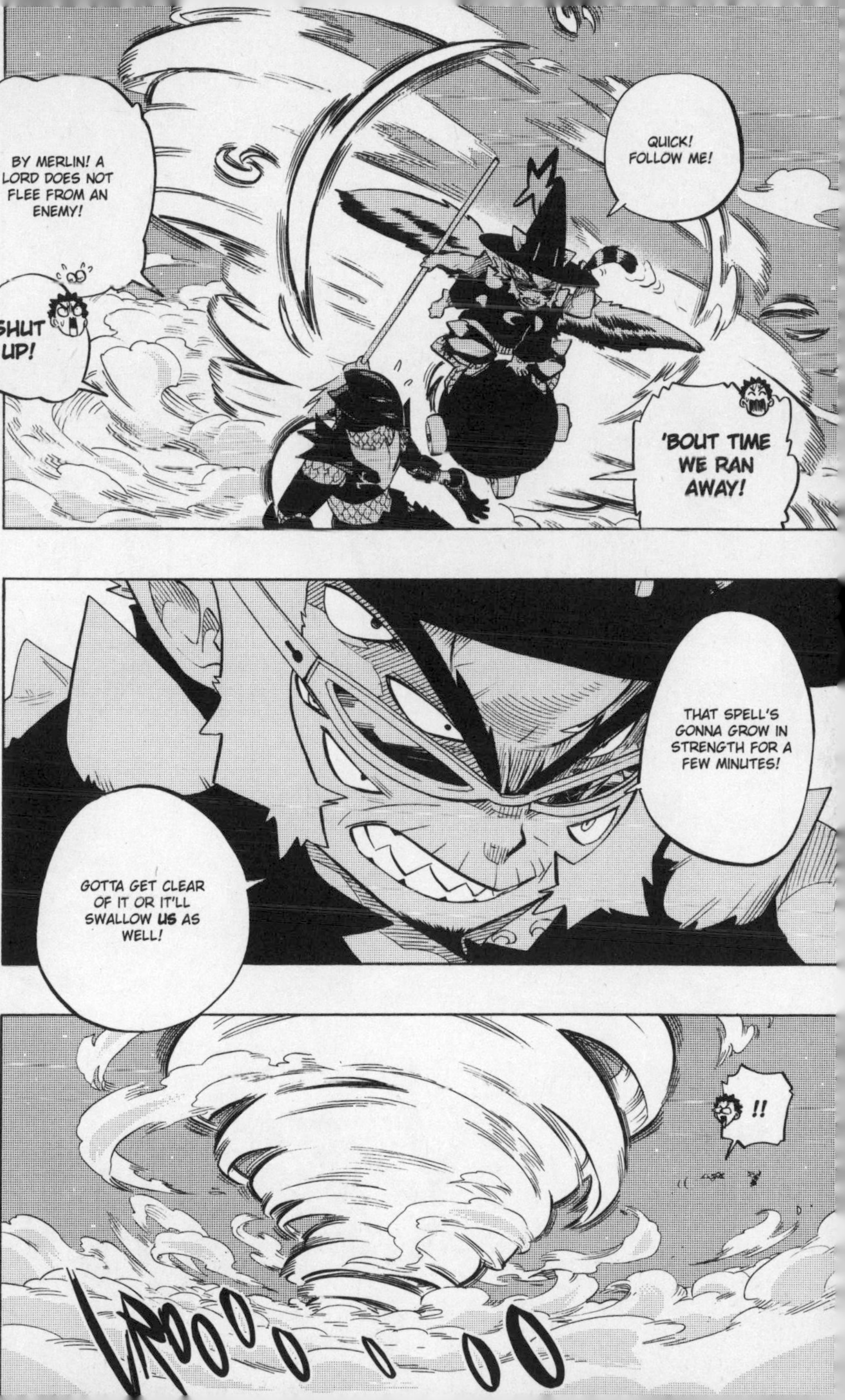
QUICK! FOLLOW ME!
BY MERLIN! A LORD DOES NOT FLEE FROM AN ENEMY!
SHUT UP!
'BOUT TIME WE RAN AWAY!
THAT SPELL'S GONNA GROW IN STRENGTH FOR A FEW MINUTES!
GOTTA GET CLEAR OF IT OR IT'LL SWALLOW US AS WELL!
!!
VROOO...OO

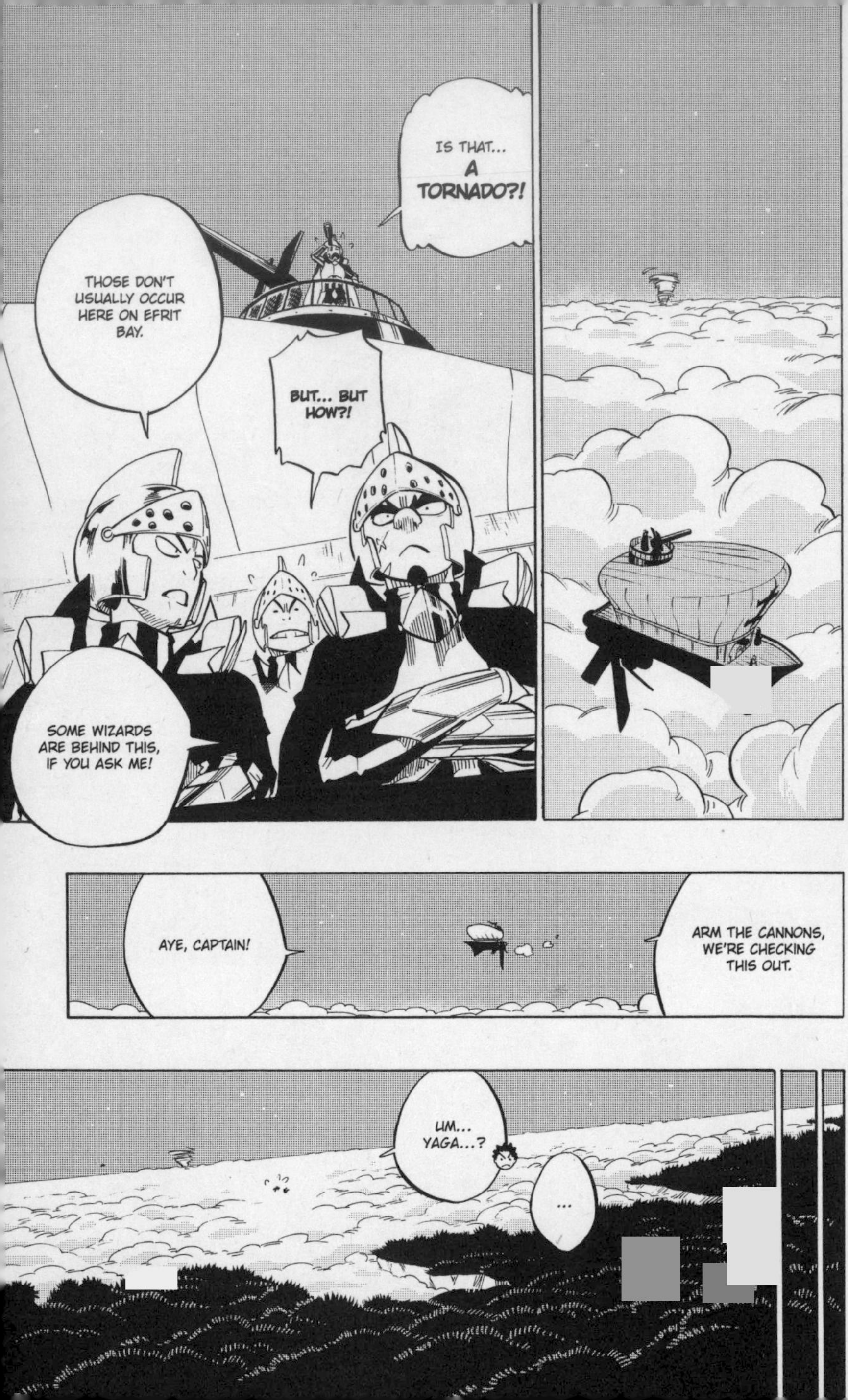
IS THAT... A TORNADO?!
THOSE DON'T USUALLY OCCUR HERE ON EFRIT BAY.
BUT... BUT HOW?!
SOME WIZARDS ARE BEHIND THIS, IF YOU ASK ME!
ARM THE CANNONS, WE'RE CHECKING THIS OUT.
AYE, CAPTAIN!
UM... YAGA...?
...

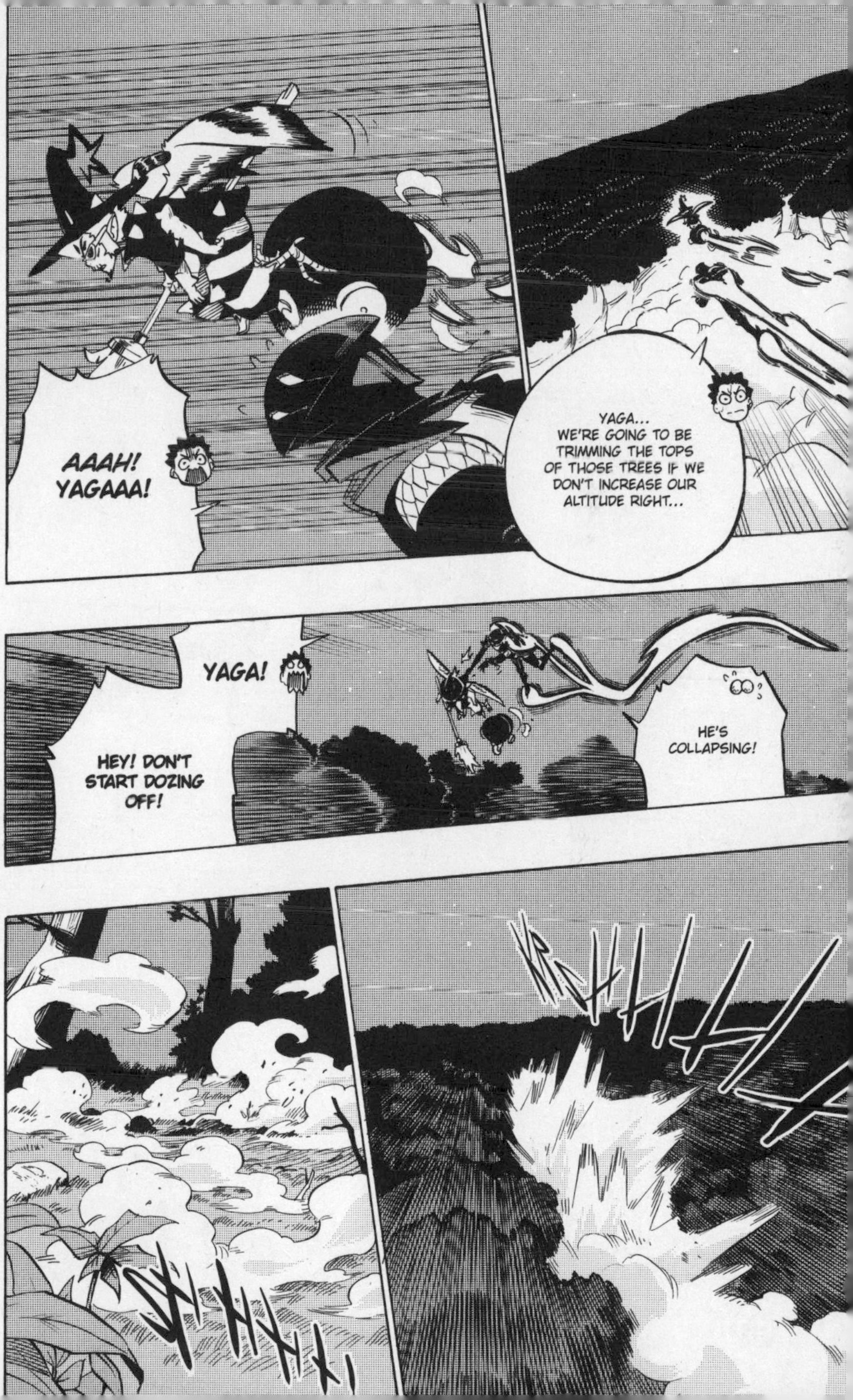
YAGA... WE'RE GOING TO BE TRIMMING THE TOPS OF THOSE TREES IF WE DON'T INCREASE OUR ALTITUDE RIGHT...
AAAH! YAGAAA!
HE'S COLLAPSING!
YAGA!
HEY! DON'T START DOZING OFF!

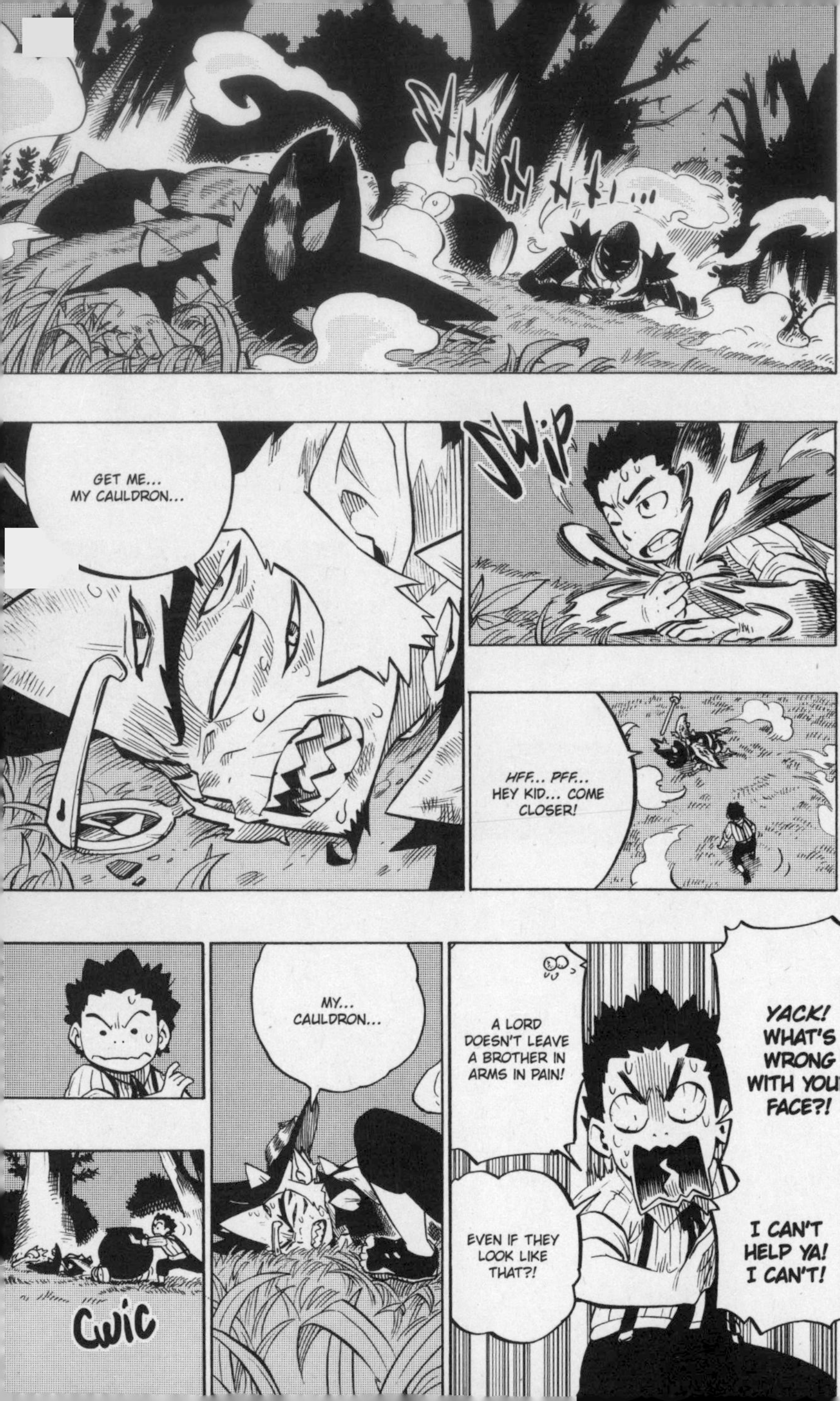
SWIP
HFF... PFF... HEY KID... COME CLOSER!
GET ME... MY CAULDRON...
YACK! WHAT'S WRONG WITH YOUR FACE?!
A LORD DOESN'T LEAVE A BROTHER IN ARMS IN PAIN!
I CAN'T HELP YA! I CAN'T!
EVEN IF THEY LOOK LIKE THAT?!
MY... CAULDRON...
CWIC

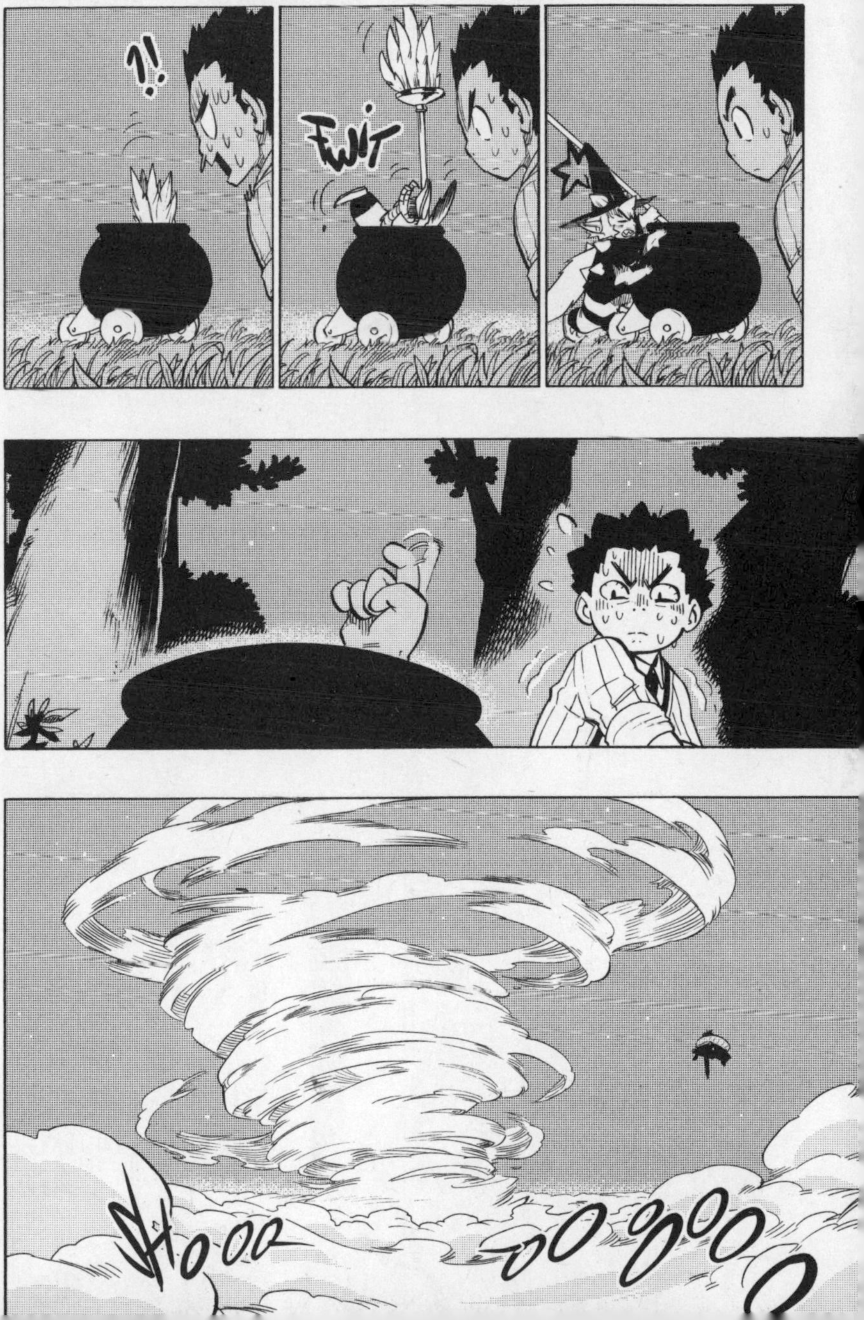
FWIT
?!
SHOOOOOOOOOOOOO

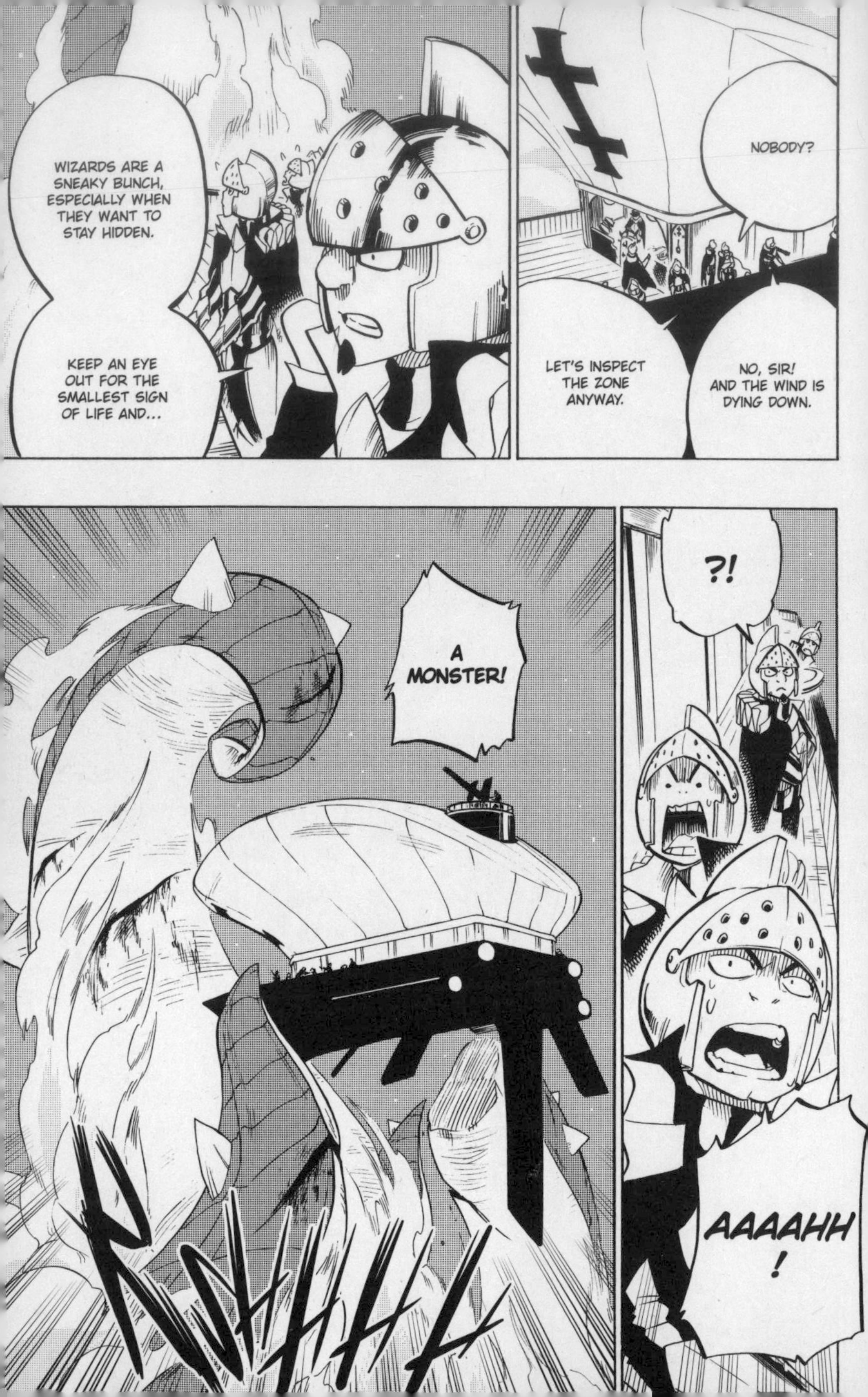
NOBODY?
NO, SIR! AND THE WIND IS DYING DOWN.
LET'S INSPECT THE ZONE ANYWAY.
WIZARDS ARE A SNEAKY BUNCH, ESPECIALLY WHEN THEY WANT TO STAY HIDDEN.
KEEP AN EYE OUT FOR THE SMALLEST SIGN OF LIFE AND...
?!
AAAAHH!
A MONSTER!

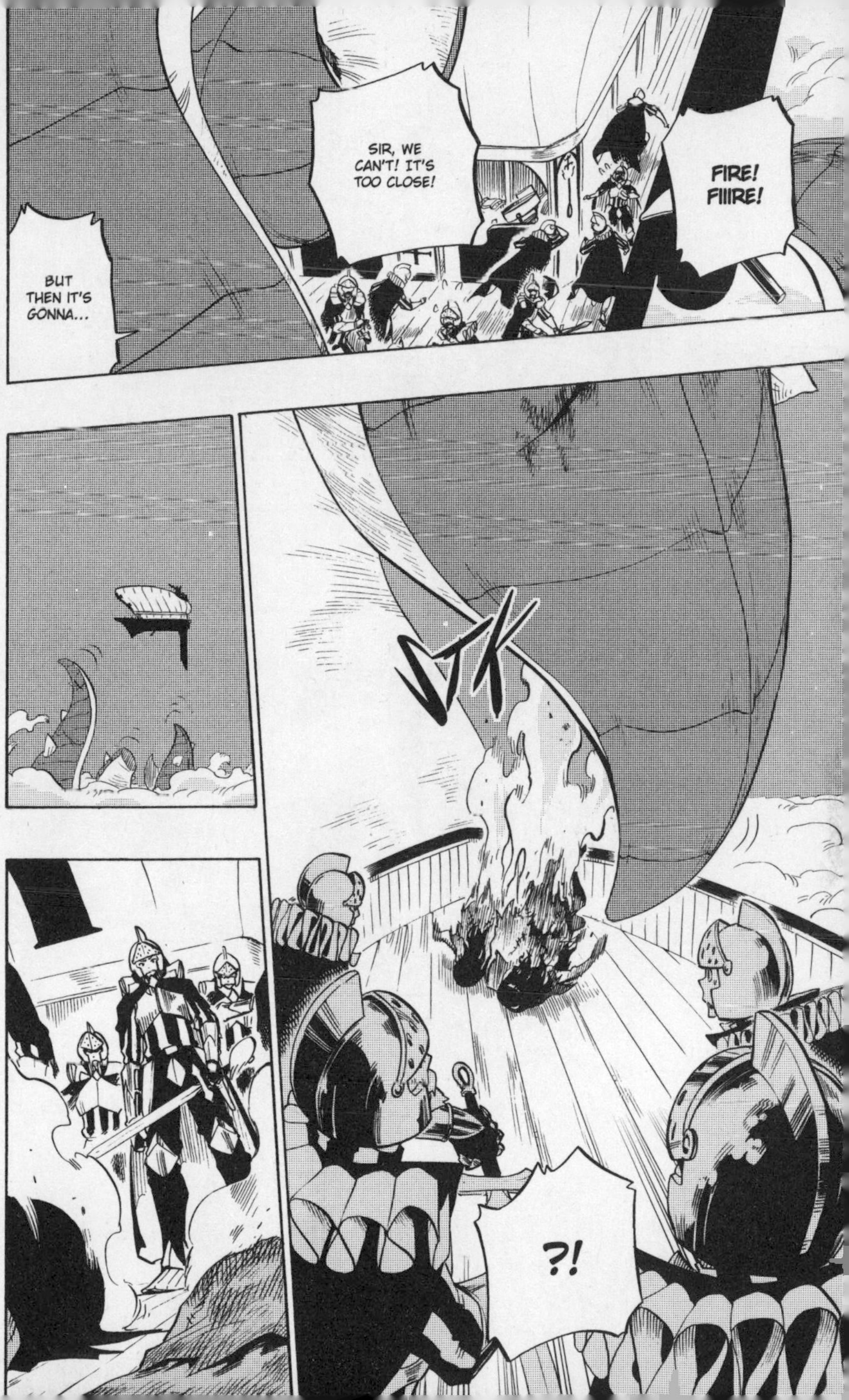
FIRE! FIIRE!
SIR, WE CAN'T! IT'S TOO CLOSE!
BUT THEN IT'S GONNA...
?!

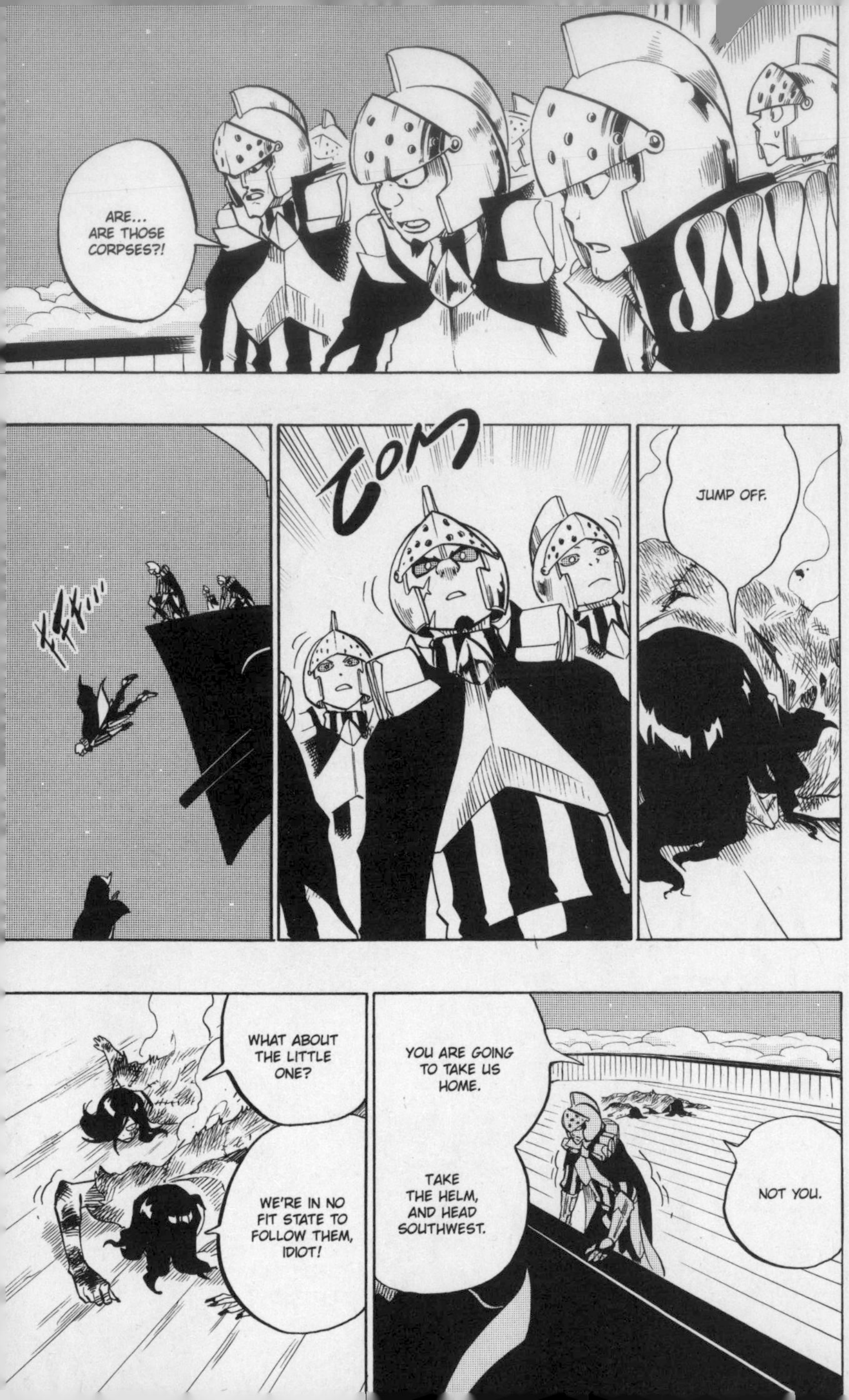
ARE... ARE THOSE CORPSES?!
JUMP OFF.
TOM
YOU ARE GOING TO TAKE US HOME.
NOT YOU.
TAKE THE HELM, AND HEAD SOUTHWEST.
WHAT ABOUT THE LITTLE ONE?
WE'RE IN NO FIT STATE TO FOLLOW THEM, IDIOT!

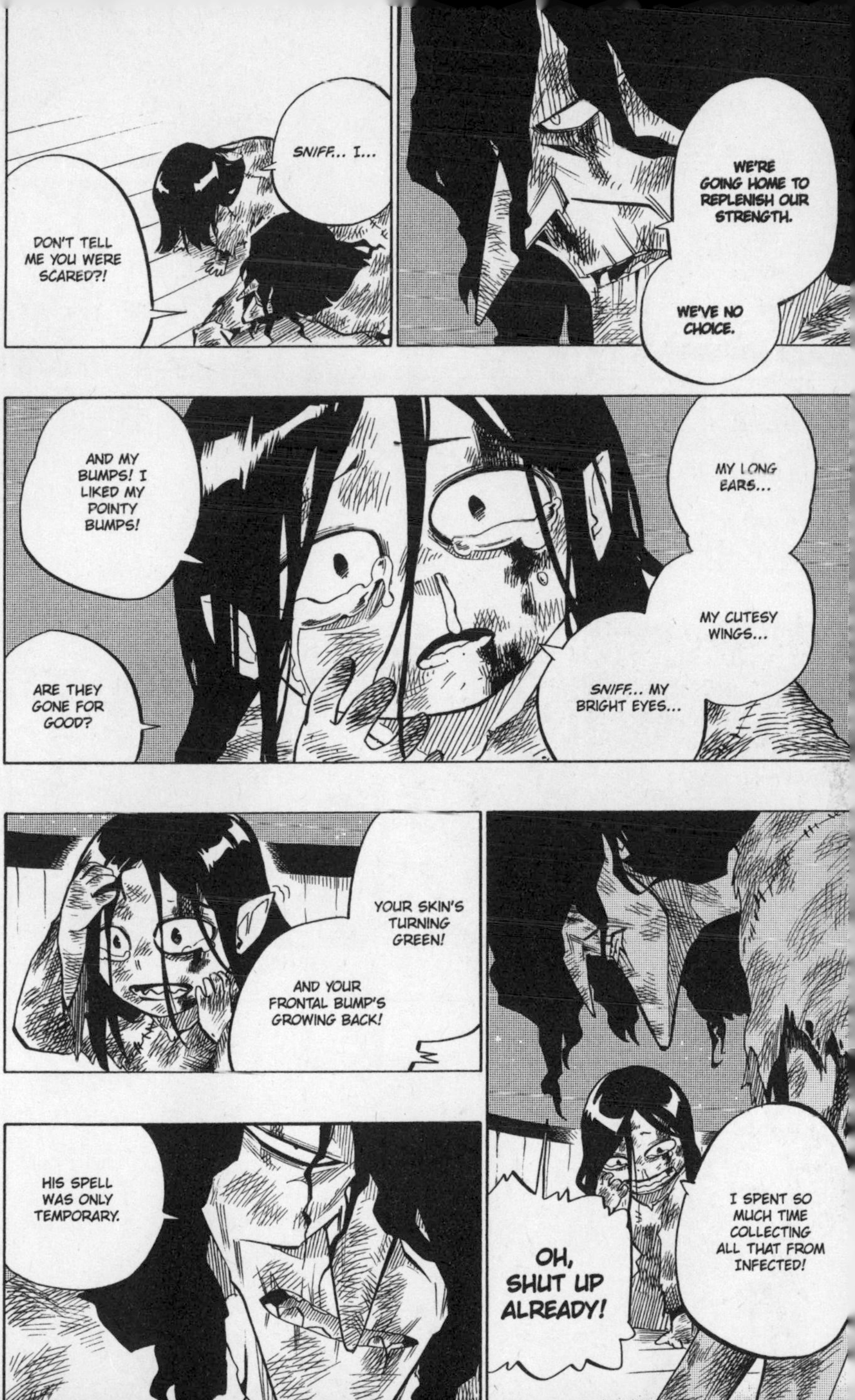
WE'RE GOING HOME TO REPLENISH OUR STRENGTH.
WE'VE NO CHOICE.
SNIFF... I...
DON'T TELL ME YOU WERE SCARED?!
MY LONG EARS...
MY CUTESY WINGS...
SNIFF... MY BRIGHT EYES...
AND MY BUMPS! I LIKED MY POINTY BUMPS!
ARE THEY GONE FOR GOOD?
I SPENT SO MUCH TIME COLLECTING ALL THAT FROM INFECTED!
OH, SHUT UP ALREADY!
YOUR SKIN'S TURNING GREEN!
AND YOUR FRONTAL BUMP'S GROWING BACK!
HIS SPELL WAS ONLY TEMPORARY.

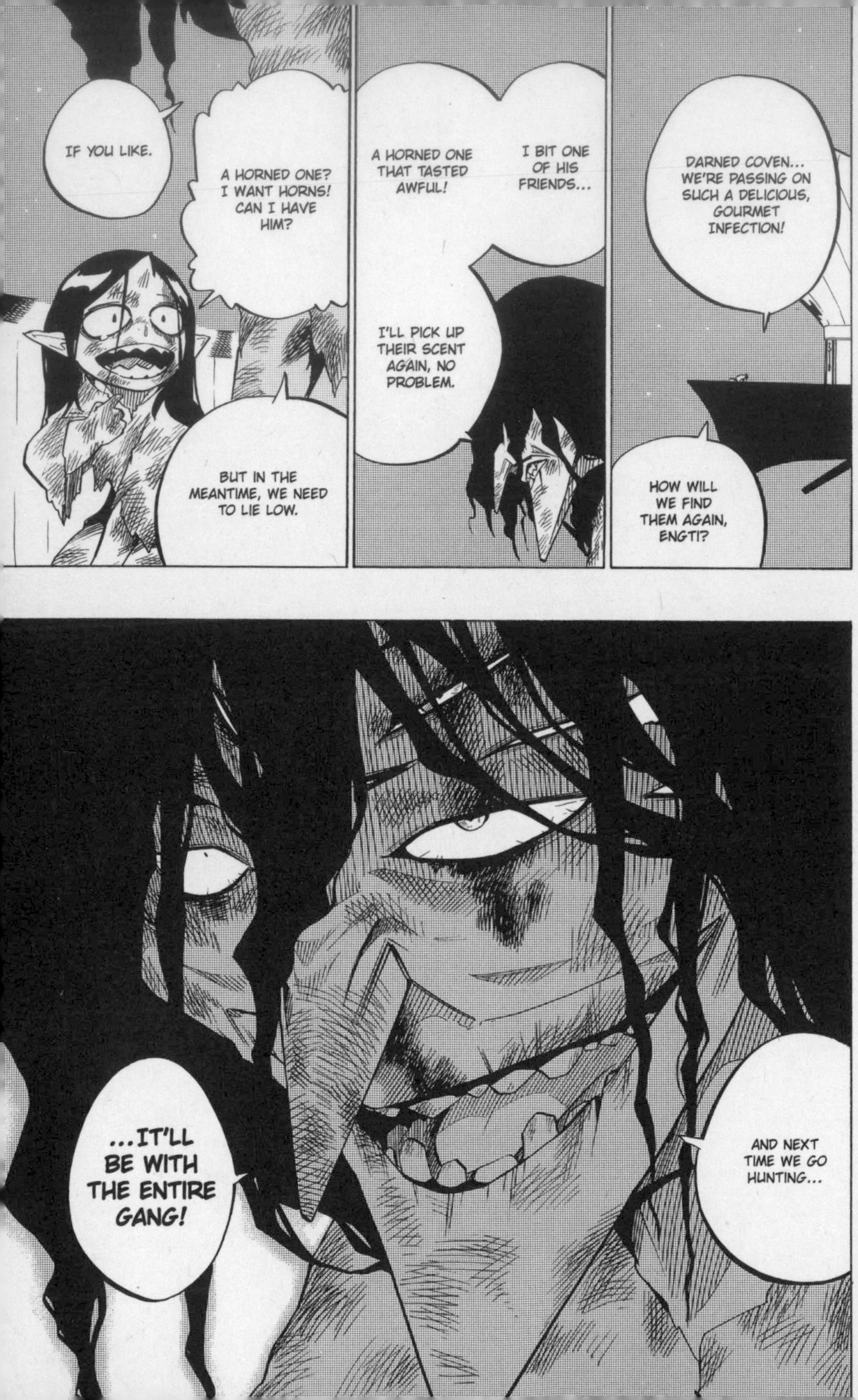
DARNED COVEN... WE'RE PASSING ON SUCH A DELICIOUS, GOURMET INFECTION!
HOW WILL WE FIND THEM AGAIN, ENGTI?
I BIT ONE OF HIS FRIENDS...
A HORNED ONE THAT TASTED AWFUL!
I'LL PICK UP THEIR SCENT AGAIN, NO PROBLEM.
A HORNED ONE? I WANT HORNS! CAN I HAVE HIM?
IF YOU LIKE.
BUT IN THE MEANTIME, WE NEED TO LIE LOW.
AND NEXT TIME WE GO HUNTING...
...IT'LL BE WITH THE ENTIRE GANG!

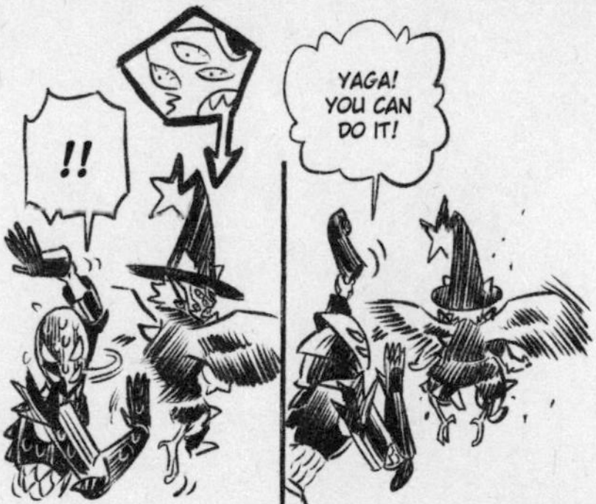
YAGA! YOU CAN DO IT!
!!

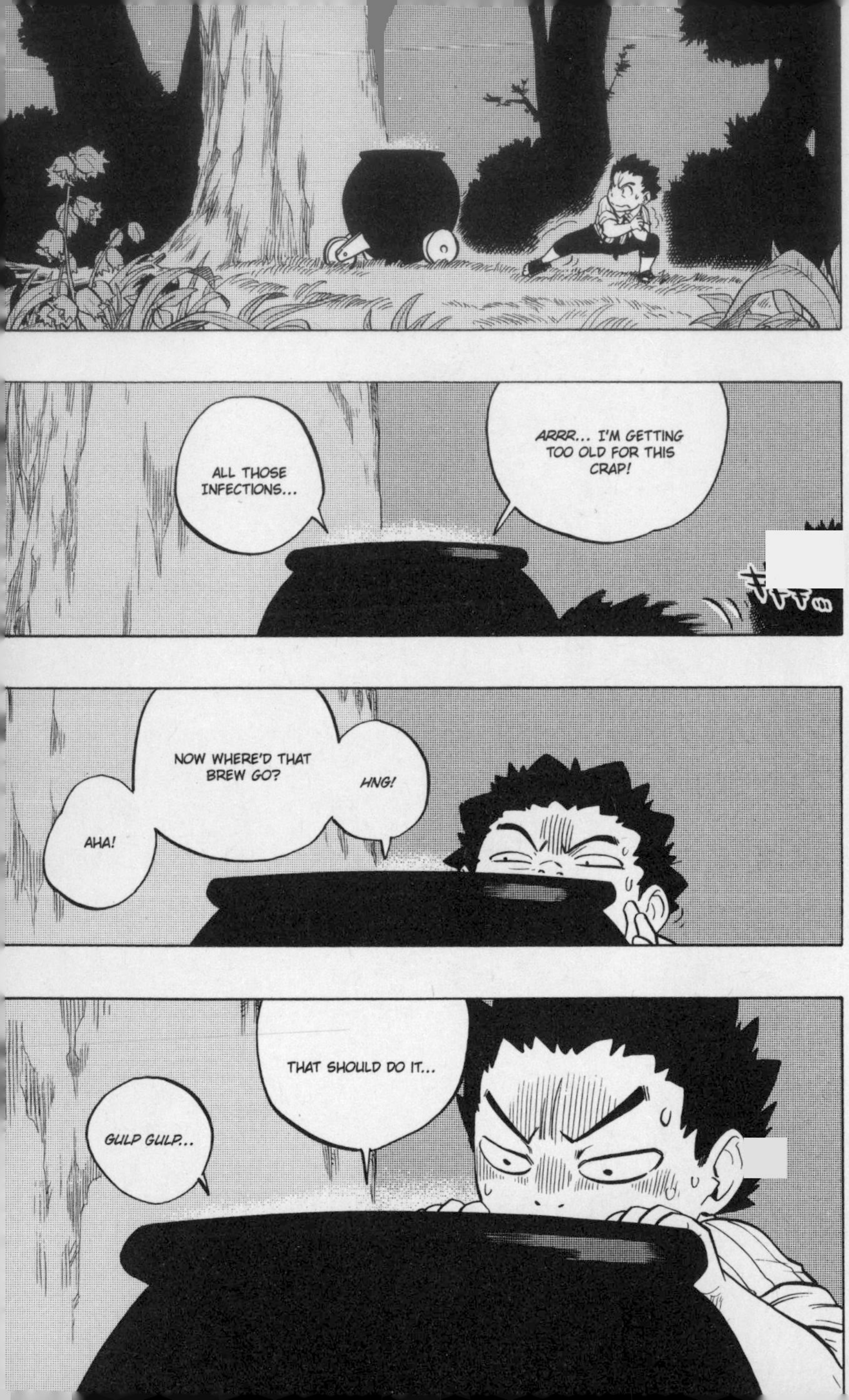
ARRR... I'M GETTING TOO OLD FOR THIS CRAP!
ALL THOSE INFECTIONS...
HNG!
NOW WHERE'D THAT BREW GO?
AHA!
THAT SHOULD DO IT...
GULP GULP...

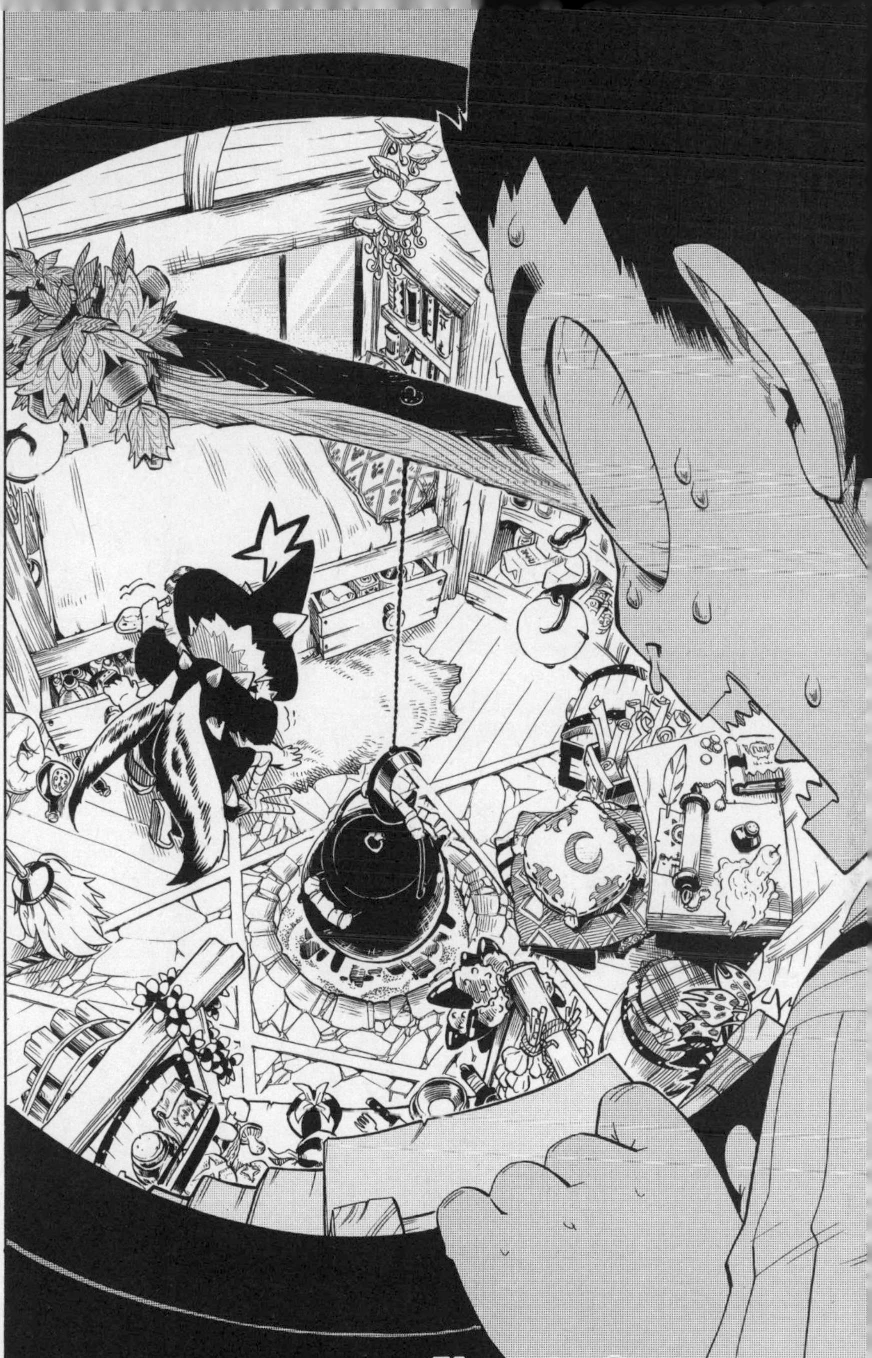

Chapter 88

Yaga's Cauldron

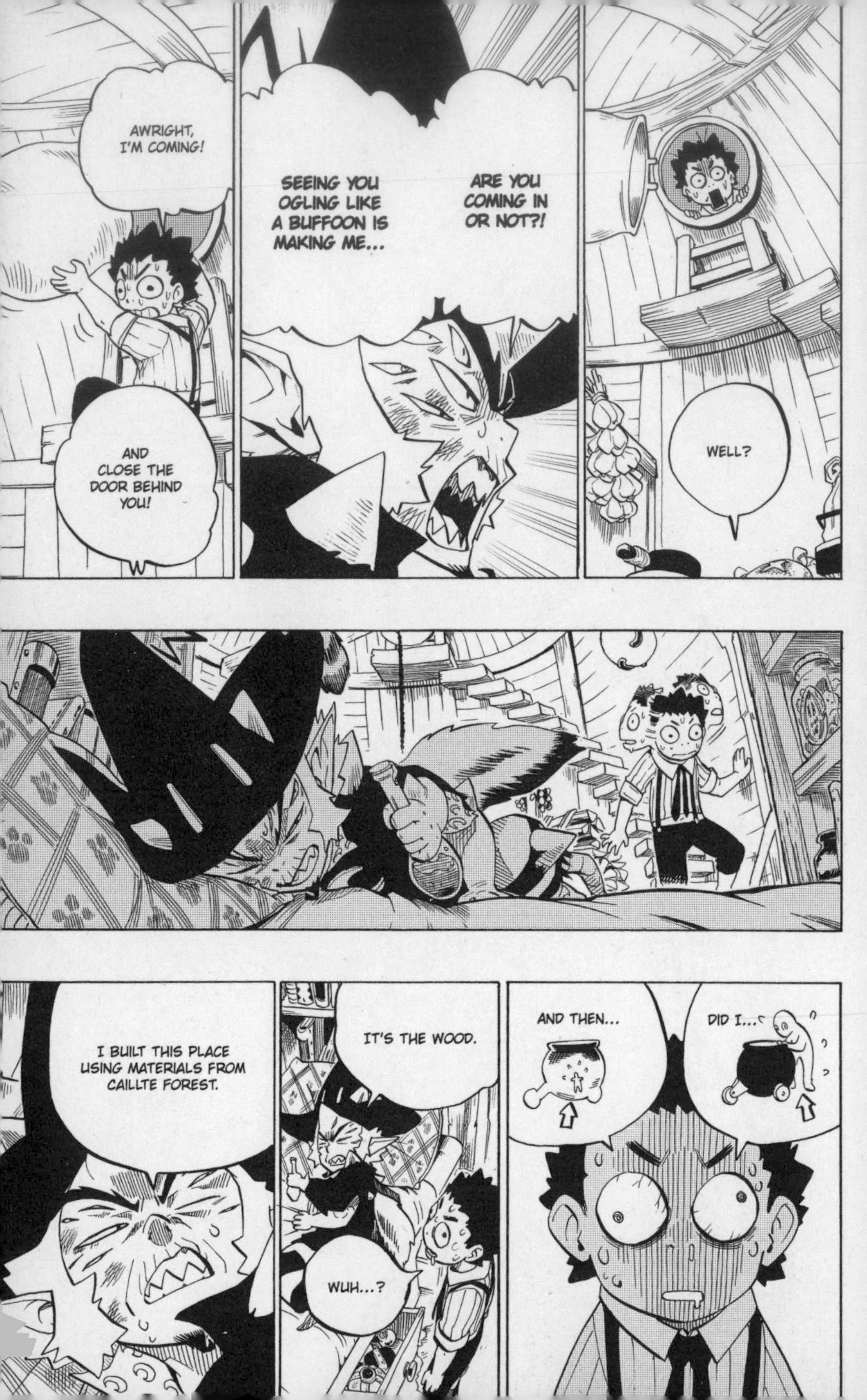
WELL?
ARE YOU COMING IN OR NOT?!
SEEING YOU OGLING LIKE A BUFFOON IS MAKING ME...
AWRIGHT, I'M COMING!
AND CLOSE THE DOOR BEHIND YOU!
DID I...?
AND THEN...
IT'S THE WOOD.
WUH...?
I BUILT THIS PLACE USING MATERIALS FROM CAILLTE FOREST.

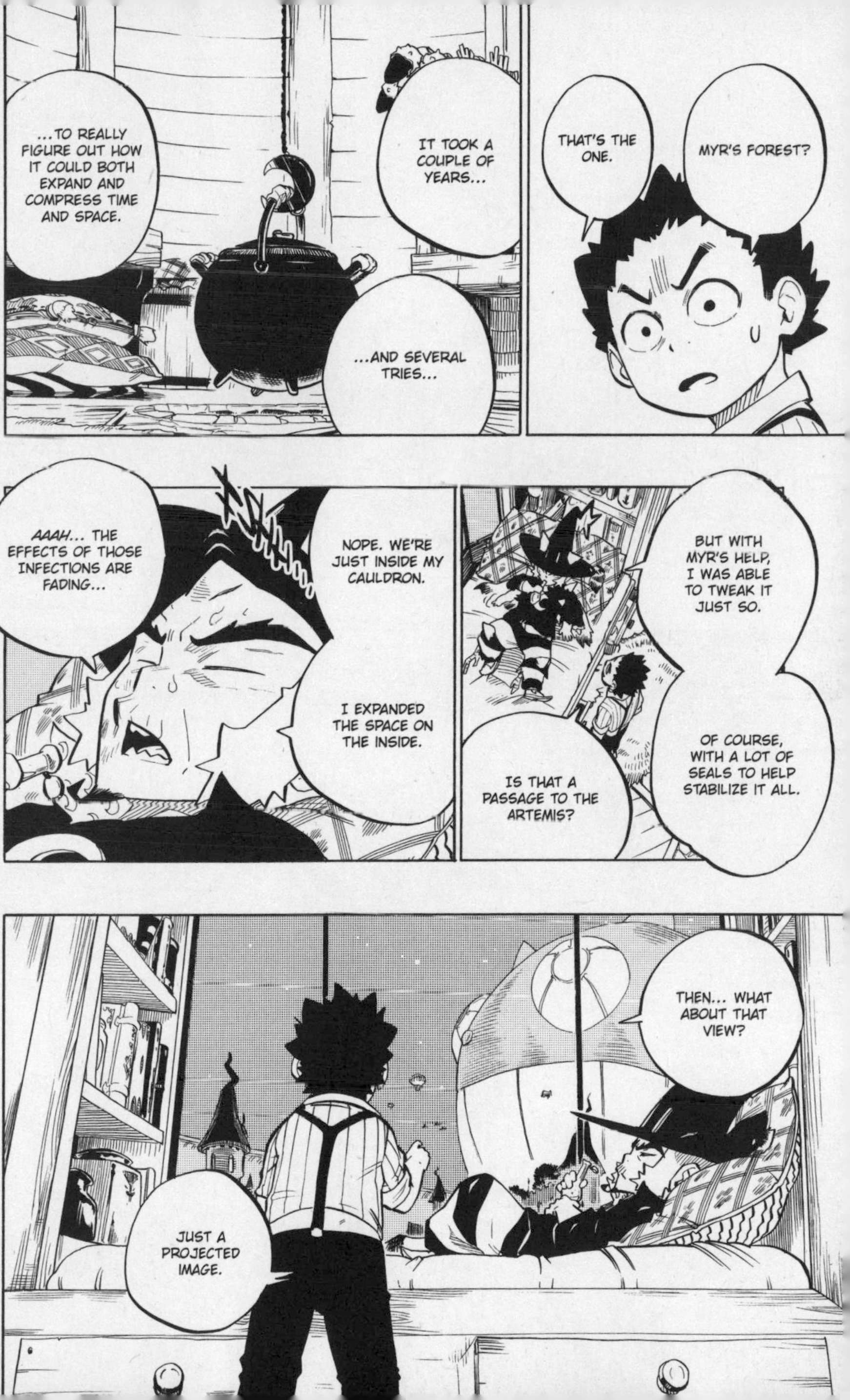
MYR'S FOREST?
THAT'S THE ONE.
IT TOOK A COUPLE OF YEARS...
...AND SEVERAL TRIES...
...TO REALLY FIGURE OUT HOW IT COULD BOTH EXPAND AND COMPRESS TIME AND SPACE.
BUT WITH MYR'S HELP, I WAS ABLE TO TWEAK IT JUST SO.
OF COURSE, WITH A LOT OF SEALS TO HELP STABILIZE IT ALL.
IS THAT A PASSAGE TO THE ARTEMIS?
NOPE. WE'RE JUST INSIDE MY CAULDRON.
I EXPANDED THE SPACE ON THE INSIDE.
AAAH... THE EFFECTS OF THOSE INFECTIONS ARE FADING...
THEN... WHAT ABOUT THAT VIEW?
JUST A PROJECTED IMAGE.

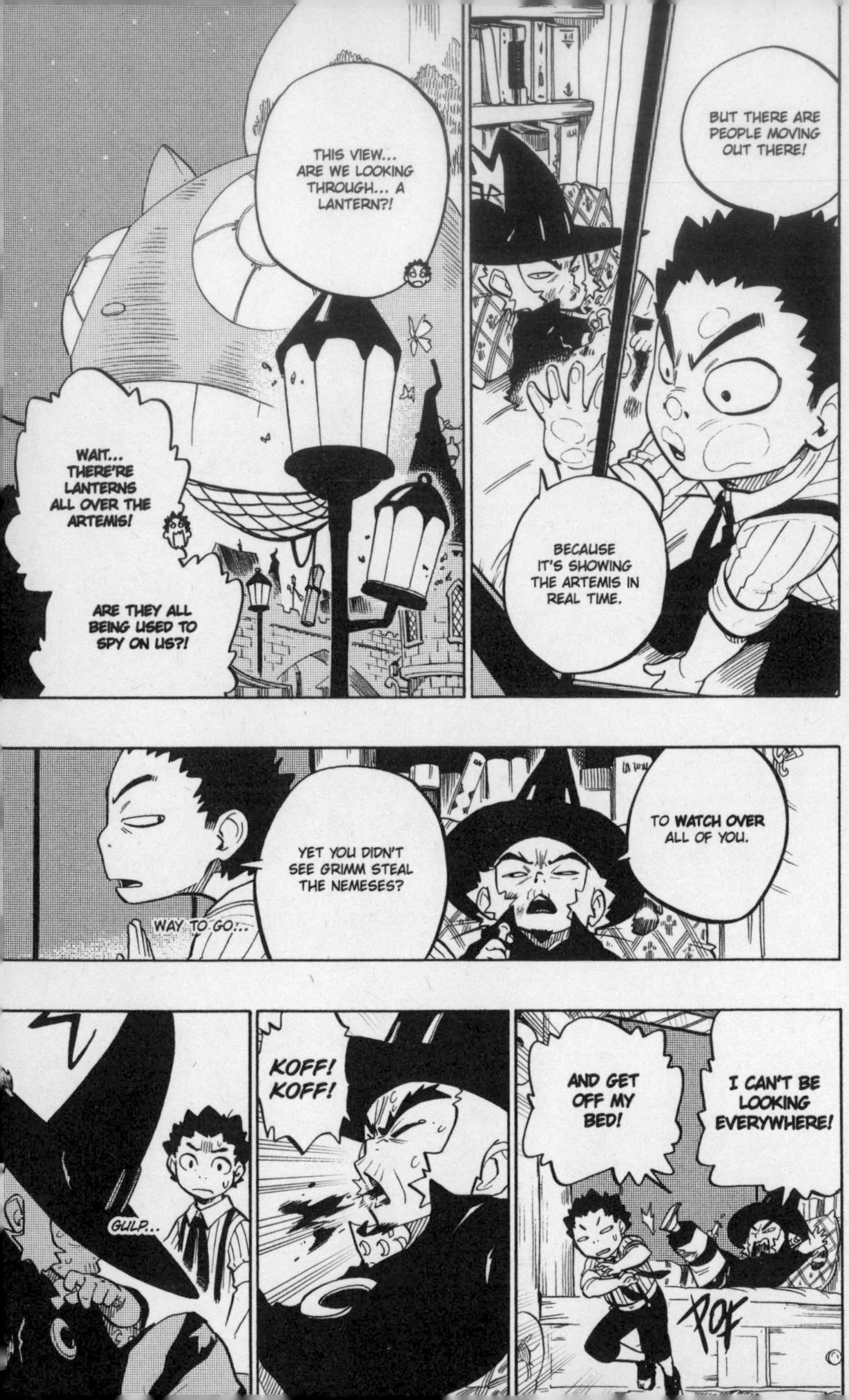
BUT THERE ARE PEOPLE MOVING OUT THERE!
BECAUSE IT'S SHOWING THE ARTEMIS IN REAL TIME.
THIS VIEW... ARE WE LOOKING THROUGH... A LANTERN?!
WAIT... THERE'RE LANTERNS ALL OVER THE ARTEMIS!
ARE THEY ALL BEING USED TO SPY ON US?!
TO WATCH OVER ALL OF YOU.
YET YOU DIDN'T SEE GRIMM STEAL THE NEMESES?
WAY TO GO...
I CAN'T BE LOOKING EVERYWHERE!
AND GET OFF MY BED!
POF
KOFF! KOFF!
GULP...

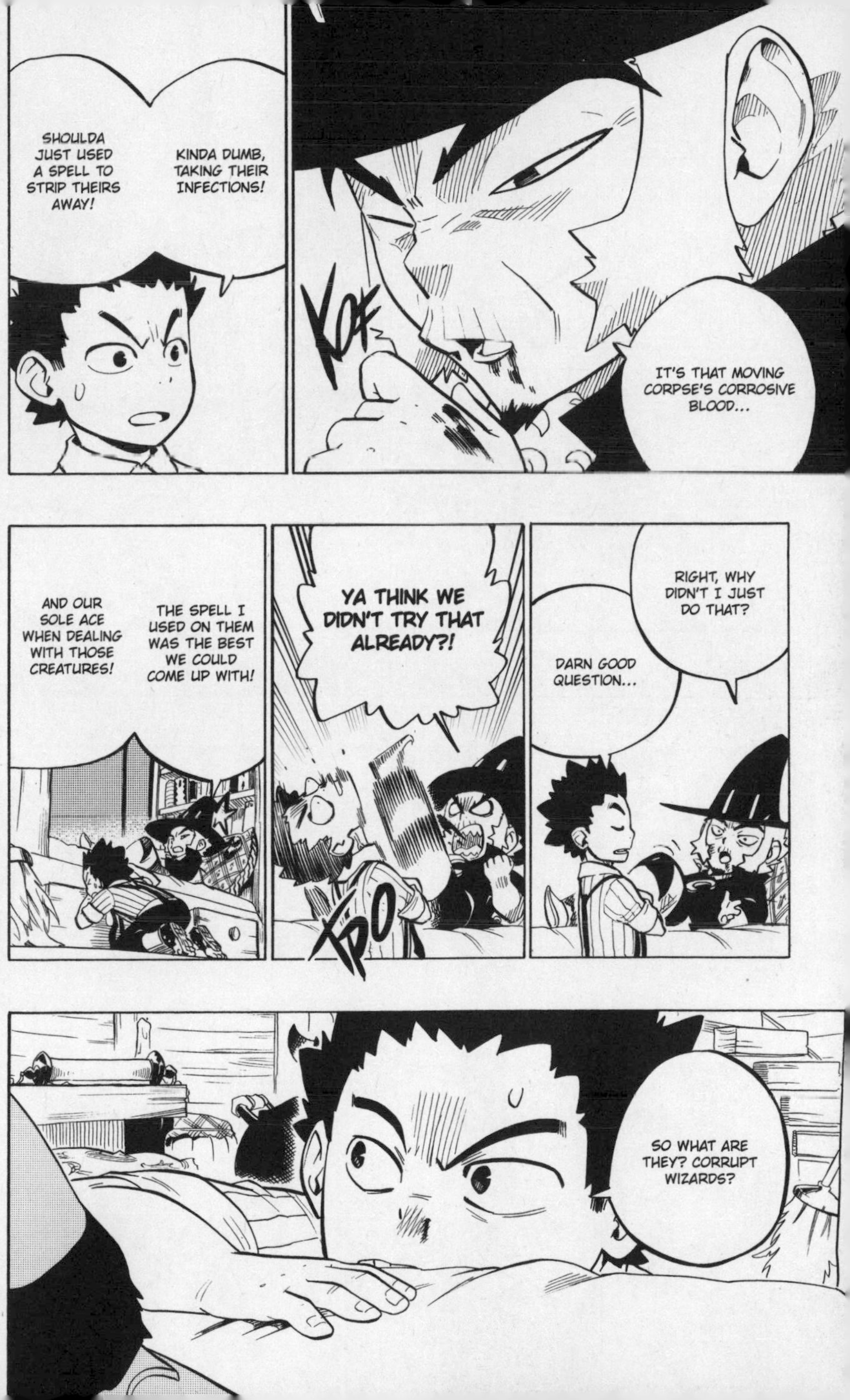
KOF
IT'S THAT MOVING CORPSE'S CORROSIVE BLOOD...
KINDA DUMB, TAKING THEIR INFECTIONS!
SHOULDA JUST USED A SPELL TO STRIP THEIRS AWAY!
RIGHT, WHY DIDN'T I JUST DO THAT?
DARN GOOD QUESTION...
YA THINK WE DIDN'T TRY THAT ALREADY?!
THE SPELL I USED ON THEM WAS THE BEST WE COULD COME UP WITH!
AND OUR SOLE ACE WHEN DEALING WITH THOSE CREATURES!
SO WHAT ARE THEY? CORRUPT WIZARDS?

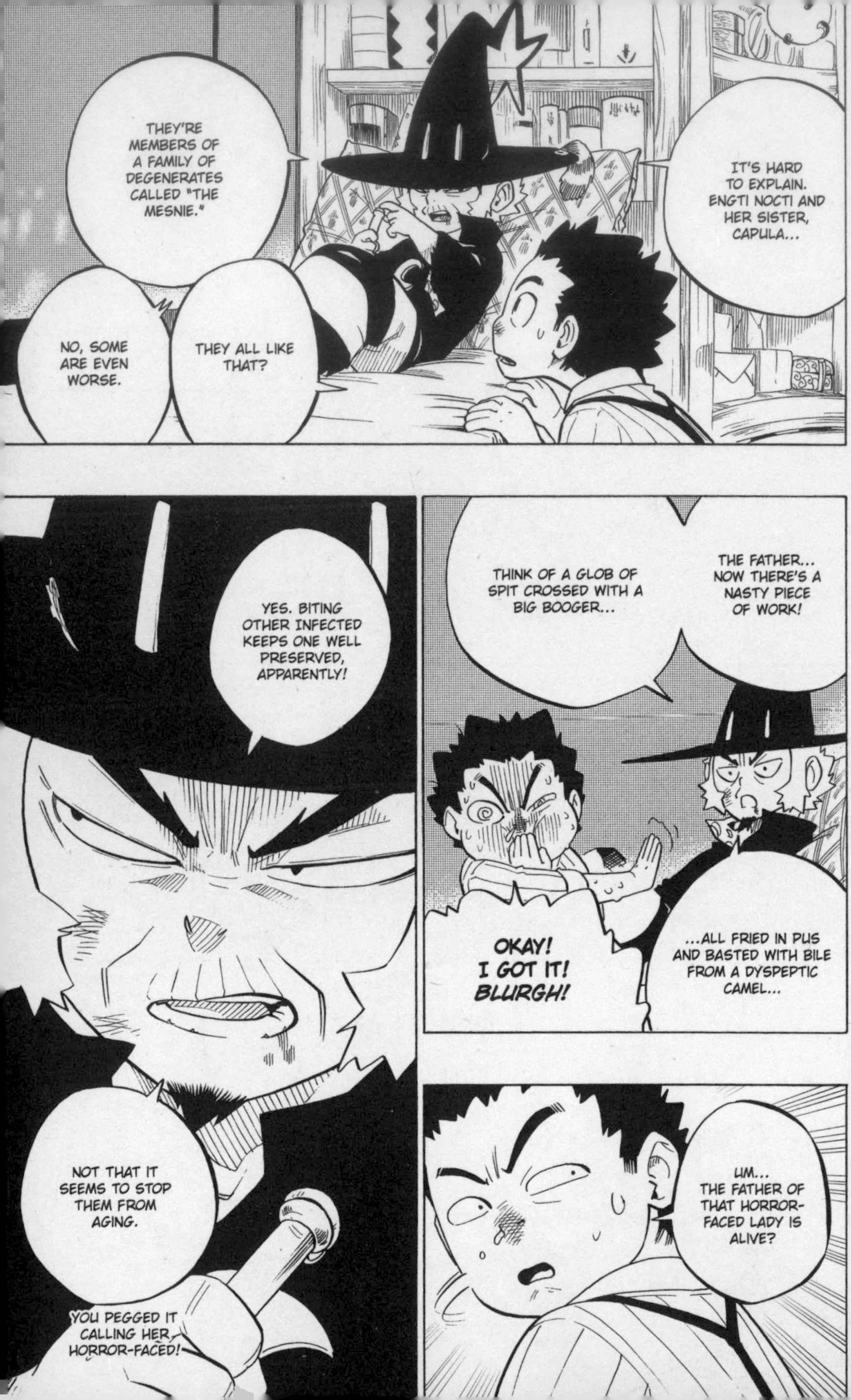
IT'S HARD TO EXPLAIN. ENGTI NOCTI AND HER SISTER, CAPULA...
THEY'RE MEMBERS OF A FAMILY OF DEGENERATES CALLED "THE MESNIE."
THEY ALL LIKE THAT?
NO, SOME ARE EVEN WORSE.
THE FATHER... NOW THERE'S A NASTY PIECE OF WORK!
THINK OF A GLOB OF SPIT CROSSED WITH A BIG BOOGER...
...ALL FRIED IN PUS AND BASTED WITH BILE FROM A DYSPEPTIC CAMEL...
OKAY! I GOT IT! BLURGH!
UM... THE FATHER OF THAT HORROR-FACED LADY IS ALIVE?
YES. BITING OTHER INFECTED KEEPS ONE WELL PRESERVED, APPARENTLY!
NOT THAT IT SEEMS TO STOP THEM FROM AGING.
YOU PEGGED IT CALLING HER HORROR-FACED!

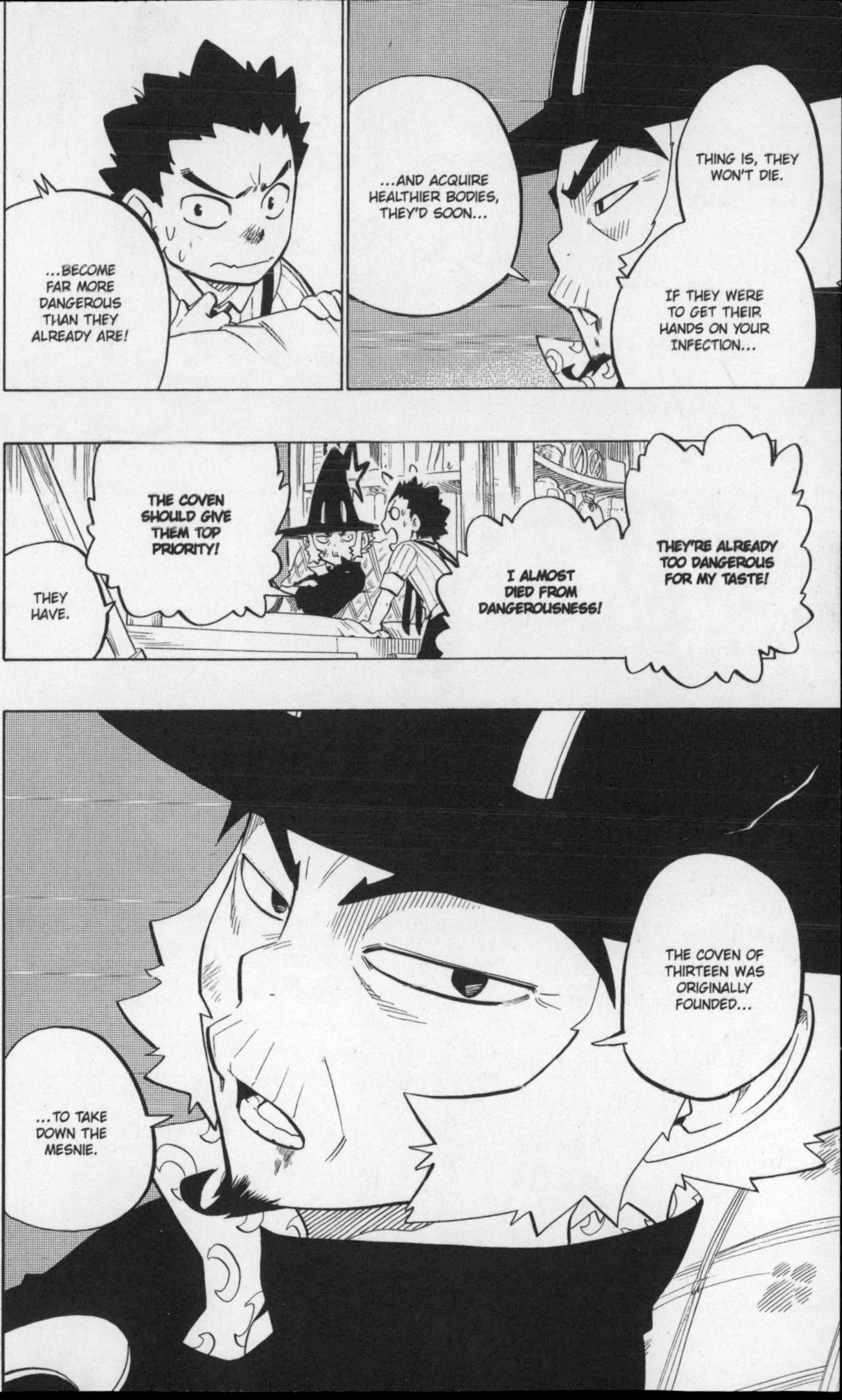
THING IS, THEY WON'T DIE.
IF THEY WERE TO GET THEIR HANDS ON YOUR INFECTION...
...AND ACQUIRE HEALTHIER BODIES, THEY'D SOON...
...BECOME FAR MORE DANGEROUS THAN THEY ALREADY ARE!
THEY'RE ALREADY TOO DANGEROUS FOR MY TASTE!
I ALMOST DIED FROM DANGEROUSNESS!
THE COVEN SHOULD GIVE THEM TOP PRIORITY!
THEY HAVE.
THE COVEN OF THIRTEEN WAS ORIGINALLY FOUNDED...
...TO TAKE DOWN THE MESNIE.

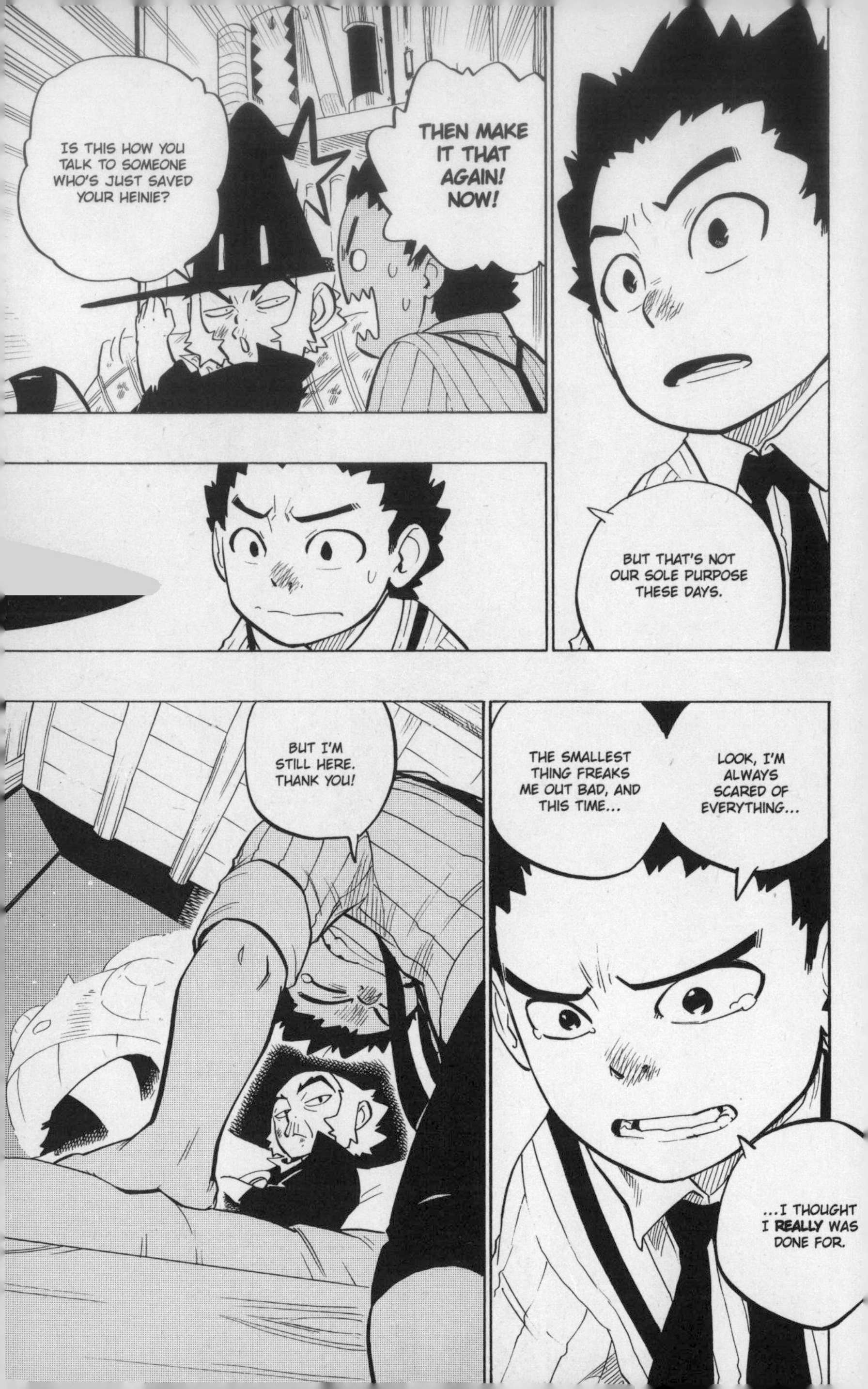
BUT THAT'S NOT OUR SOLE PURPOSE THESE DAYS.
THEN MAKE IT THAT AGAIN! NOW!
IS THIS HOW YOU TALK TO SOMEONE WHO'S JUST SAVED YOUR HEINIE?
LOOK, I'M ALWAYS SCARED OF EVERYTHING...
THE SMALLEST THING FREAKS ME OUT BAD, AND THIS TIME...
...I THOUGHT I **REALLY** WAS DONE FOR.
BUT I'M STILL HERE. THANK YOU!

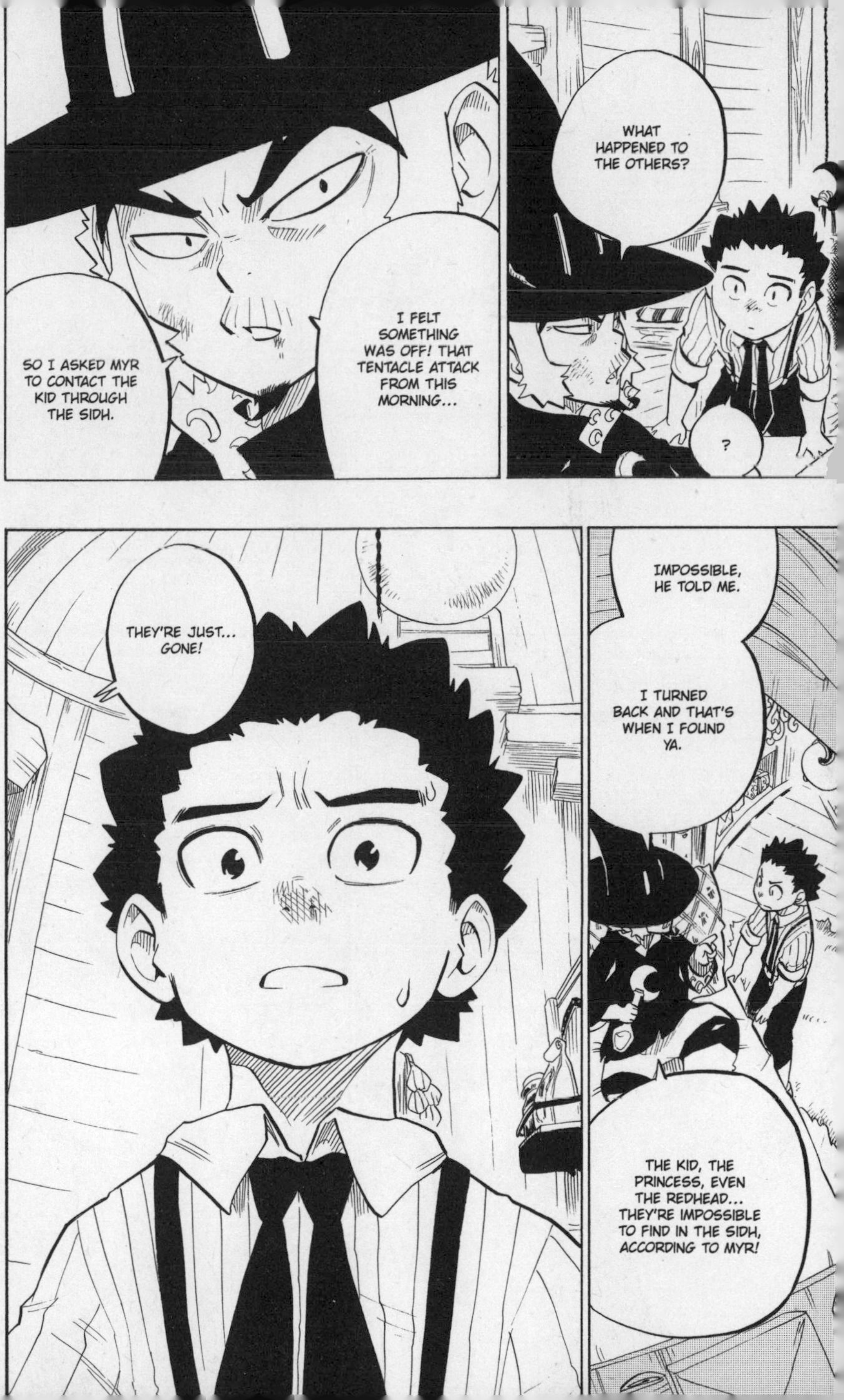
WHAT HAPPENED TO THE OTHERS?
?
I FELT SOMETHING WAS OFF! THAT TENTACLE ATTACK FROM THIS MORNING...
SO I ASKED MYR TO CONTACT THE KID THROUGH THE SIDH.
IMPOSSIBLE, HE TOLD ME.
I TURNED BACK AND THAT'S WHEN I FOUND YA.
THE KID, THE PRINCESS, EVEN THE REDHEAD... THEY'RE IMPOSSIBLE TO FIND IN THE SIDH, ACCORDING TO MYR!
THEY'RE JUST... GONE!

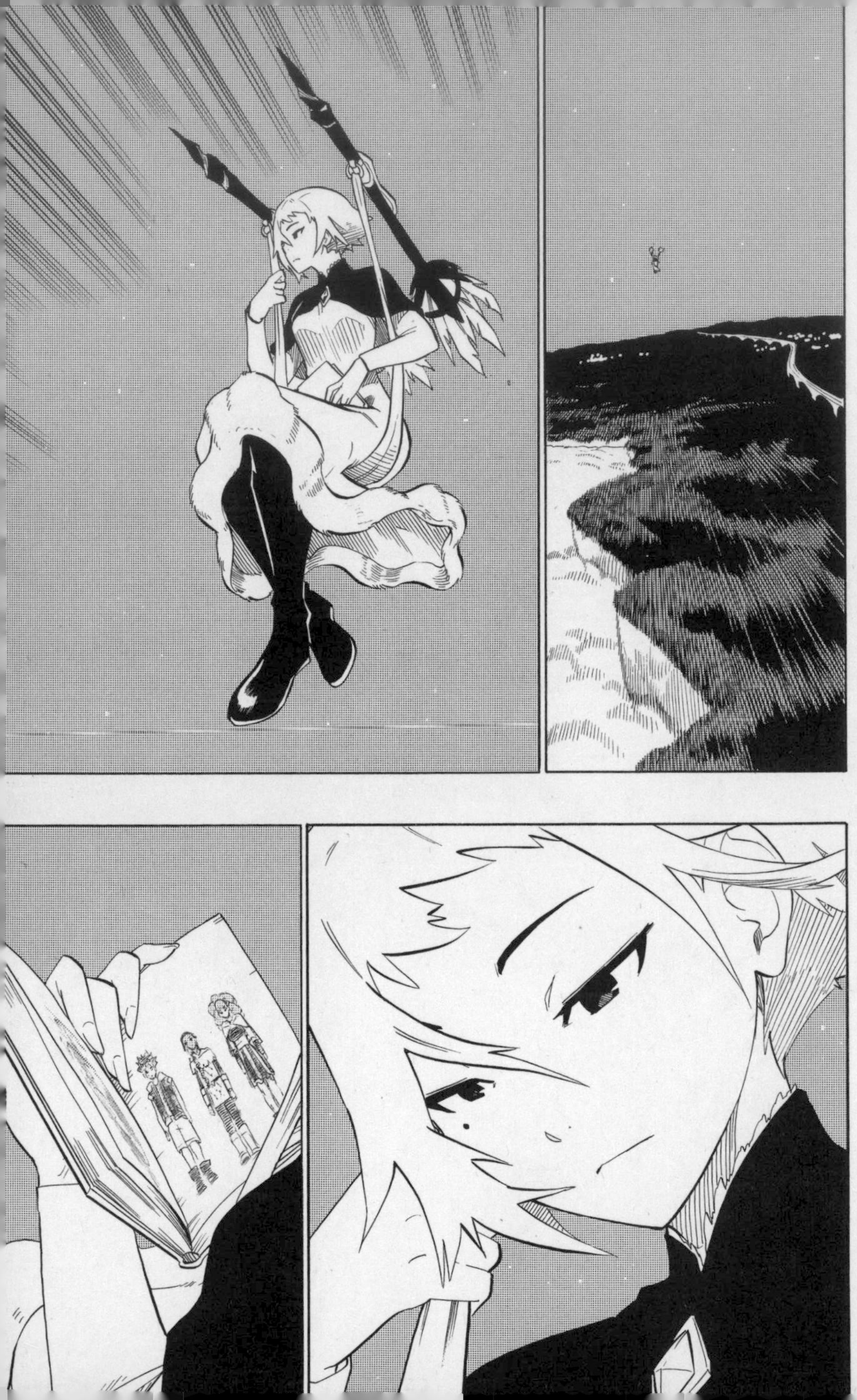

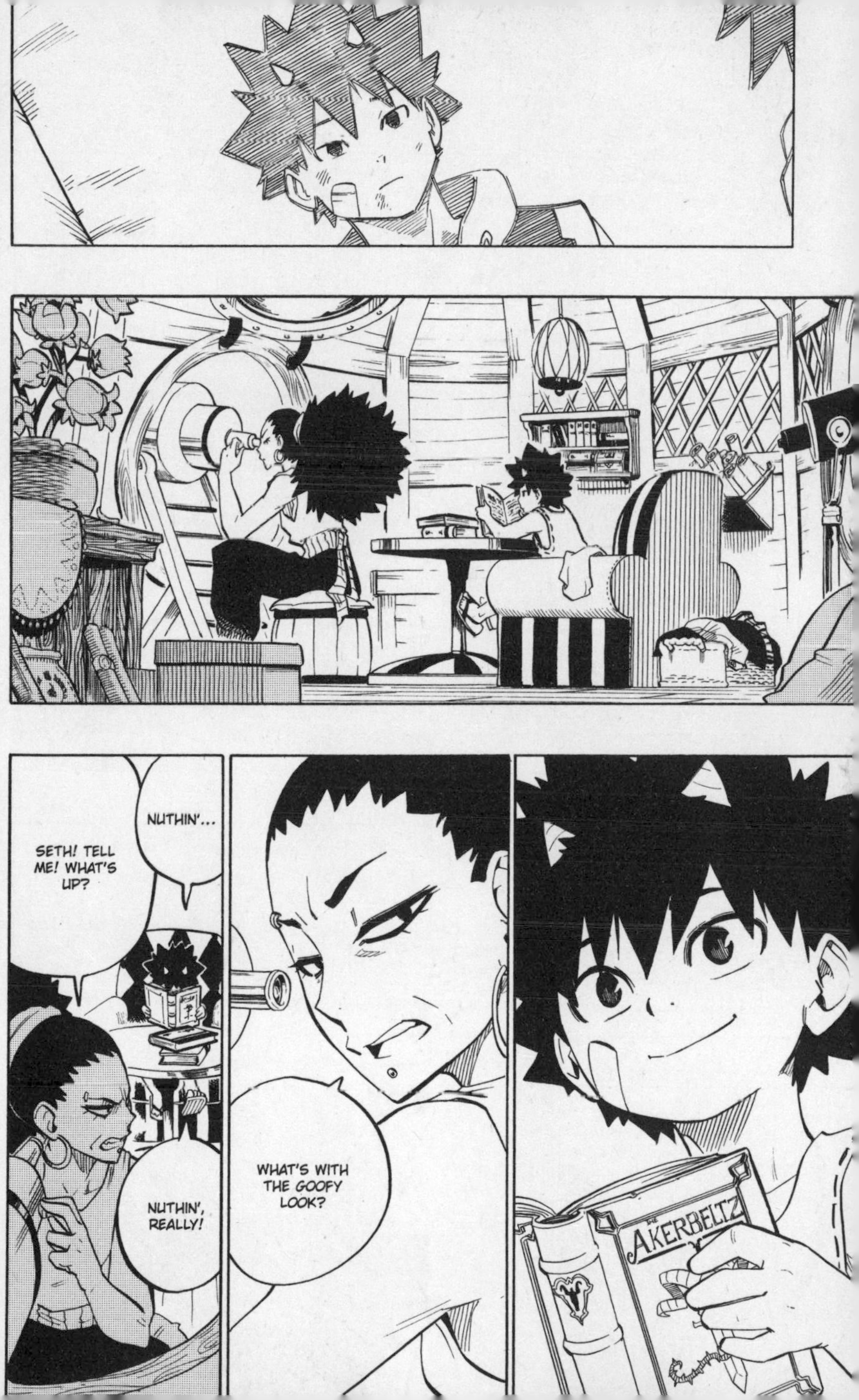
AKERBELTZ
WHAT'S WITH THE GOOFY LOOK?
NUTHIN'...
SETH! TELL ME! WHAT'S UP?
NUTHIN', REALLY!

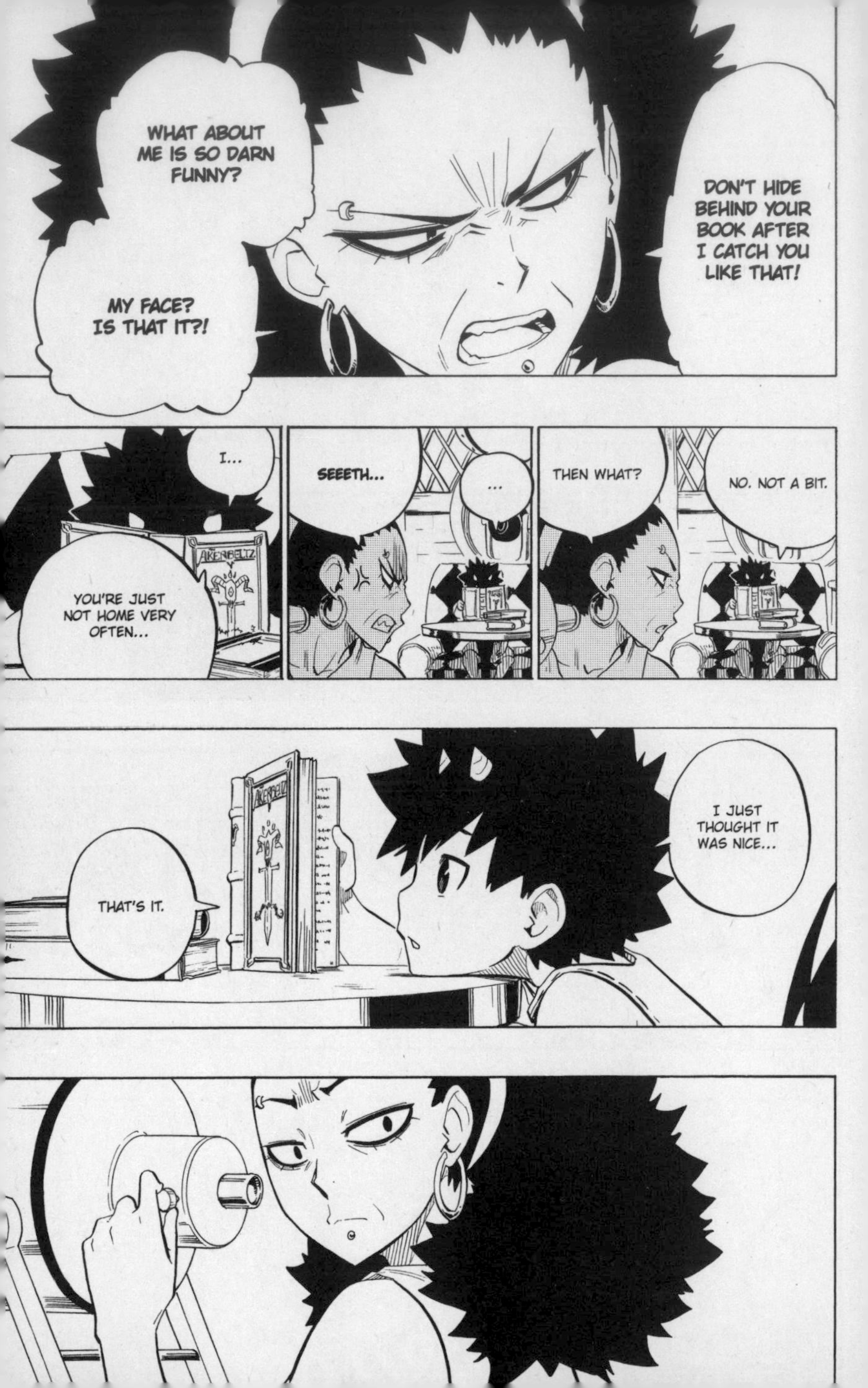
DON'T HIDE BEHIND YOUR BOOK AFTER I CATCH YOU LIKE THAT!
WHAT ABOUT ME IS SO DARN FUNNY?
MY FACE? IS THAT IT?!
NO. NOT A BIT.
THEN WHAT?
...
SEEETH...
I...
YOU'RE JUST NOT HOME VERY OFTEN...
I JUST THOUGHT IT WAS NICE...
THAT'S IT.

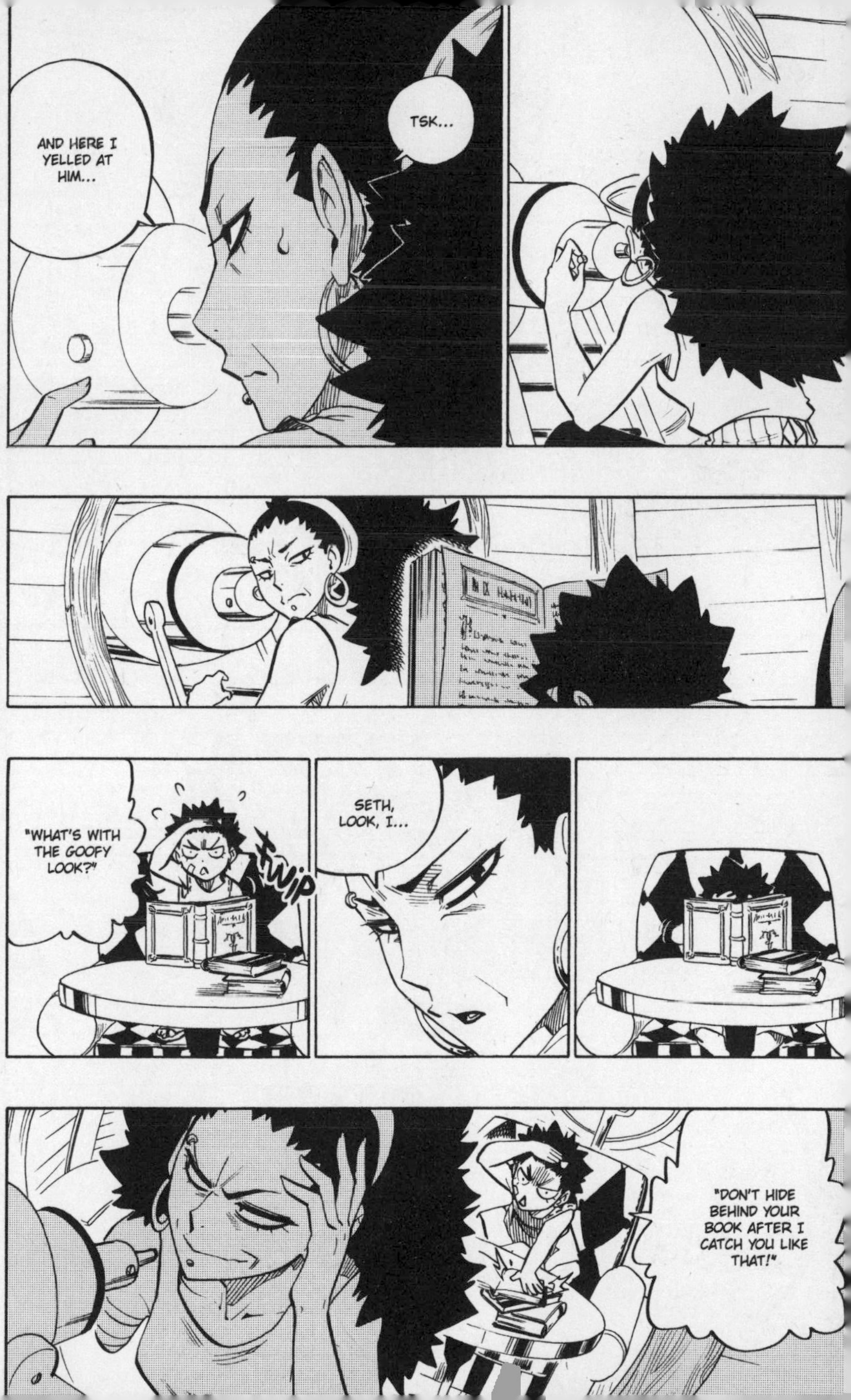
TSK...
AND HERE I YELLED AT HIM...
SETH, LOOK, I...
"WHAT'S WITH THE GOOFY LOOK?"
FWIP
"DON'T HIDE BEHIND YOUR BOOK AFTER I CATCH YOU LIKE THAT!"

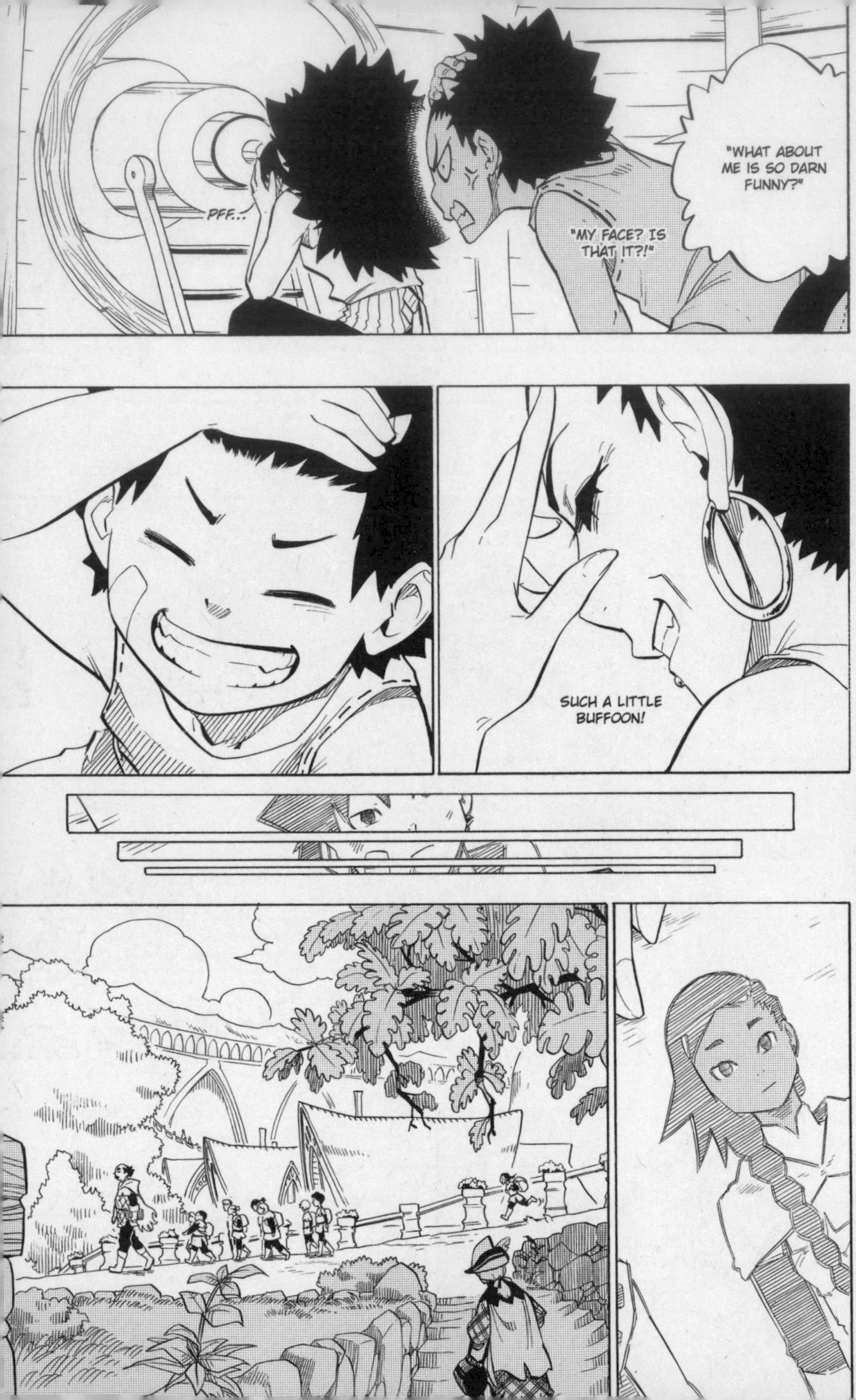
"WHAT ABOUT ME IS SO DARN FUNNY?"
"MY FACE? IS THAT IT?!"
PFF...
SUCH A LITTLE BUFFOON!

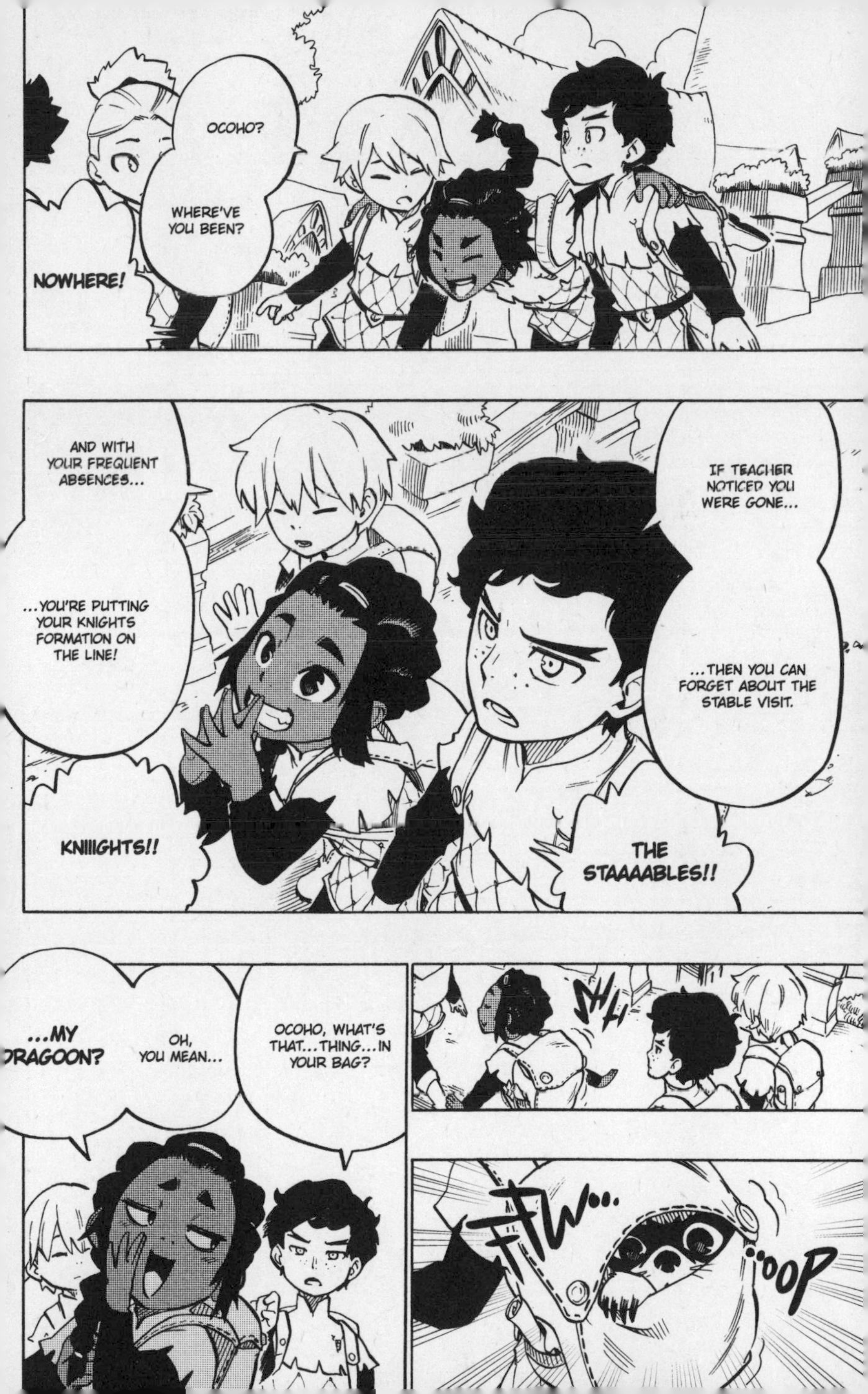
OCOHO?
WHERE'VE YOU BEEN?
NOWHERE!
IF TEACHER NOTICED YOU WERE GONE...
...THEN YOU CAN FORGET ABOUT THE STABLE VISIT.
AND WITH YOUR FREQUENT ABSENCES...
...YOU'RE PUTTING YOUR KNIGHTS FORMATION ON THE LINE!
THE STAAAABLES!!
KNIIIGHTS!!
FW...
...OOP
OCOHO, WHAT'S THAT...THING...IN YOUR BAG?
OH, YOU MEAN...
...MY DRAGOON?

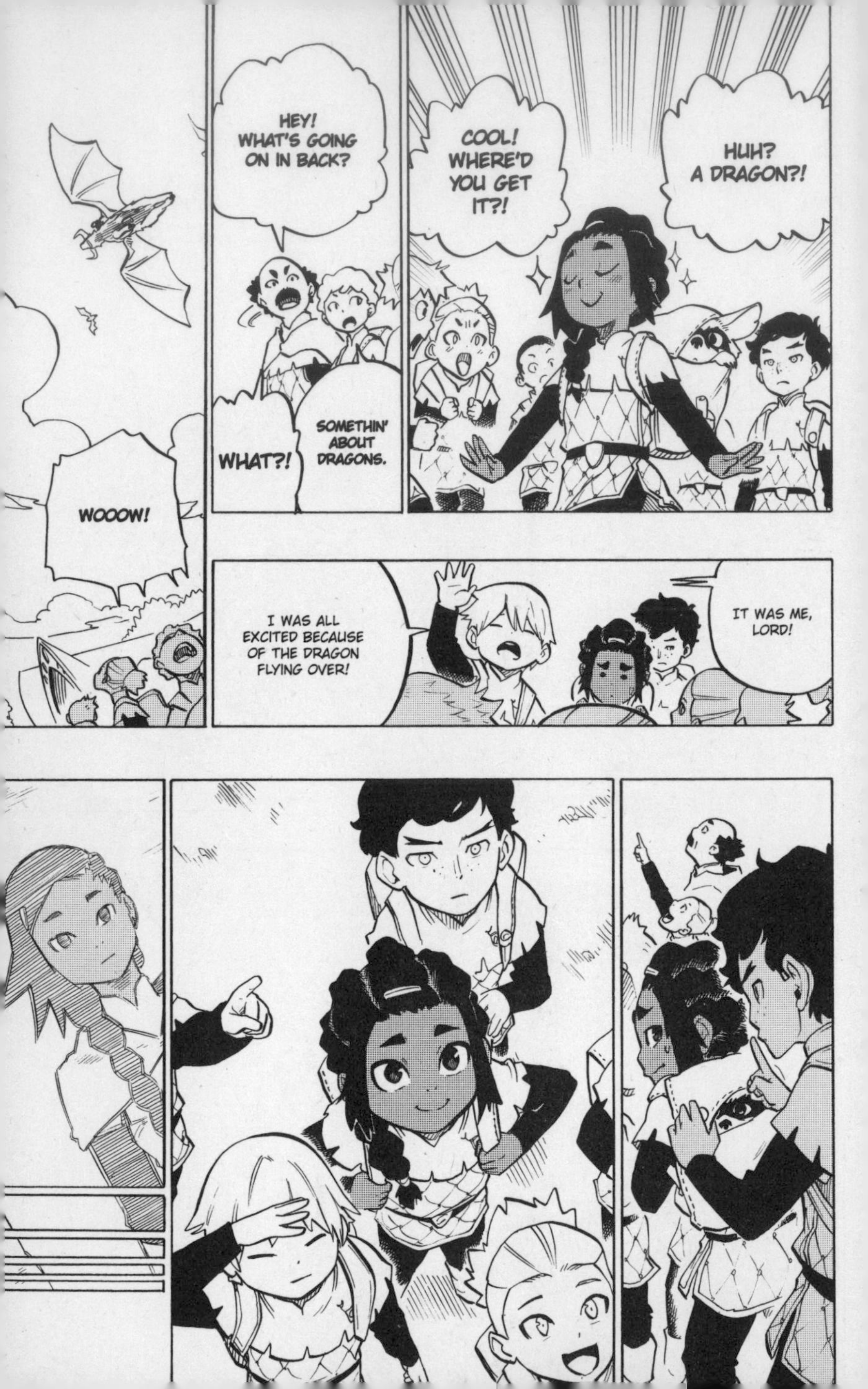
HUH? A DRAGON?!
COOL! WHERE'D YOU GET IT?!
HEY! WHAT'S GOING ON IN BACK?
SOMETHIN' ABOUT DRAGONS.
WHAT?!
IT WAS ME, LORD!
I WAS ALL EXCITED BECAUSE OF THE DRAGON FLYING OVER!
WOOOW!

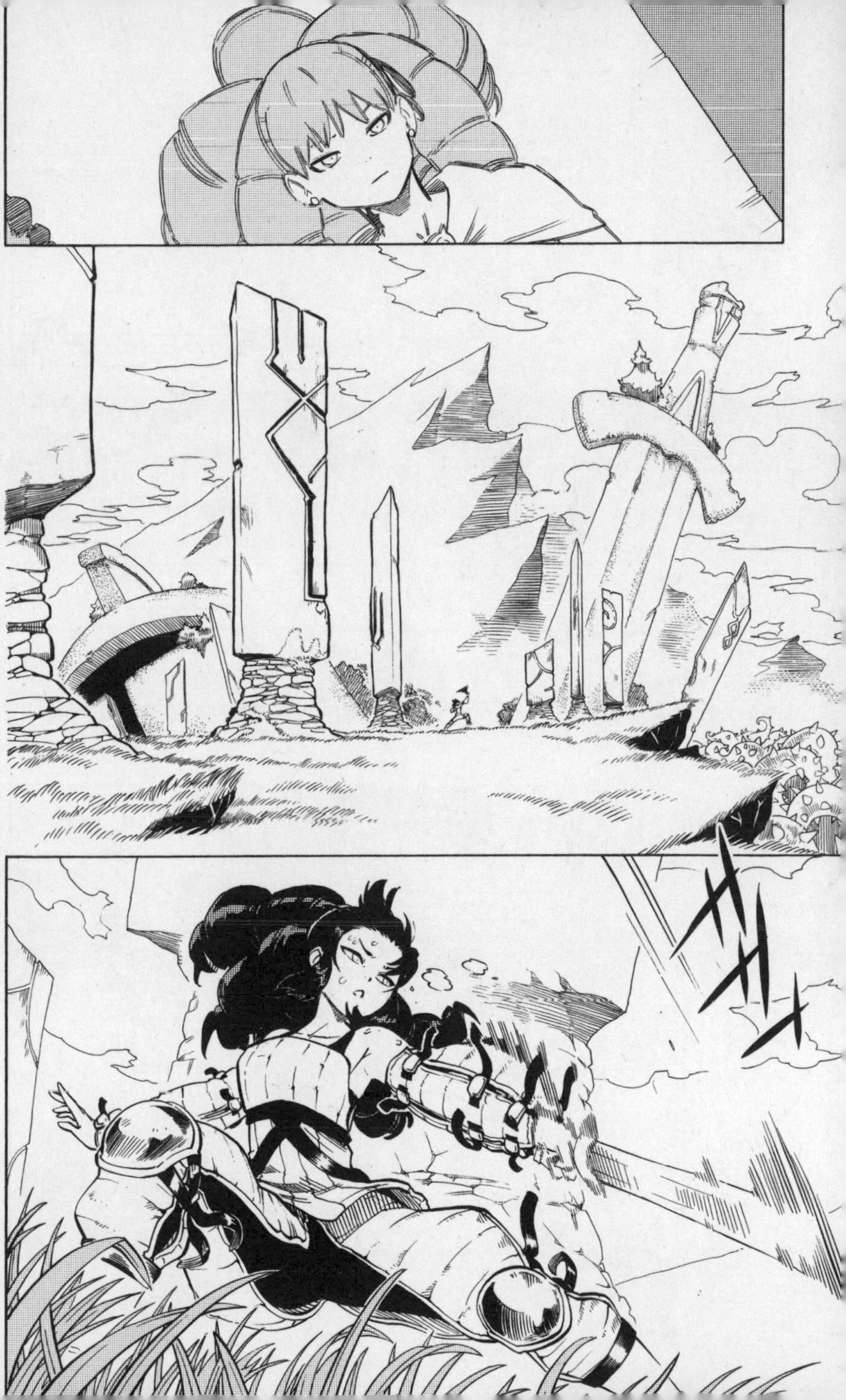

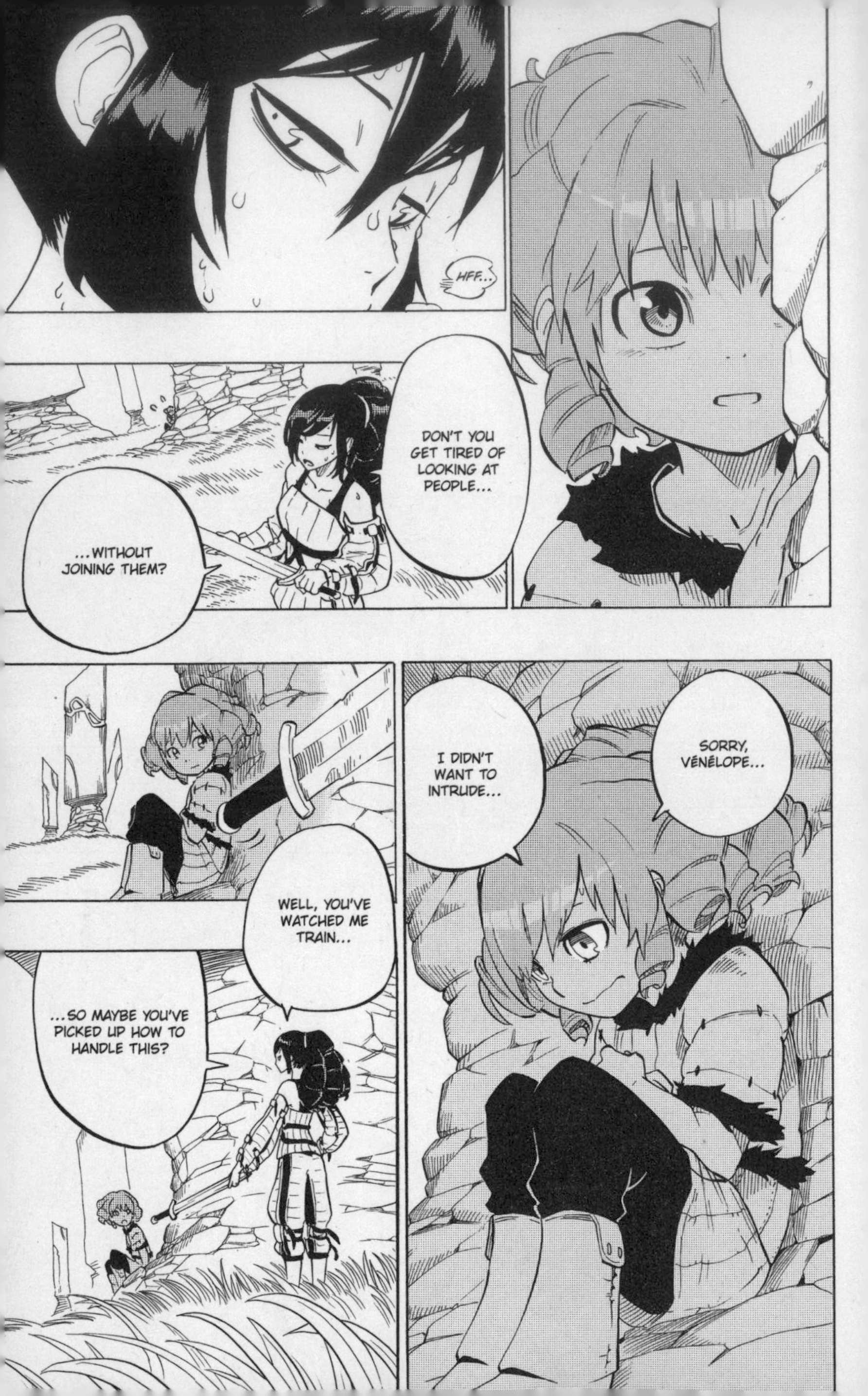
HFF...
DON'T YOU GET TIRED OF LOOKING AT PEOPLE...
...WITHOUT JOINING THEM?
SORRY, VENÉLOPE...
I DIDN'T WANT TO INTRUDE...
WELL, YOU'VE WATCHED ME TRAIN...
...SO MAYBE YOU'VE PICKED UP HOW TO HANDLE THIS?

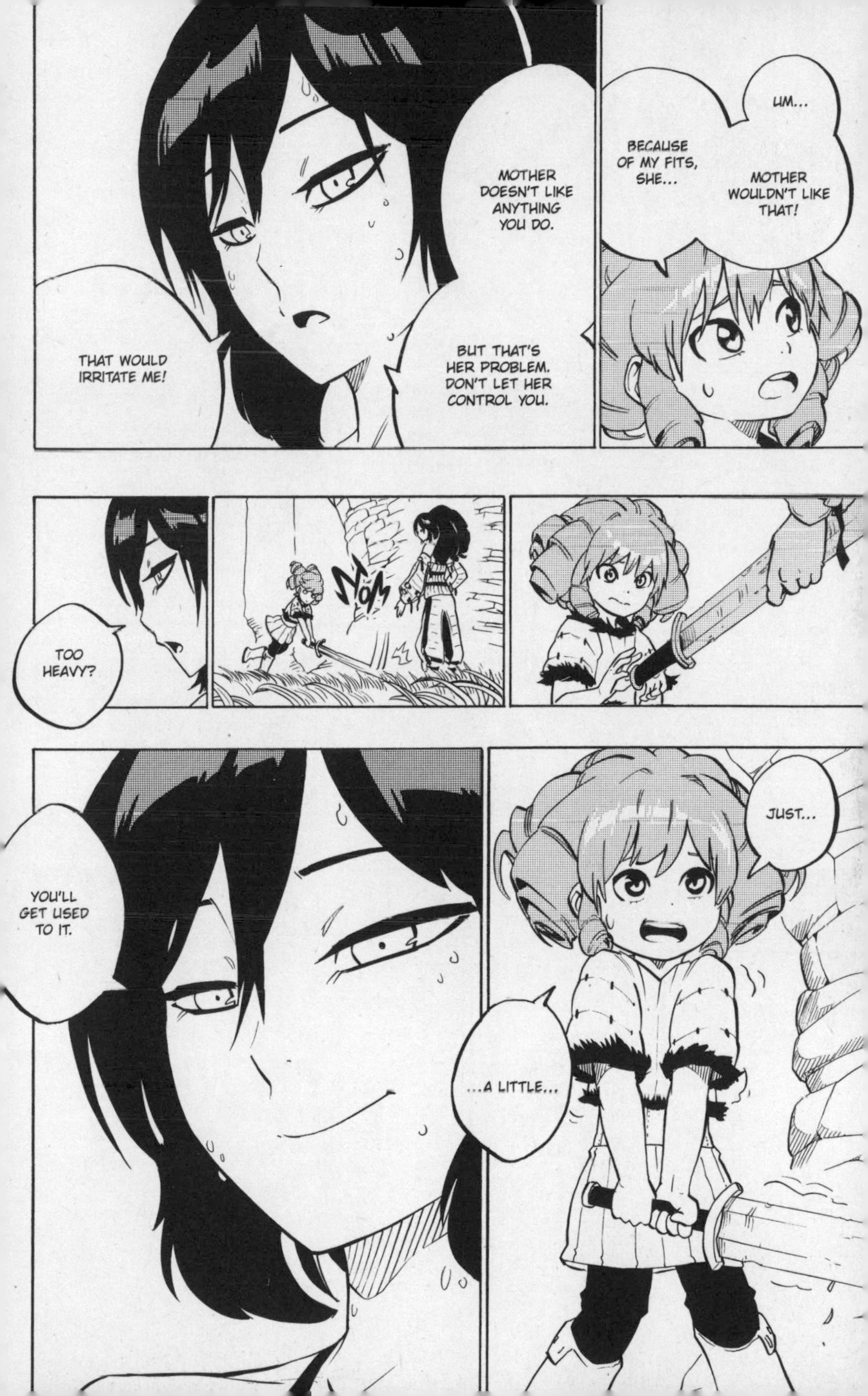
UM...
MOTHER WOULDN'T LIKE THAT!
BECAUSE OF MY FITS, SHE...
MOTHER DOESN'T LIKE ANYTHING YOU DO.
BUT THAT'S HER PROBLEM. DON'T LET HER CONTROL YOU.
THAT WOULD IRRITATE ME!
STOM
TOO HEAVY?
JUST...
...A LITTLE...
YOU'LL GET USED TO IT.

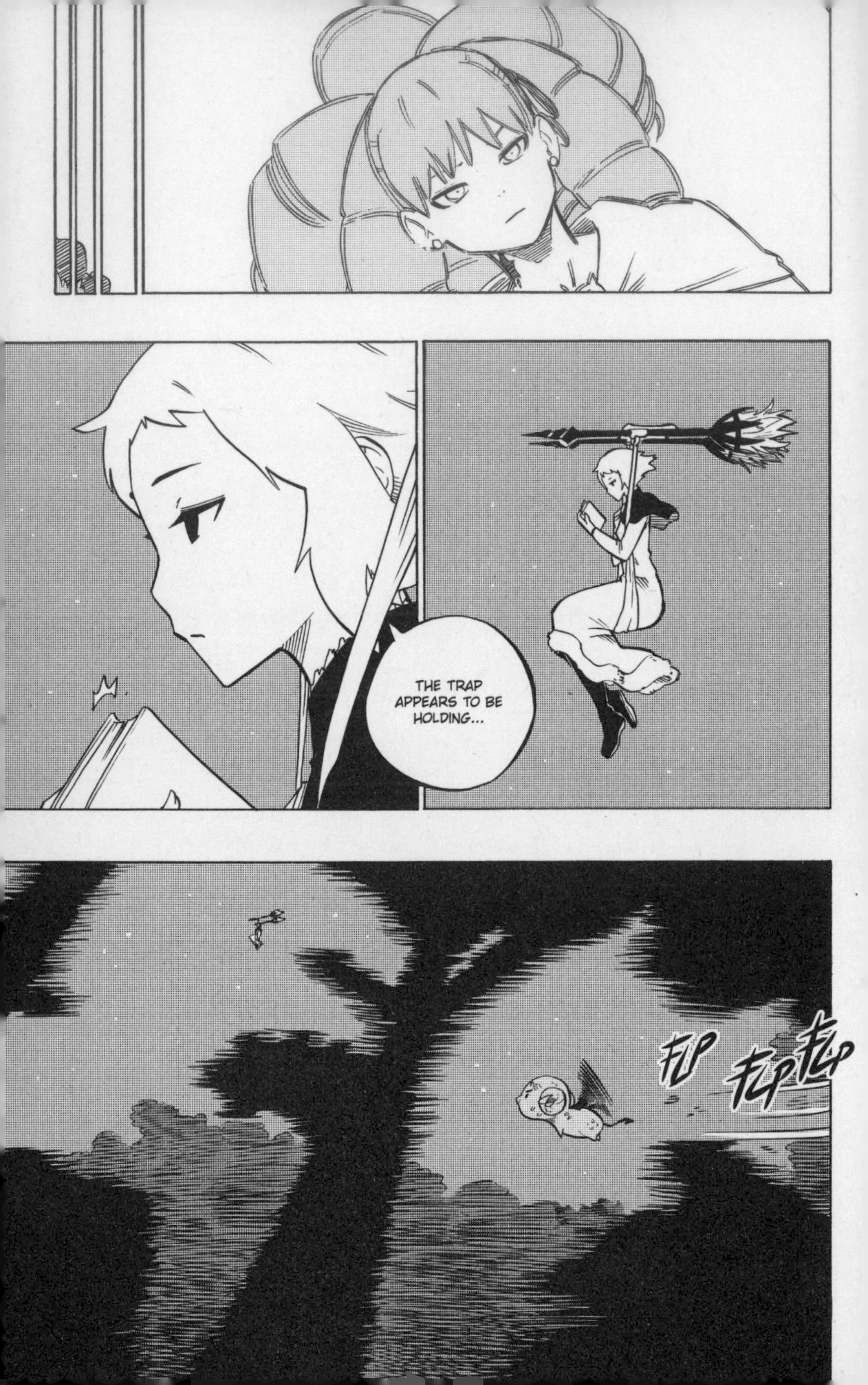
THE TRAP APPEARS TO BE HOLDING...
FLP FLP FLP

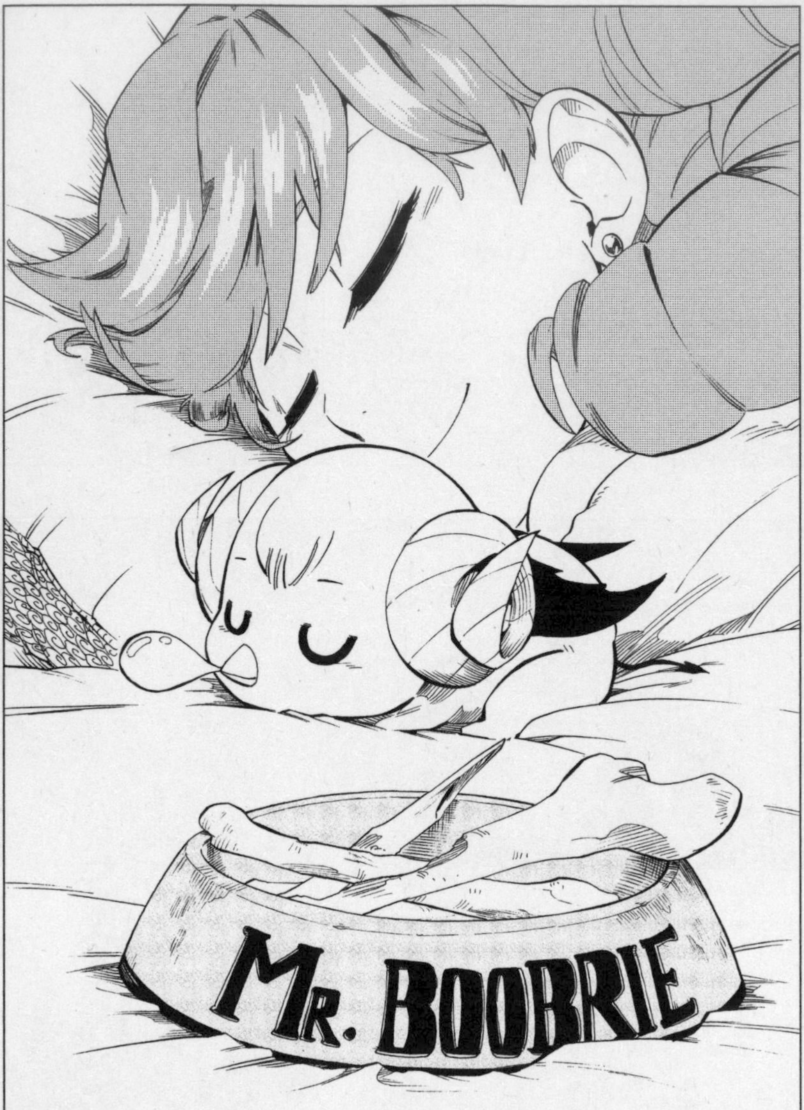
MR. BOOBRIE

CHAPTER 89

BOUND

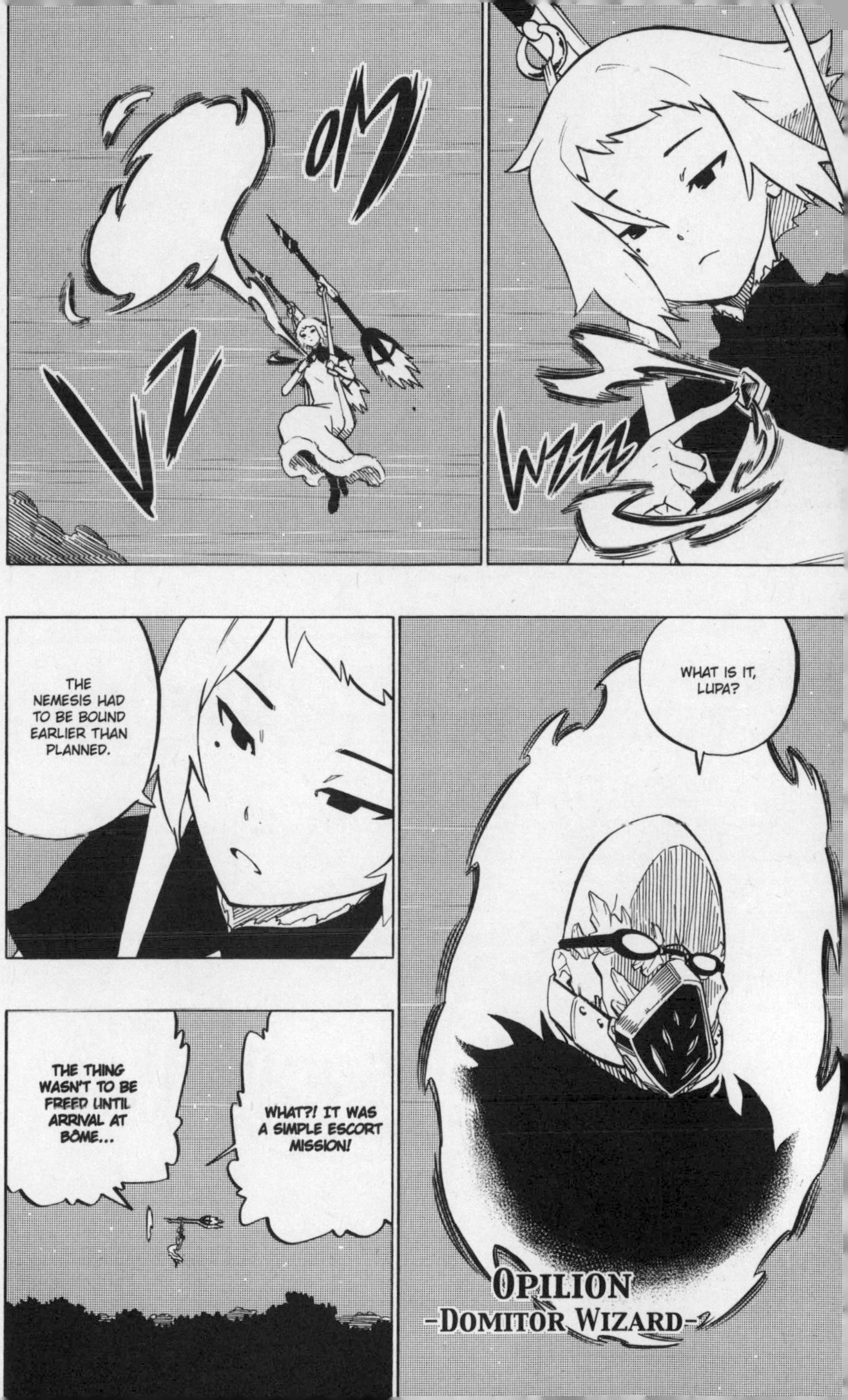
WZZZ
WHAT IS IT, LUPA?
OPILION
-DOMITOR WIZARD-
THE NEMESIS HAD TO BE BOUND EARLIER THAN PLANNED.
WHAT?! IT WAS A SIMPLE ESCORT MISSION!
THE THING WASN'T TO BE FREED UNTIL ARRIVAL AT BÔME...

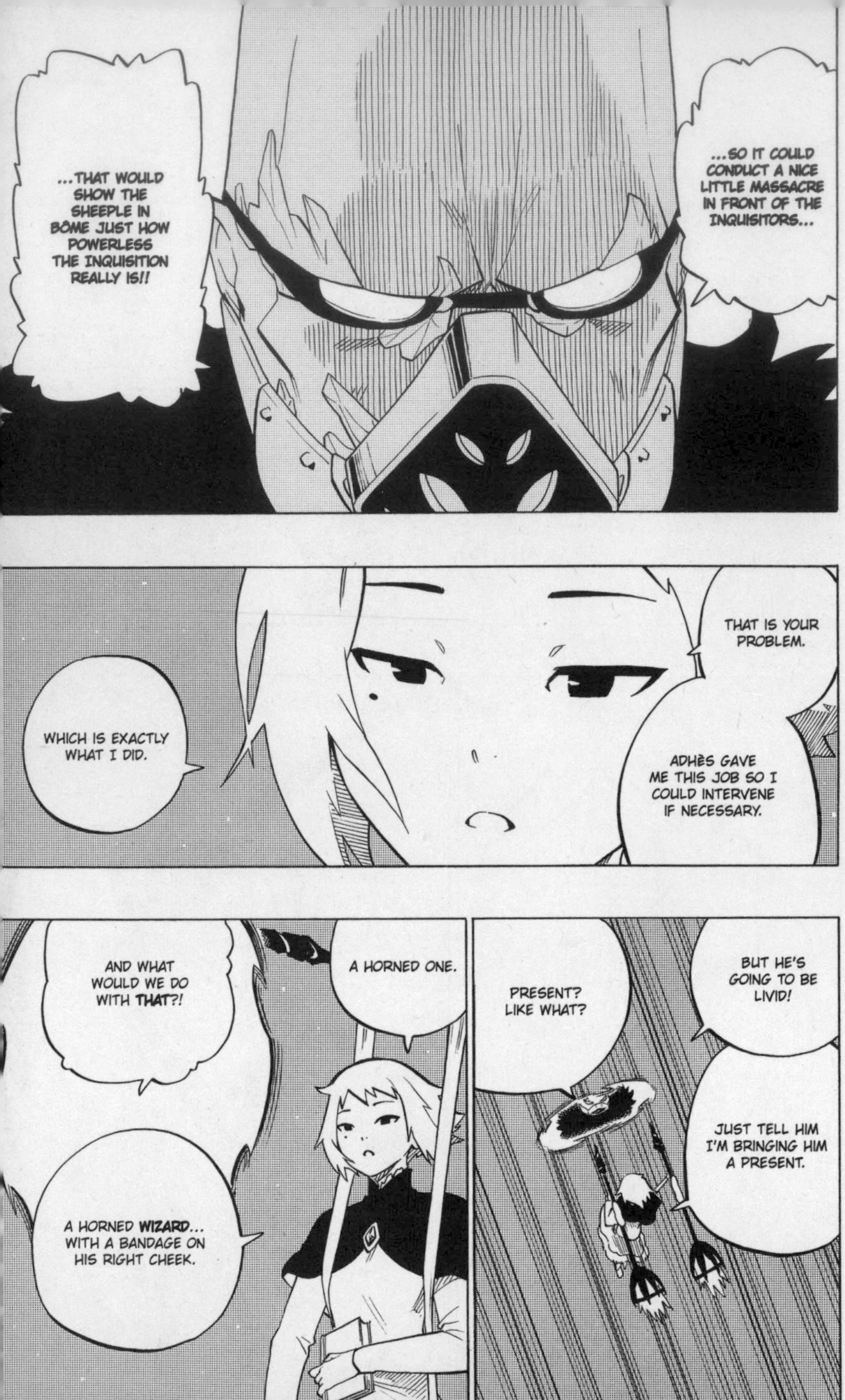
...SO IT COULD CONDUCT A NICE LITTLE MASSACRE IN FRONT OF THE INQUISITORS...
...THAT WOULD SHOW THE SHEEPLE IN BÔME JUST HOW POWERLESS THE INQUISITION REALLY IS!!
THAT IS YOUR PROBLEM.
ADHÈS GAVE ME THIS JOB SO I COULD INTERVENE IF NECESSARY.
WHICH IS EXACTLY WHAT I DID.
BUT HE'S GOING TO BE LIVID!
JUST TELL HIM I'M BRINGING HIM A PRESENT.
PRESENT? LIKE WHAT?
A HORNED ONE.
AND WHAT WOULD WE DO WITH THAT?!
A HORNED WIZARD... WITH A BANDAGE ON HIS RIGHT CHEEK.

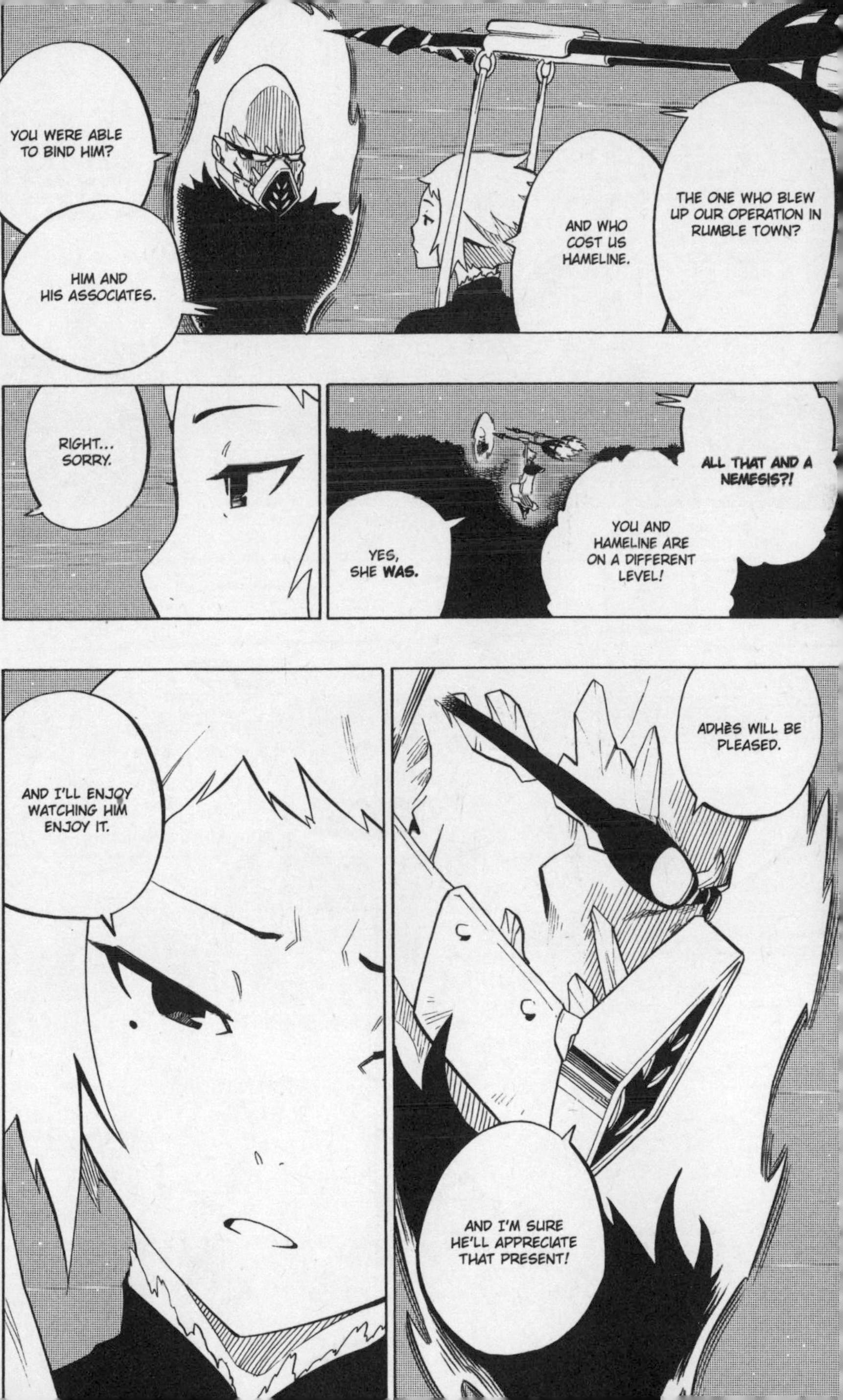
THE ONE WHO BLEW UP OUR OPERATION IN RUMBLE TOWN?
AND WHO COST US HAMELINE.
YOU WERE ABLE TO BIND HIM?
HIM AND HIS ASSOCIATES.
ALL THAT AND A NEMESIS?!
YOU AND HAMELINE ARE ON A DIFFERENT LEVEL!
YES, SHE WAS.
RIGHT... SORRY.
ADHÈS WILL BE PLEASED.
AND I'M SURE HE'LL APPRECIATE THAT PRESENT!
AND I'LL ENJOY WATCHING HIM ENJOY IT.

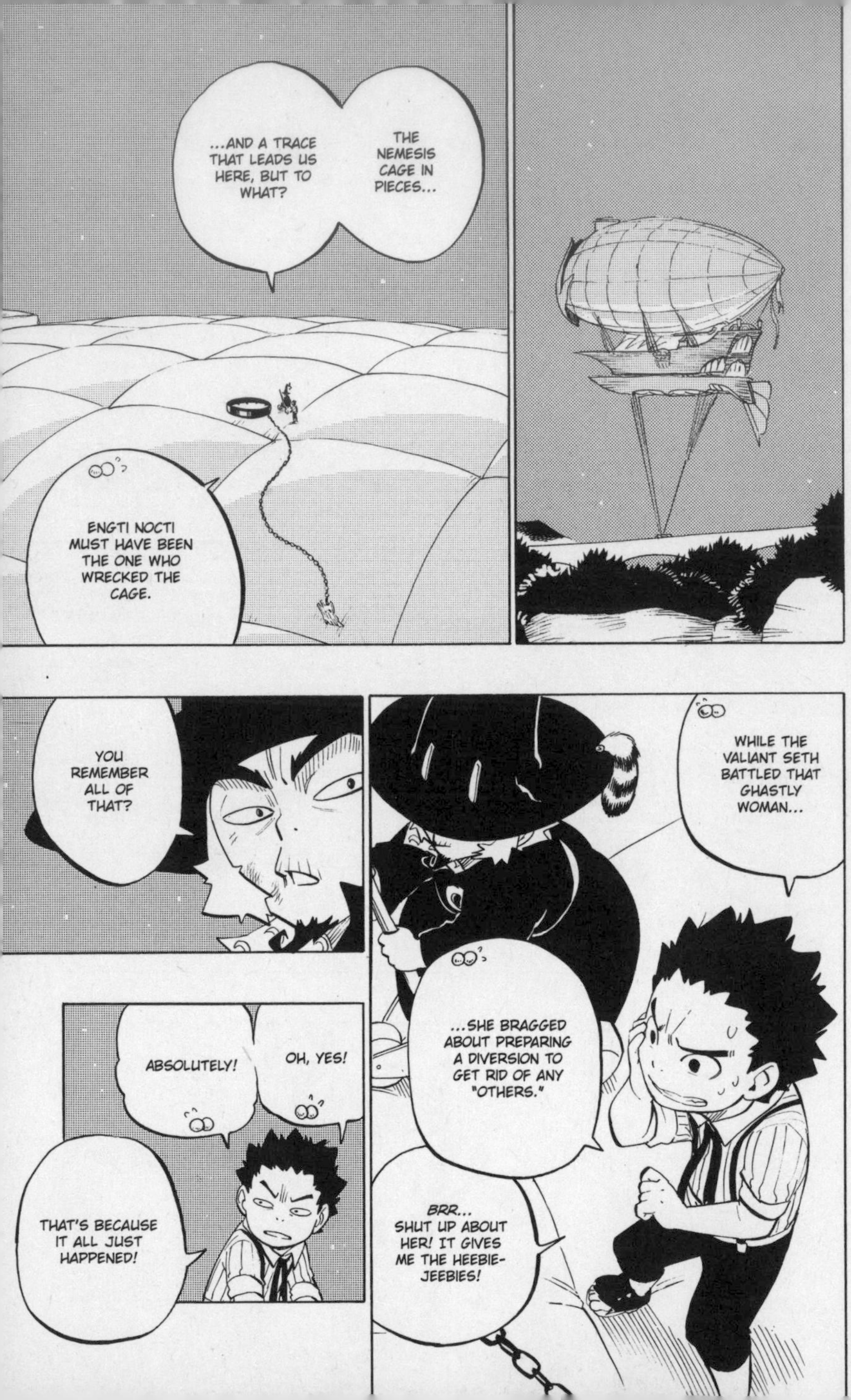
THE NEMESIS CAGE IN PIECES...
...AND A TRACE THAT LEADS US HERE, BUT TO WHAT?
ENGTI NOCTI MUST HAVE BEEN THE ONE WHO WRECKED THE CAGE.
WHILE THE VALIANT SETH BATTLED THAT GHASTLY WOMAN...
...SHE BRAGGED ABOUT PREPARING A DIVERSION TO GET RID OF ANY "OTHERS."
BRR... SHUT UP ABOUT HER! IT GIVES ME THE HEEBIE-JEEBIES!
YOU REMEMBER ALL OF THAT?
OH, YES!
ABSOLUTELY!
THAT'S BECAUSE IT ALL JUST HAPPENED!

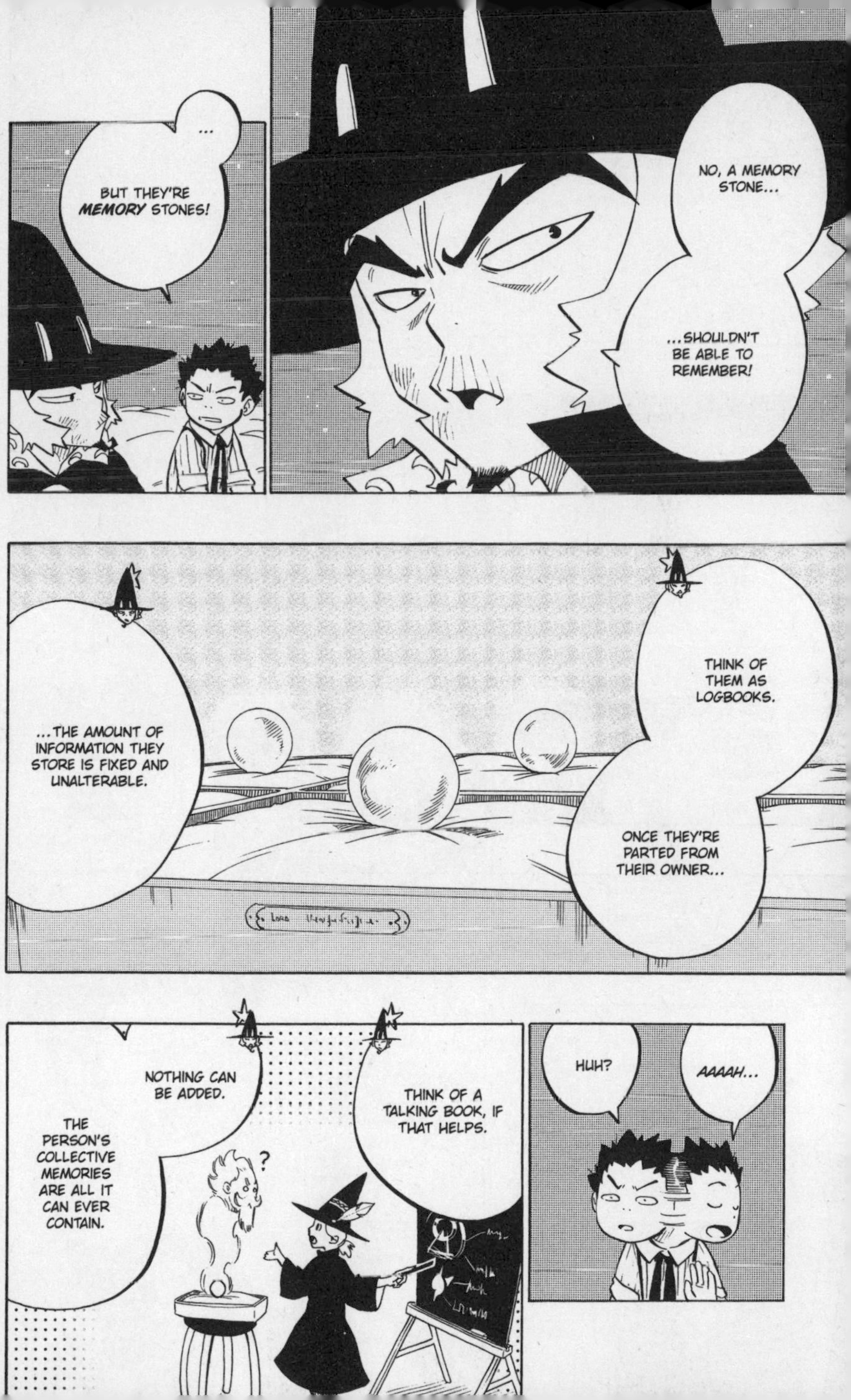

NO, A MEMORY STONE...
...SHOULDN'T BE ABLE TO REMEMBER!
...
BUT THEY'RE MEMORY STONES!
THINK OF THEM AS LOGBOOKS.
ONCE THEY'RE PARTED FROM THEIR OWNER...
...THE AMOUNT OF INFORMATION THEY STORE IS FIXED AND UNALTERABLE.
AAAAH...
HUH?
THINK OF A TALKING BOOK, IF THAT HELPS.
NOTHING CAN BE ADDED.
THE PERSON'S COLLECTIVE MEMORIES ARE ALL IT CAN EVER CONTAIN.

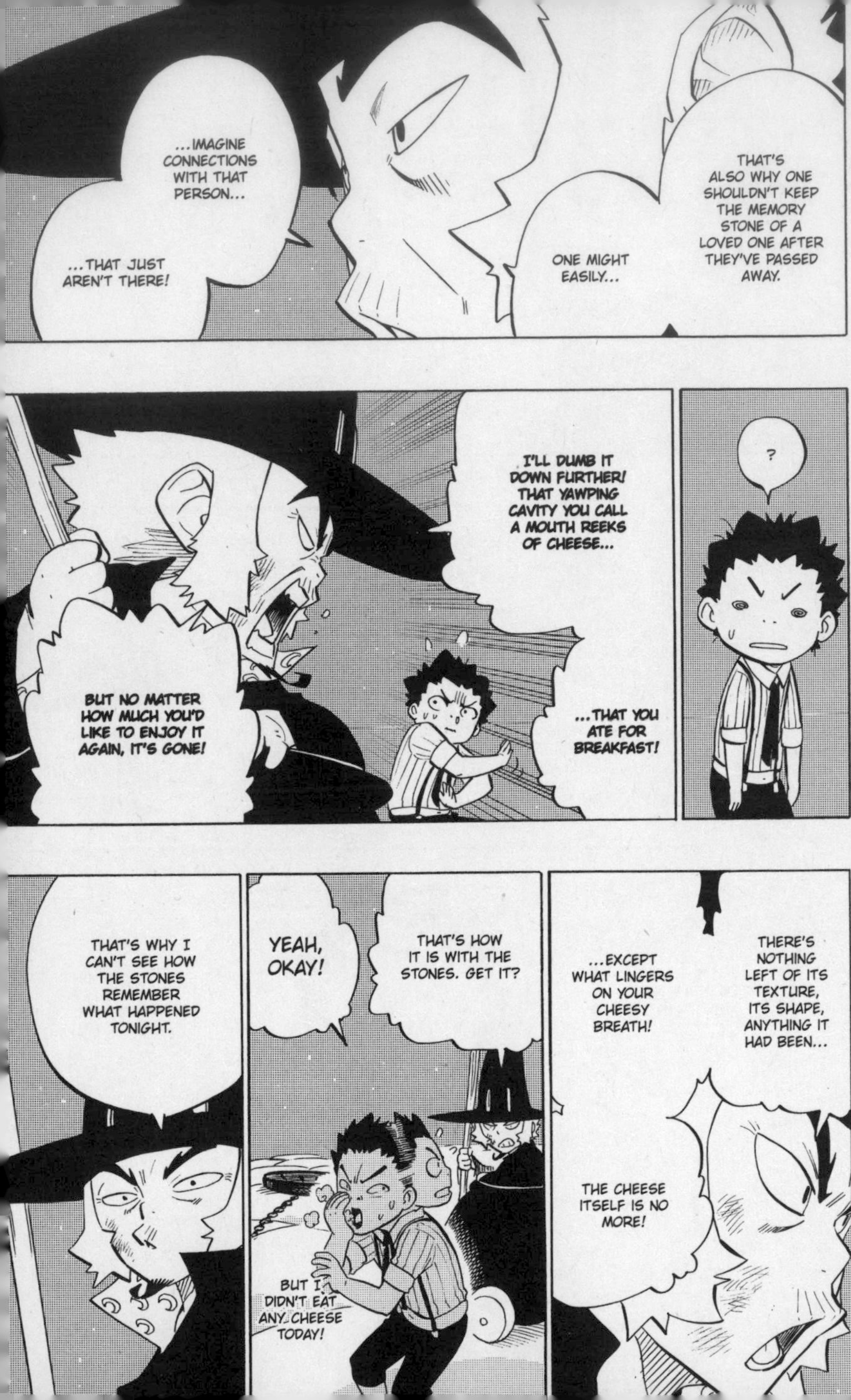
THAT'S ALSO WHY ONE SHOULDN'T KEEP THE MEMORY STONE OF A LOVED ONE AFTER THEY'VE PASSED AWAY.
ONE MIGHT EASILY...
...IMAGINE CONNECTIONS WITH THAT PERSON...
...THAT JUST AREN'T THERE!
?
I'LL DUMB IT DOWN FURTHER! THAT YAWPING CAVITY YOU CALL A MOUTH REEKS OF CHEESE...
...THAT YOU ATE FOR BREAKFAST!
BUT NO MATTER HOW MUCH YOU'D LIKE TO ENJOY IT AGAIN, IT'S GONE!
THERE'S NOTHING LEFT OF ITS TEXTURE, ITS SHAPE, ANYTHING IT HAD BEEN...
...EXCEPT WHAT LINGERS ON YOUR CHEESY BREATH!
THE CHEESE ITSELF IS NO MORE!
THAT'S HOW IT IS WITH THE STONES. GET IT?
YEAH, OKAY!
BUT I DIDN'T EAT ANY CHEESE TODAY!
THAT'S WHY I CAN'T SEE HOW THE STONES REMEMBER WHAT HAPPENED TONIGHT.

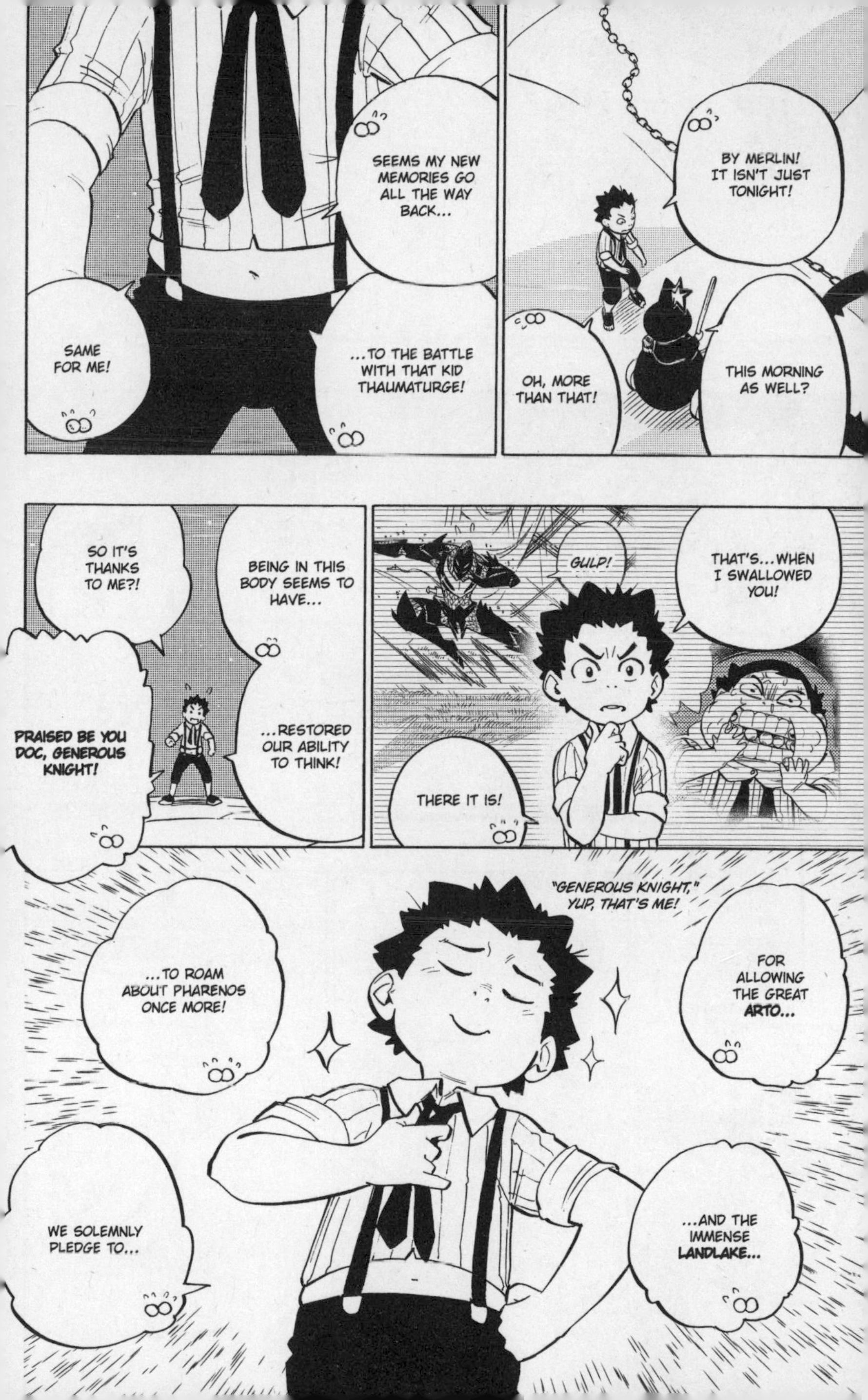

BY MERLIN! IT ISN'T JUST TONIGHT!
THIS MORNING AS WELL?
OH, MORE THAN THAT!
SEEMS MY NEW MEMORIES GO ALL THE WAY BACK...
...TO THE BATTLE WITH THAT KID THAUMATURGE!
SAME FOR ME!
THAT'S...WHEN I SWALLOWED YOU!
GULP!
THERE IT IS!
BEING IN THIS BODY SEEMS TO HAVE...
...RESTORED OUR ABILITY TO THINK!
SO IT'S THANKS TO ME?!
PRAISED BE YOU DOC, GENEROUS KNIGHT!
"GENEROUS KNIGHT," YUP, THAT'S ME!
FOR ALLOWING THE GREAT **ARTO...**
...TO ROAM ABOUT PHARENOS ONCE MORE!
...AND THE IMMENSE **LANDLAKE...**
WE SOLEMNLY PLEDGE TO...

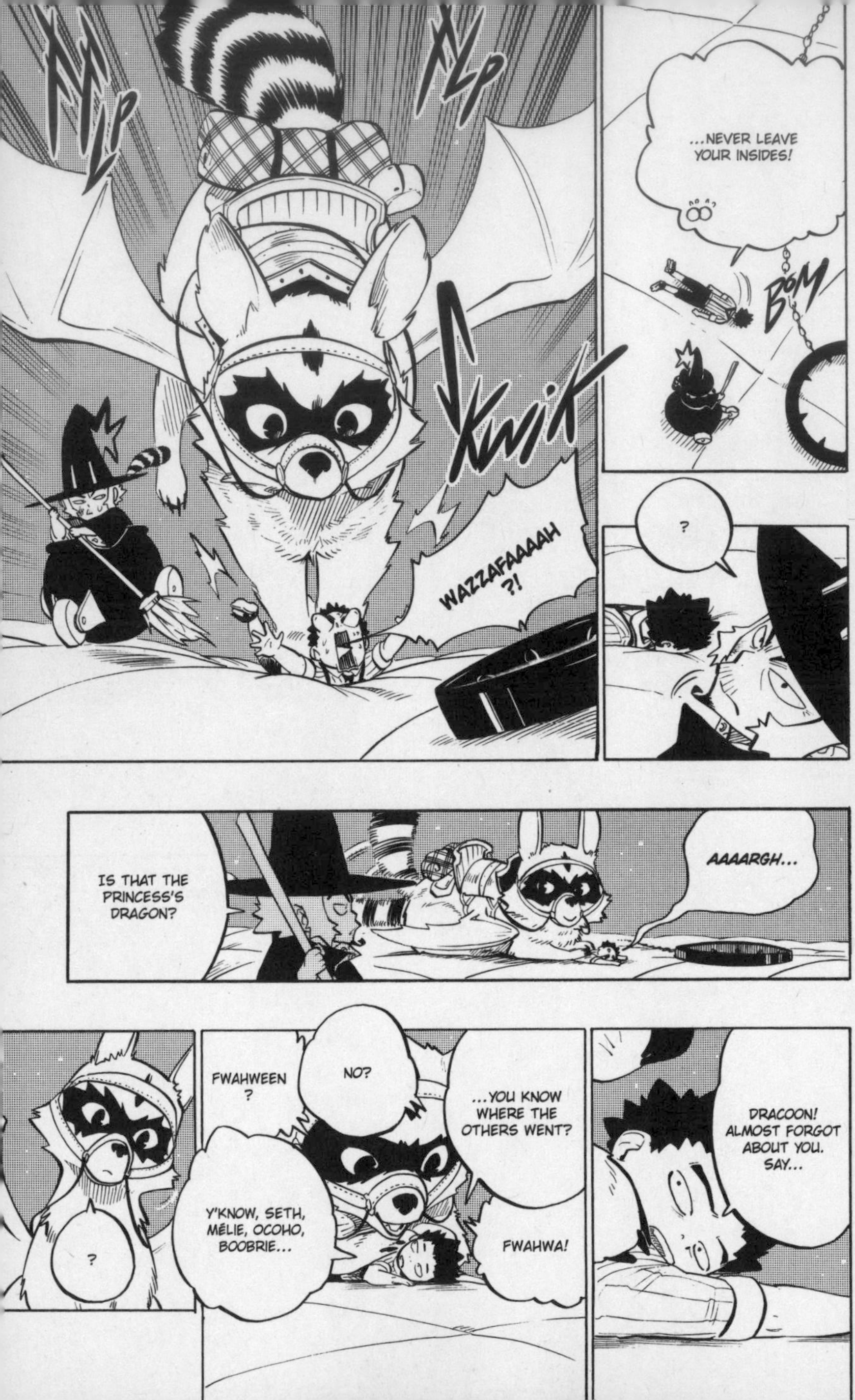
...NEVER LEAVE YOUR INSIDES!
BOM
?
FLIP
FLIP
SKWIK
WAZZAFAAAAH ?!
AAAARGH...
IS THAT THE PRINCESS'S DRAGON?
DRACOON! ALMOST FORGOT ABOUT YOU. SAY...
...YOU KNOW WHERE THE OTHERS WENT?
FWAHWEEN ?
Y'KNOW, SETH, MÉLIE, OCOHO, BOOBRIE...
FWAHWA!
NO?
?

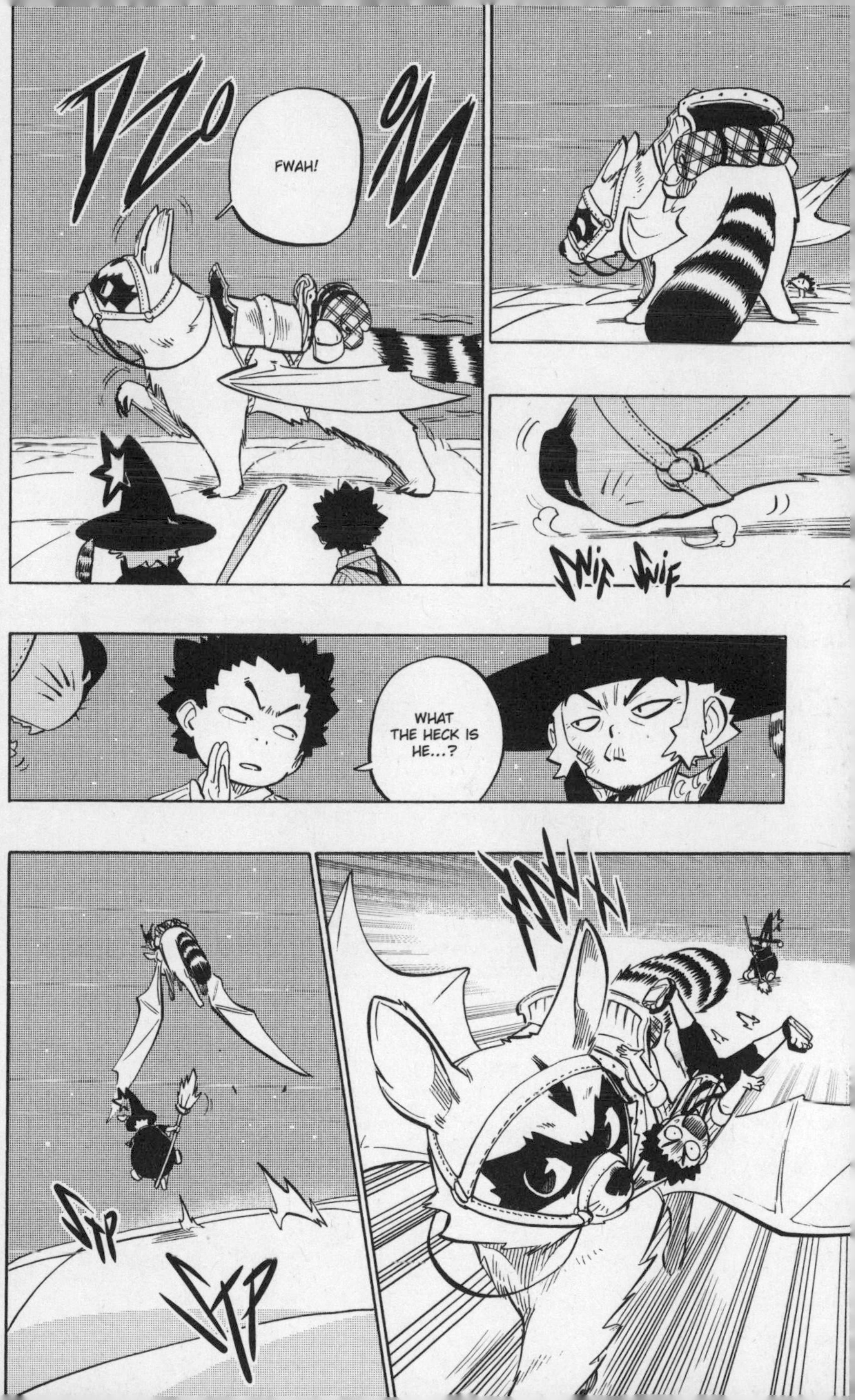

SNIF SNIF
DZOOM
FWAH!
WHAT THE HECK IS HE...?

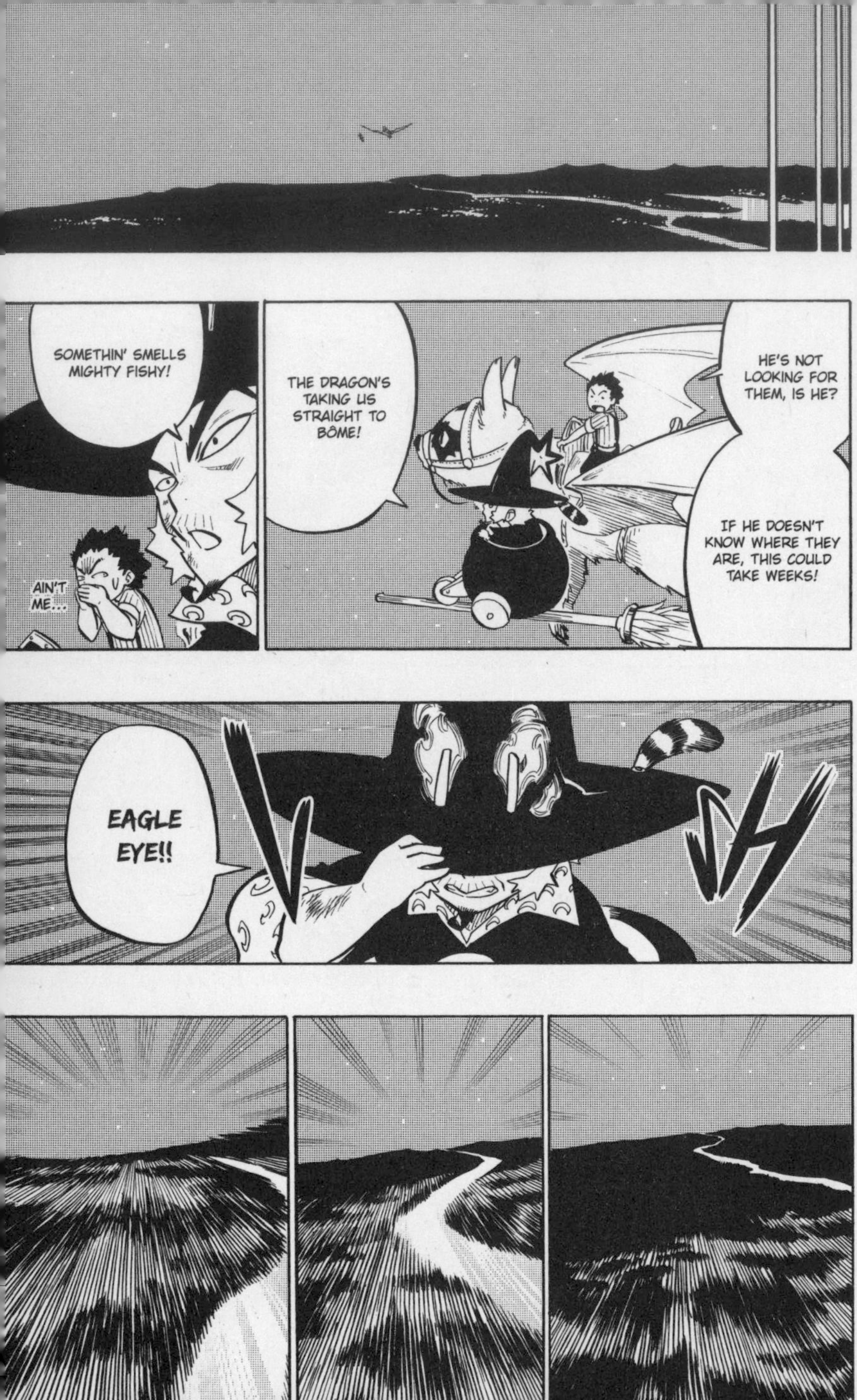

HE'S NOT LOOKING FOR THEM, IS HE?
IF HE DOESN'T KNOW WHERE THEY ARE, THIS COULD TAKE WEEKS!
THE DRAGON'S TAKING US STRAIGHT TO BÔME!
SOMETHIN' SMELLS MIGHTY FISHY!
AIN'T ME...
EAGLE EYE!!

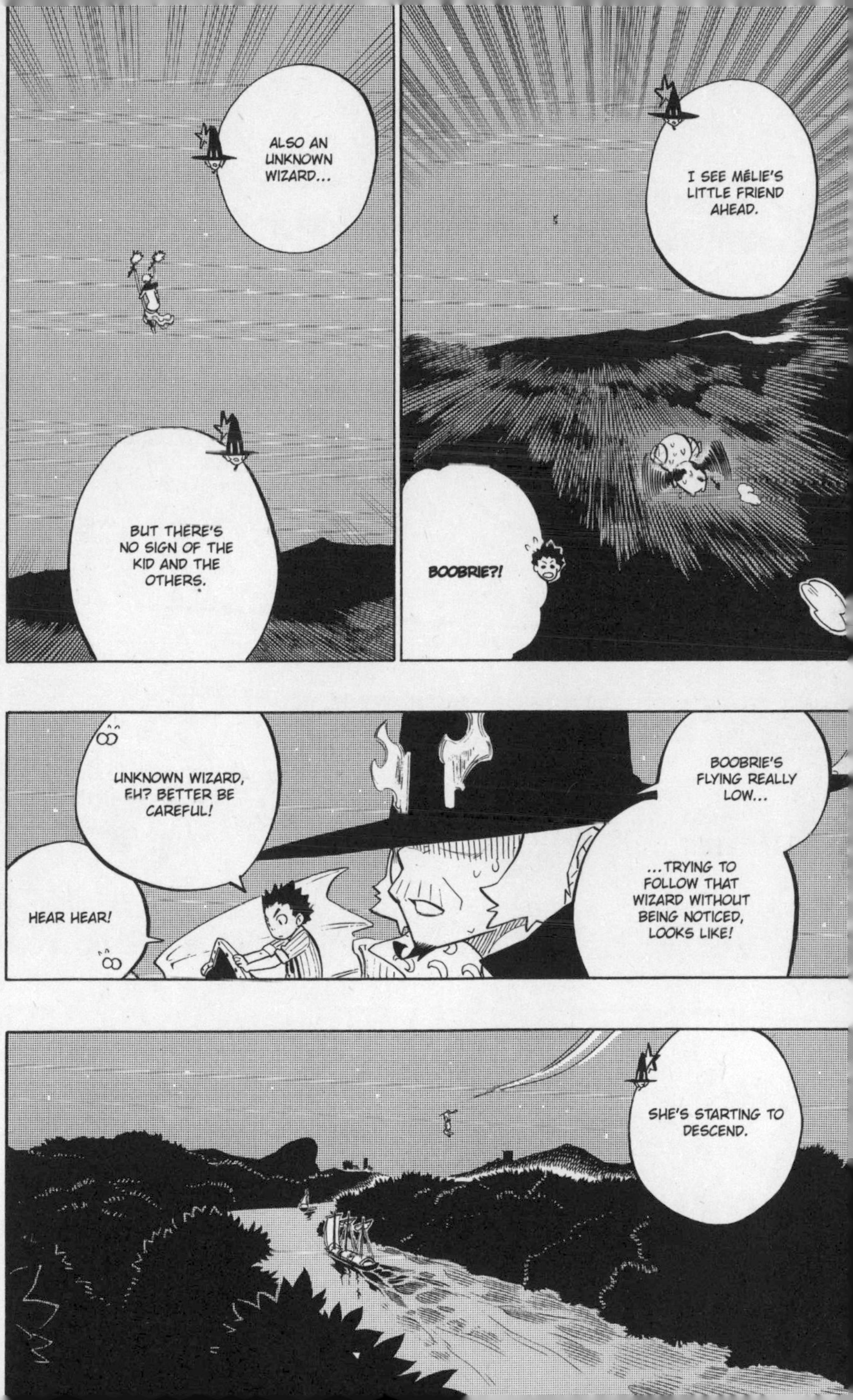
I SEE MÉLIE'S LITTLE FRIEND AHEAD.
BOOBRIE?!
ALSO AN UNKNOWN WIZARD...
BUT THERE'S NO SIGN OF THE KID AND THE OTHERS.
BOOBRIE'S FLYING REALLY LOW...
...TRYING TO FOLLOW THAT WIZARD WITHOUT BEING NOTICED, LOOKS LIKE!
UNKNOWN WIZARD, EH? BETTER BE CAREFUL!
HEAR HEAR!
SHE'S STARTING TO DESCEND.

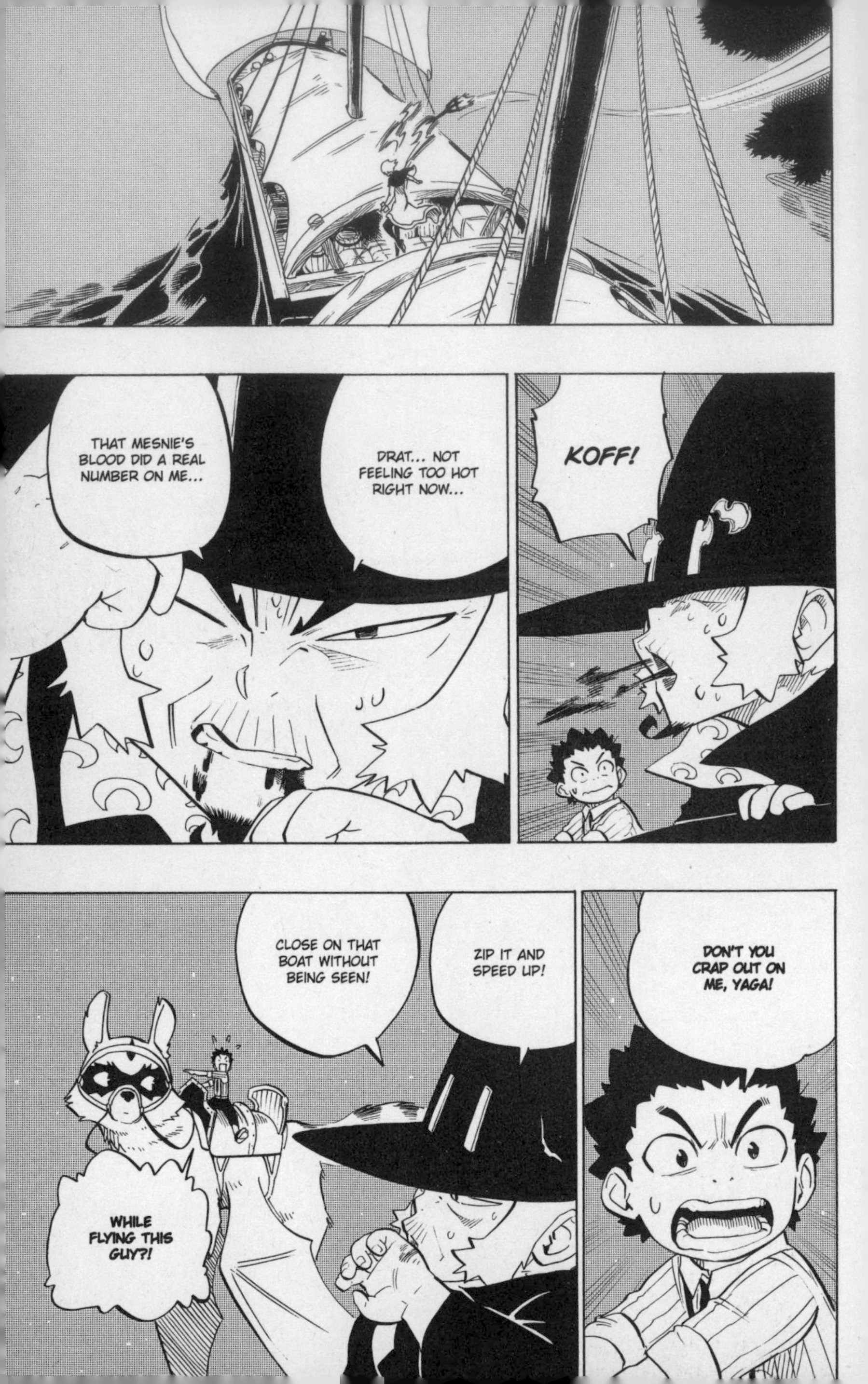
KOFF!
DRAT... NOT FEELING TOO HOT RIGHT NOW...
THAT MESNIE'S BLOOD DID A REAL NUMBER ON ME...
DON'T YOU CRAP OUT ON ME, YAGA!
ZIP IT AND SPEED UP!
CLOSE ON THAT BOAT WITHOUT BEING SEEN!
WHILE FLYING THIS GUY?!

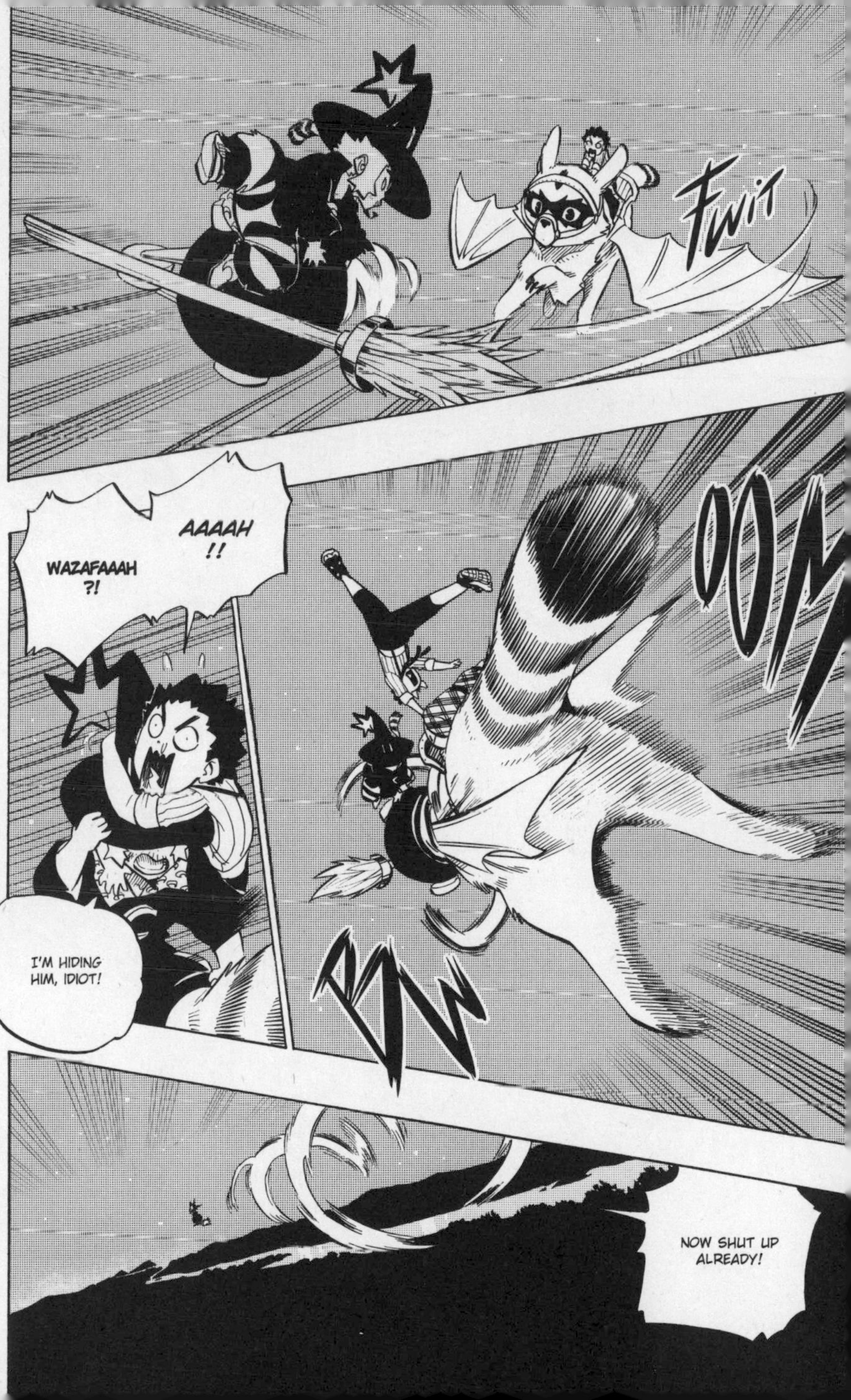
FWIT
AAAAH!!
WAZAFAAAH?!
I'M HIDING HIM, IDIOT!
NOW SHUT UP ALREADY!

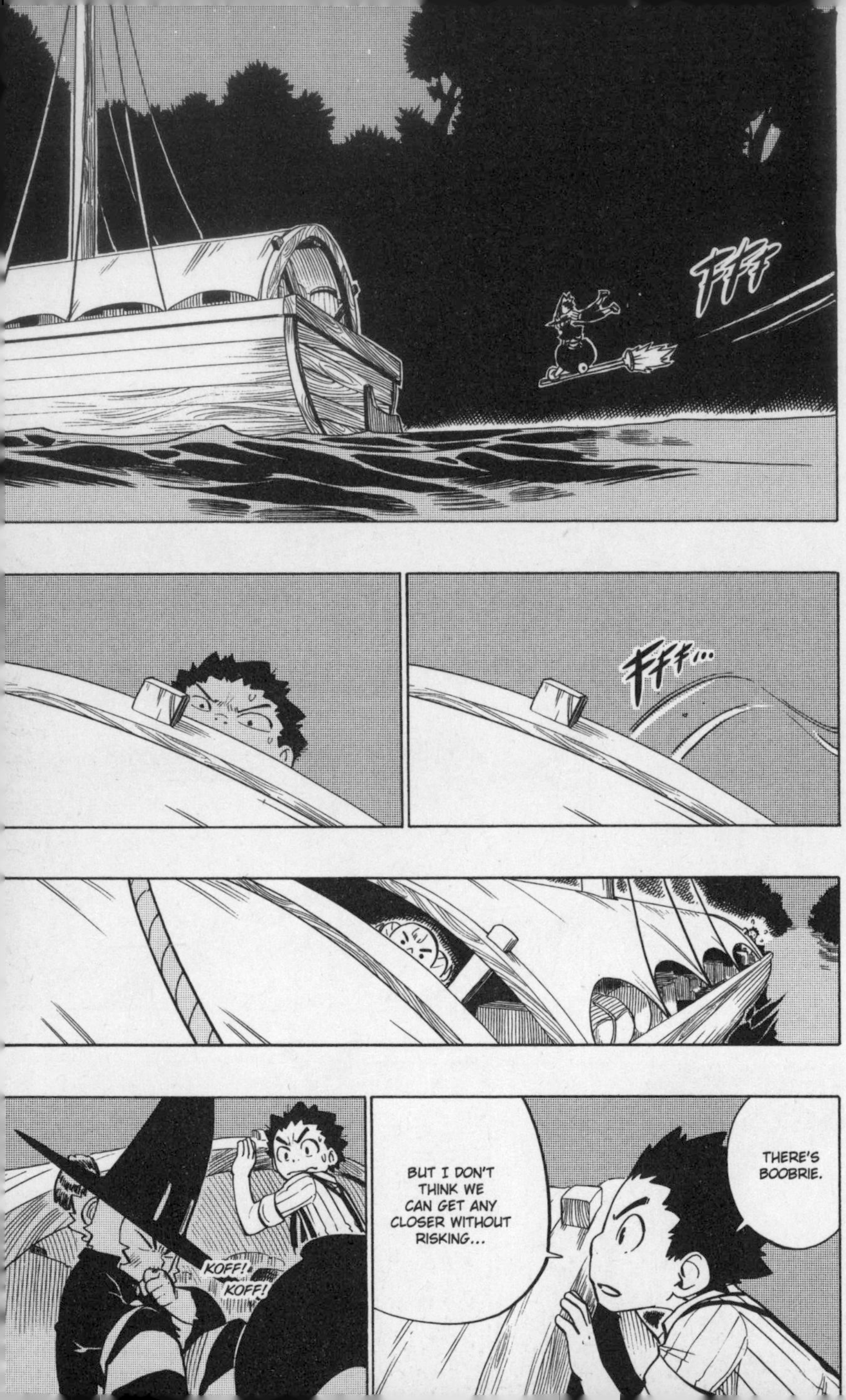
THERE'S BOOBRIE.
BUT I DON'T THINK WE CAN GET ANY CLOSER WITHOUT RISKING...
KOFF! KOFF!

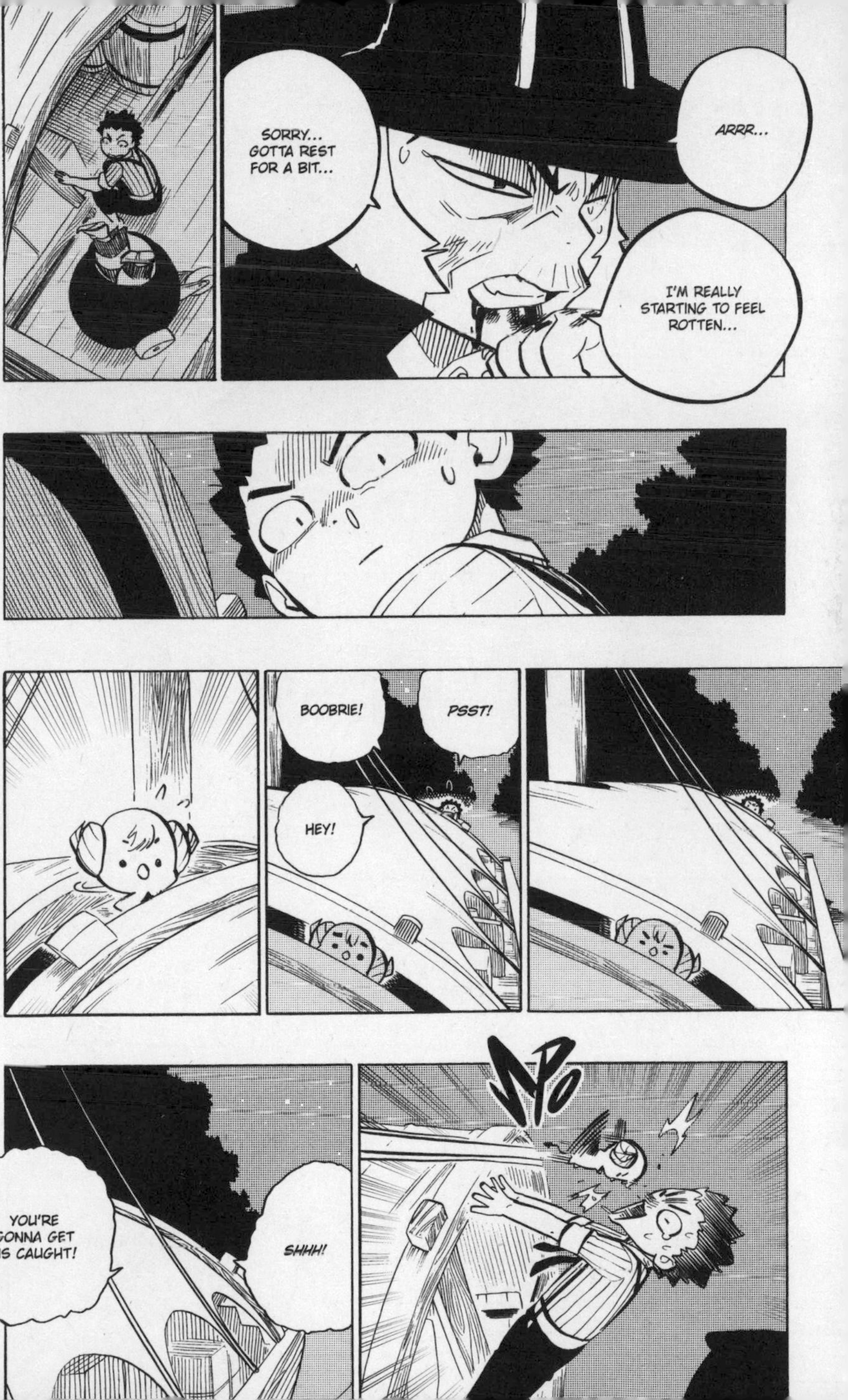
ARRR...
I'M REALLY STARTING TO FEEL ROTTEN...
SORRY... GOTTA REST FOR A BIT...
PSST!
BOOBRIE!
HEY!
SPO
SHHH!
YOU'RE GONNA GET US CAUGHT!

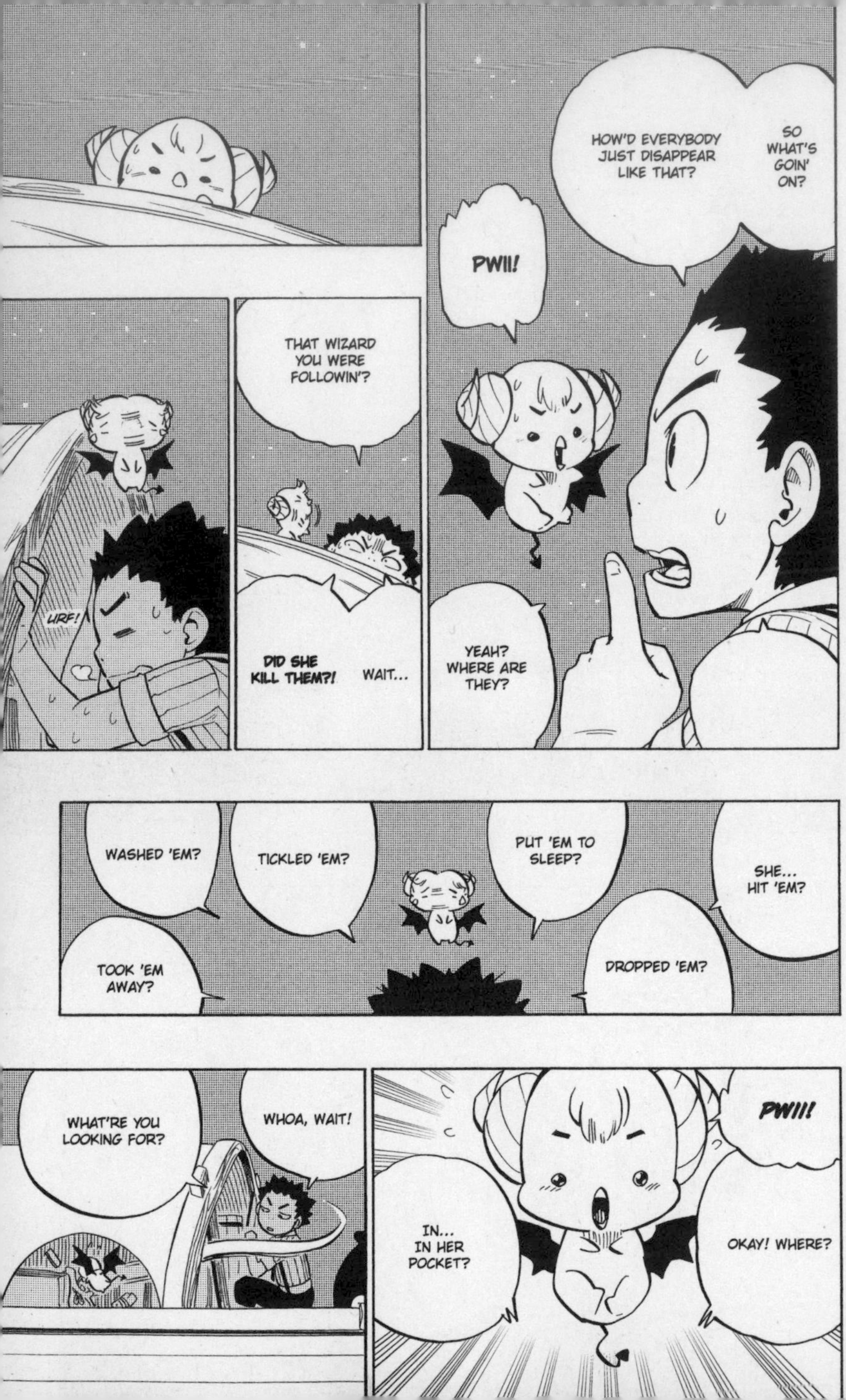
SO WHAT'S GOIN' ON?
HOW'D EVERYBODY JUST DISAPPEAR LIKE THAT?
PWII!
YEAH? WHERE ARE THEY?
THAT WIZARD YOU WERE FOLLOWIN'?
WAIT...
DID SHE KILL THEM?!
URF!
SHE... HIT 'EM?
DROPPED 'EM?
PUT 'EM TO SLEEP?
TICKLED 'EM?
WASHED 'EM?
TOOK 'EM AWAY?
PWII!
OKAY! WHERE?
IN... IN HER POCKET?
WHOA, WAIT!
WHAT'RE YOU LOOKING FOR?

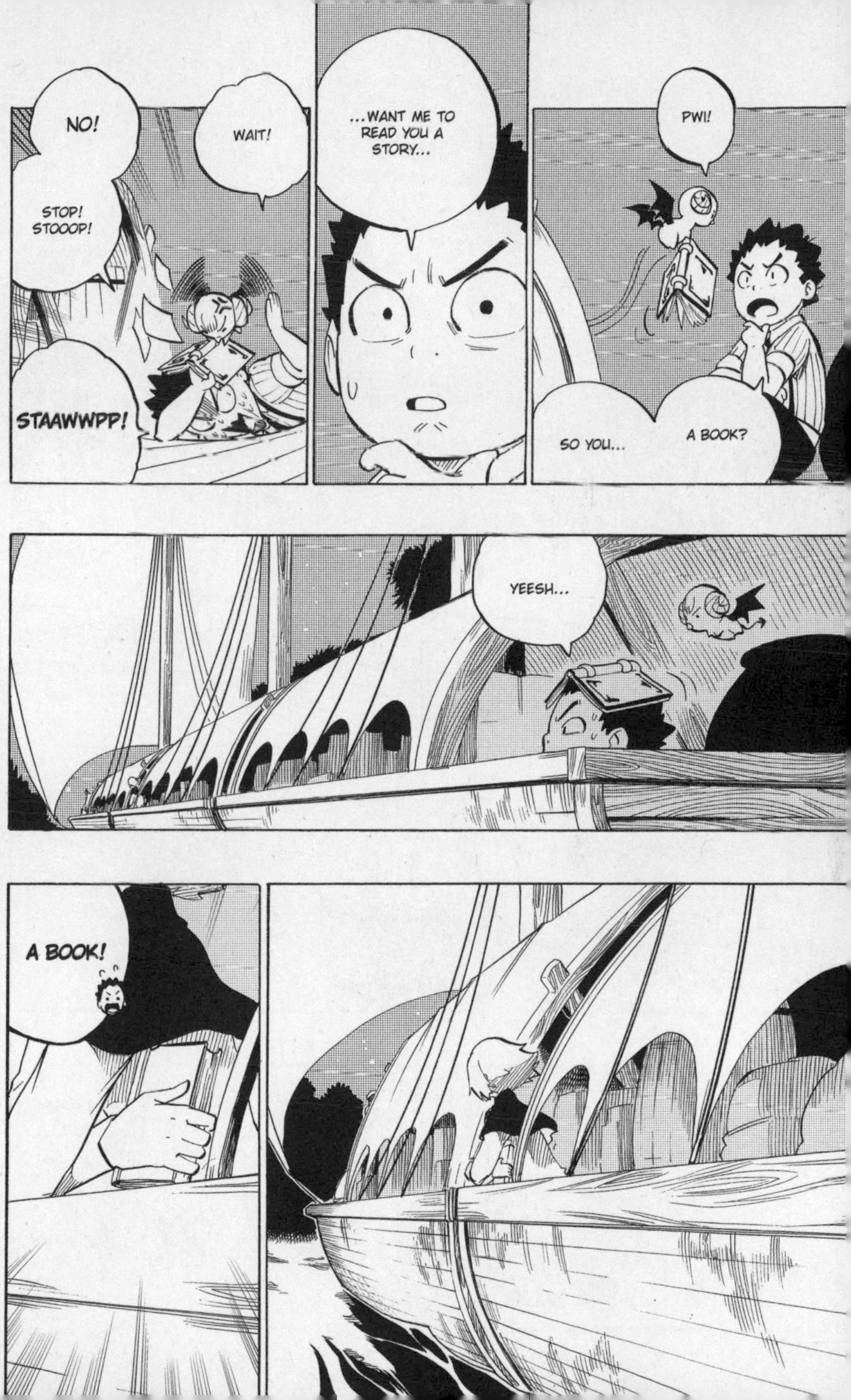
PWI!
A BOOK?
SO YOU...
...WANT ME TO READ YOU A STORY...
WAIT!
NO!
STOP! STOOOP!
STAAWWPP!
YEESH...
A BOOK!

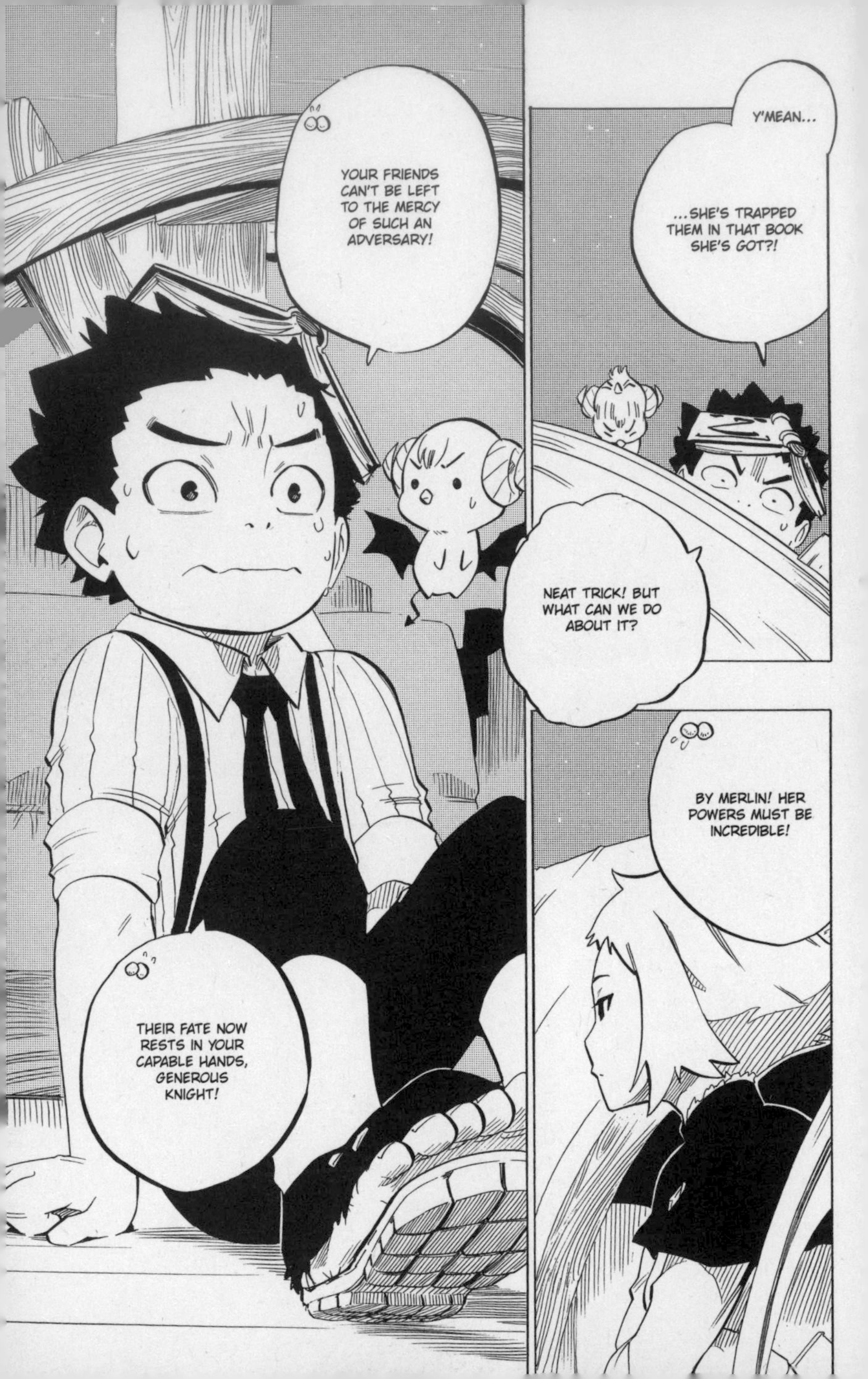
Y'MEAN...
...SHE'S TRAPPED THEM IN THAT BOOK SHE'S GOT?!
NEAT TRICK! BUT WHAT CAN WE DO ABOUT IT?
BY MERLIN! HER POWERS MUST BE INCREDIBLE!
YOUR FRIENDS CAN'T BE LEFT TO THE MERCY OF SUCH AN ADVERSARY!
THEIR FATE NOW RESTS IN YOUR CAPABLE HANDS, GENEROUS KNIGHT!

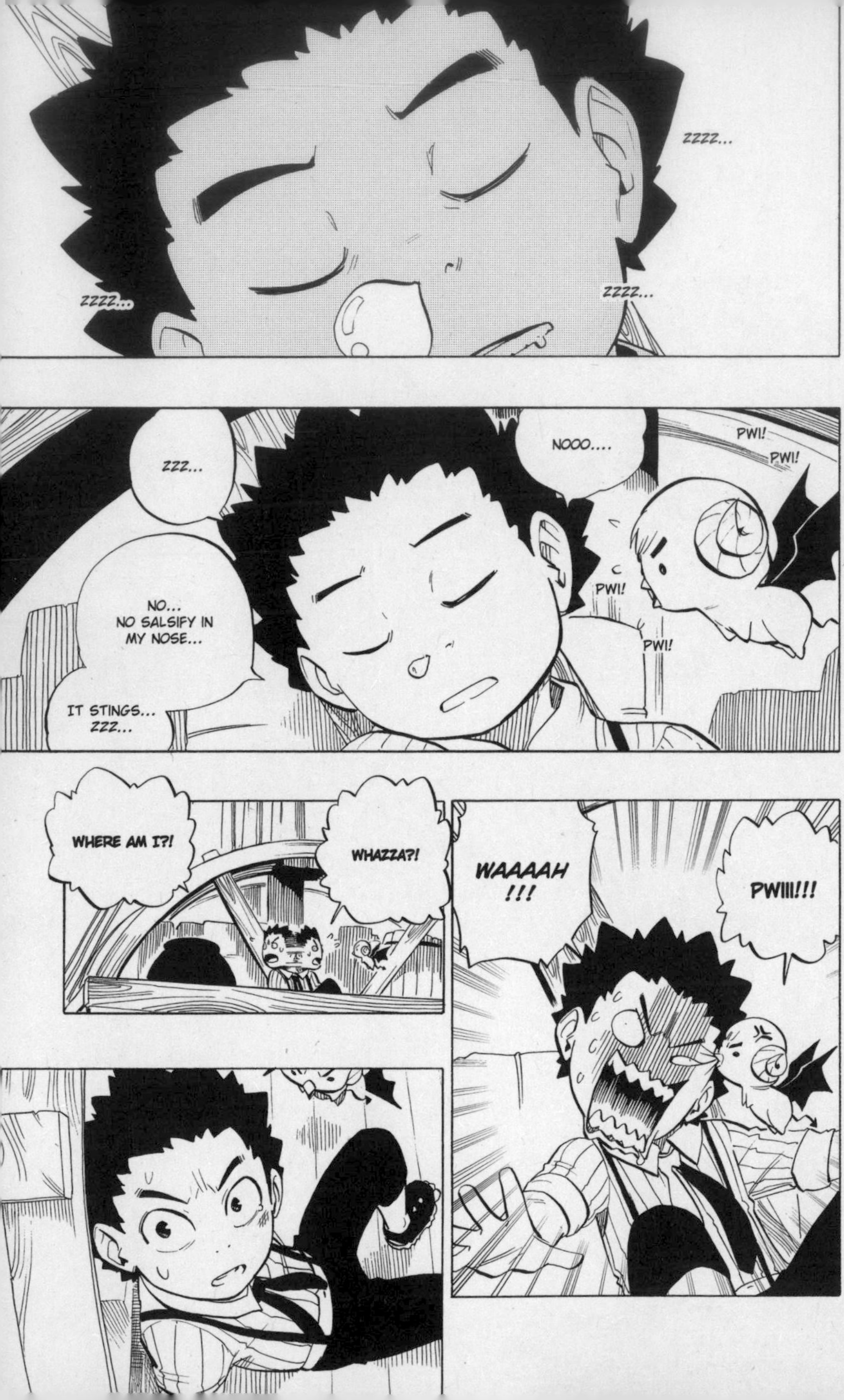
ZZZZ...
ZZZZ...
ZZZZ...
PWI!
PWI!
NOOO....
ZZZ...
PWI!
NO...
NO SALSIFY IN
MY NOSE...
PWI!
IT STINGS...
ZZZ...
PWIII!!!
WAAAAH
!!!
WHAZZA?!
WHERE AM I?!

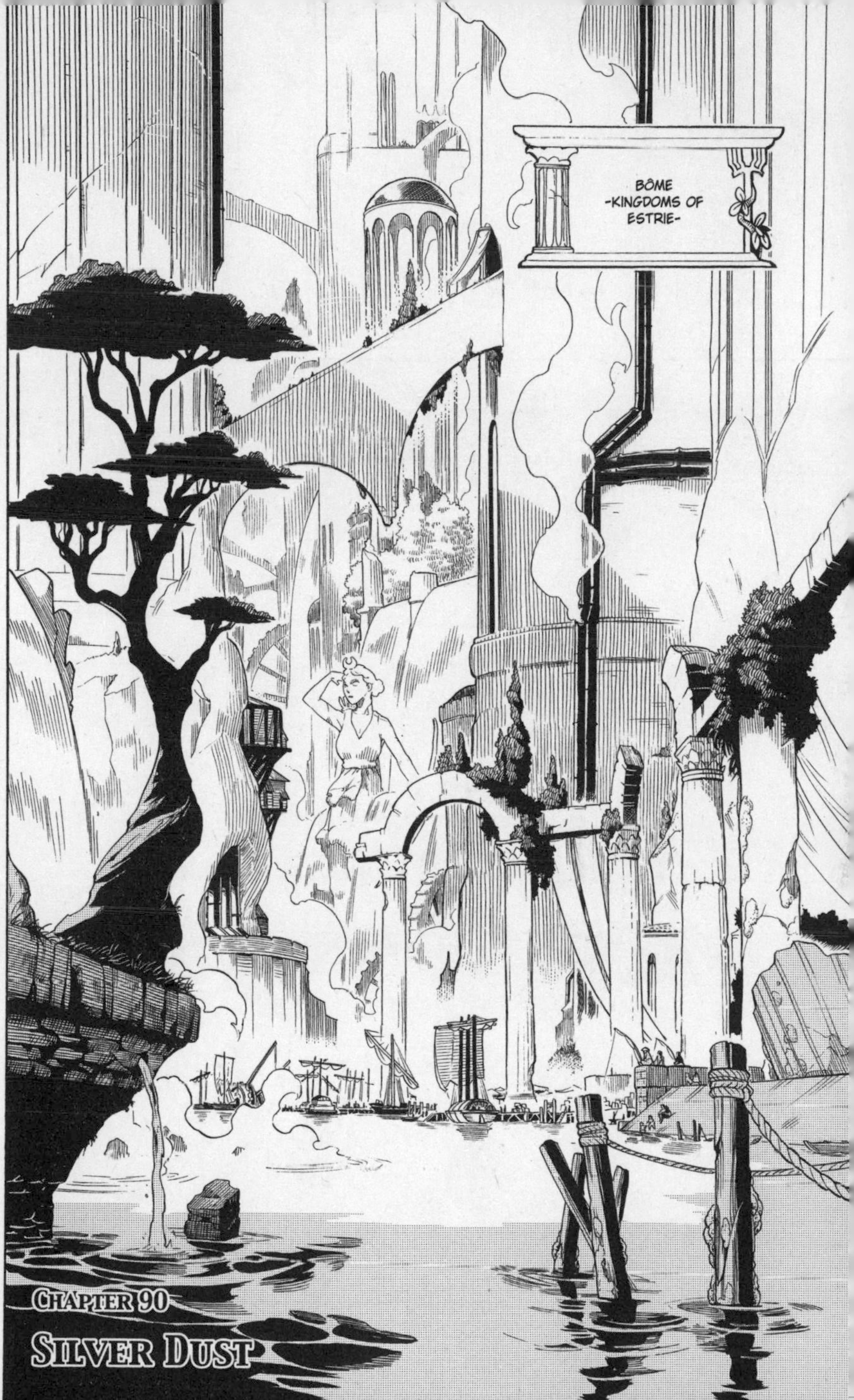
BÔME
-KINGDOMS OF ESTRIE-
CHAPTER 90
SILVER DUST

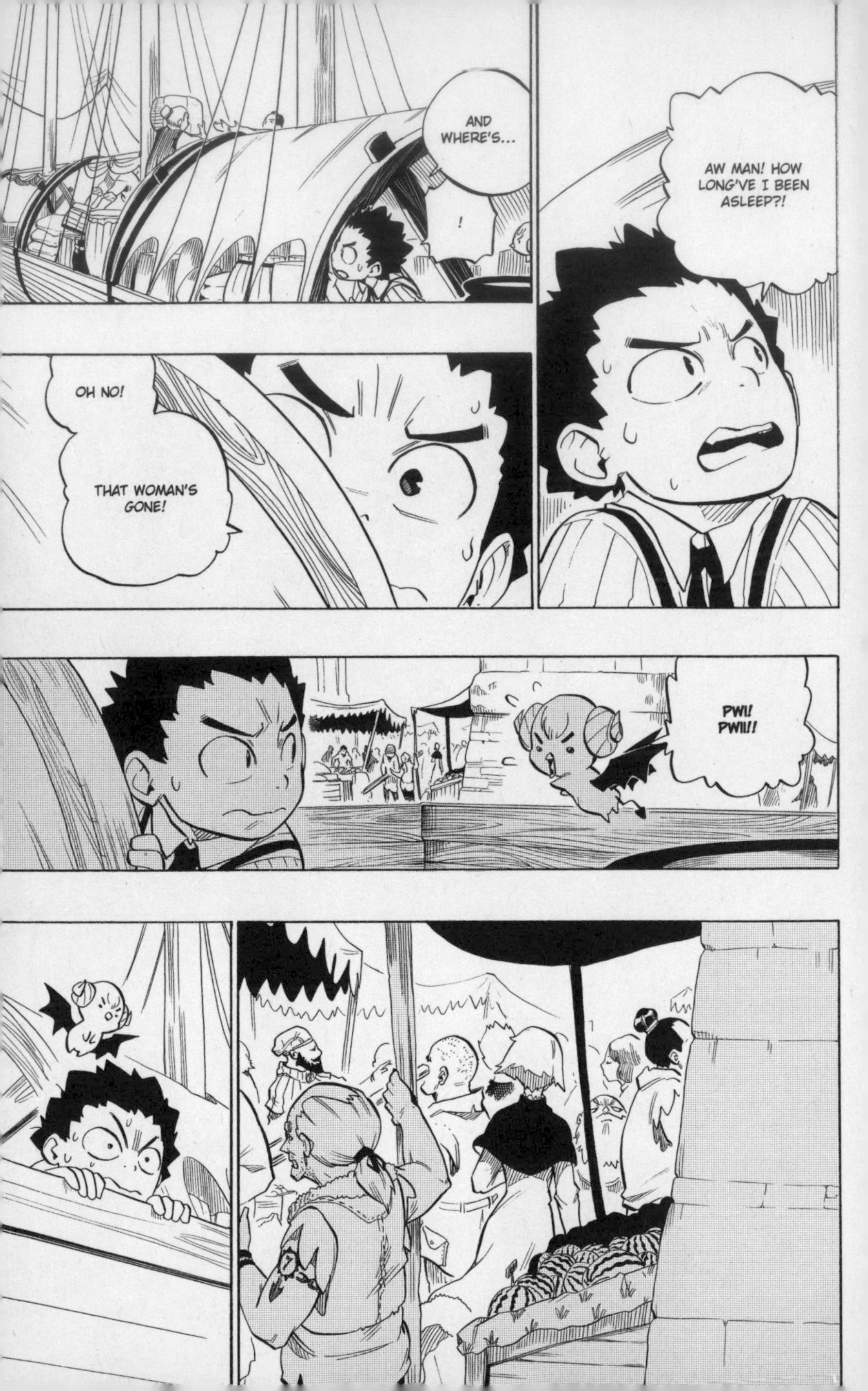
AW MAN! HOW LONG'VE I BEEN ASLEEP?!
AND WHERE'S...
!
OH NO!
THAT WOMAN'S GONE!
PWI! PWII!!

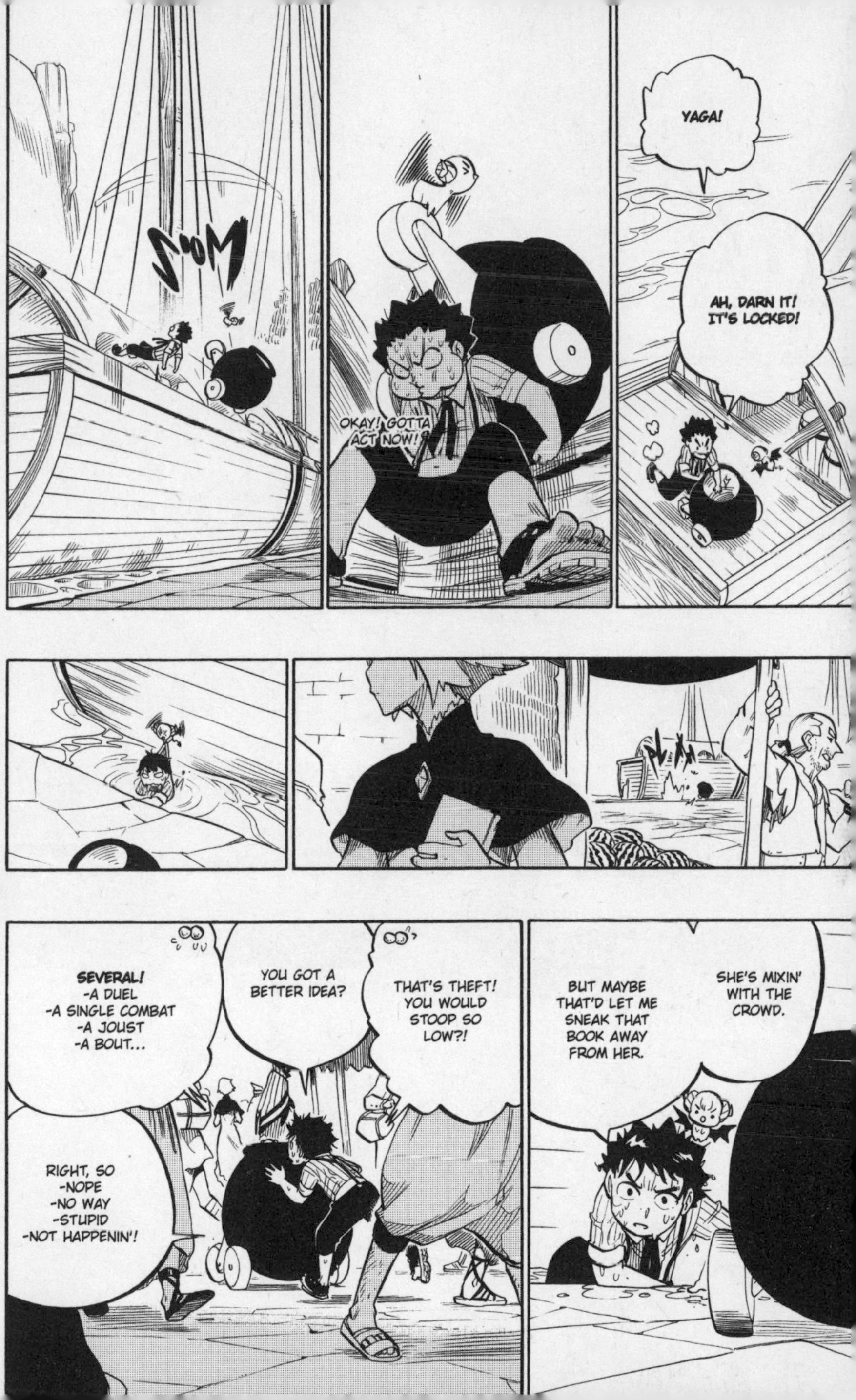
YAGA!
AH, DARN IT! IT'S LOCKED!
OKAY! GOTTA ACT NOW!
SHE'S MIXIN' WITH THE CROWD.
BUT MAYBE THAT'D LET ME SNEAK THAT BOOK AWAY FROM HER.
THAT'S THEFT! YOU WOULD STOOP SO LOW?!
YOU GOT A BETTER IDEA?
SEVERAL! -A DUEL -A SINGLE COMBAT -A JOUST -A BOUT...
RIGHT, SO -NOPE -NO WAY -STUPID -NOT HAPPENIN'!

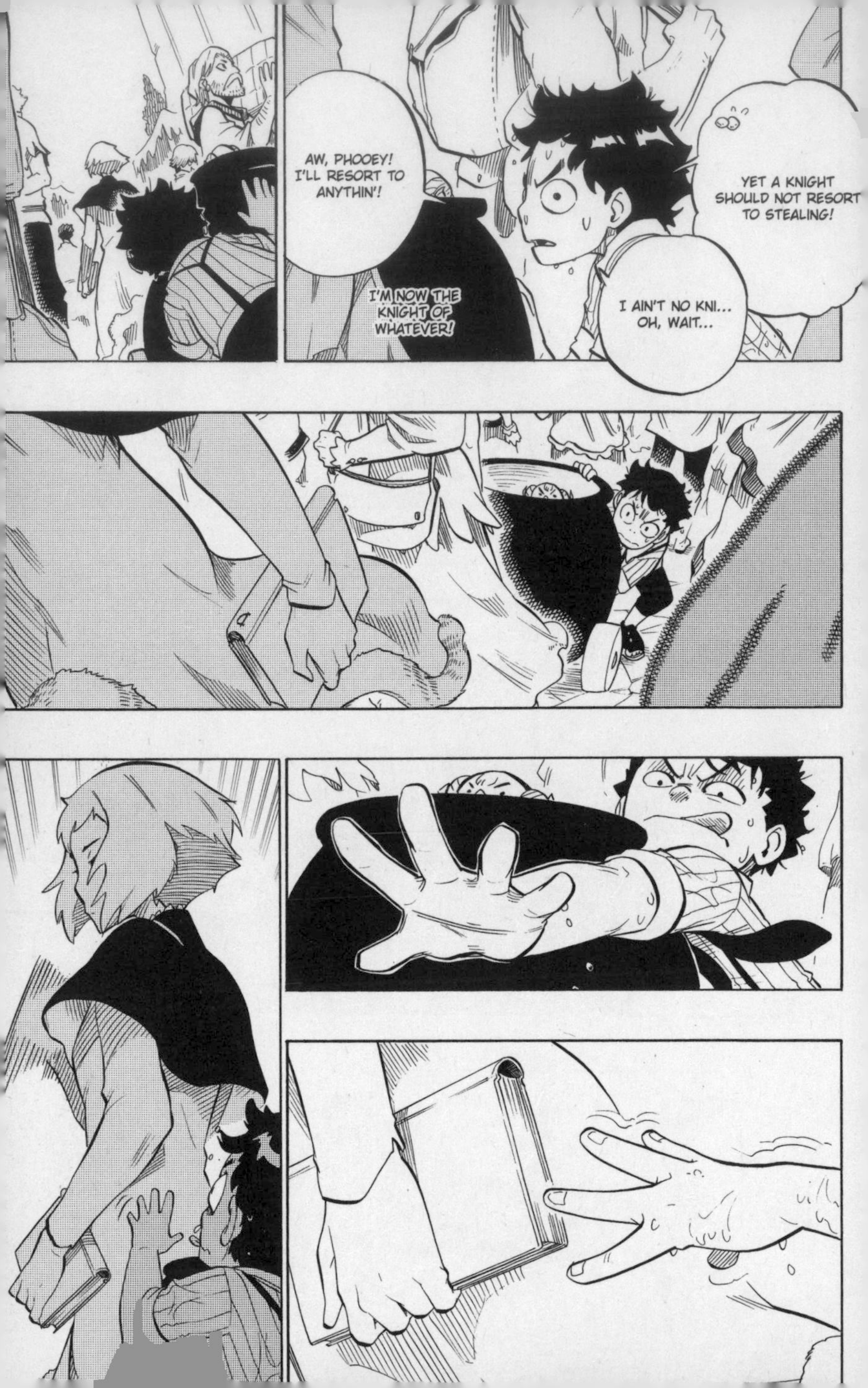
YET A KNIGHT SHOULD NOT RESORT TO STEALING!
I AIN'T NO KNI... OH, WAIT...
I'M NOW THE KNIGHT OF WHATEVER!
AW, PHOOEY! I'LL RESORT TO ANYTHIN'!

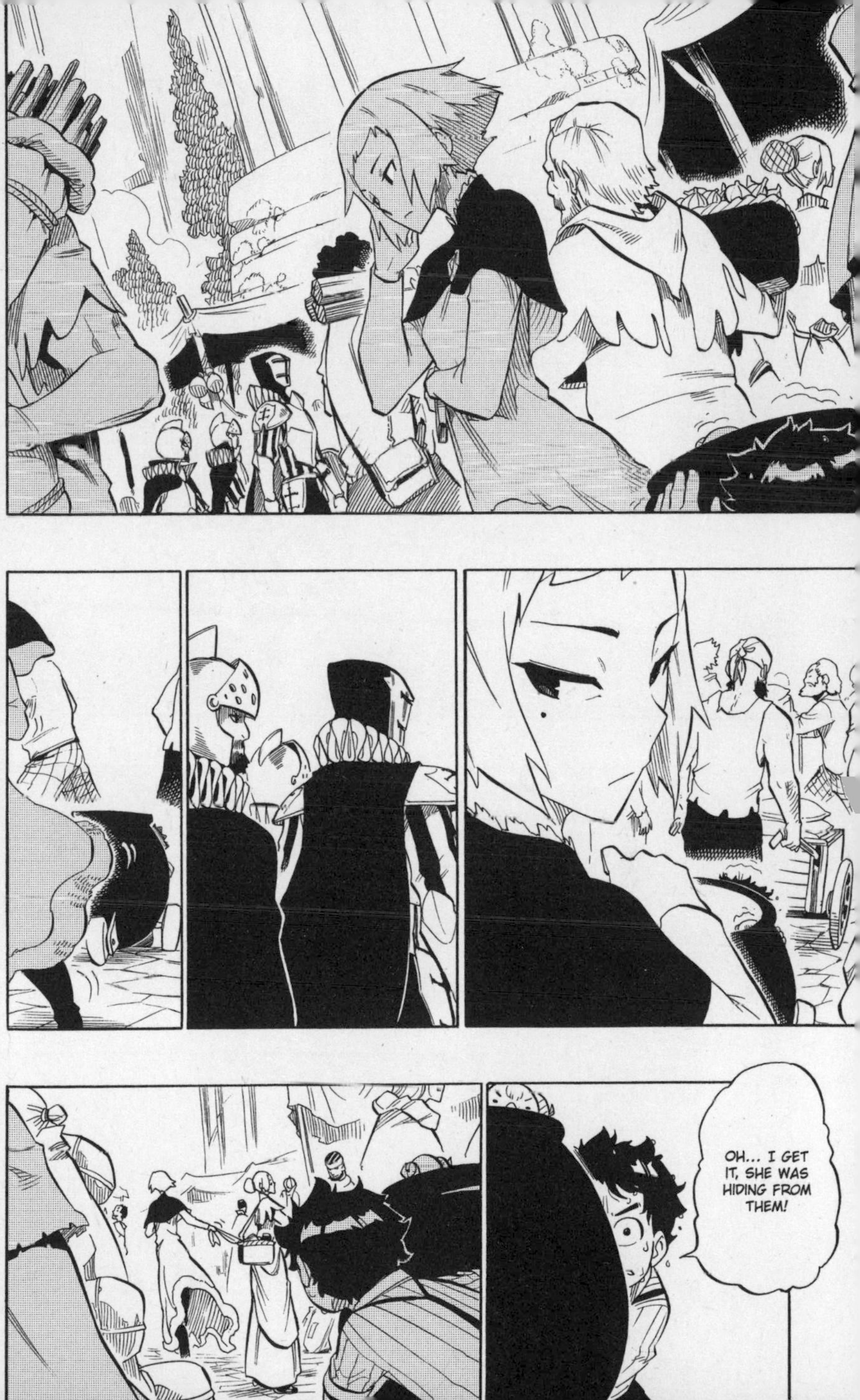
OH... I GET IT, SHE WAS HIDING FROM THEM!

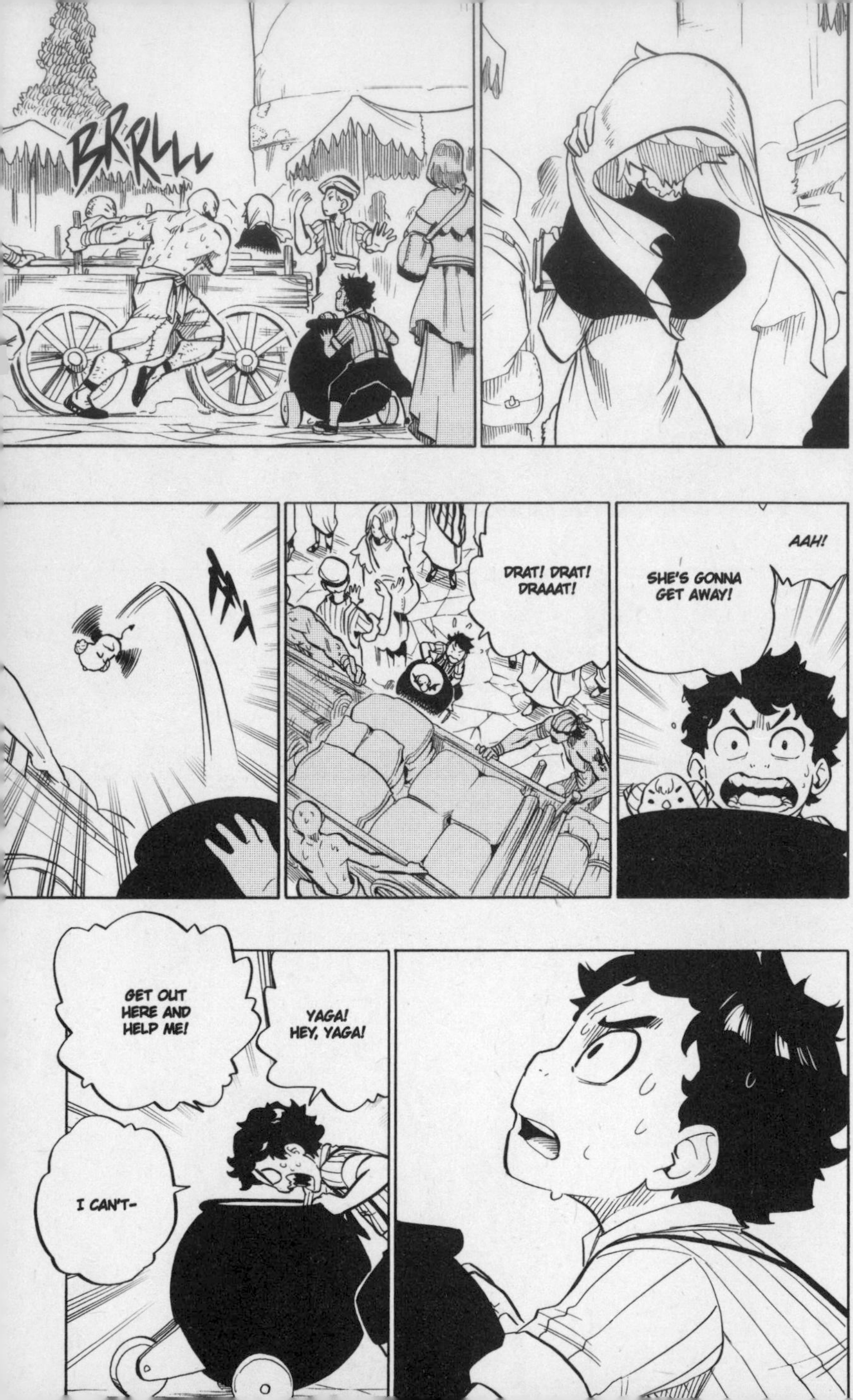
BRRLLL
AAH!
SHE'S GONNA GET AWAY!
DRAT! DRAT! DRAAAT!
YAGA! HEY, YAGA!
GET OUT HERE AND HELP ME!
I CAN'T-

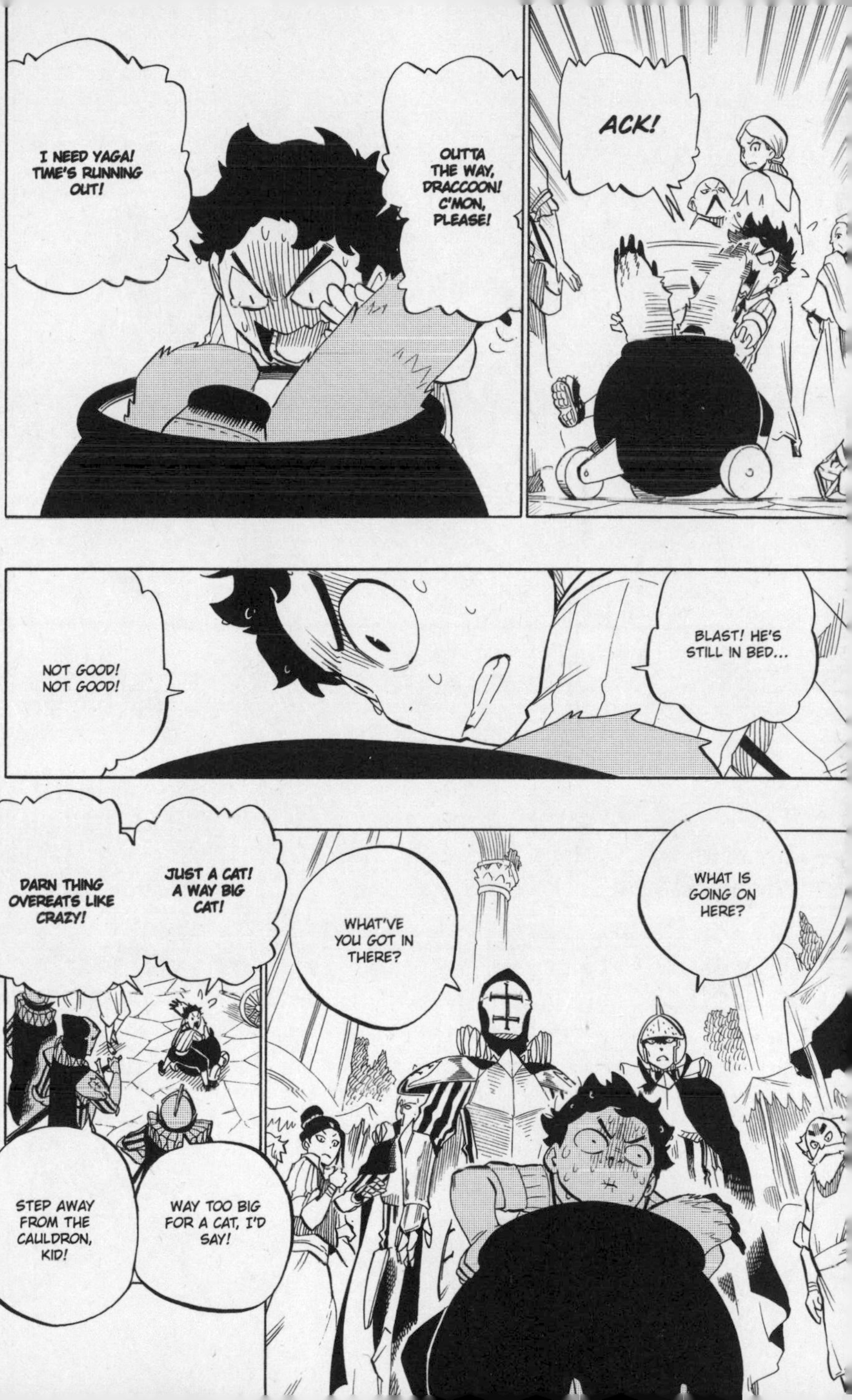
ACK!
OUTTA THE WAY, DRACCOON! C'MON, PLEASE!
I NEED YAGA! TIME'S RUNNING OUT!
BLAST! HE'S STILL IN BED...
NOT GOOD! NOT GOOD!
WHAT IS GOING ON HERE?
WHAT'VE YOU GOT IN THERE?
JUST A CAT! A WAY BIG CAT!
DARN THING OVEREATS LIKE CRAZY!
WAY TOO BIG FOR A CAT, I'D SAY!
STEP AWAY FROM THE CAULDRON, KID!

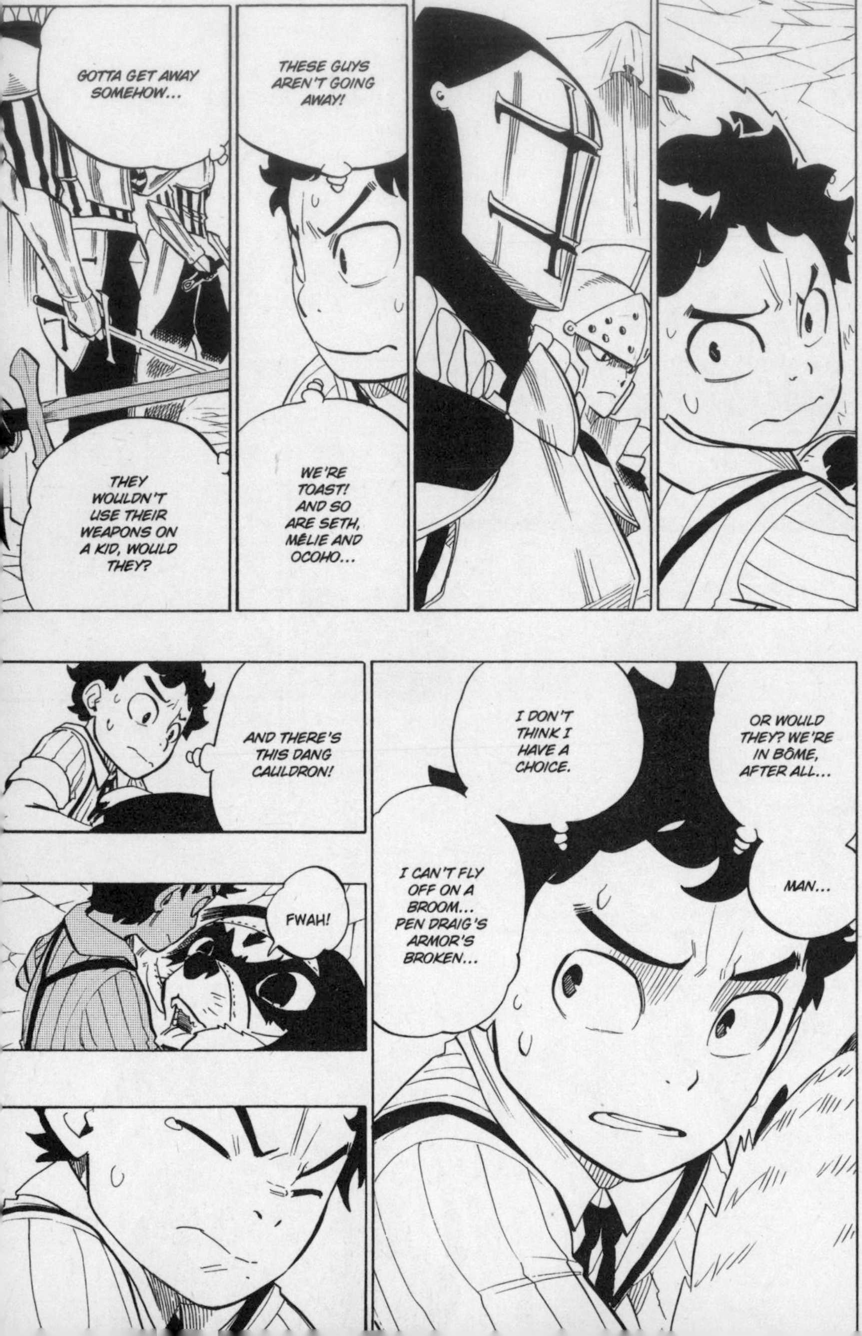
THESE GUYS AREN'T GOING AWAY!
WE'RE TOAST! AND SO ARE SETH, MÊLIE AND OCOHO...
GOTTA GET AWAY SOMEHOW...
THEY WOULDN'T USE THEIR WEAPONS ON A KID, WOULD THEY?
OR WOULD THEY? WE'RE IN BÔME, AFTER ALL...
I DON'T THINK I HAVE A CHOICE.
MAN...
I CAN'T FLY OFF ON A BROOM... PEN DRAIG'S ARMOR'S BROKEN...
AND THERE'S THIS DANG CAULDRON!
FWAH!

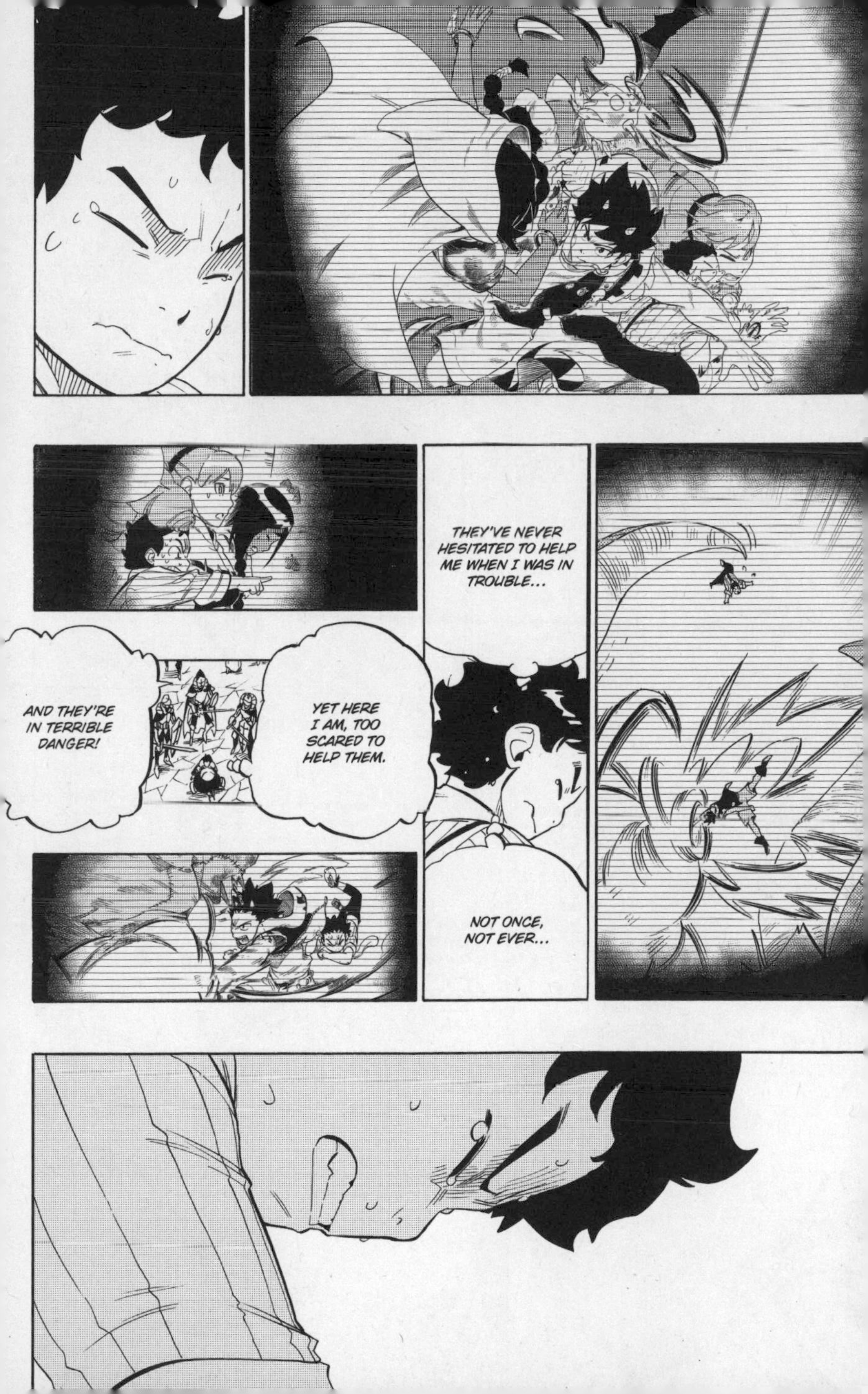
THEY'VE NEVER HESITATED TO HELP ME WHEN I WAS IN TROUBLE...
NOT ONCE, NOT EVER...
YET HERE I AM, TOO SCARED TO HELP THEM.
AND THEY'RE IN TERRIBLE DANGER!

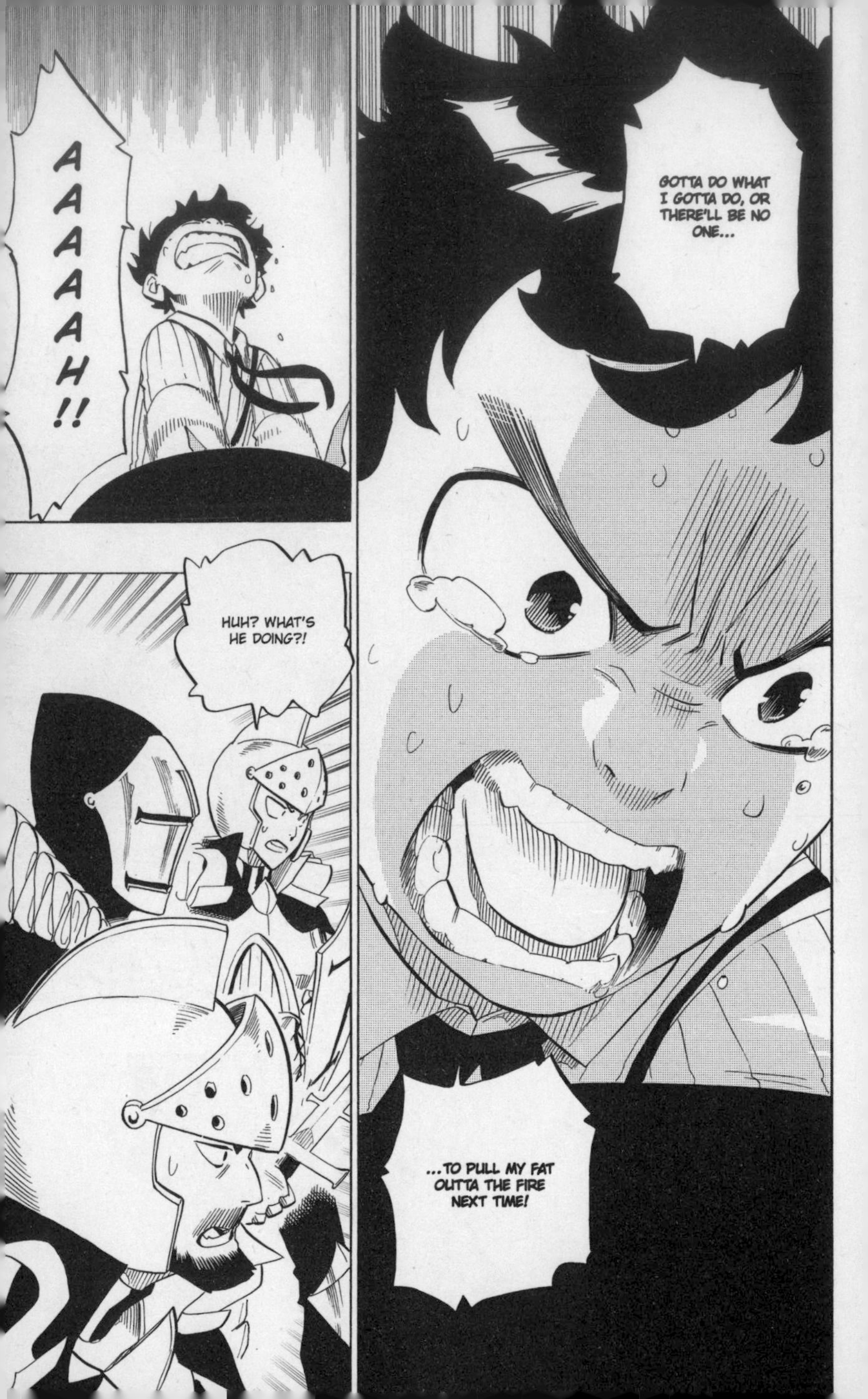
GOTTA DO WHAT I GOTTA DO, OR THERE'LL BE NO ONE...
...TO PULL MY FAT OUTTA THE FIRE NEXT TIME!
AAAAAAH!!
HUH? WHAT'S HE DOING?!

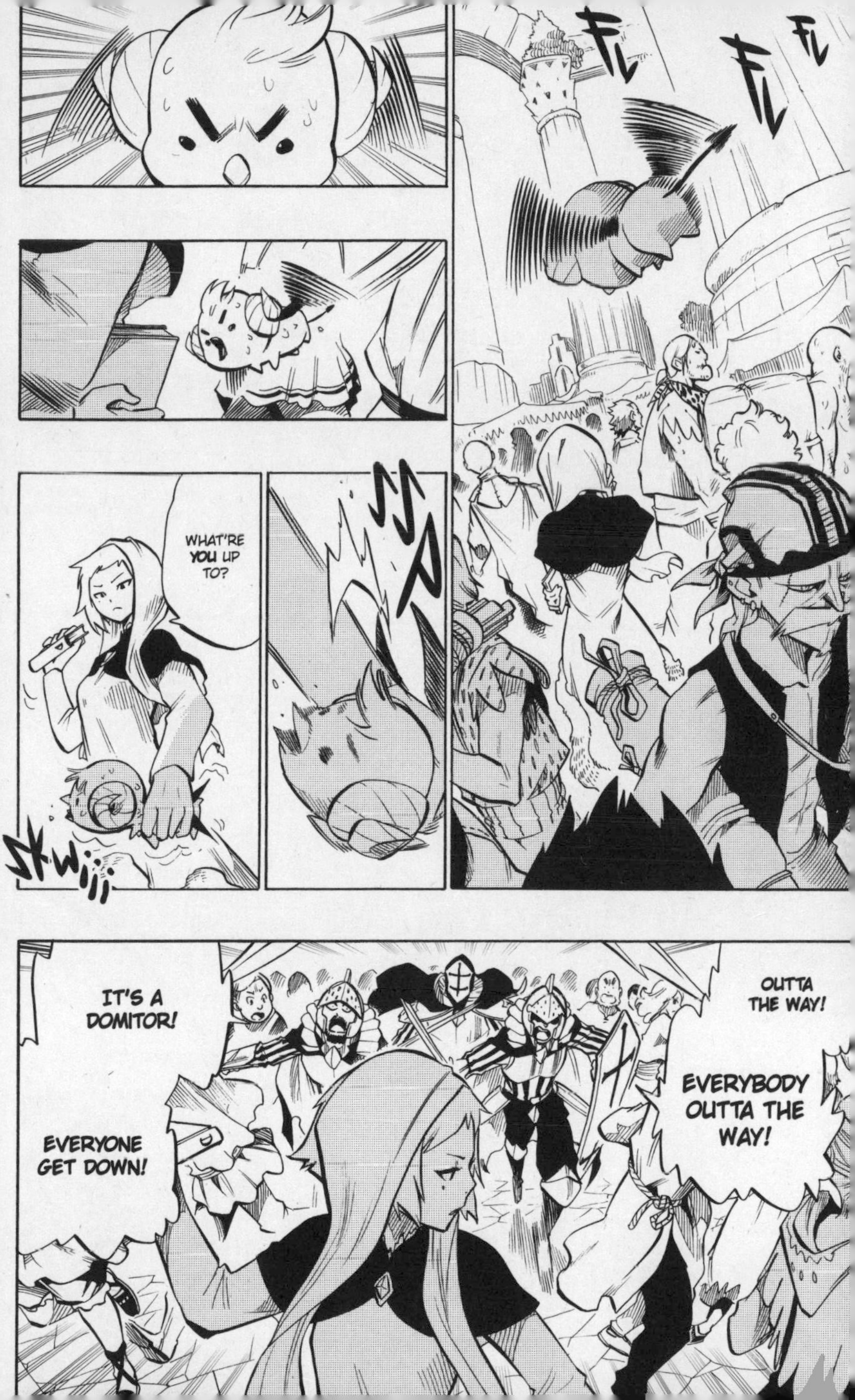
FL FL FL
WHAT'RE YOU UP TO?
SKWiiii
OUTTA THE WAY!
EVERYBODY OUTTA THE WAY!
IT'S A DOMITOR!
EVERYONE GET DOWN!

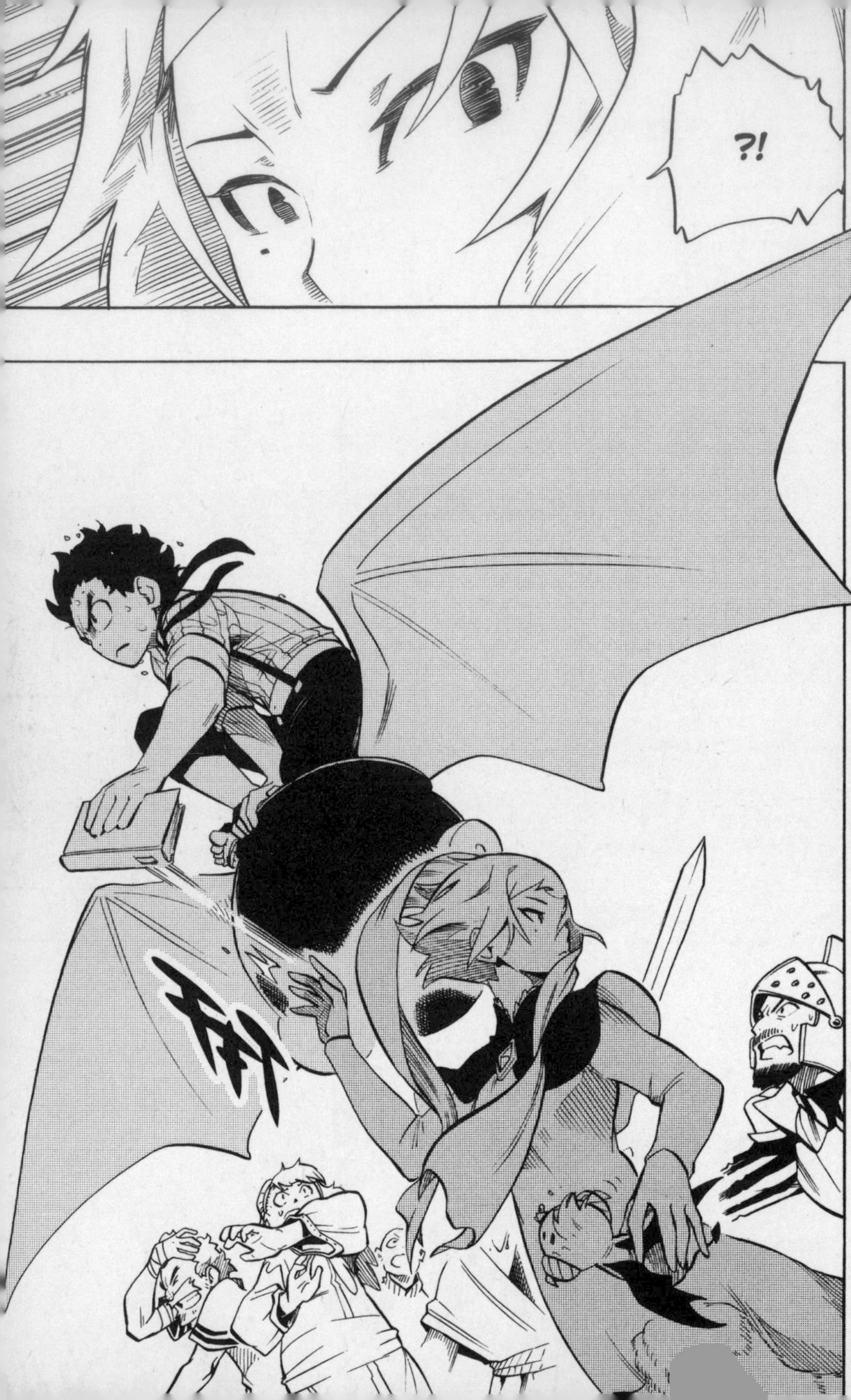
?!

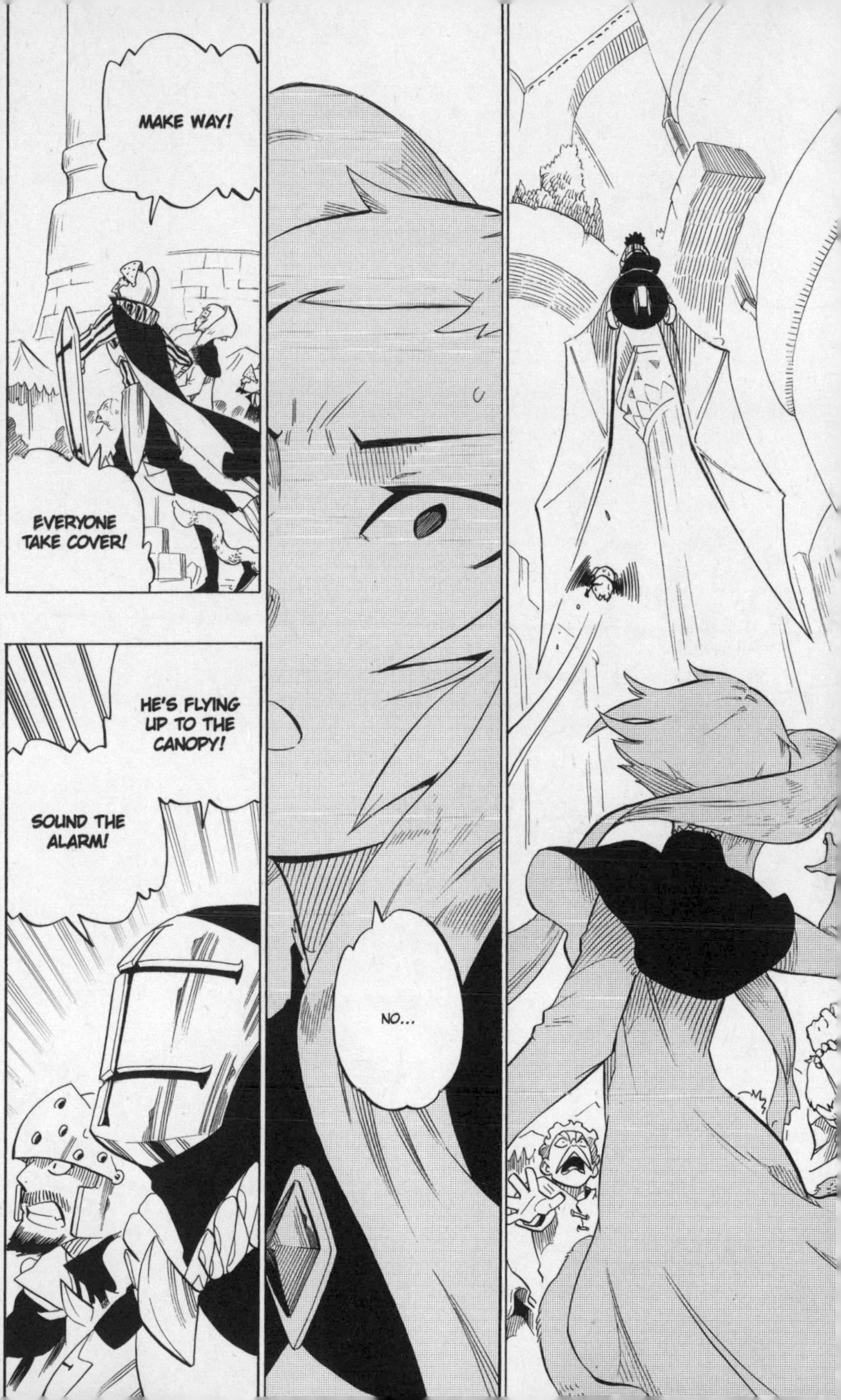
NO...
MAKE WAY!
EVERYONE TAKE COVER!
HE'S FLYING UP TO THE CANOPY!
SOUND THE ALARM!

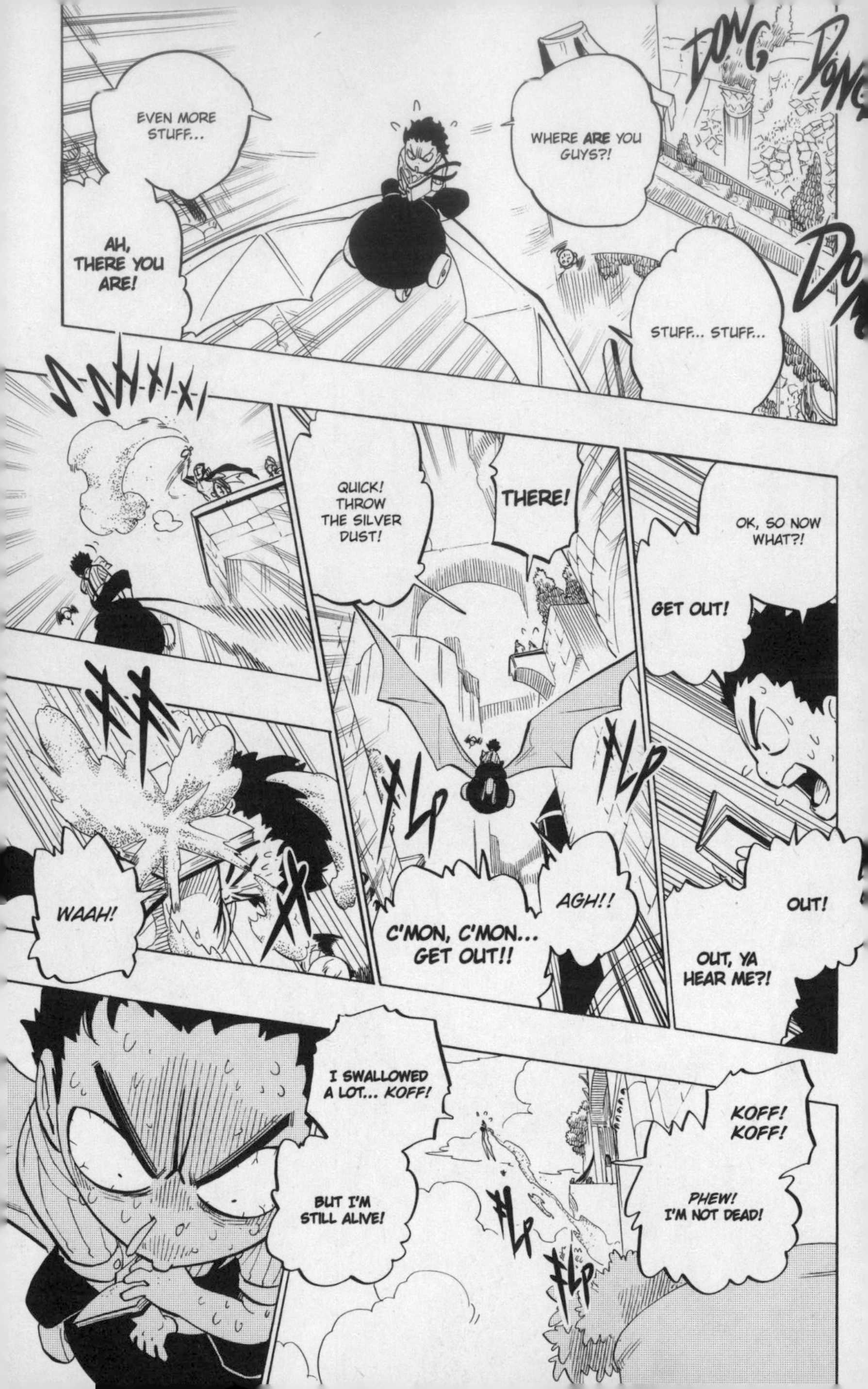
DONG DONG
WHERE **ARE** YOU GUYS?!
EVEN MORE STUFF...
STUFF... STUFF...
AH, THERE YOU ARE!
OK, SO NOW WHAT?!
GET OUT!
OUT!
OUT, YA HEAR ME?!
THERE!
QUICK! THROW THE SILVER DUST!
FLP
FLP
AGH!!
C'MON, C'MON... GET OUT!!
S-SH-X-X-X
WAAH!
KOFF! KOFF!
PHEW! I'M NOT DEAD!
FLP
FLP
I SWALLOWED A LOT... KOFF!
BUT I'M STILL ALIVE!

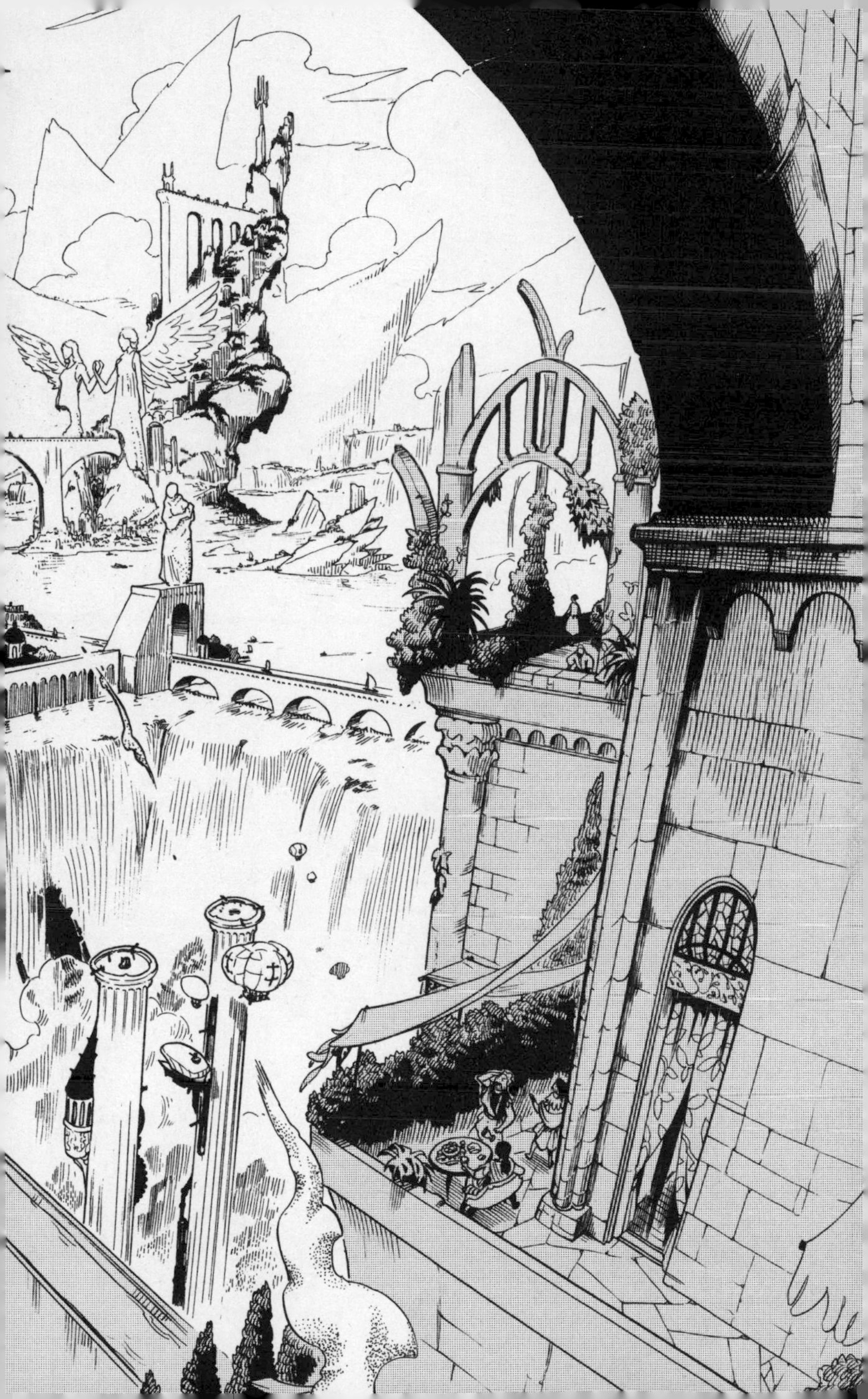

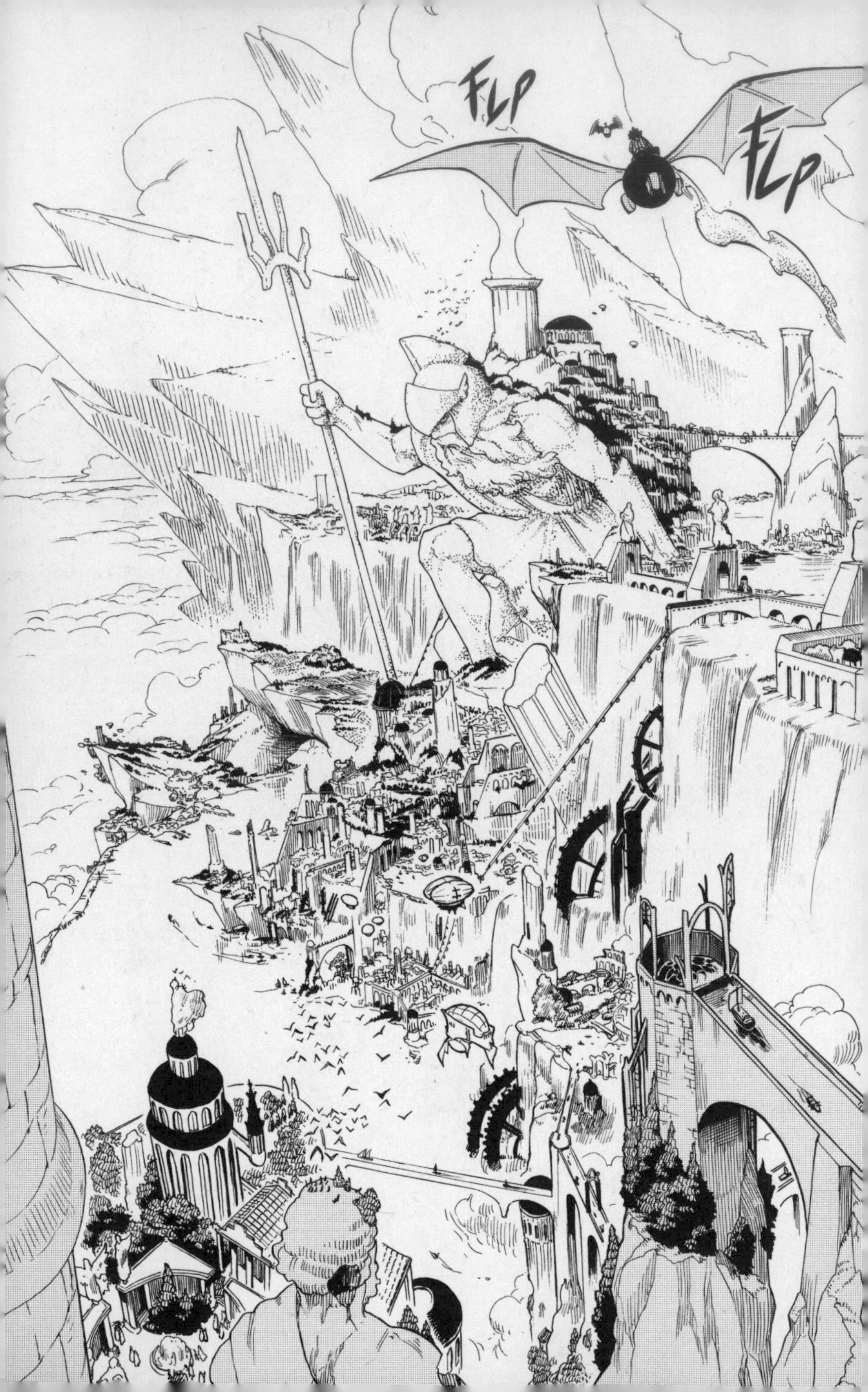
FLP
FLP

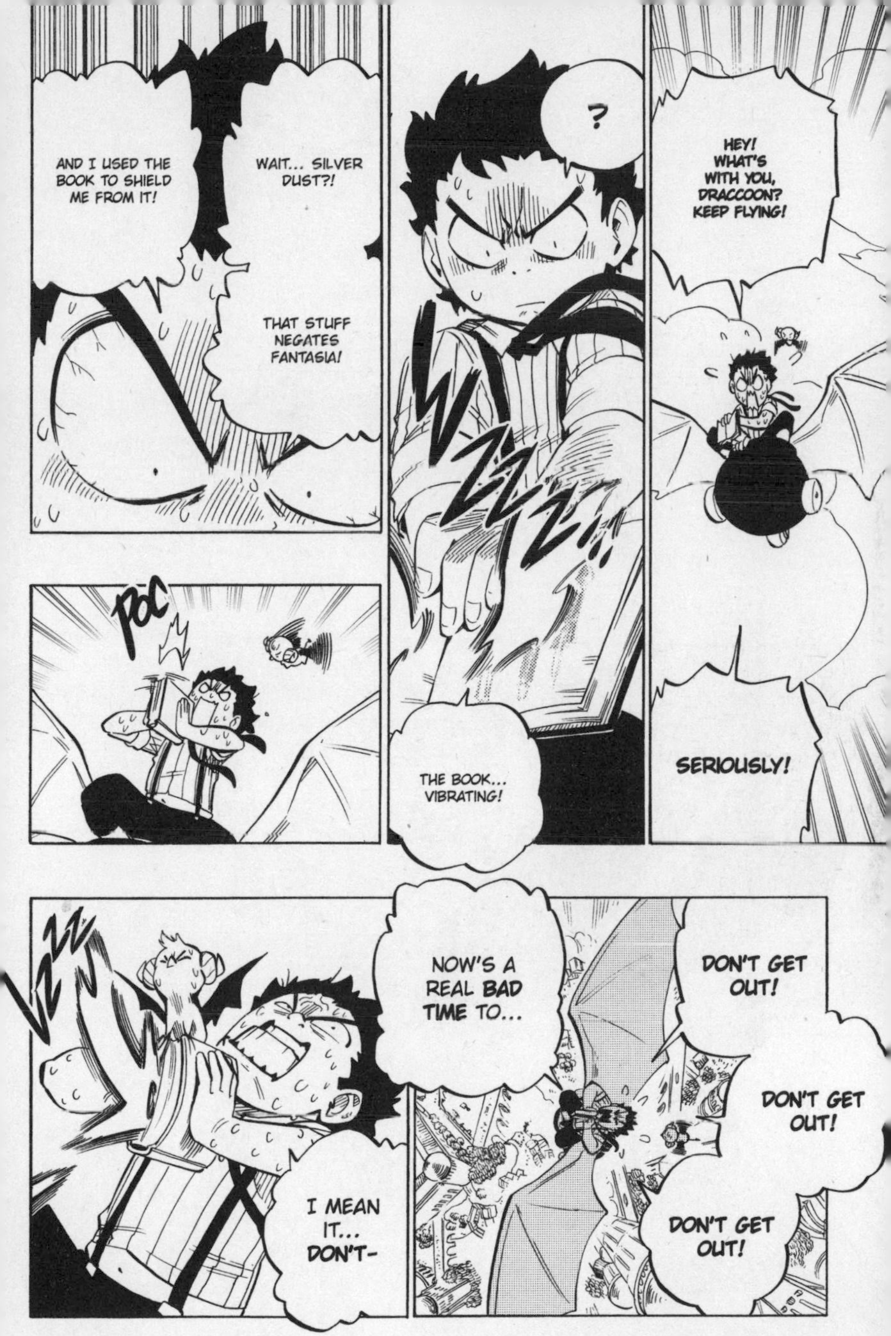
HEY! WHAT'S WITH YOU, DRACCOON? KEEP FLYING!
SERIOUSLY!
?
ZZZZ!!
THE BOOK... VIBRATING!
WAIT... SILVER DUST?!
AND I USED THE BOOK TO SHIELD ME FROM IT!
THAT STUFF NEGATES FANTASIA!
POC
DON'T GET OUT!
DON'T GET OUT!
DON'T GET OUT!
NOW'S A REAL BAD TIME TO...
ZZZZ
I MEAN IT... DON'T-

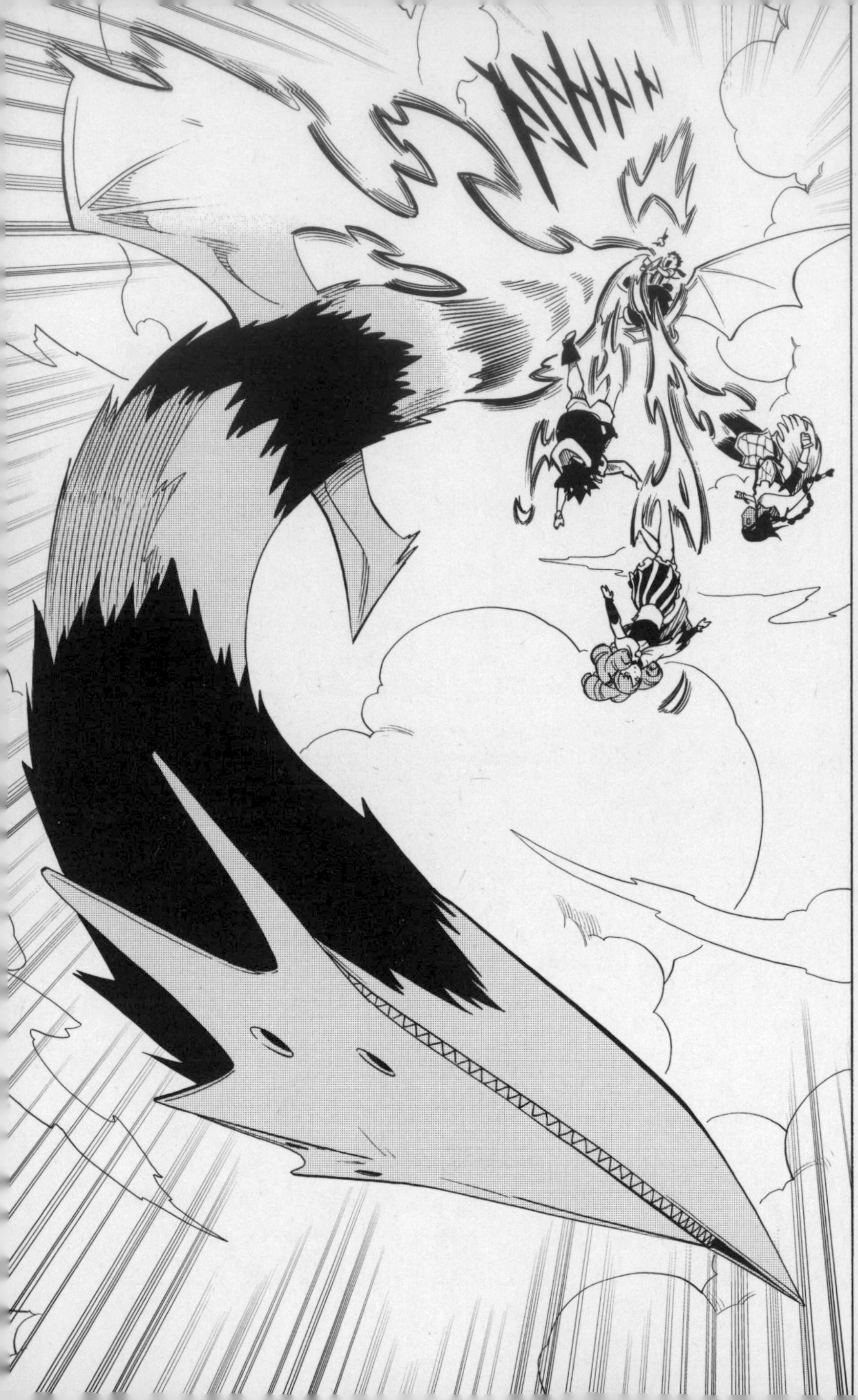

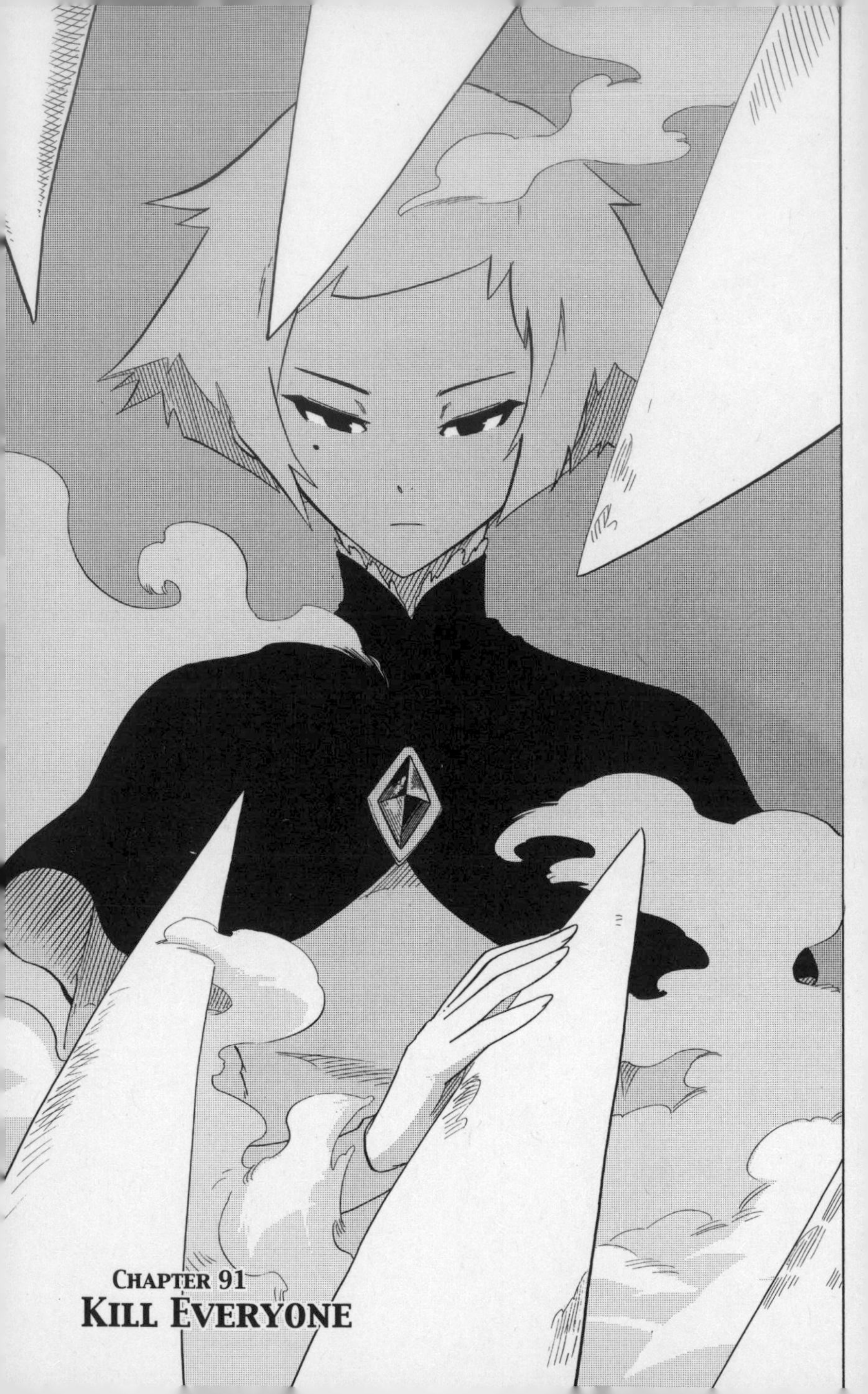
Chapter 91
Kill Everyone

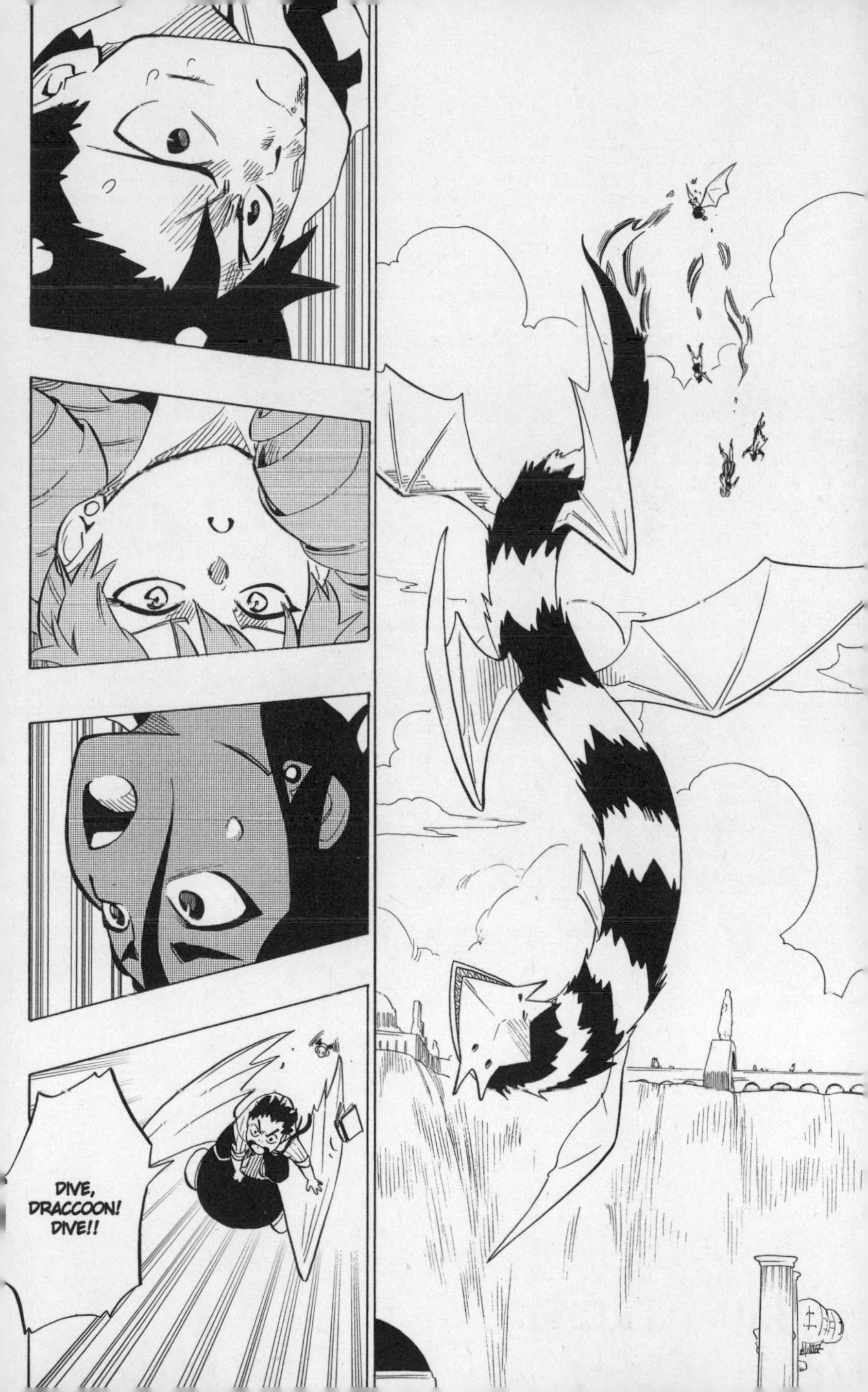
DIVE, DRACCOON! DIVE!!

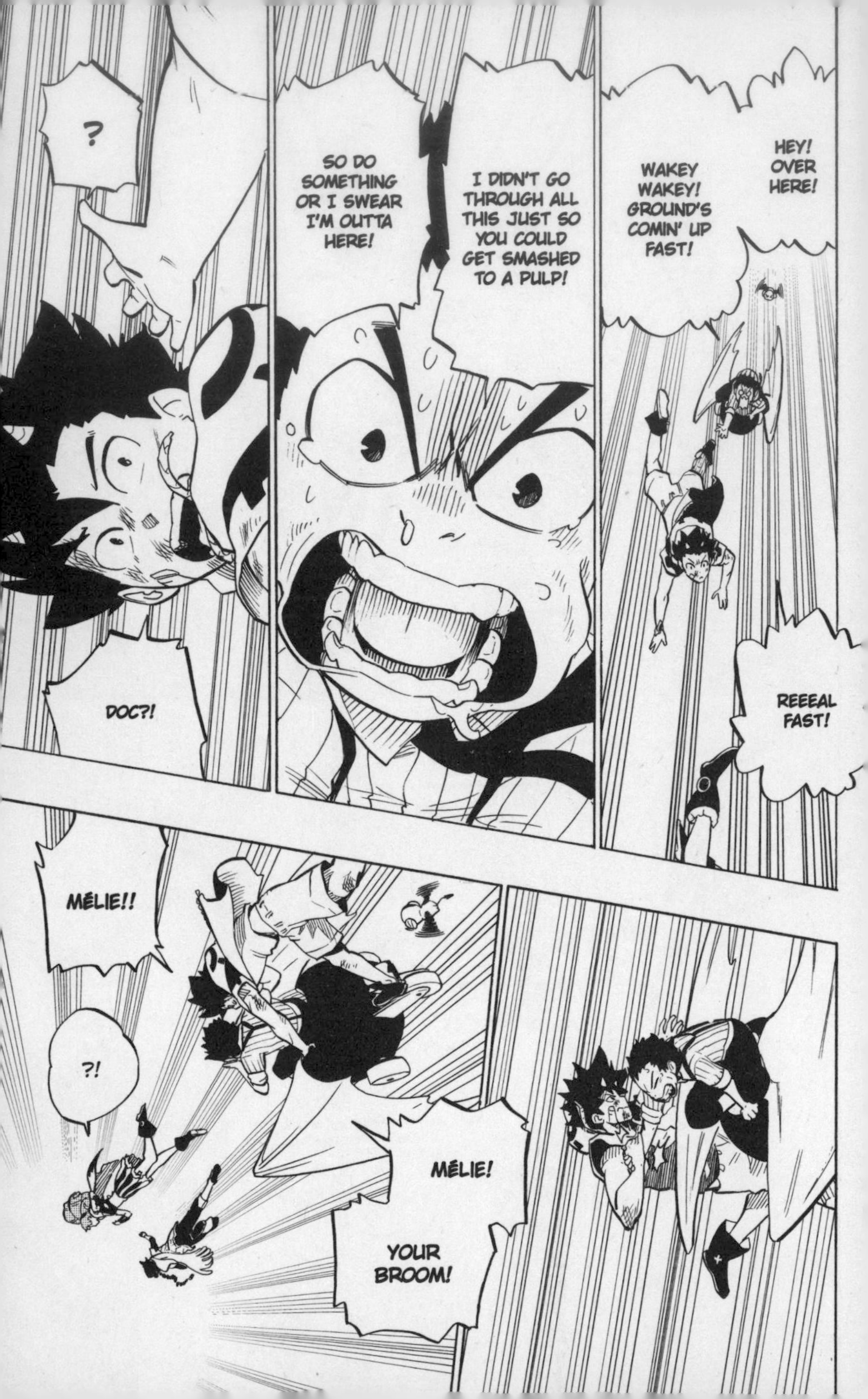
HEY! OVER HERE!
WAKEY WAKEY! GROUND'S COMIN' UP FAST!
REEEAL FAST!
I DIDN'T GO THROUGH ALL THIS JUST SO YOU COULD GET SMASHED TO A PULP!
SO DO SOMETHING OR I SWEAR I'M OUTTA HERE!
?
DOC?!
MÉLIE!!
?!
MÉLIE!
YOUR BROOM!

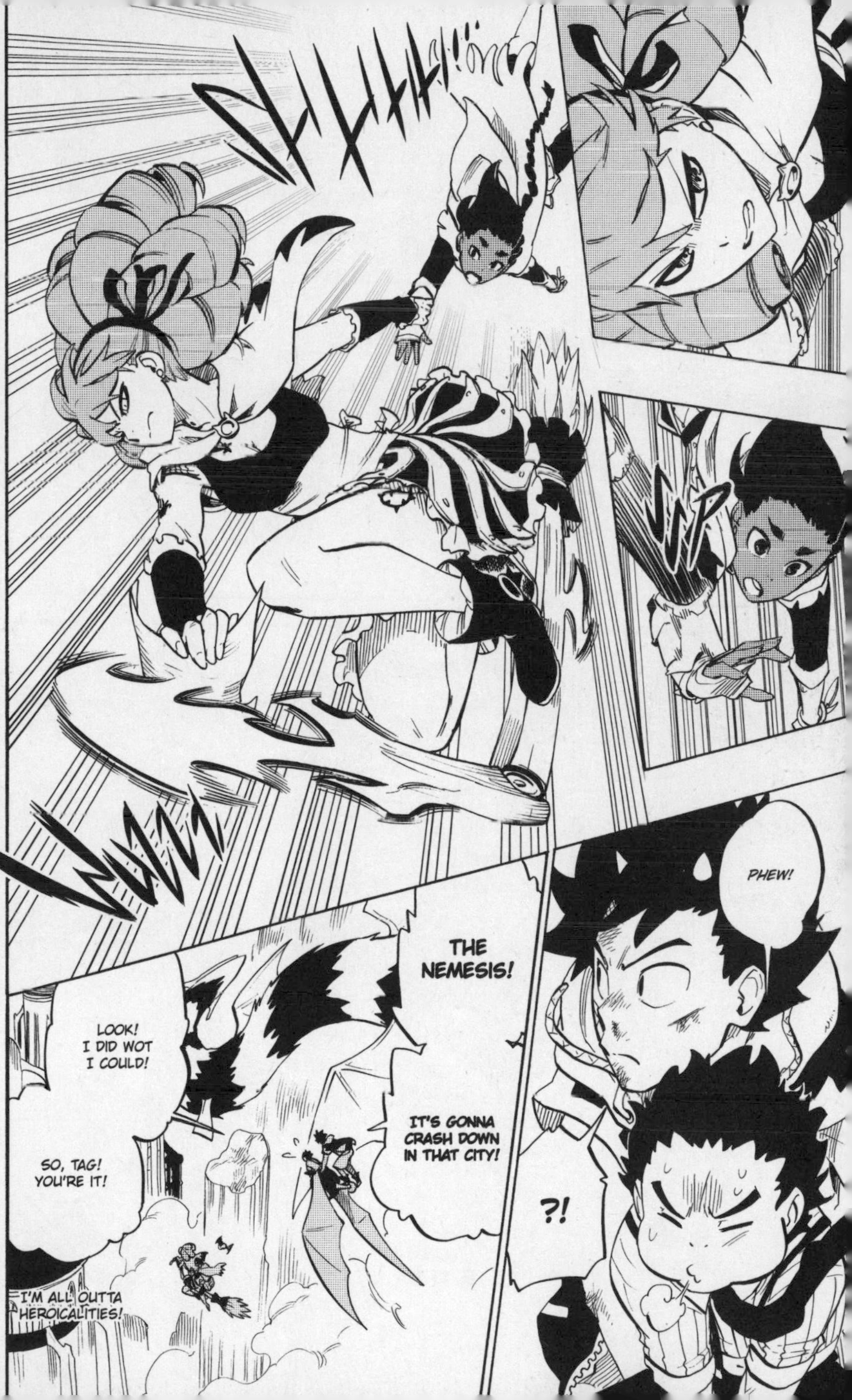
PHEW!
?!
THE NEMESIS!
IT'S GONNA CRASH DOWN IN THAT CITY!
LOOK! I DID WOT I COULD!
SO, TAG! YOU'RE IT!
I'M ALL OUTTA HEROICALITIES!

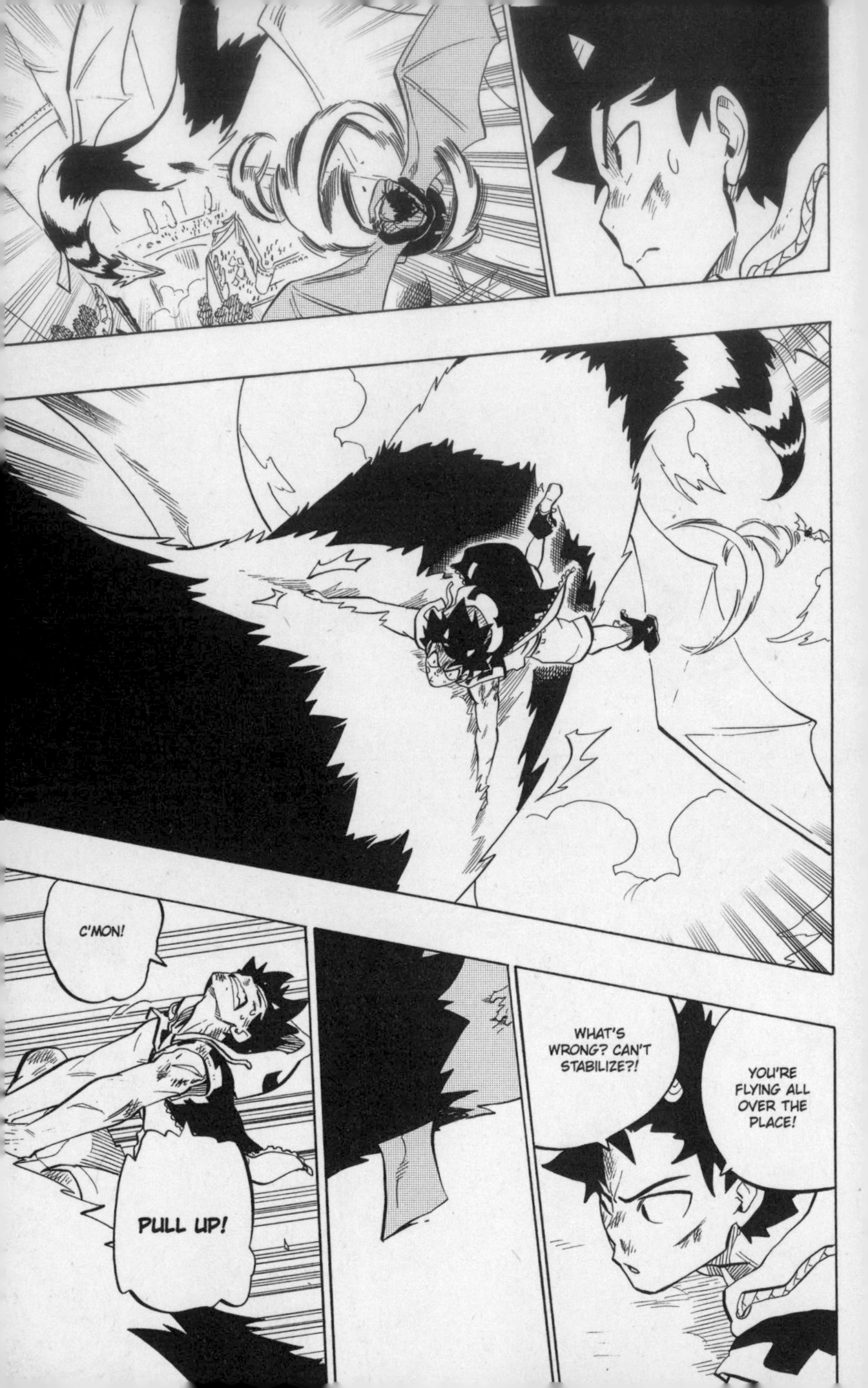
WHAT'S WRONG? CAN'T STABILIZE?!
YOU'RE FLYING ALL OVER THE PLACE!
C'MON!
PULL UP!

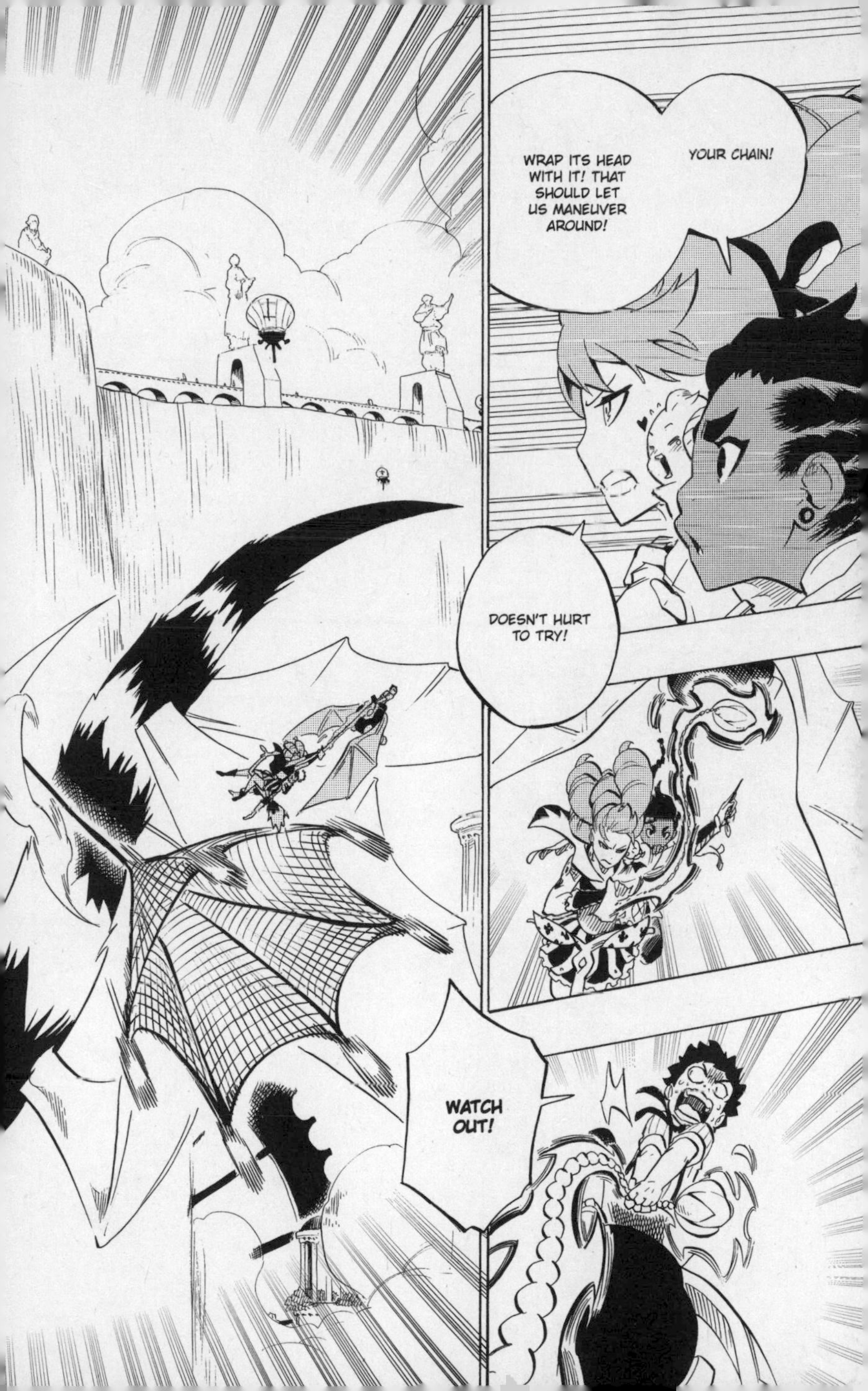
YOUR CHAIN!
WRAP ITS HEAD WITH IT! THAT SHOULD LET US MANEUVER AROUND!
DOESN'T HURT TO TRY!
WATCH OUT!

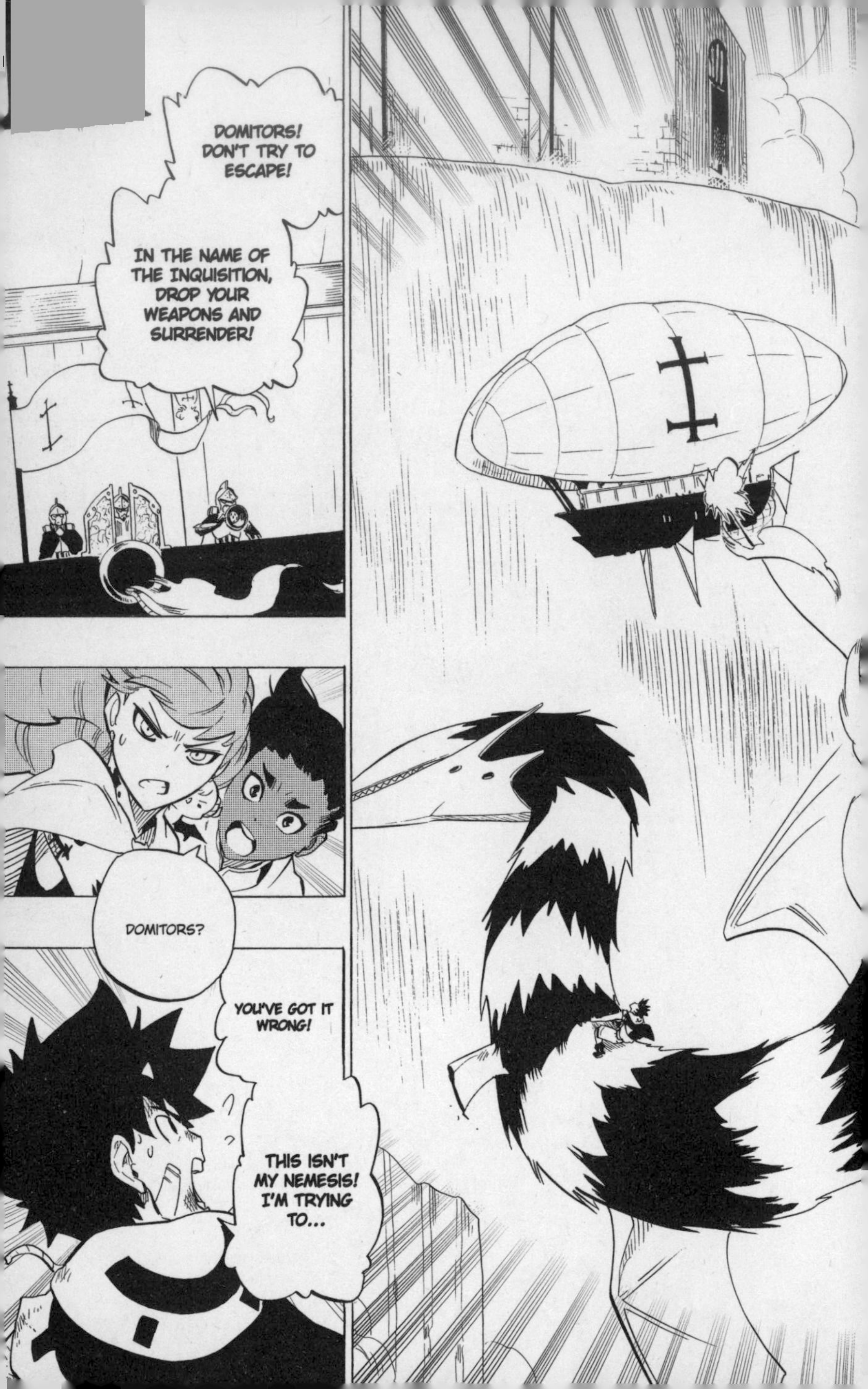
DOMITORS! DON'T TRY TO ESCAPE!
IN THE NAME OF THE INQUISITION, DROP YOUR WEAPONS AND SURRENDER!
DOMITORS?
YOU'VE GOT IT WRONG!
THIS ISN'T MY NEMESIS! I'M TRYING TO...

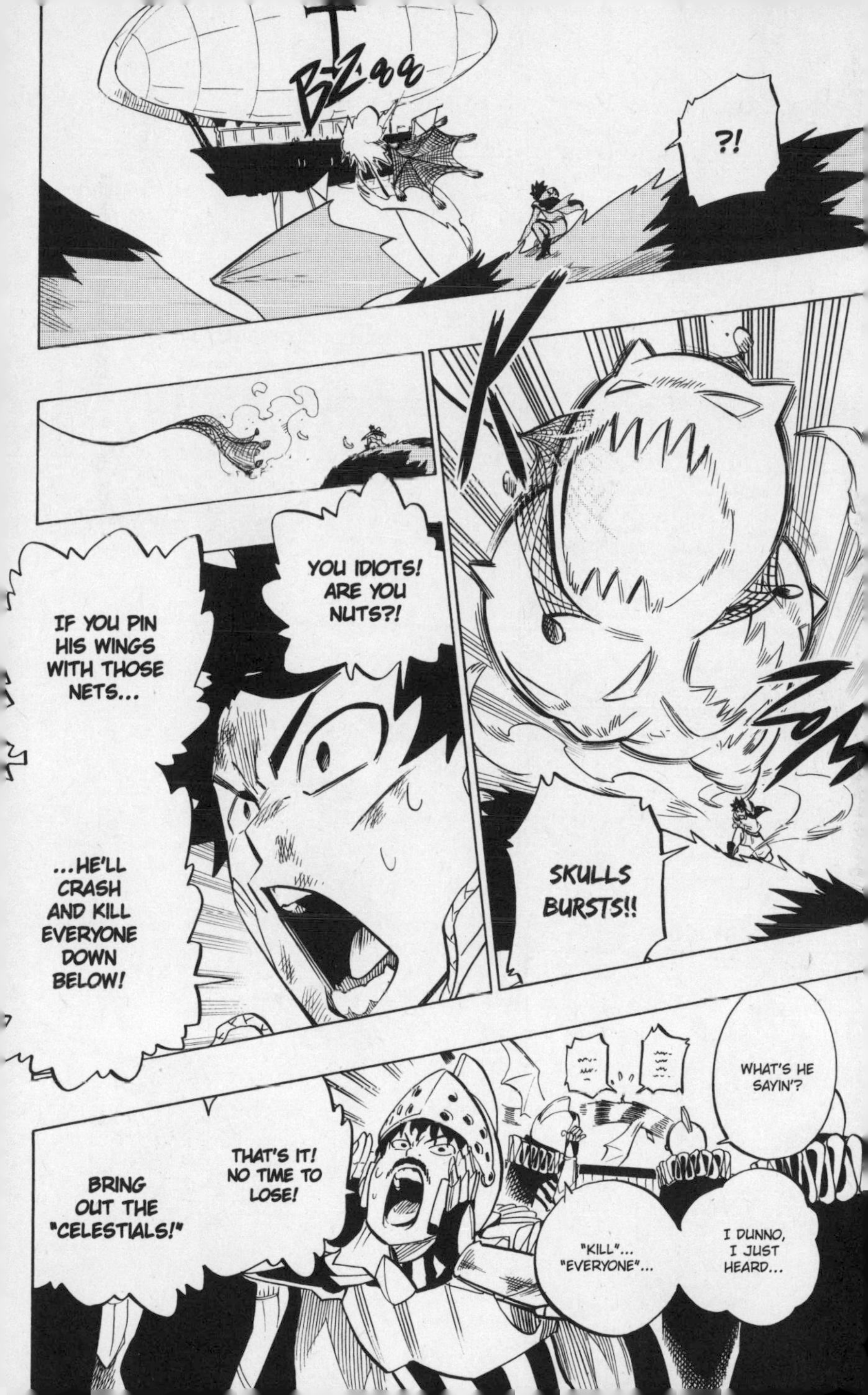
?!
SKULLS BURSTS!!
YOU IDIOTS! ARE YOU NUTS?!
IF YOU PIN HIS WINGS WITH THOSE NETS...
...HE'LL CRASH AND KILL EVERYONE DOWN BELOW!
WHAT'S HE SAYIN'?
I DUNNO, I JUST HEARD...
"KILL"... "EVERYONE"...
THAT'S IT! NO TIME TO LOSE!
BRING OUT THE "CELESTIALS!"

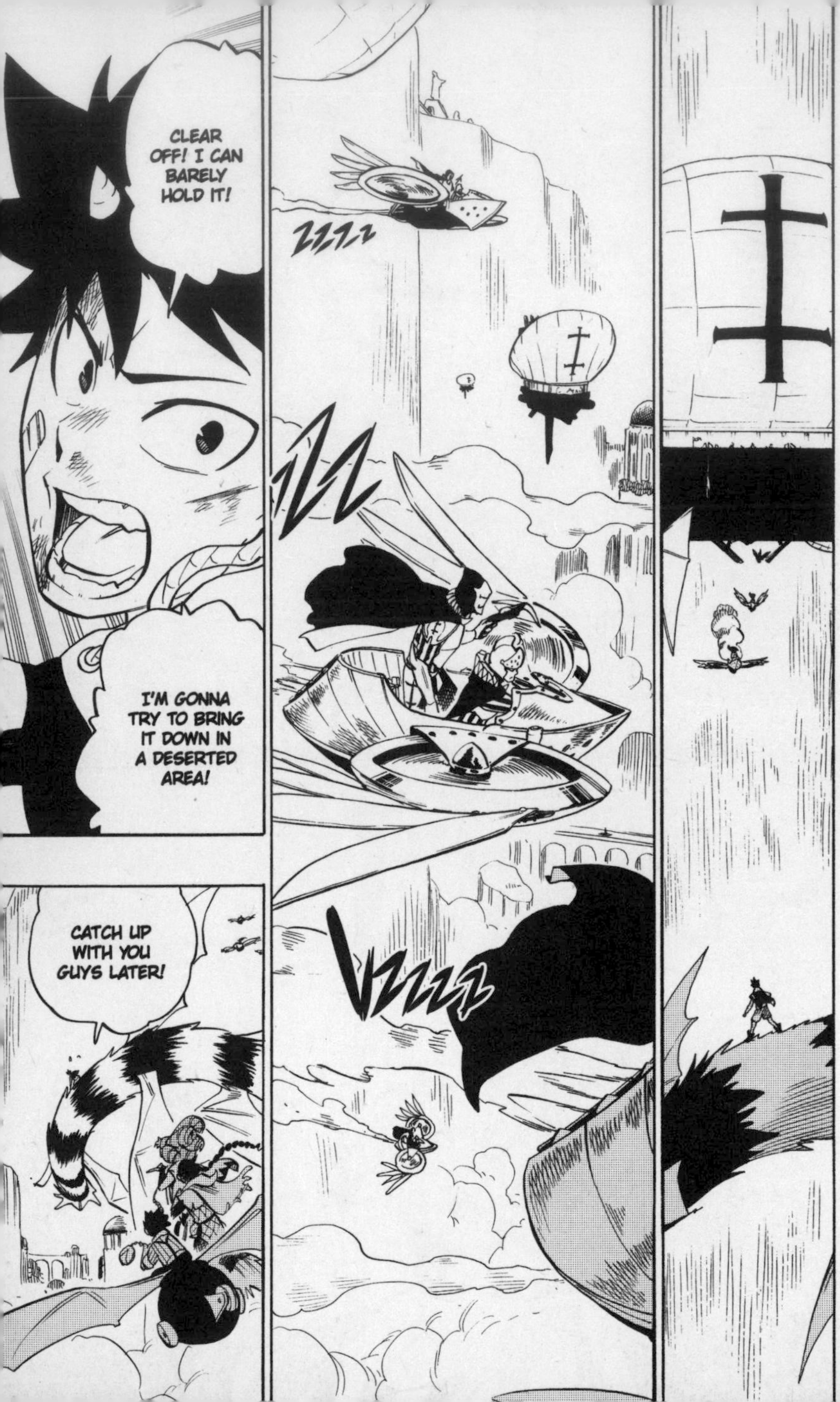
ZZZZ
VZZZZ
CLEAR OFF! I CAN BARELY HOLD IT!
I'M GONNA TRY TO BRING IT DOWN IN A DESERTED AREA!
CATCH UP WITH YOU GUYS LATER!

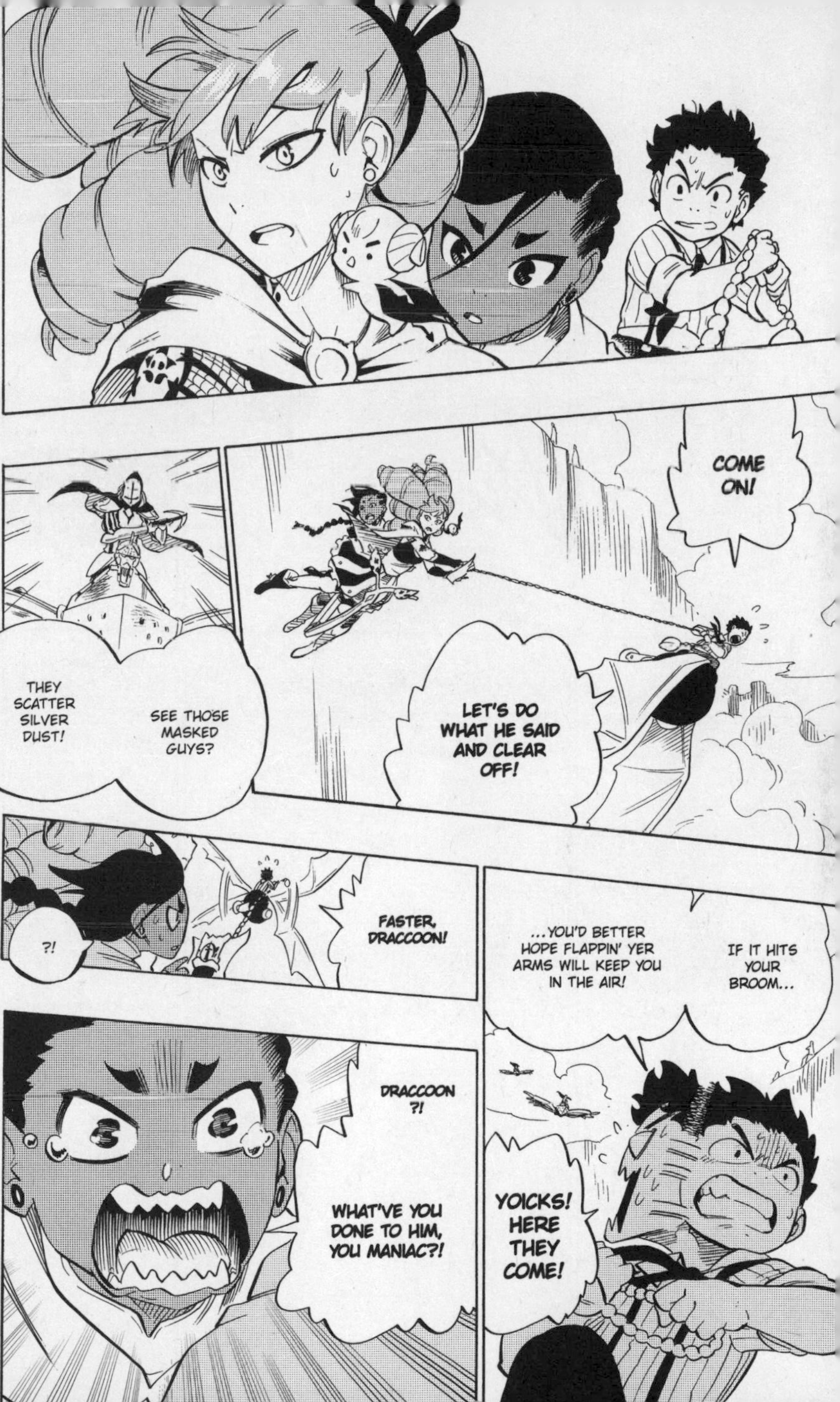
COME ON!
LET'S DO WHAT HE SAID AND CLEAR OFF!
SEE THOSE MASKED GUYS?
THEY SCATTER SILVER DUST!
IF IT HITS YOUR BROOM...
...YOU'D BETTER HOPE FLAPPIN' YER ARMS WILL KEEP YOU IN THE AIR!
YOICKS! HERE THEY COME!
FASTER, DRACCOON!
?!
DRACCOON?!
WHAT'VE YOU DONE TO HIM, YOU MANIAC?!

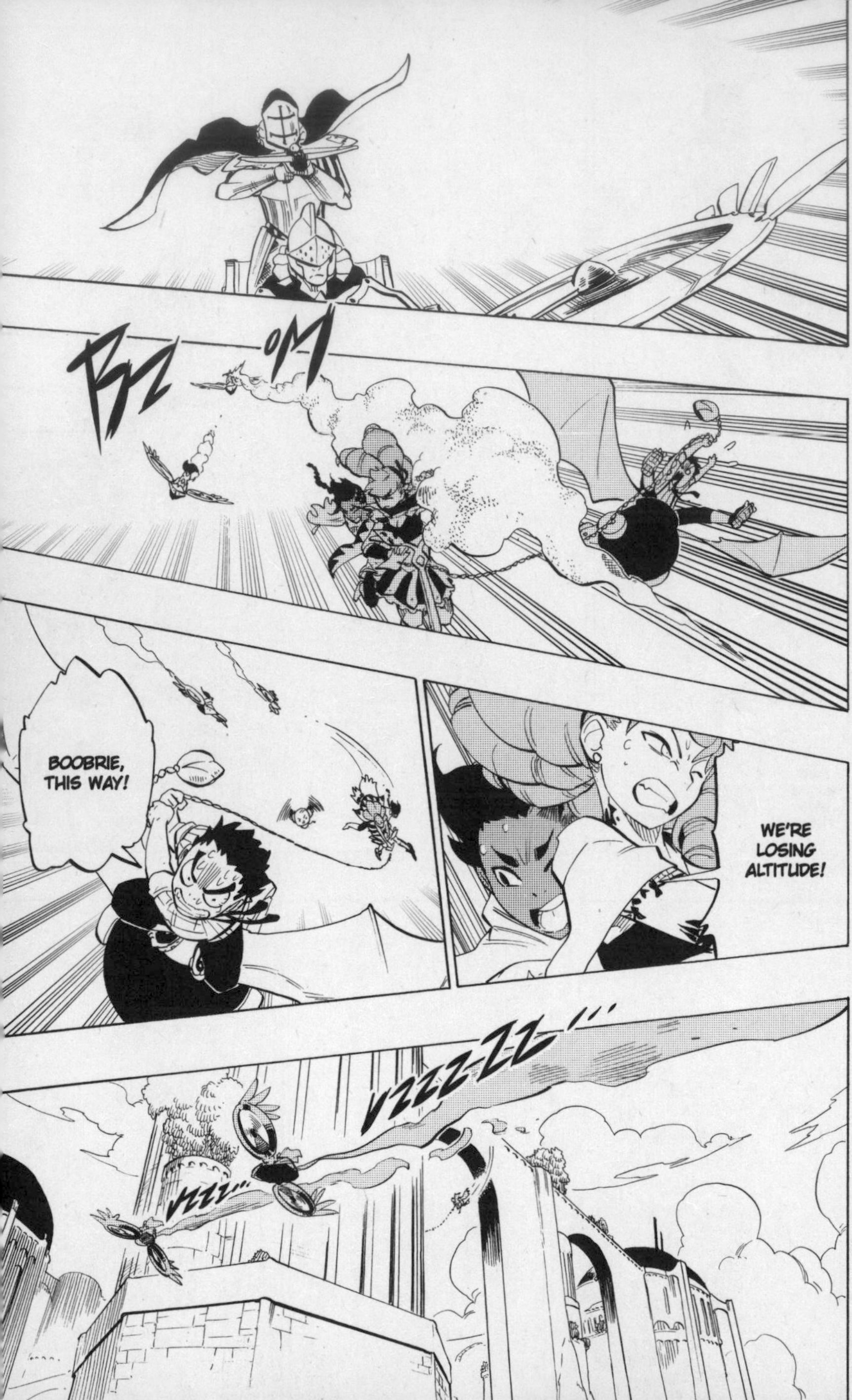
BZOOM
WE'RE LOSING ALTITUDE!
BOOBRIE, THIS WAY!
VZZZ-Z-Z-Z...
VZZZ...

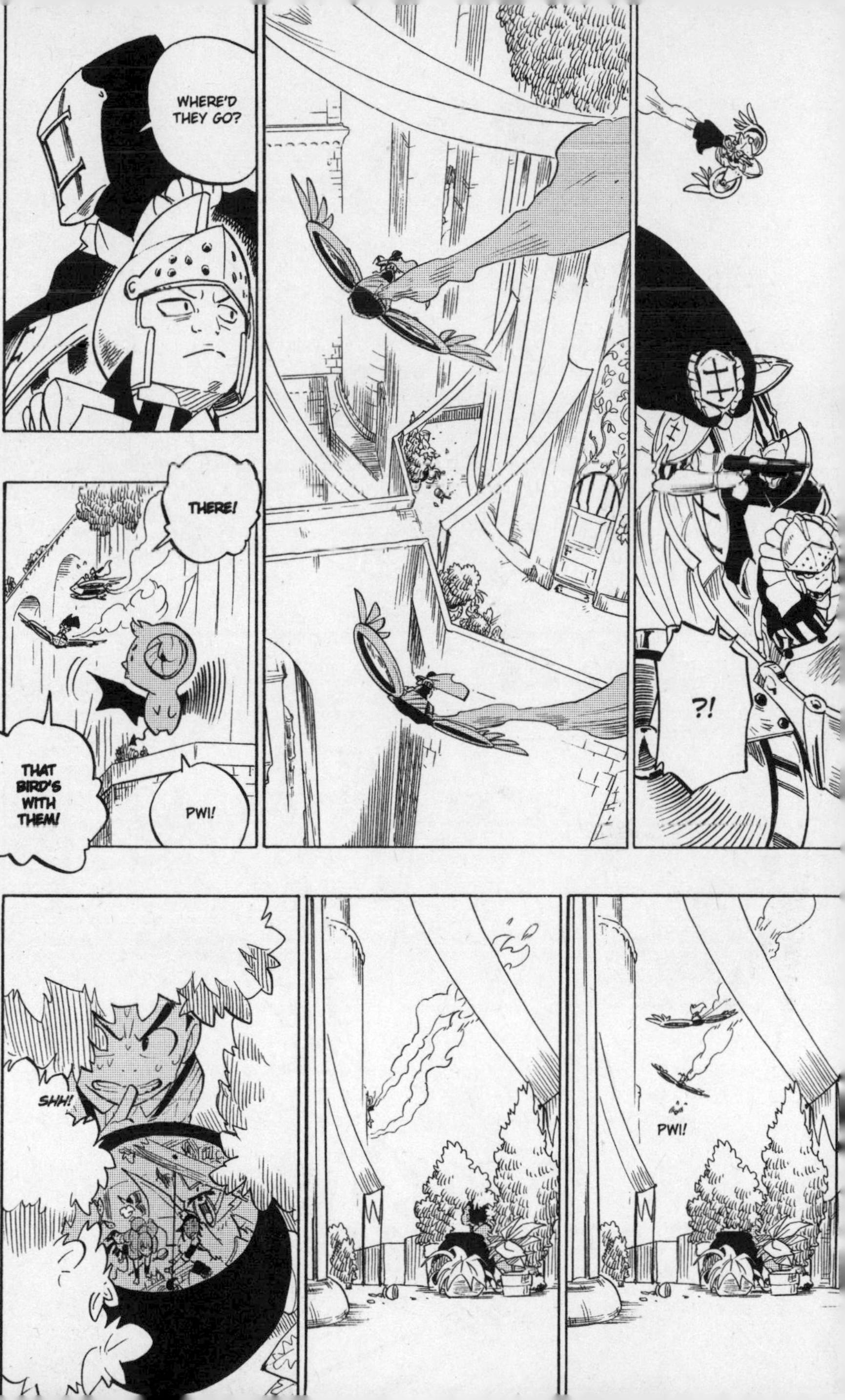
?!
WHERE'D THEY GO?
THERE!
THAT BIRD'S WITH THEM!
PWI!
PWI!
SHH!

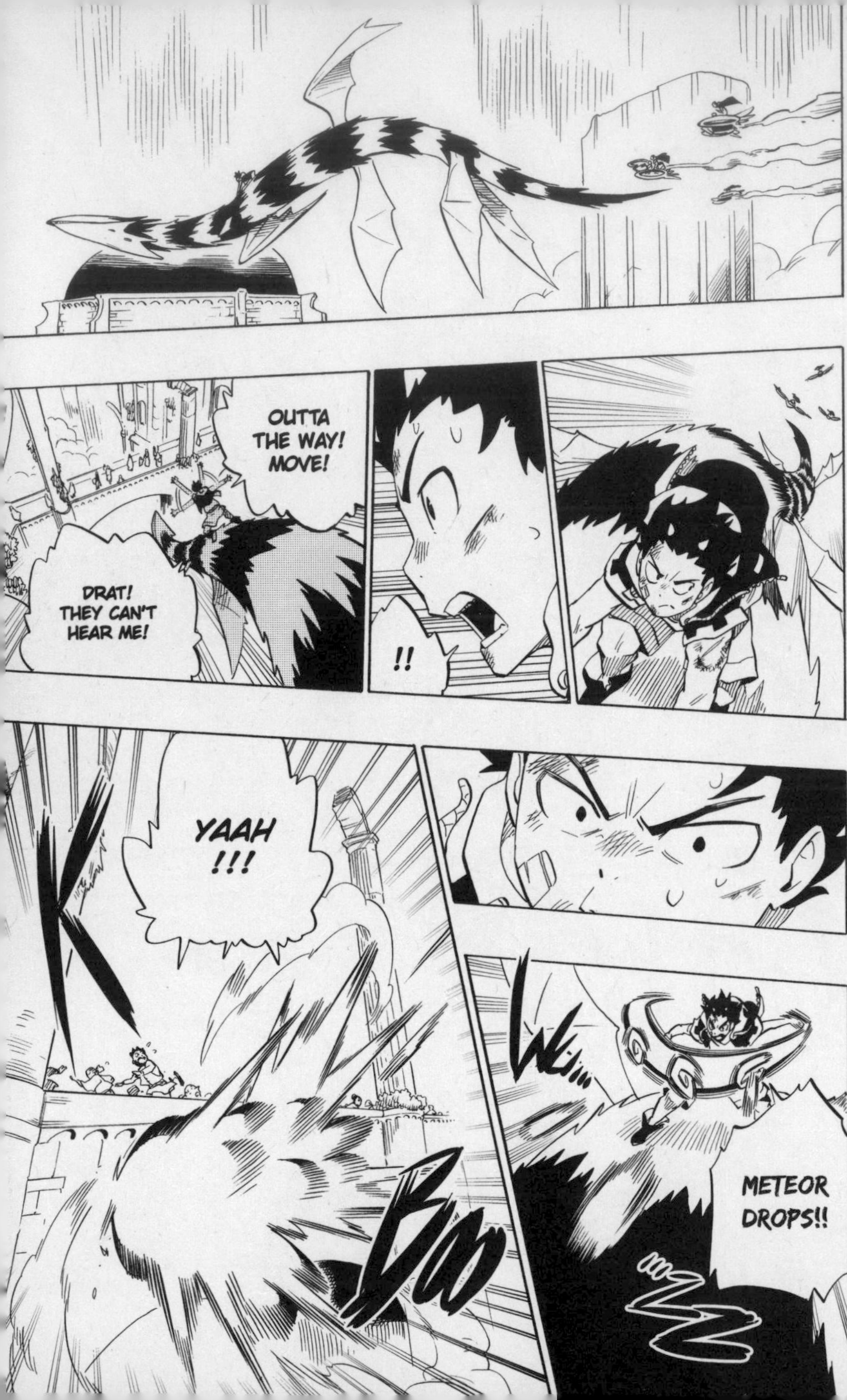
!!
OUTTA THE WAY! MOVE!
DRAT! THEY CAN'T HEAR ME!
METEOR DROPS!!
YAAH !!!

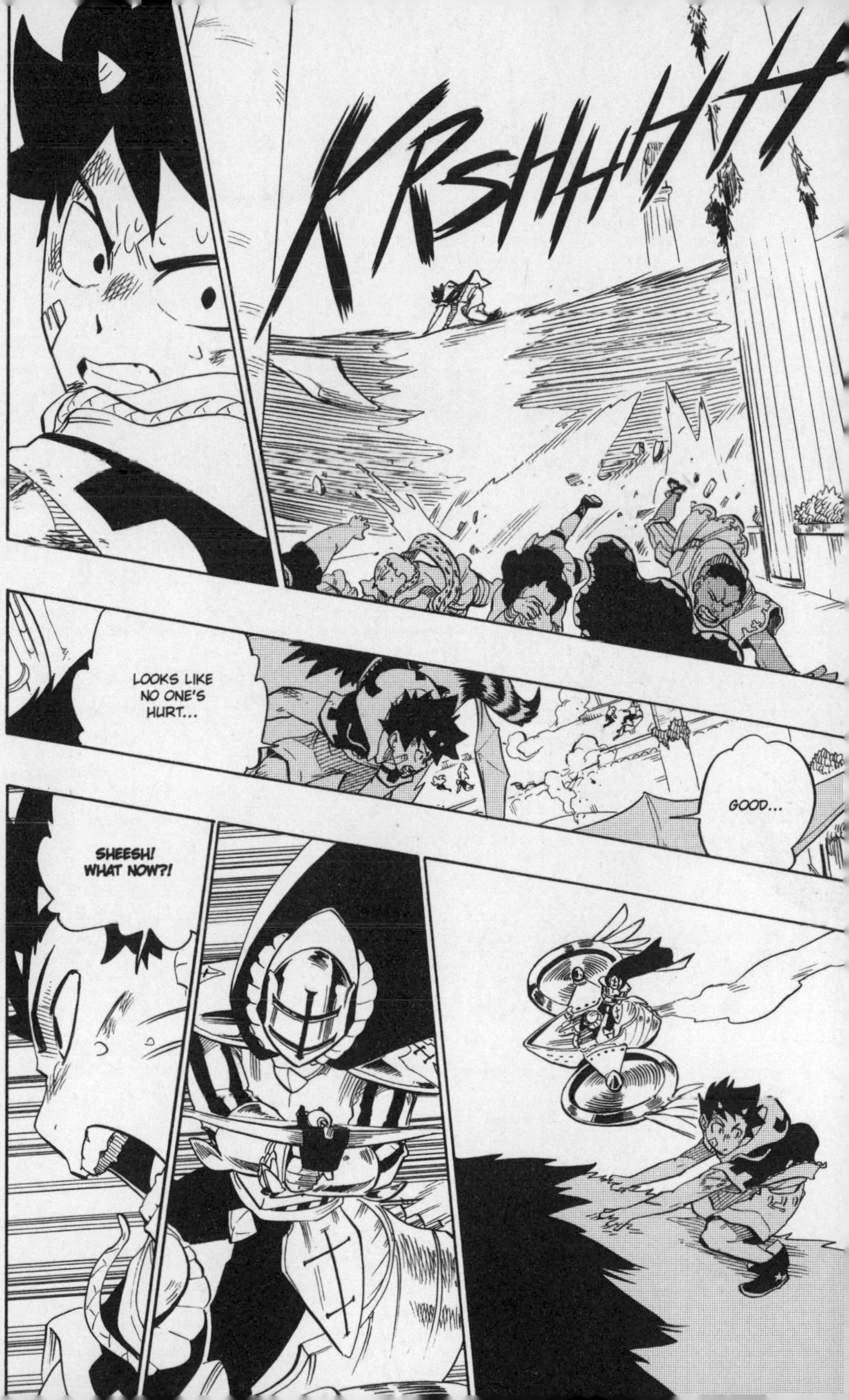
KRSHHHH!!
LOOKS LIKE NO ONE'S HURT...
GOOD...
SHEESH! WHAT NOW?!

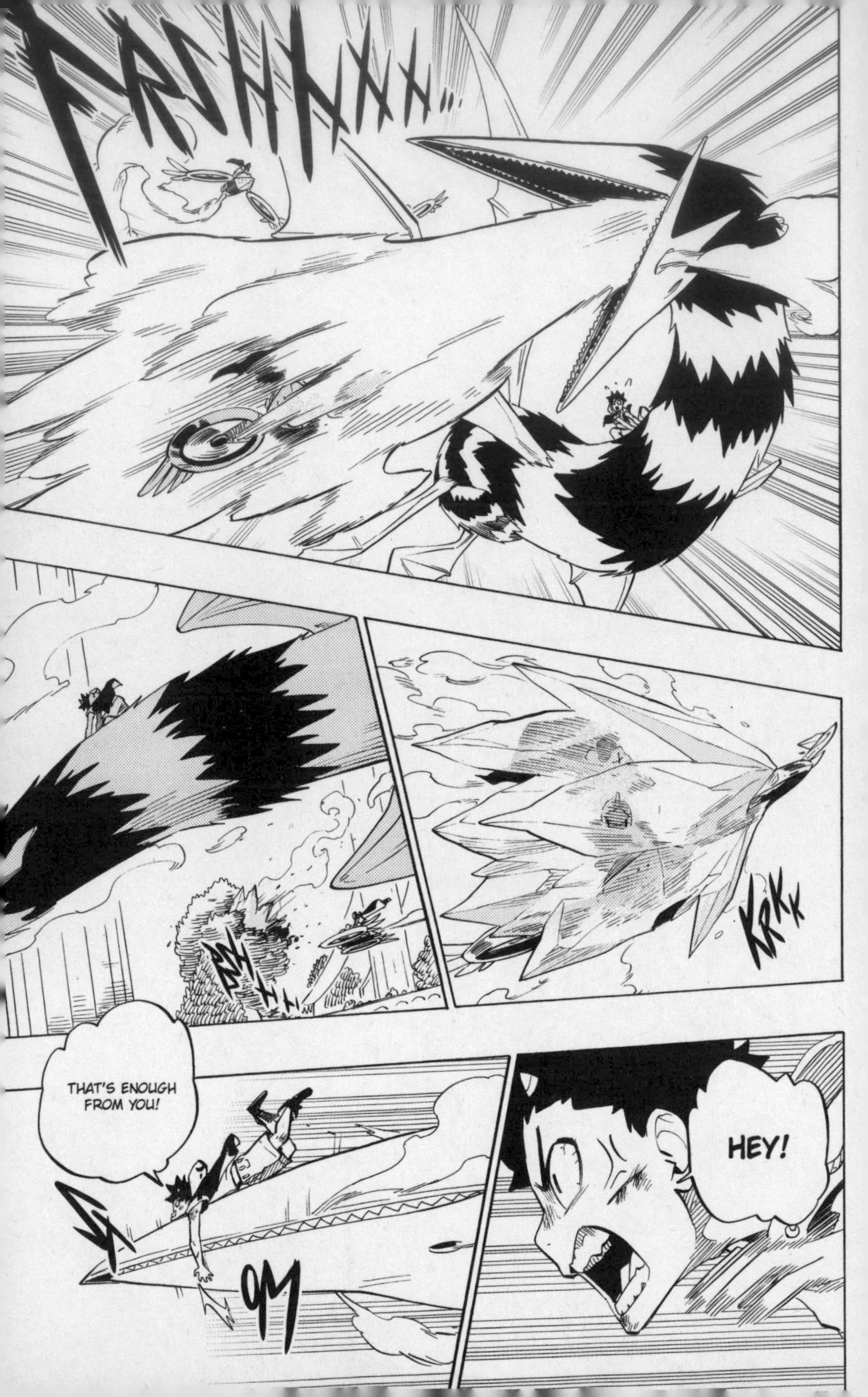
HEY!
THAT'S ENOUGH FROM YOU!

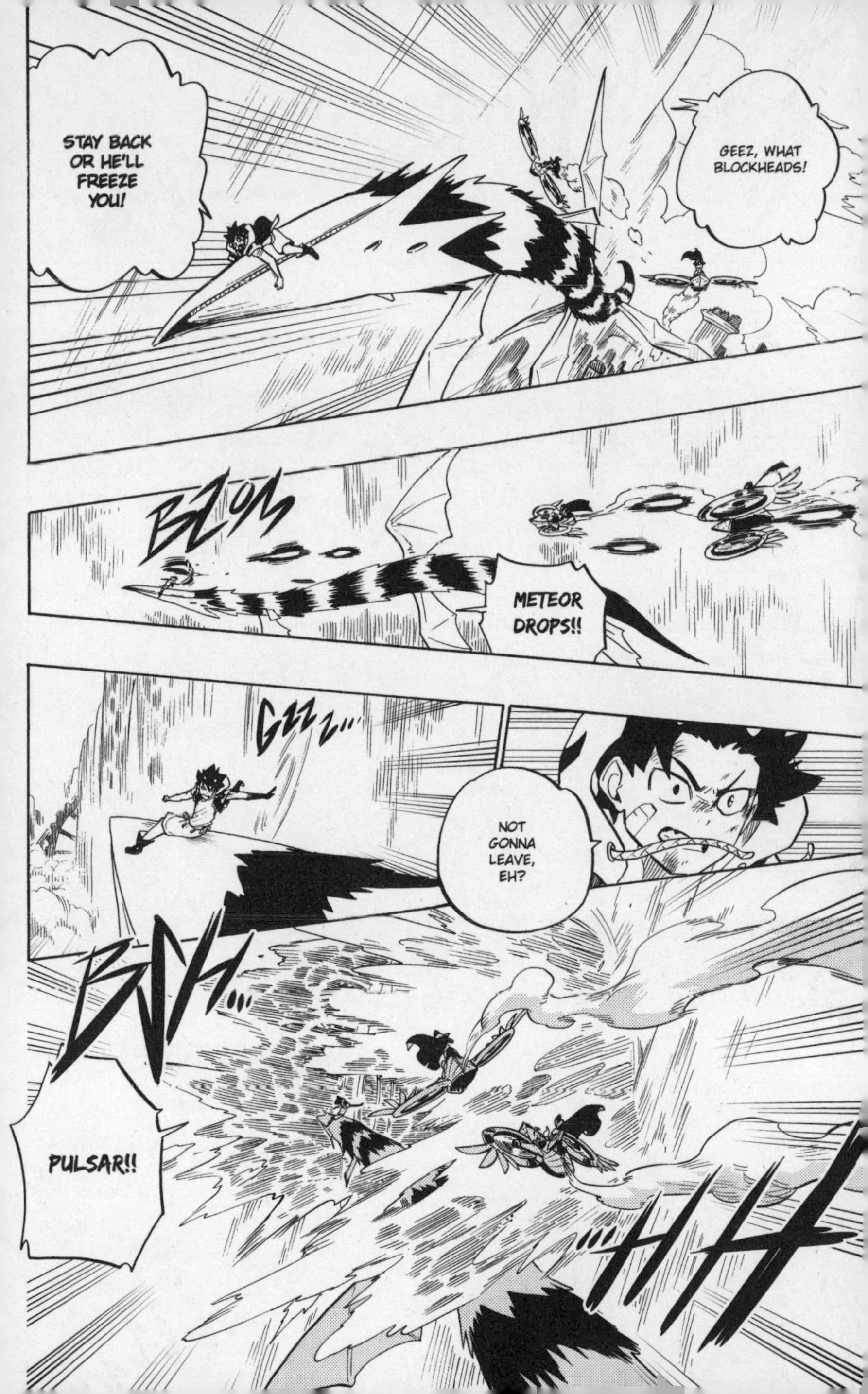
GEEZ, WHAT BLOCKHEADS!
STAY BACK OR HE'LL FREEZE YOU!
METEOR DROPS!!
BZOM
NOT GONNA LEAVE, EH?
GZZZ...
PULSAR!!

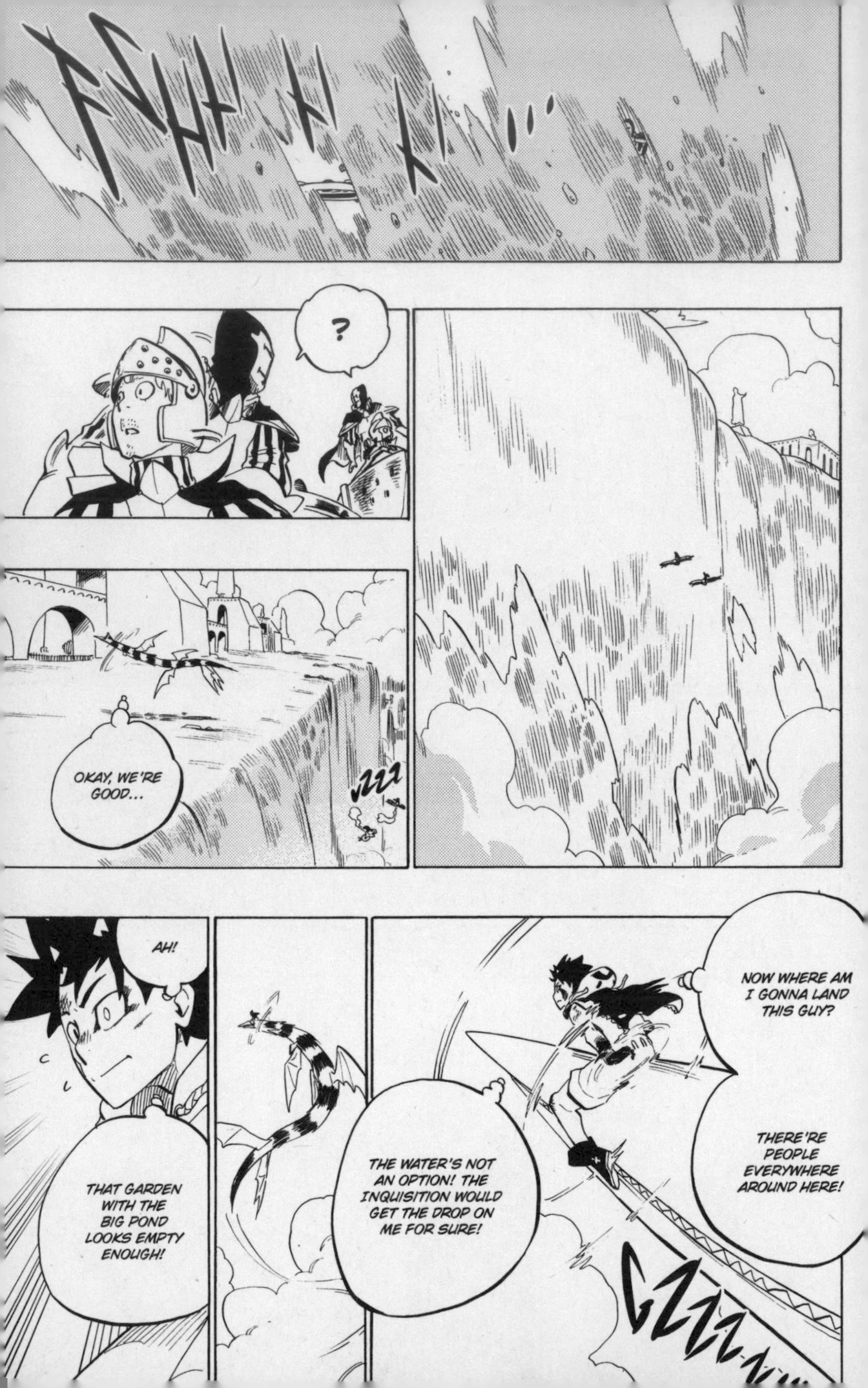
?
OKAY, WE'RE GOOD...
NOW WHERE AM I GONNA LAND THIS GUY?
THERE'RE PEOPLE EVERYWHERE AROUND HERE!
THE WATER'S NOT AN OPTION! THE INQUISITION WOULD GET THE DROP ON ME FOR SURE!
AH!
THAT GARDEN WITH THE BIG POND LOOKS EMPTY ENOUGH!

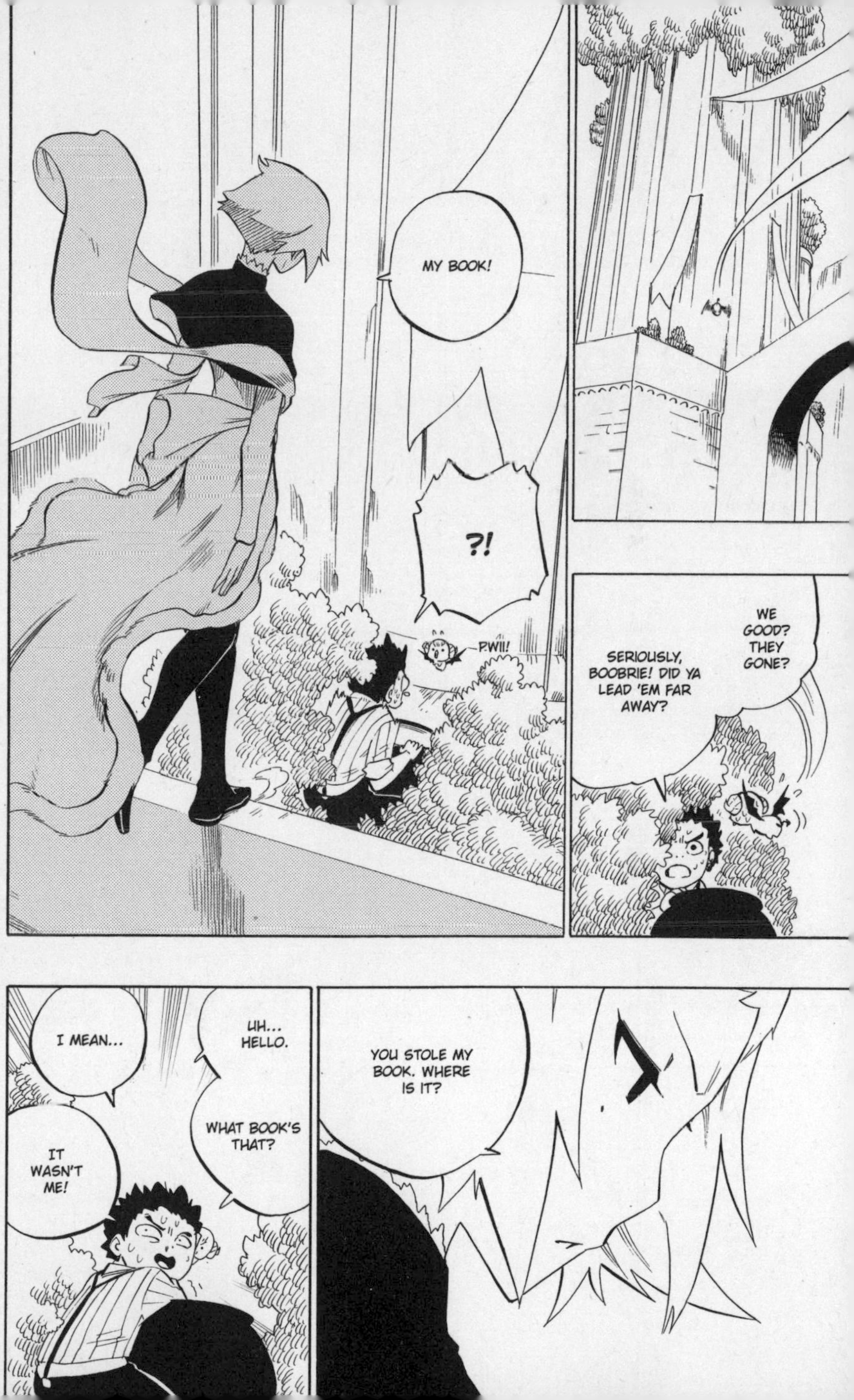
WE GOOD? THEY GONE?
SERIOUSLY, BOOBRIE! DID YA LEAD 'EM FAR AWAY?
MY BOOK!
?!
PWII!
YOU STOLE MY BOOK. WHERE IS IT?
UH... HELLO.
I MEAN...
WHAT BOOK'S THAT?
IT WASN'T ME!

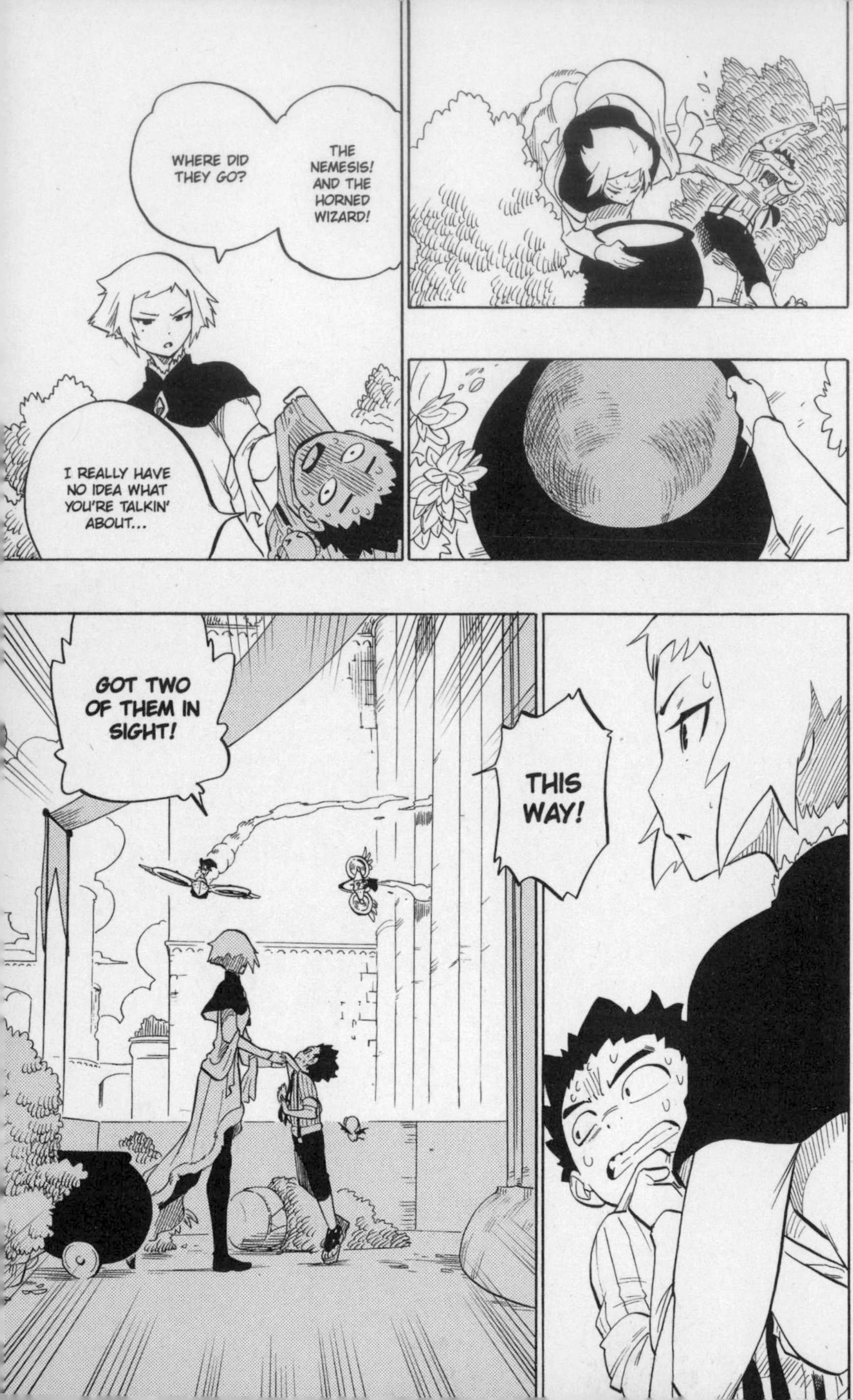
WHERE DID THEY GO?
THE NEMESIS! AND THE HORNED WIZARD!
I REALLY HAVE NO IDEA WHAT YOU'RE TALKIN' ABOUT...
THIS WAY!
GOT TWO OF THEM IN SIGHT!

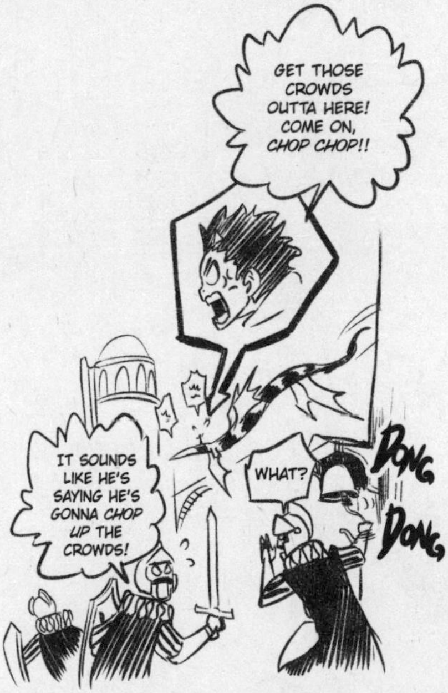
GET THOSE CROWDS OUTTA HERE! COME ON, *CHOP CHOP*!!
DONG
DONG
WHAT?
IT SOUNDS LIKE HE'S SAYING HE'S GONNA *CHOP UP* THE CROWDS!

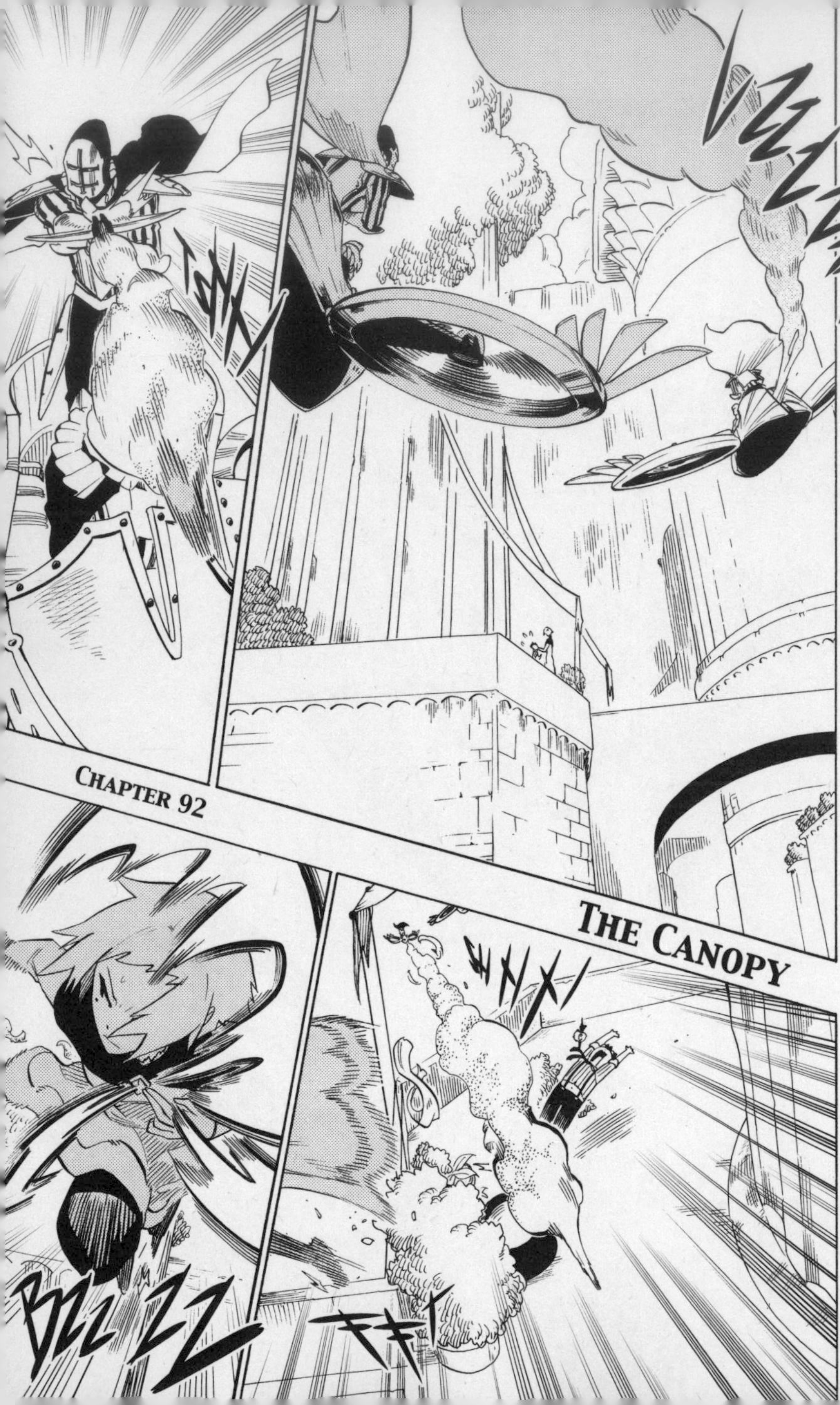
CHAPTER 92
THE CANOPY

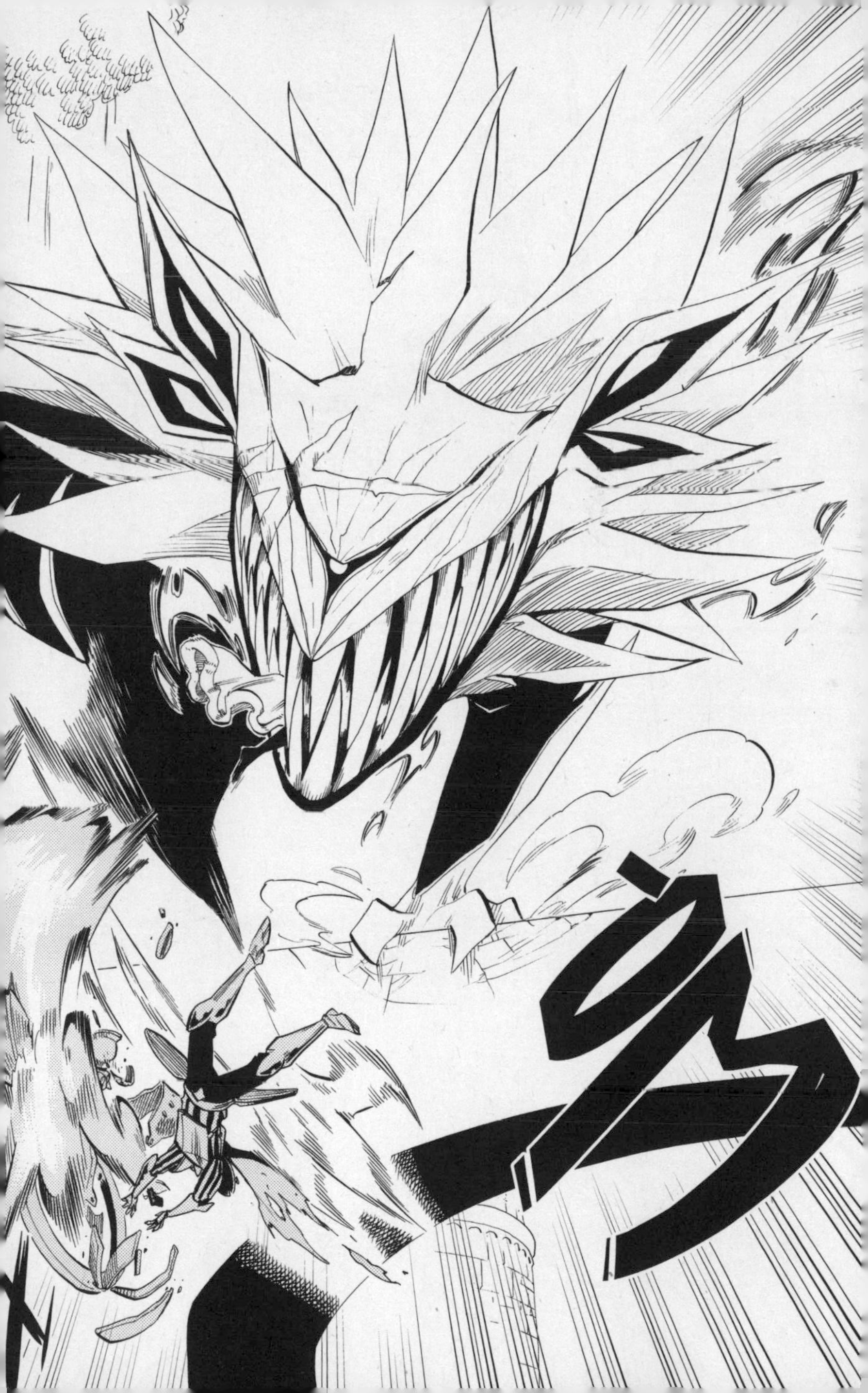

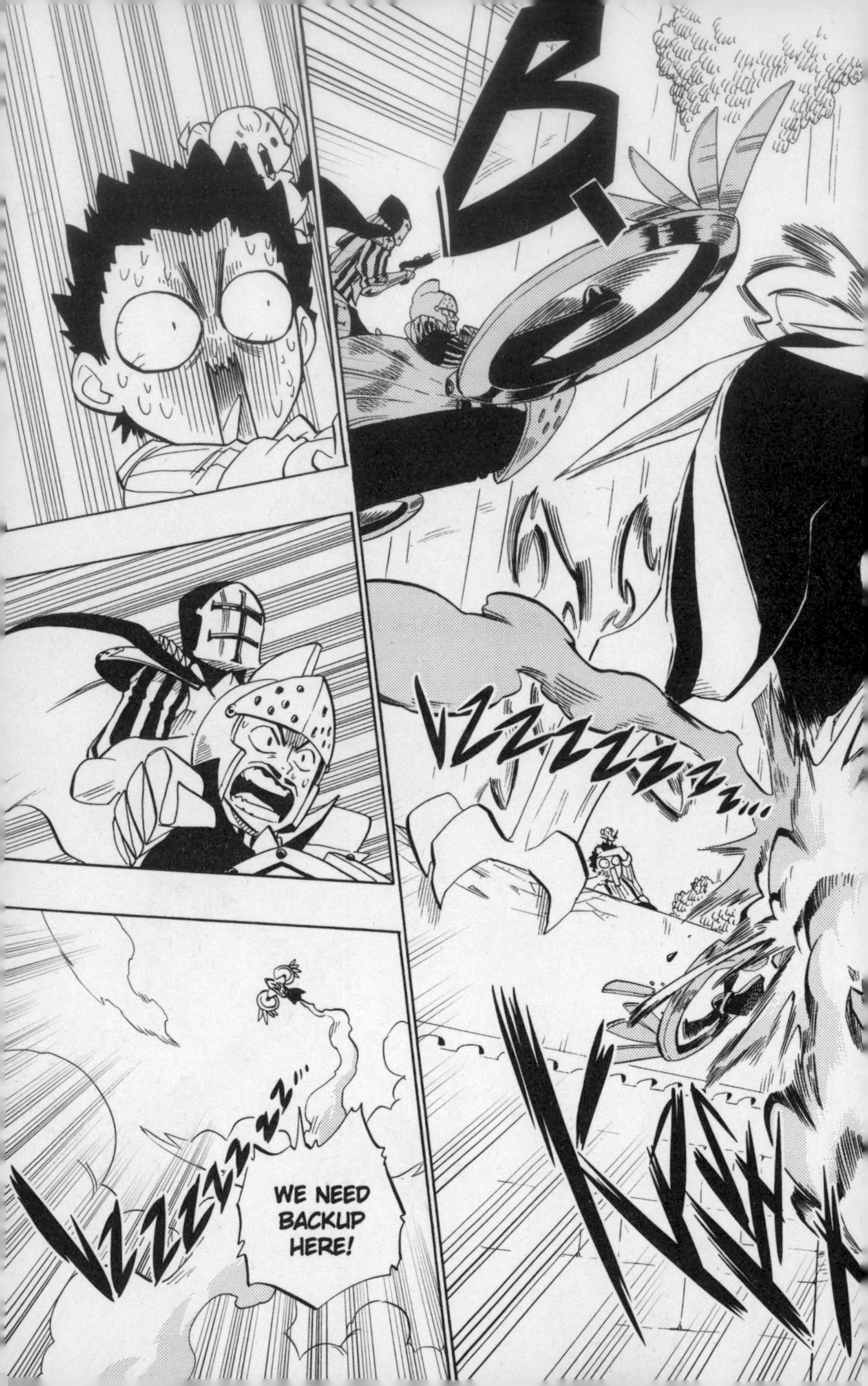
VZZZZZZZZZ...
WE NEED BACKUP HERE!

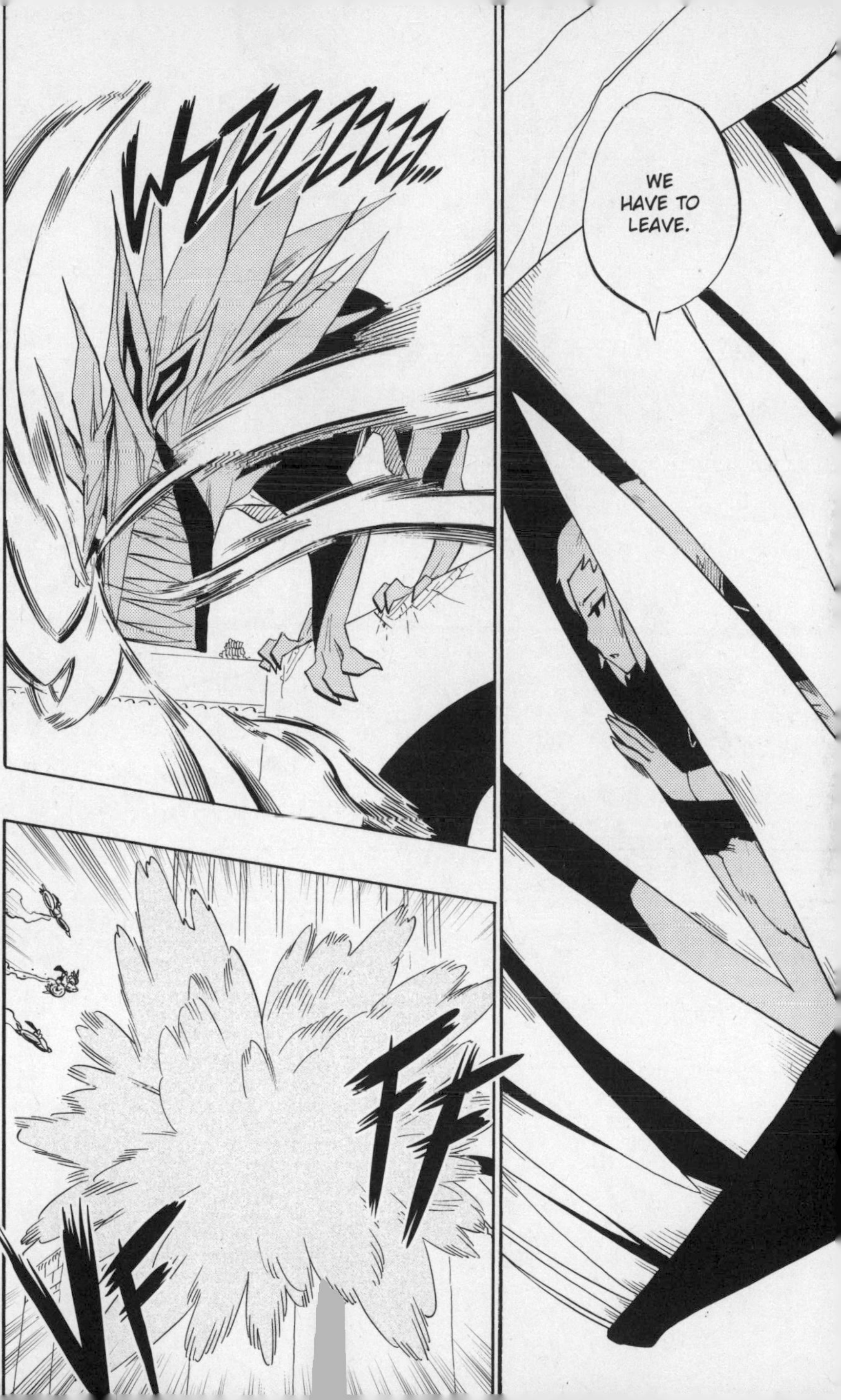
WE HAVE TO LEAVE.

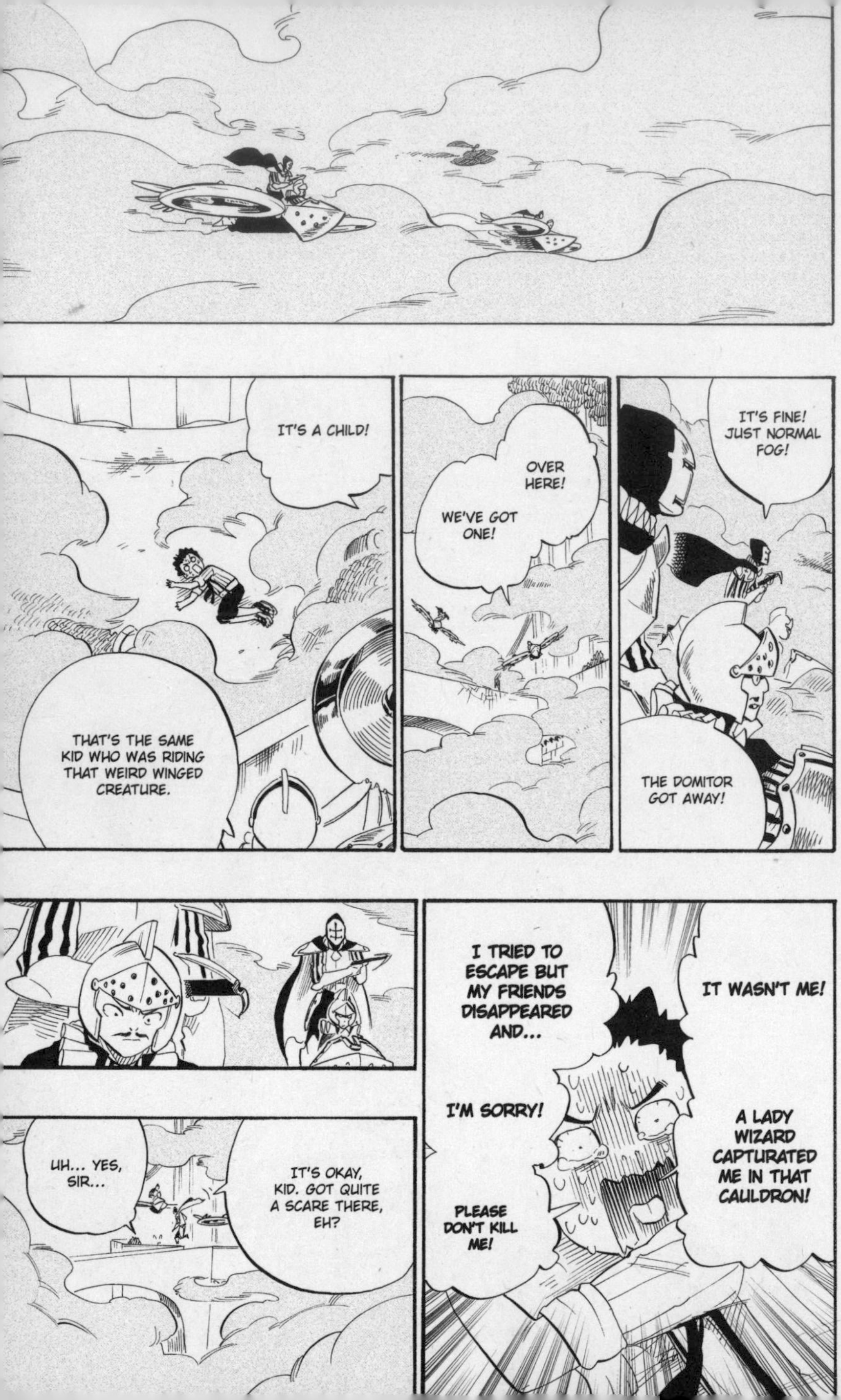
IT'S FINE! JUST NORMAL FOG!
THE DOMITOR GOT AWAY!
OVER HERE!
WE'VE GOT ONE!
IT'S A CHILD!
THAT'S THE SAME KID WHO WAS RIDING THAT WEIRD WINGED CREATURE.
IT WASN'T ME!
I TRIED TO ESCAPE BUT MY FRIENDS DISAPPEARED AND...
A LADY WIZARD CAPTURATED ME IN THAT CAULDRON!
I'M SORRY!
PLEASE DON'T KILL ME!
IT'S OKAY, KID. GOT QUITE A SCARE THERE, EH?
UH... YES, SIR...

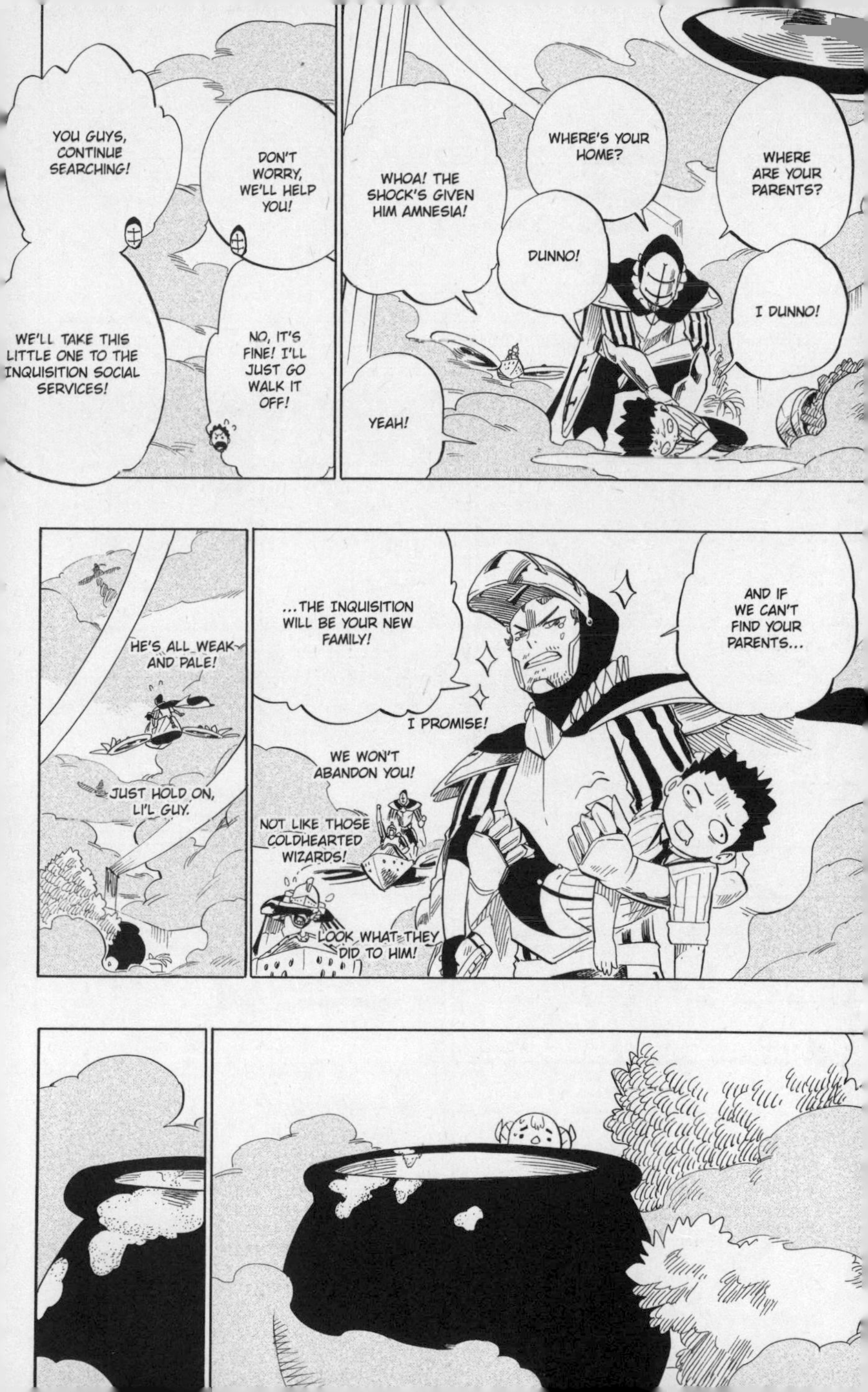
WHERE ARE YOUR PARENTS?
I DUNNO!
WHERE'S YOUR HOME?
DUNNO!
WHOA! THE SHOCK'S GIVEN HIM AMNESIA!
YEAH!
DON'T WORRY, WE'LL HELP YOU!
YOU GUYS, CONTINUE SEARCHING!
NO, IT'S FINE! I'LL JUST GO WALK IT OFF!
WE'LL TAKE THIS LITTLE ONE TO THE INQUISITION SOCIAL SERVICES!
AND IF WE CAN'T FIND YOUR PARENTS...
...THE INQUISITION WILL BE YOUR NEW FAMILY!
I PROMISE!
WE WON'T ABANDON YOU!
NOT LIKE THOSE COLDHEARTED WIZARDS!
LOOK WHAT THEY DID TO HIM!
HE'S ALL WEAK AND PALE!
JUST HOLD ON, LI'L GUY.

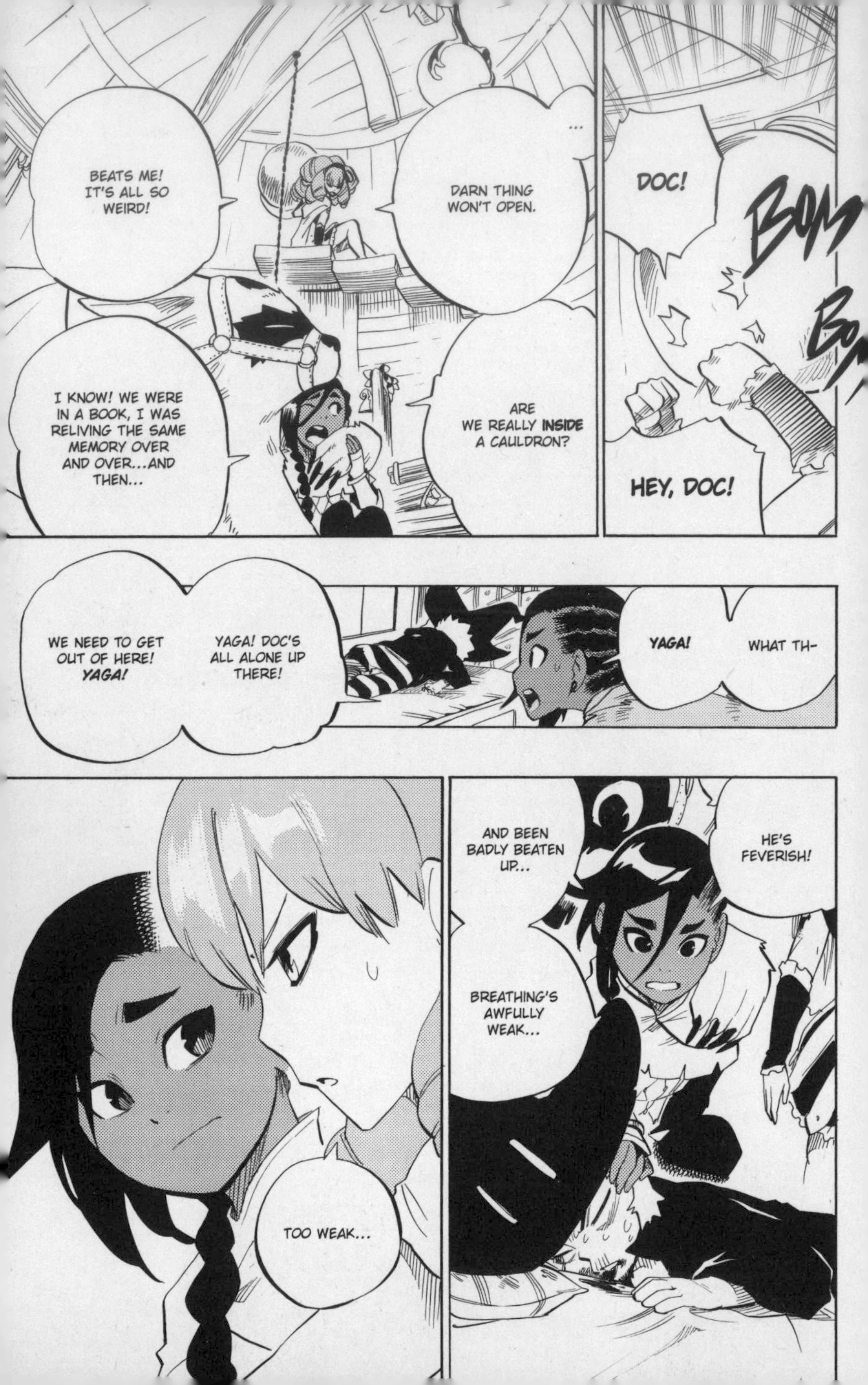

DOC!
BOM
BOM
HEY, DOC!
...
DARN THING WON'T OPEN.
BEATS ME! IT'S ALL SO WEIRD!
ARE WE REALLY **INSIDE** A CAULDRON?
I KNOW! WE WERE IN A BOOK, I WAS RELIVING THE SAME MEMORY OVER AND OVER...AND THEN...
WHAT TH-
YAGA!
YAGA! DOC'S ALL ALONE UP THERE!
WE NEED TO GET OUT OF HERE! **YAGA!**
HE'S FEVERISH!
AND BEEN BADLY BEATEN UP...
BREATHING'S AWFULLY WEAK...
TOO WEAK...

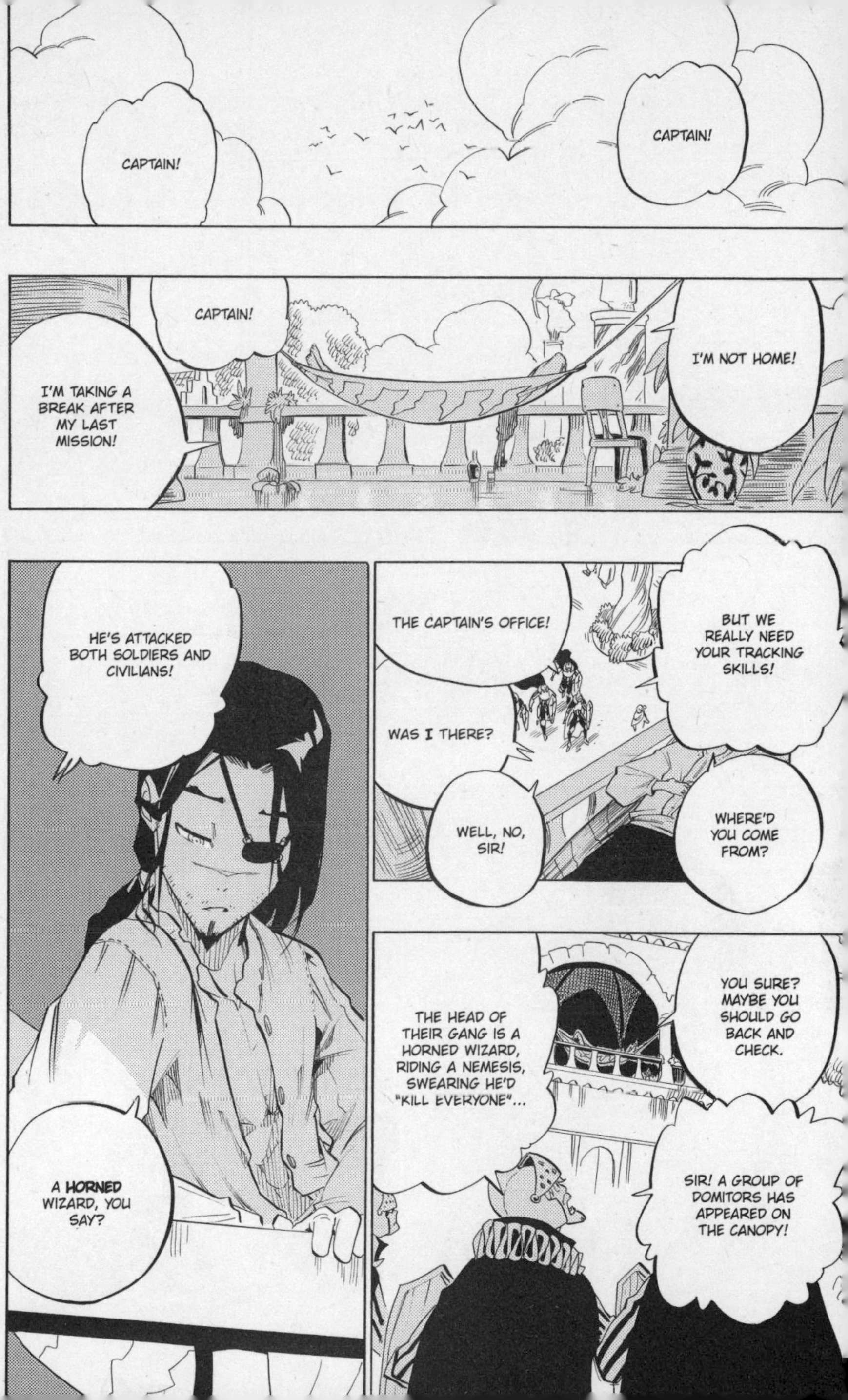
CAPTAIN!
CAPTAIN!
CAPTAIN!
I'M NOT HOME!
I'M TAKING A BREAK AFTER MY LAST MISSION!
WHERE'D YOU COME FROM?
THE CAPTAIN'S OFFICE!
WAS I THERE?
WELL, NO, SIR!
BUT WE REALLY NEED YOUR TRACKING SKILLS!
YOU SURE? MAYBE YOU SHOULD GO BACK AND CHECK.
SIR! A GROUP OF DOMITORS HAS APPEARED ON THE CANOPY!
THE HEAD OF THEIR GANG IS A HORNED WIZARD, RIDING A NEMESIS, SWEARING HE'D "KILL EVERYONE"...
HE'S ATTACKED BOTH SOLDIERS AND CIVILIANS!
A **HORNED** WIZARD, YOU SAY?

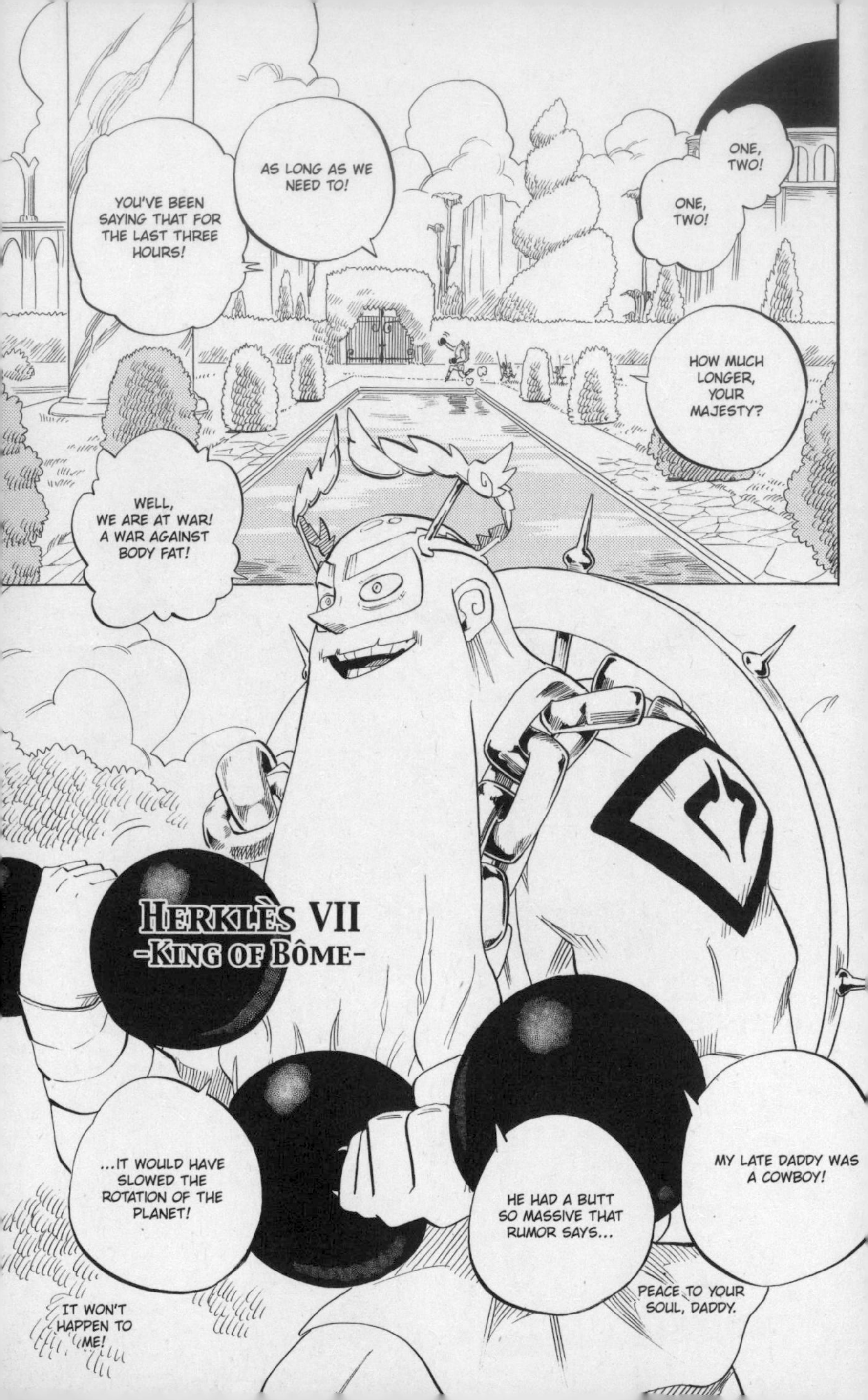
ONE, TWO!
ONE, TWO!
HOW MUCH LONGER, YOUR MAJESTY?
AS LONG AS WE NEED TO!
YOU'VE BEEN SAYING THAT FOR THE LAST THREE HOURS!
WELL, WE ARE AT WAR! A WAR AGAINST BODY FAT!
HERKLÈS VII -KING OF BÔME-
MY LATE DADDY WAS A COWBOY!
HE HAD A BUTT SO MASSIVE THAT RUMOR SAYS...
...IT WOULD HAVE SLOWED THE ROTATION OF THE PLANET!
PEACE TO YOUR SOUL, DADDY.
IT WON'T HAPPEN TO ME!

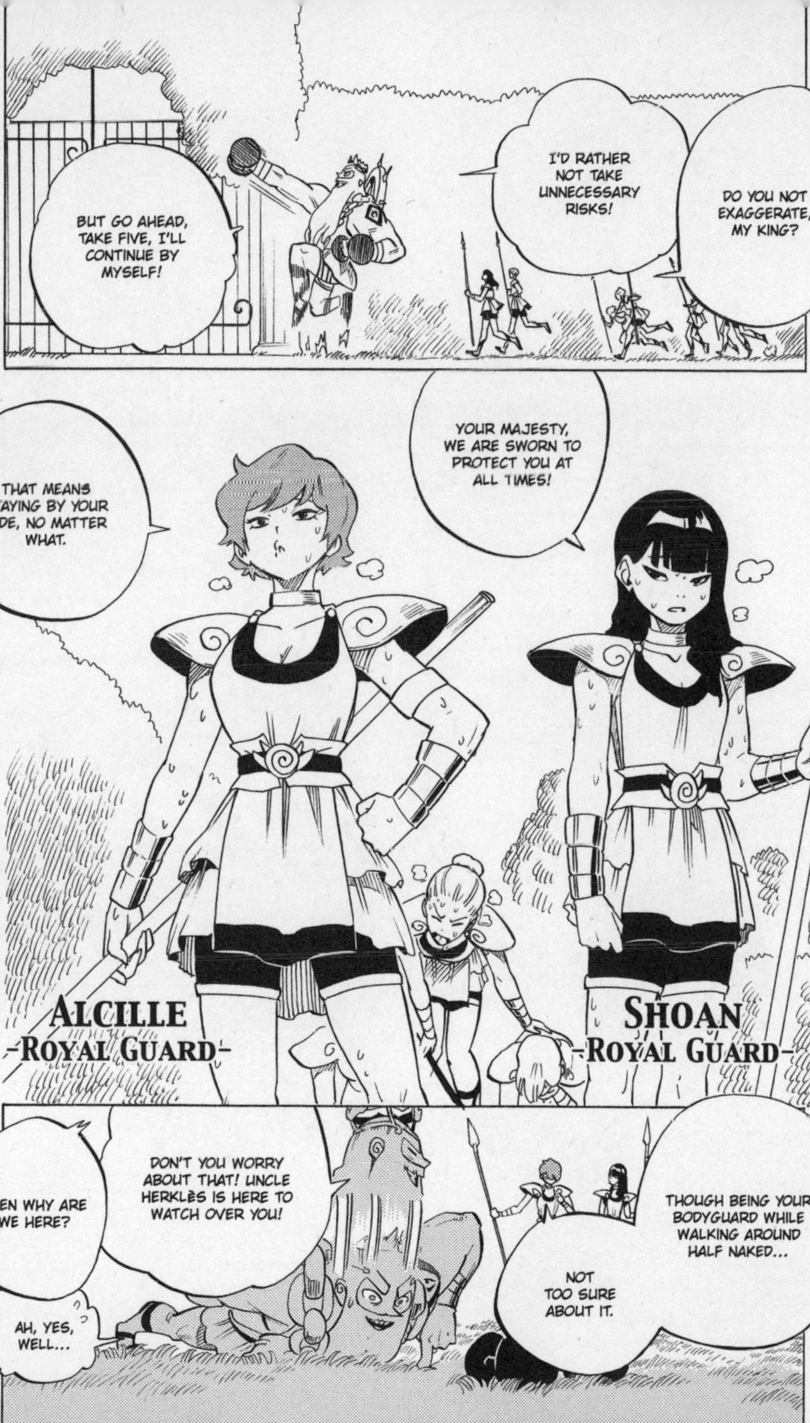
DO YOU NOT EXAGGERATE, MY KING?
I'D RATHER NOT TAKE UNNECESSARY RISKS!
BUT GO AHEAD, TAKE FIVE, I'LL CONTINUE BY MYSELF!
YOUR MAJESTY, WE ARE SWORN TO PROTECT YOU AT ALL TIMES!
THAT MEANS STAYING BY YOUR SIDE, NO MATTER WHAT.
SHOAN
-ROYAL GUARD-
ALCILLE
-ROYAL GUARD-
THOUGH BEING YOUR BODYGUARD WHILE WALKING AROUND HALF NAKED...
NOT TOO SURE ABOUT IT.
DON'T YOU WORRY ABOUT THAT! UNCLE HERKLÈS IS HERE TO WATCH OVER YOU!
THEN WHY ARE WE HERE?
AH, YES, WELL...

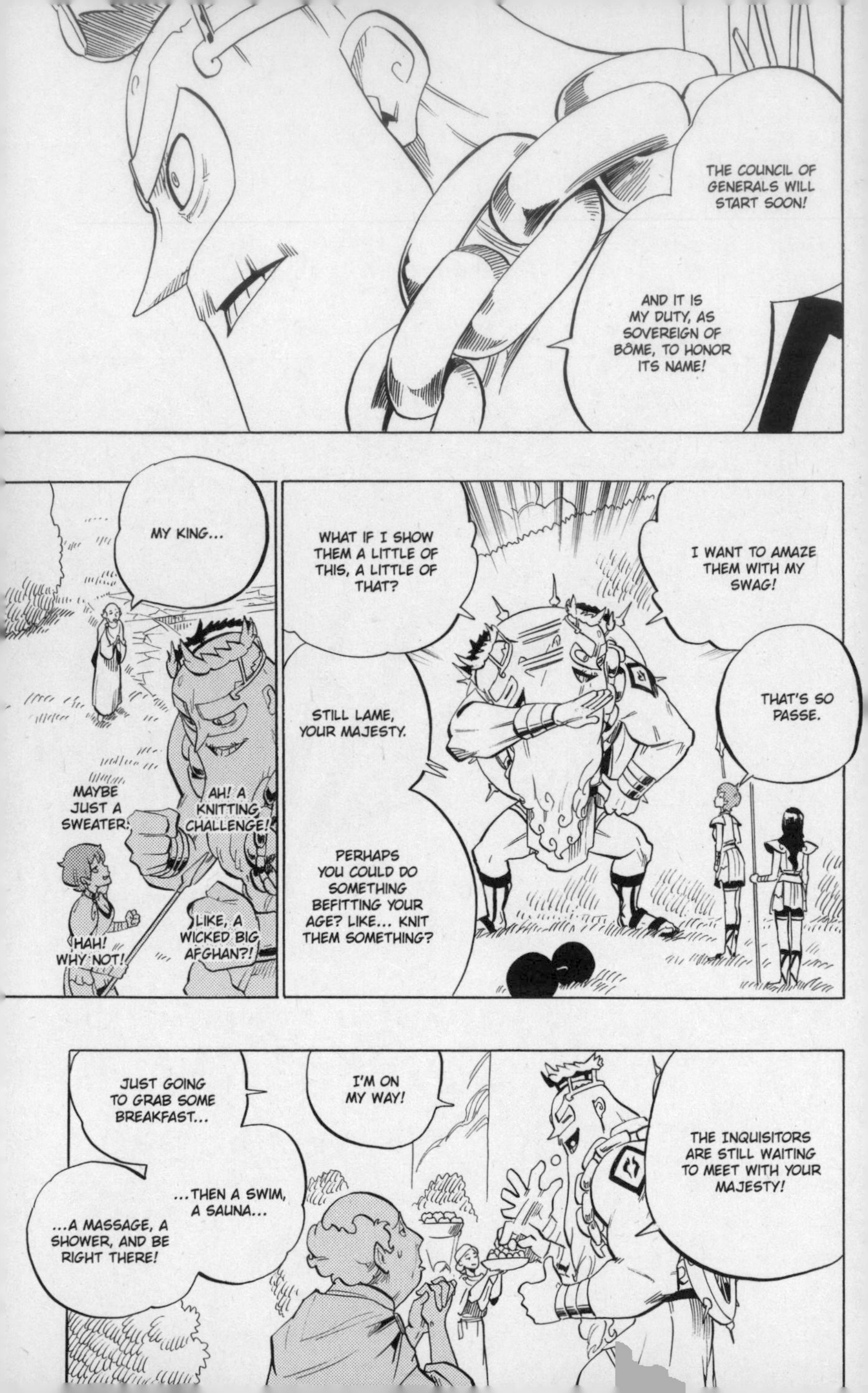
THE COUNCIL OF GENERALS WILL START SOON!
AND IT IS MY DUTY, AS SOVEREIGN OF BÔME, TO HONOR ITS NAME!
I WANT TO AMAZE THEM WITH MY SWAG!
WHAT IF I SHOW THEM A LITTLE OF THIS, A LITTLE OF THAT?
THAT'S SO PASSE.
STILL LAME, YOUR MAJESTY.
PERHAPS YOU COULD DO SOMETHING BEFITTING YOUR AGE? LIKE... KNIT THEM SOMETHING?
MY KING...
AH! A KNITTING CHALLENGE!
MAYBE JUST A SWEATER!
LIKE, A WICKED BIG AFGHAN?!
HAH! WHY NOT!
THE INQUISITORS ARE STILL WAITING TO MEET WITH YOUR MAJESTY!
I'M ON MY WAY!
JUST GOING TO GRAB SOME BREAKFAST...
...THEN A SWIM, A SAUNA...
...A MASSAGE, A SHOWER, AND BE RIGHT THERE!

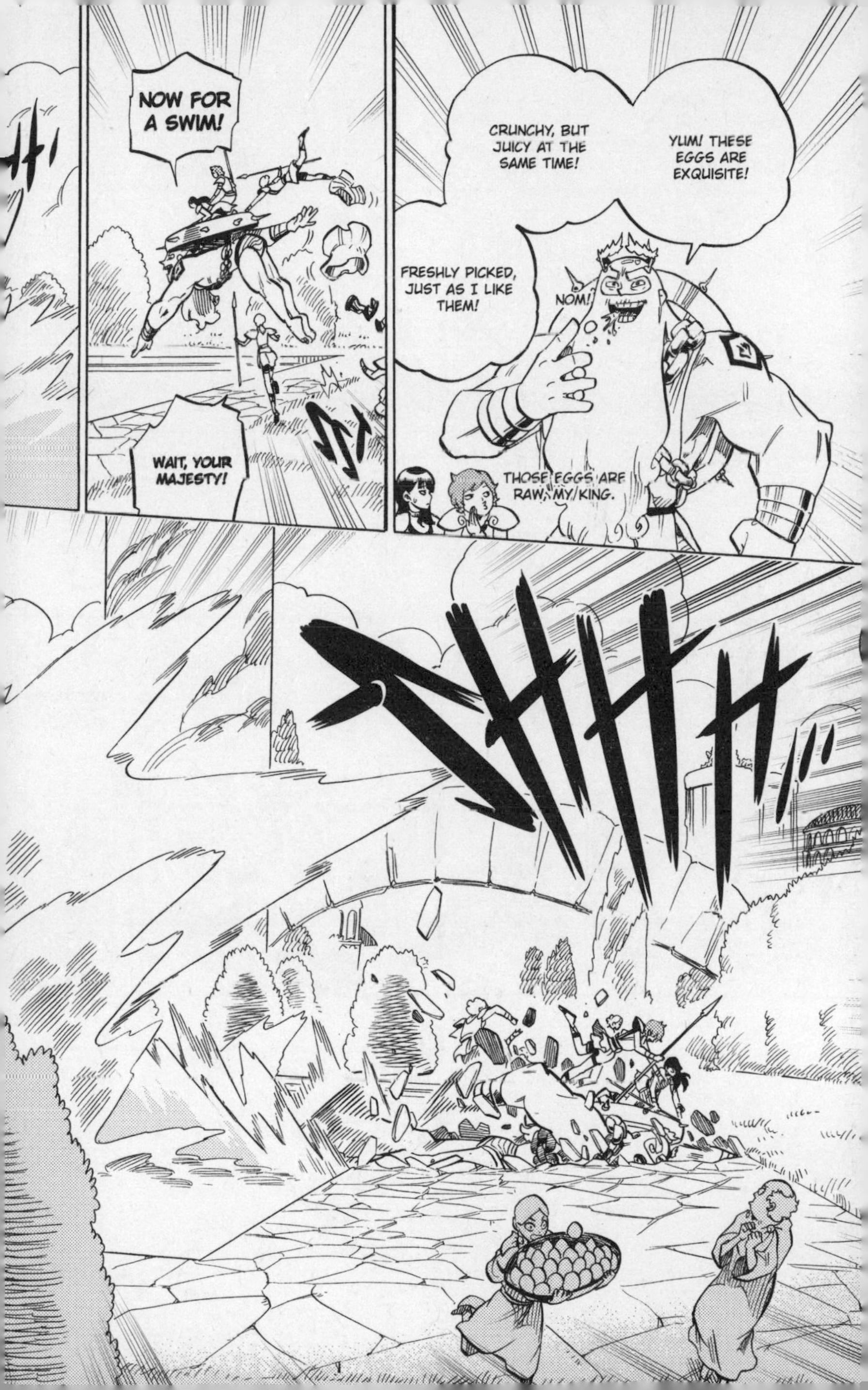
YUM! THESE EGGS ARE EXQUISITE!
CRUNCHY, BUT JUICY AT THE SAME TIME!
NOM!
FRESHLY PICKED, JUST AS I LIKE THEM!
THOSE EGGS ARE RAW, MY KING.
NOW FOR A SWIM!
WAIT, YOUR MAJESTY!

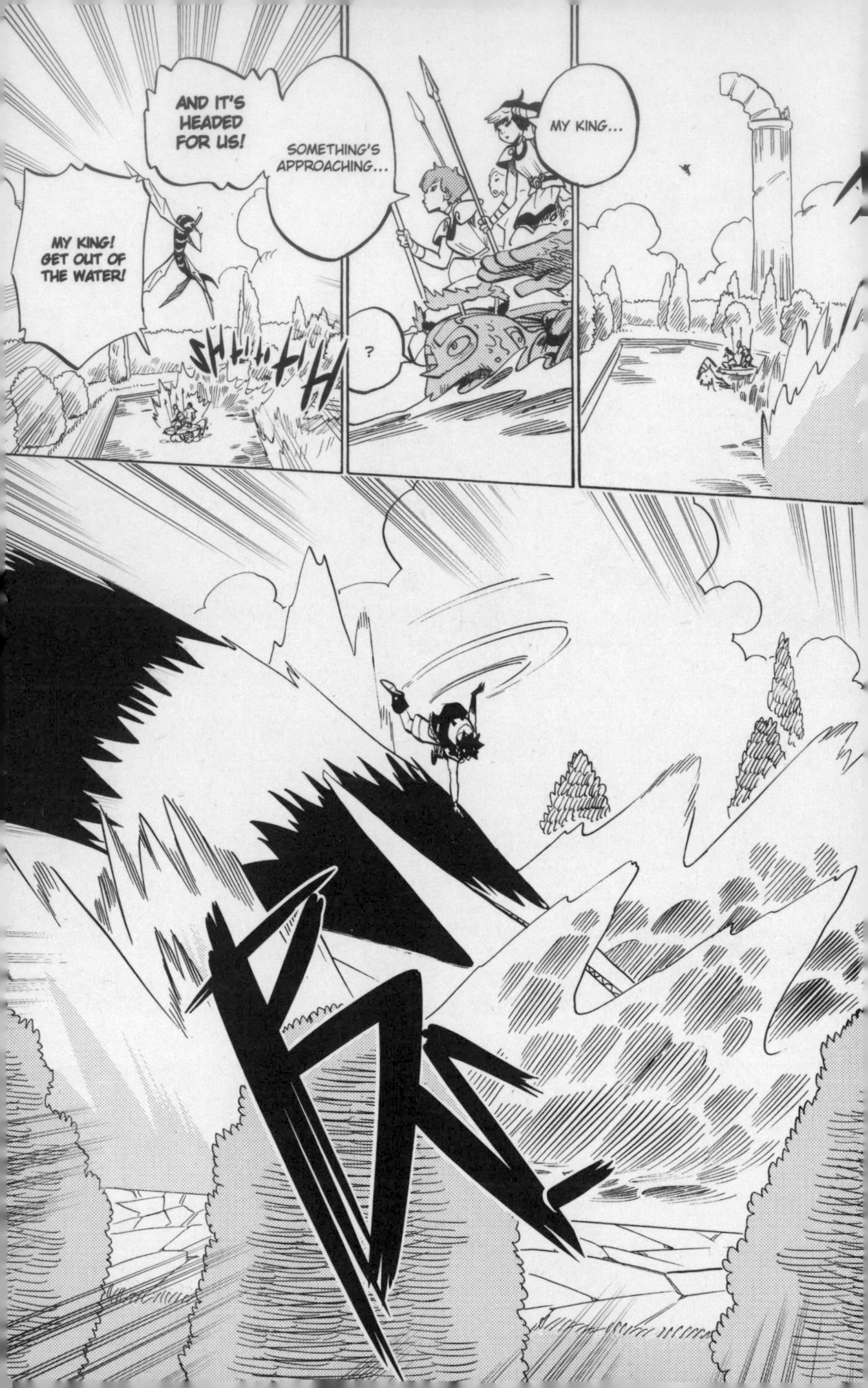
MY KING...
SOMETHING'S APPROACHING...
?
AND IT'S HEADED FOR US!
MY KING! GET OUT OF THE WATER!

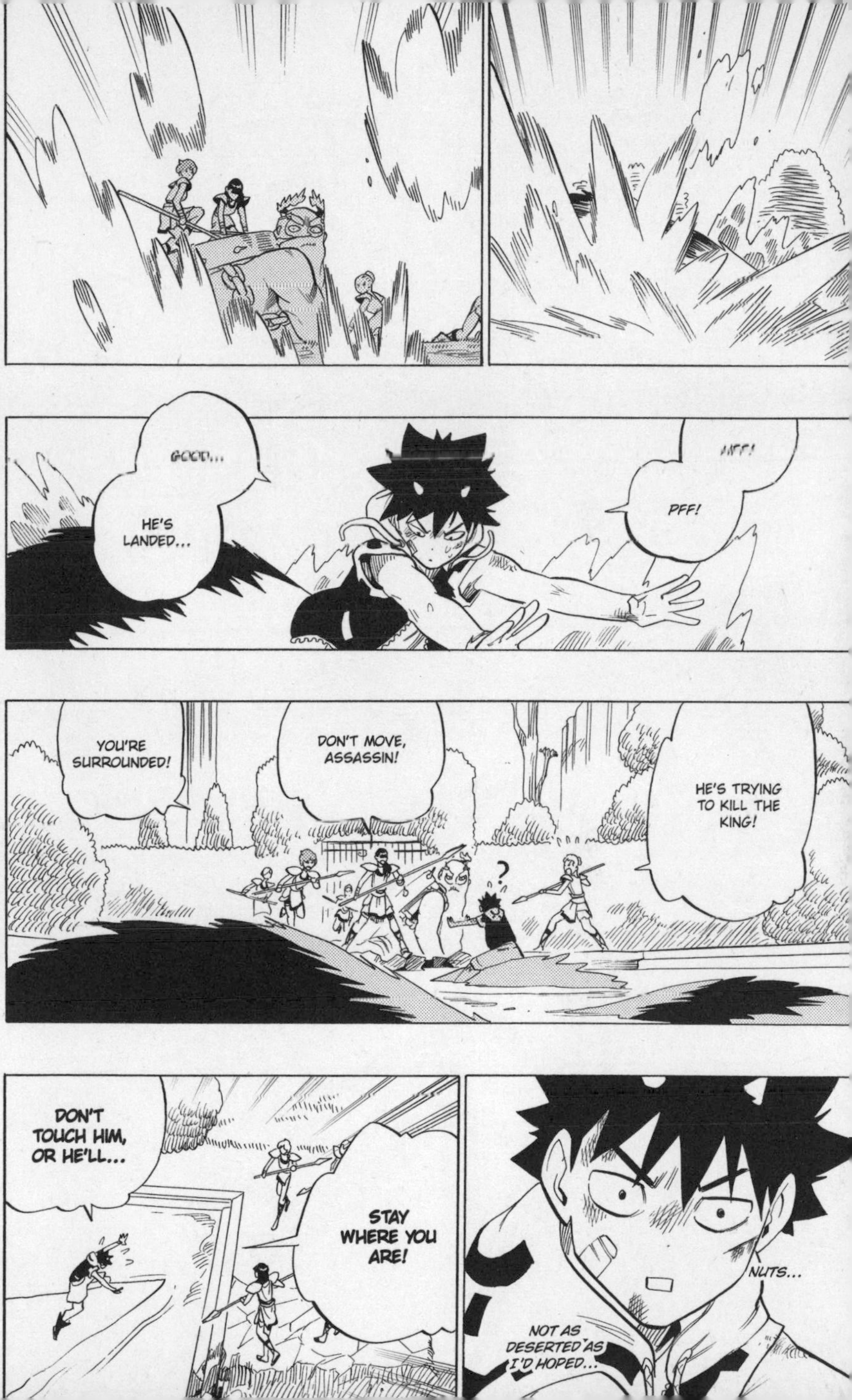
MFF! PFF!
GOOD... HE'S LANDED...
HE'S TRYING TO KILL THE KING!
DON'T MOVE, ASSASSIN!
YOU'RE SURROUNDED!
NUTS...
NOT AS DESERTED AS I'D HOPED...
STAY WHERE YOU ARE!
DON'T TOUCH HIM, OR HE'LL...

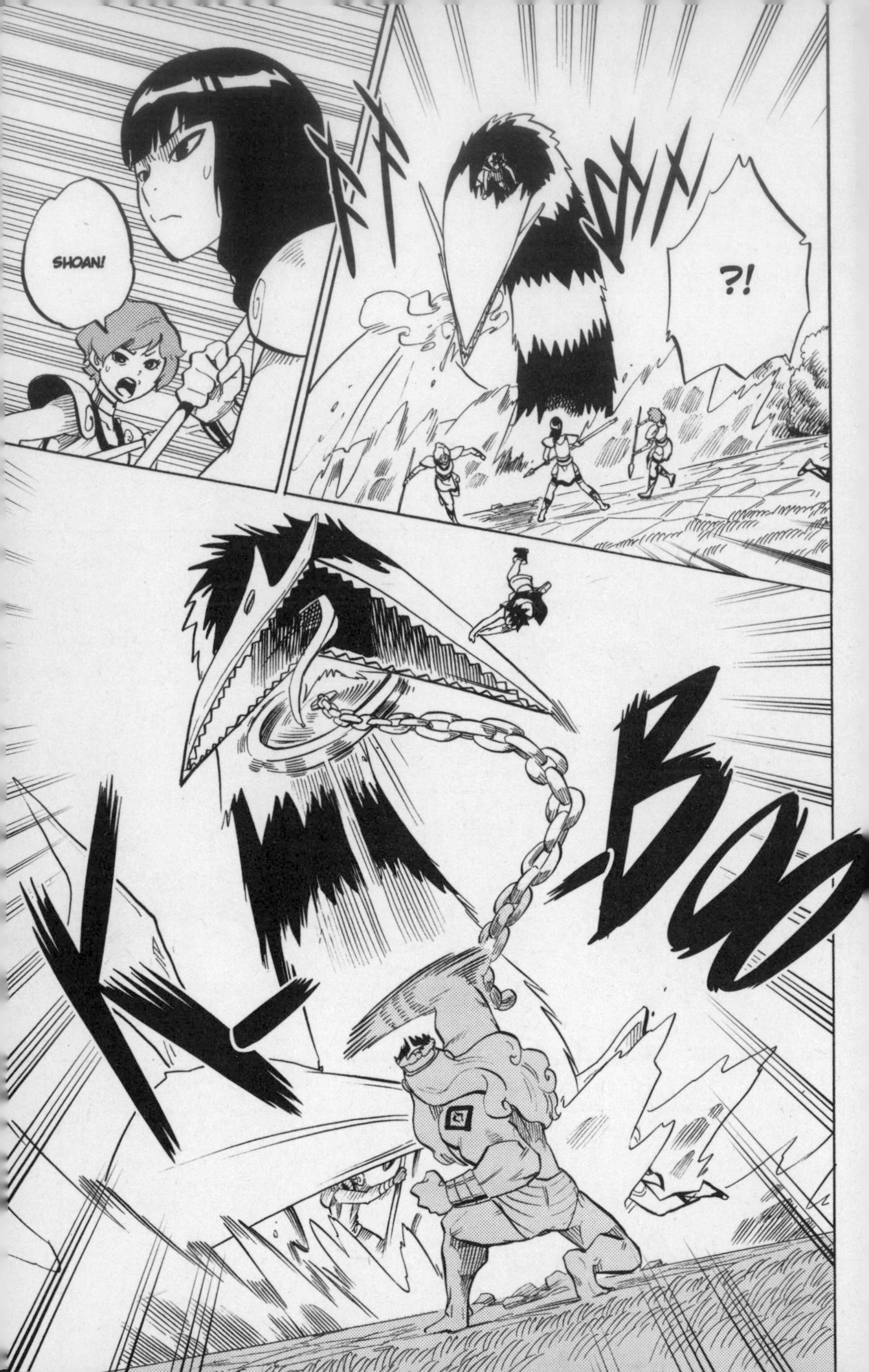

?!
SHOAN!

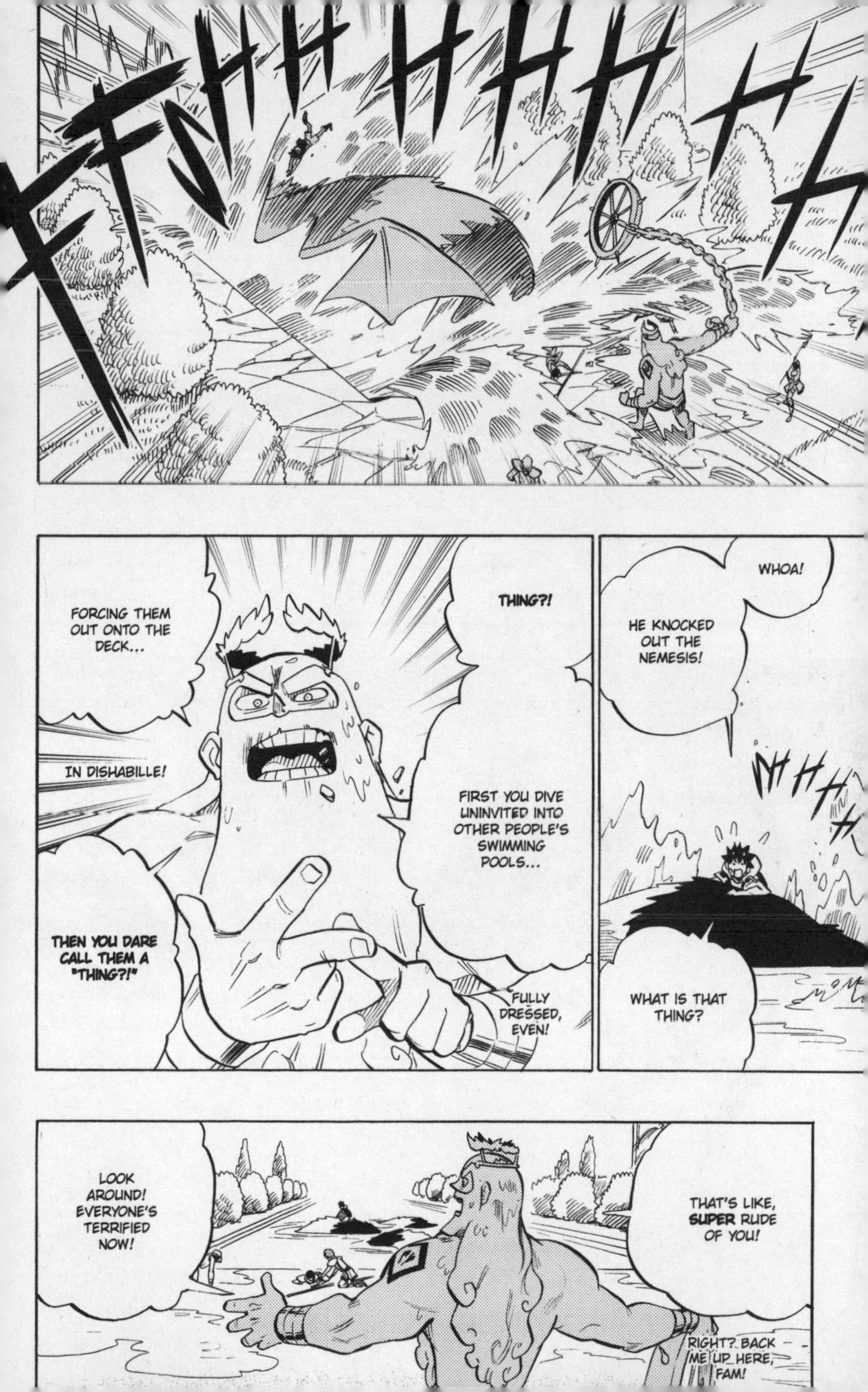
WHOA!
HE KNOCKED OUT THE NEMESIS!
WHAT IS THAT THING?
THING?!
FIRST YOU DIVE UNINVITED INTO OTHER PEOPLE'S SWIMMING POOLS...
FULLY DRESSED, EVEN!
FORCING THEM OUT ONTO THE DECK...
IN DISHABILLE!
THEN YOU DARE CALL THEM A "THING?!"
THAT'S LIKE, **SUPER** RUDE OF YOU!
LOOK AROUND! EVERYONE'S TERRIFIED NOW!
RIGHT? BACK ME UP HERE, FAM!

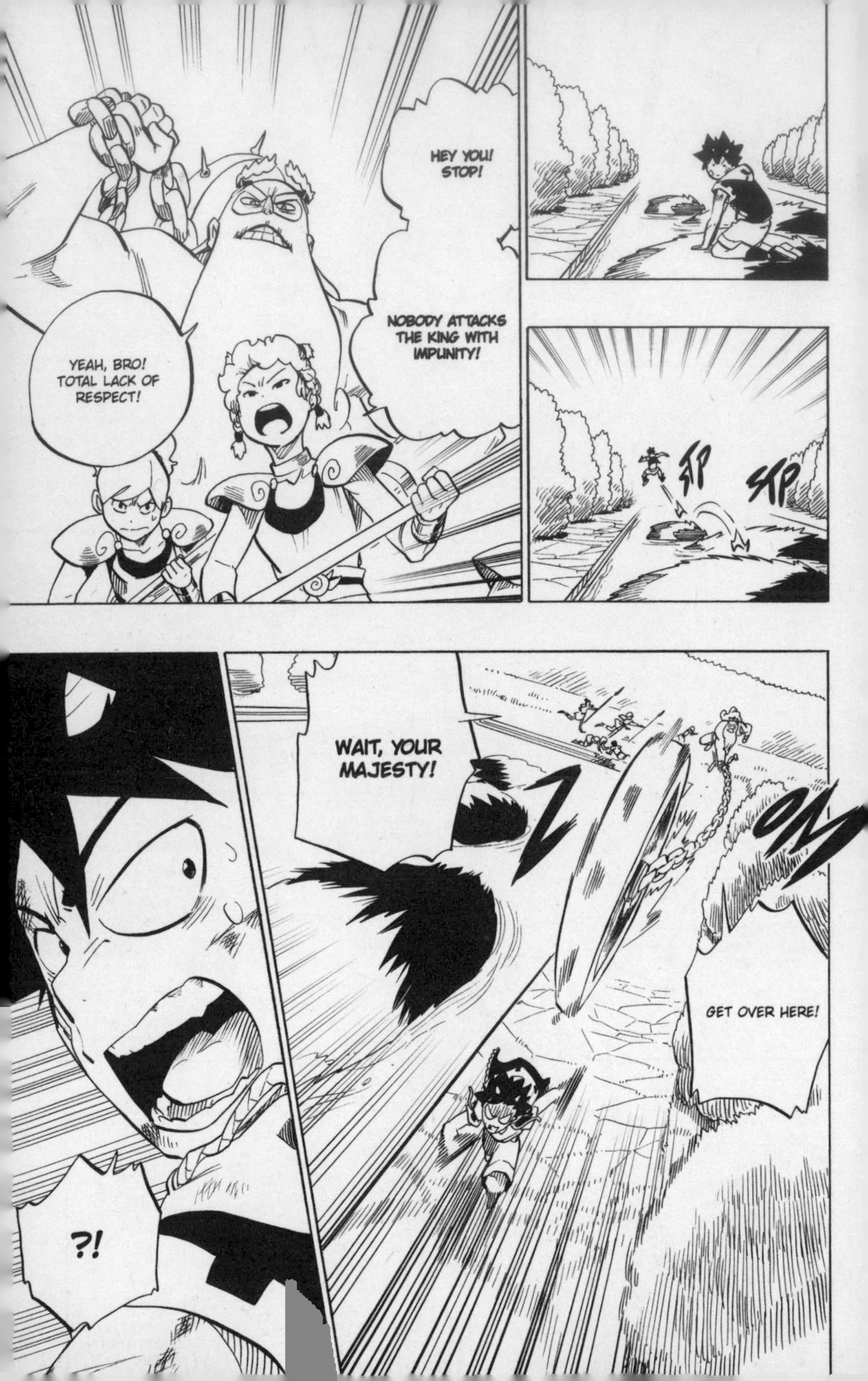
STP
STP
HEY YOU! STOP!
NOBODY ATTACKS THE KING WITH IMPUNITY!
YEAH, BRO! TOTAL LACK OF RESPECT!
WAIT, YOUR MAJESTY!
GET OVER HERE!
?!

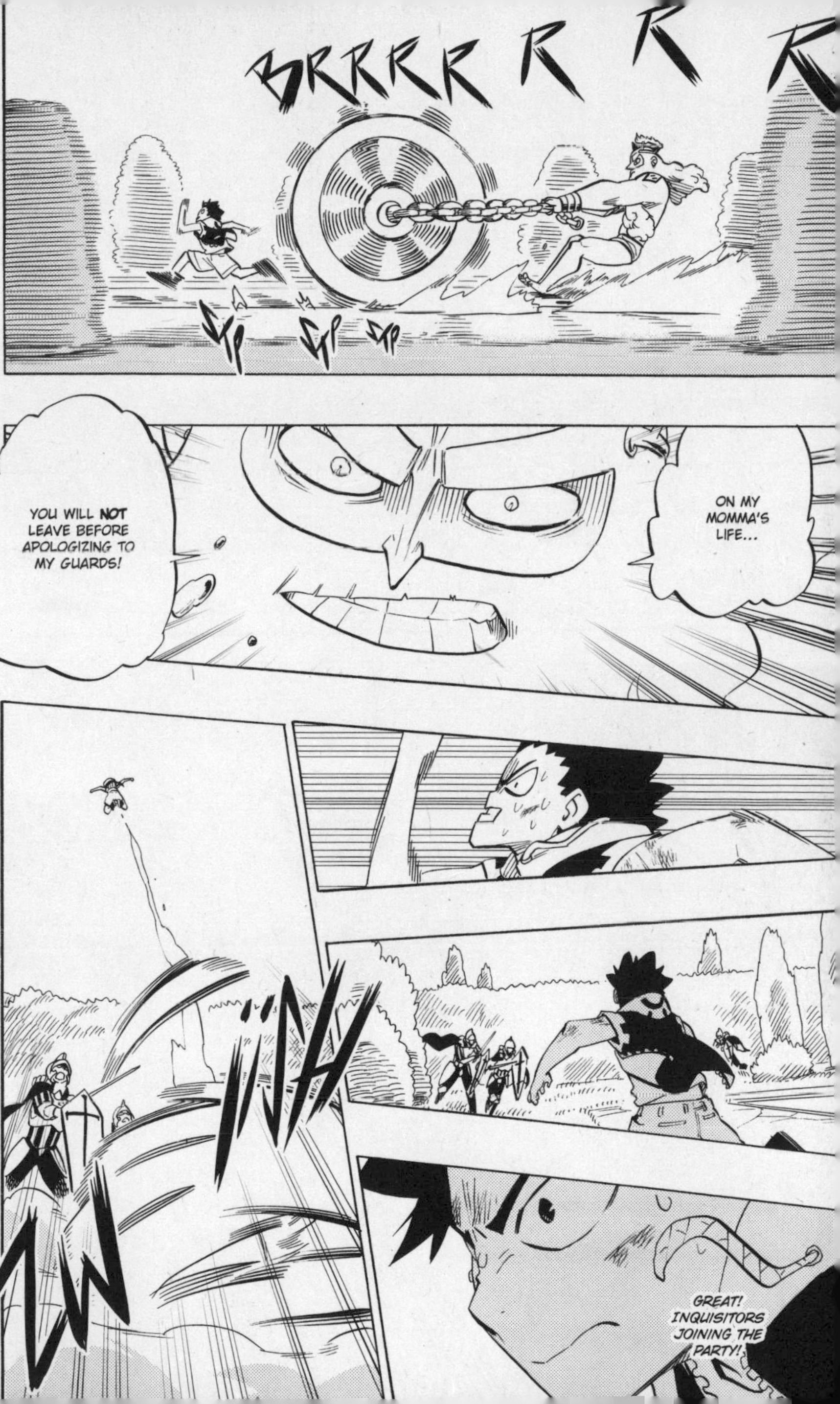
BRRRR R R R
SKP SKP SKP
ON MY MOMMA'S LIFE...
YOU WILL NOT LEAVE BEFORE APOLOGIZING TO MY GUARDS!
ZWISH
GREAT! INQUISITORS JOINING THE PARTY!

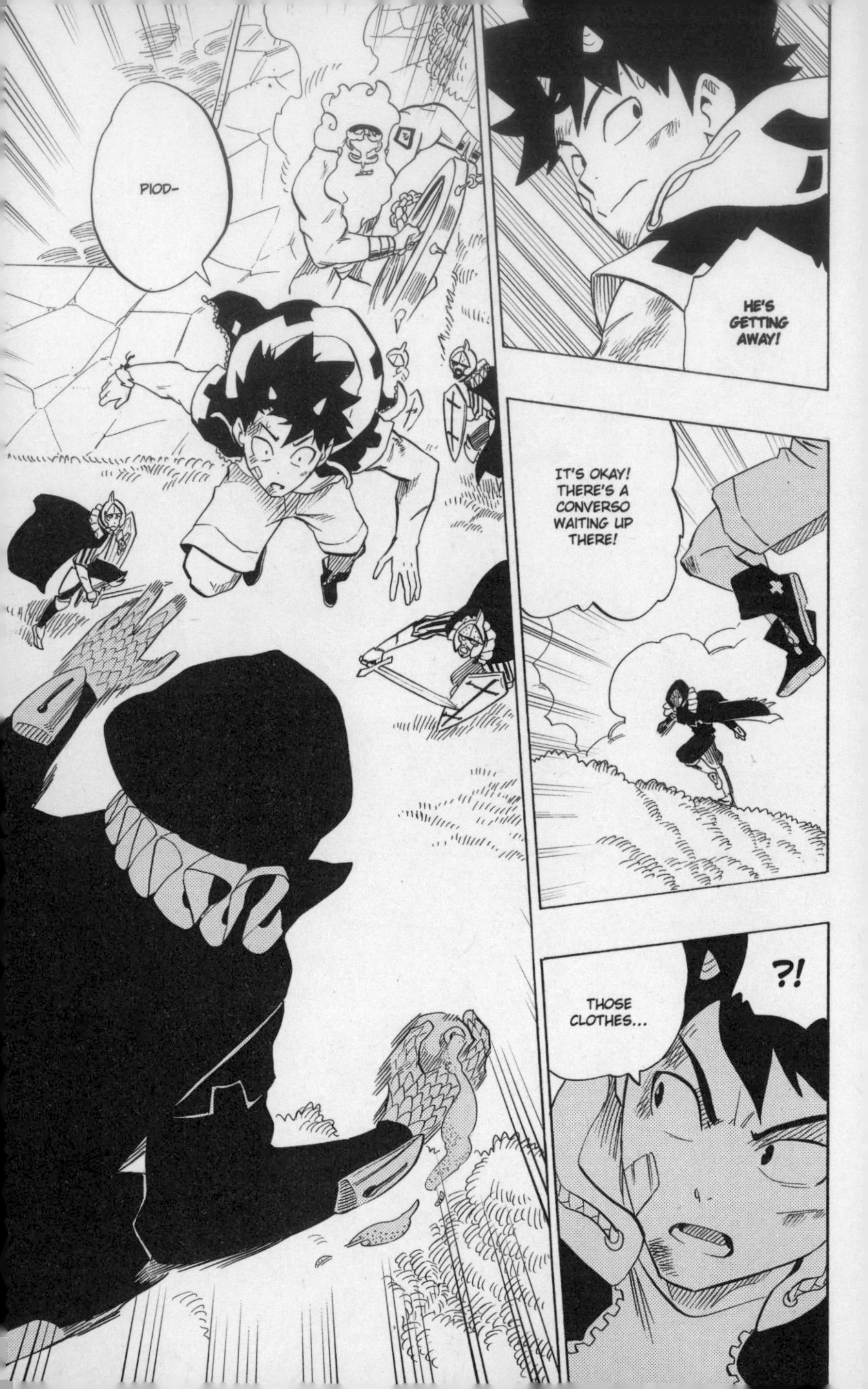
HE'S GETTING AWAY!
IT'S OKAY! THERE'S A CONVERSO WAITING UP THERE!
?!
THOSE CLOTHES...
PIOD-

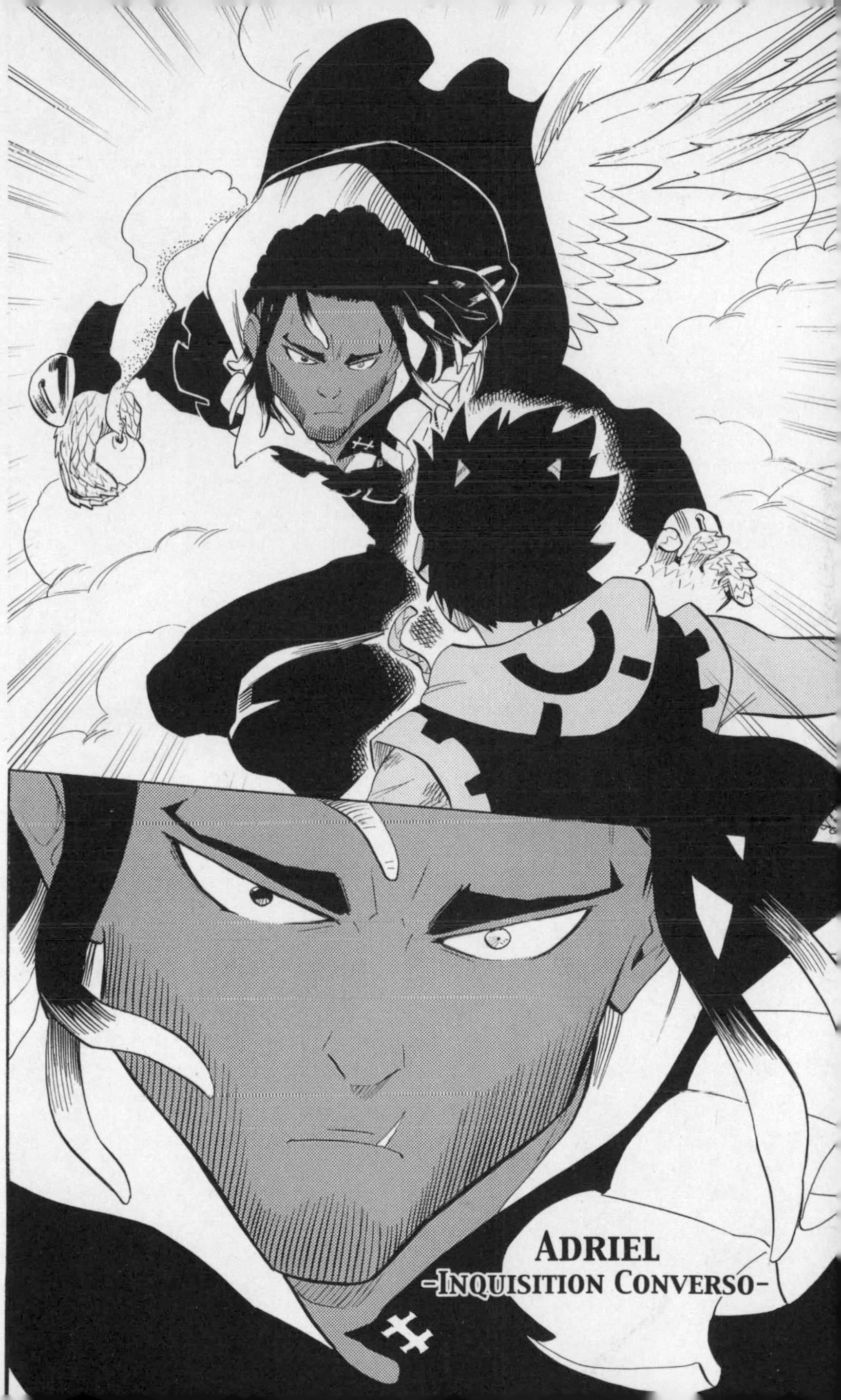
ADRIEL
-INQUISITION CONVERSO-

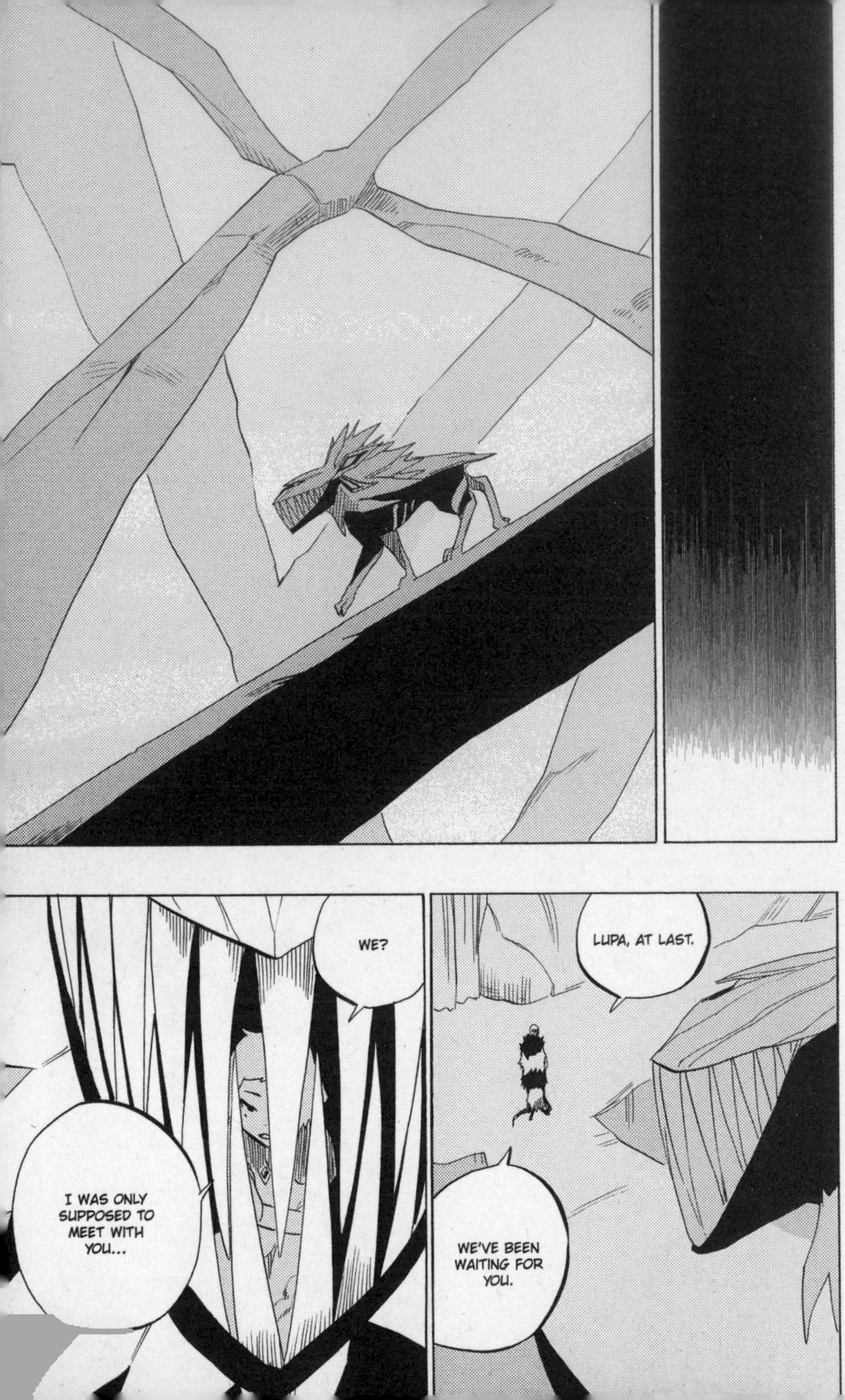
LUPA, AT LAST.
WE'VE BEEN WAITING FOR YOU.
WE?
I WAS ONLY SUPPOSED TO MEET WITH YOU...

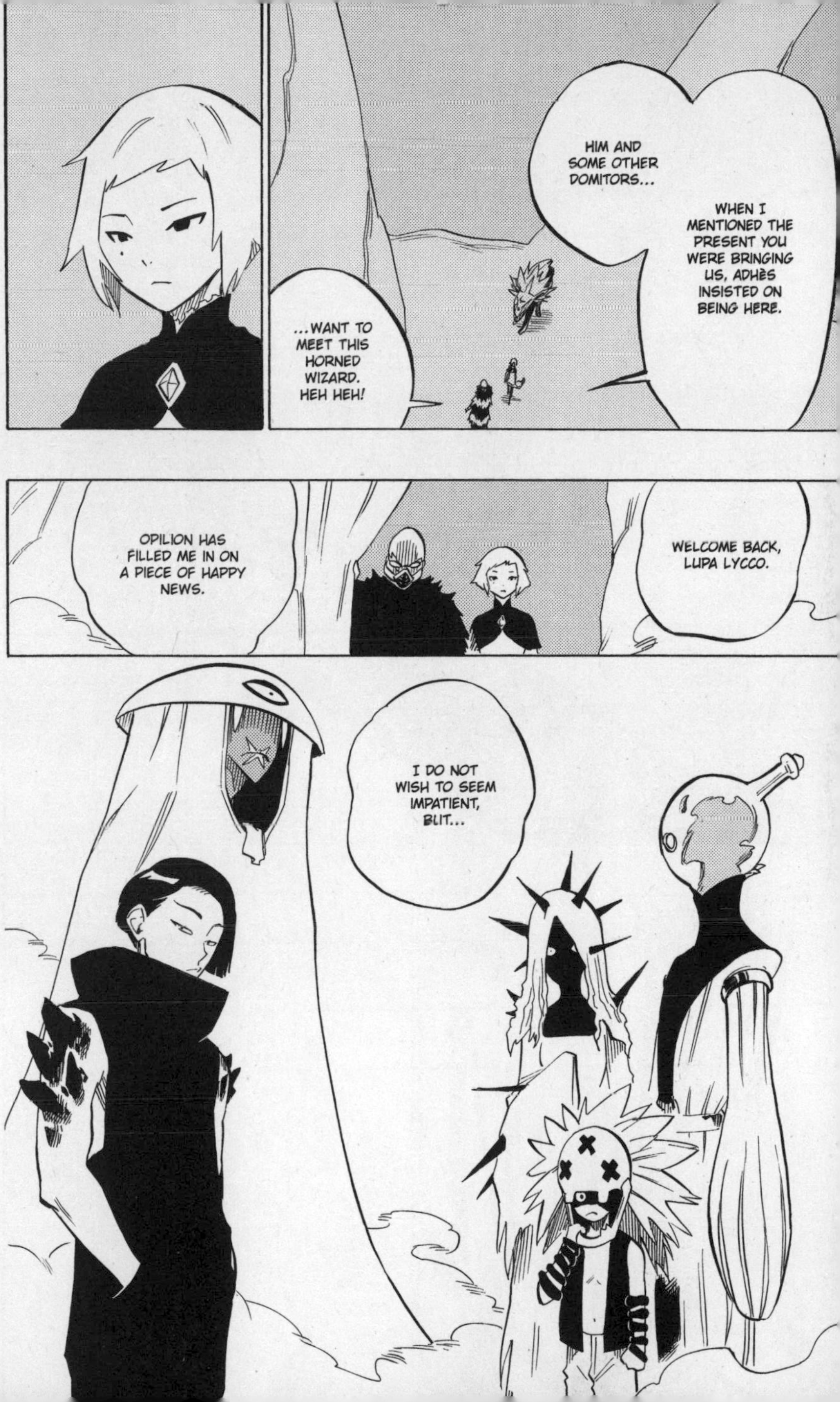
WHEN I MENTIONED THE PRESENT YOU WERE BRINGING US, ADHÈS INSISTED ON BEING HERE.
HIM AND SOME OTHER DOMITORS...
...WANT TO MEET THIS HORNED WIZARD. HEH HEH!
WELCOME BACK, LUPA LYCCO.
OPILION HAS FILLED ME IN ON A PIECE OF HAPPY NEWS.
I DO NOT WISH TO SEEM IMPATIENT, BUT...

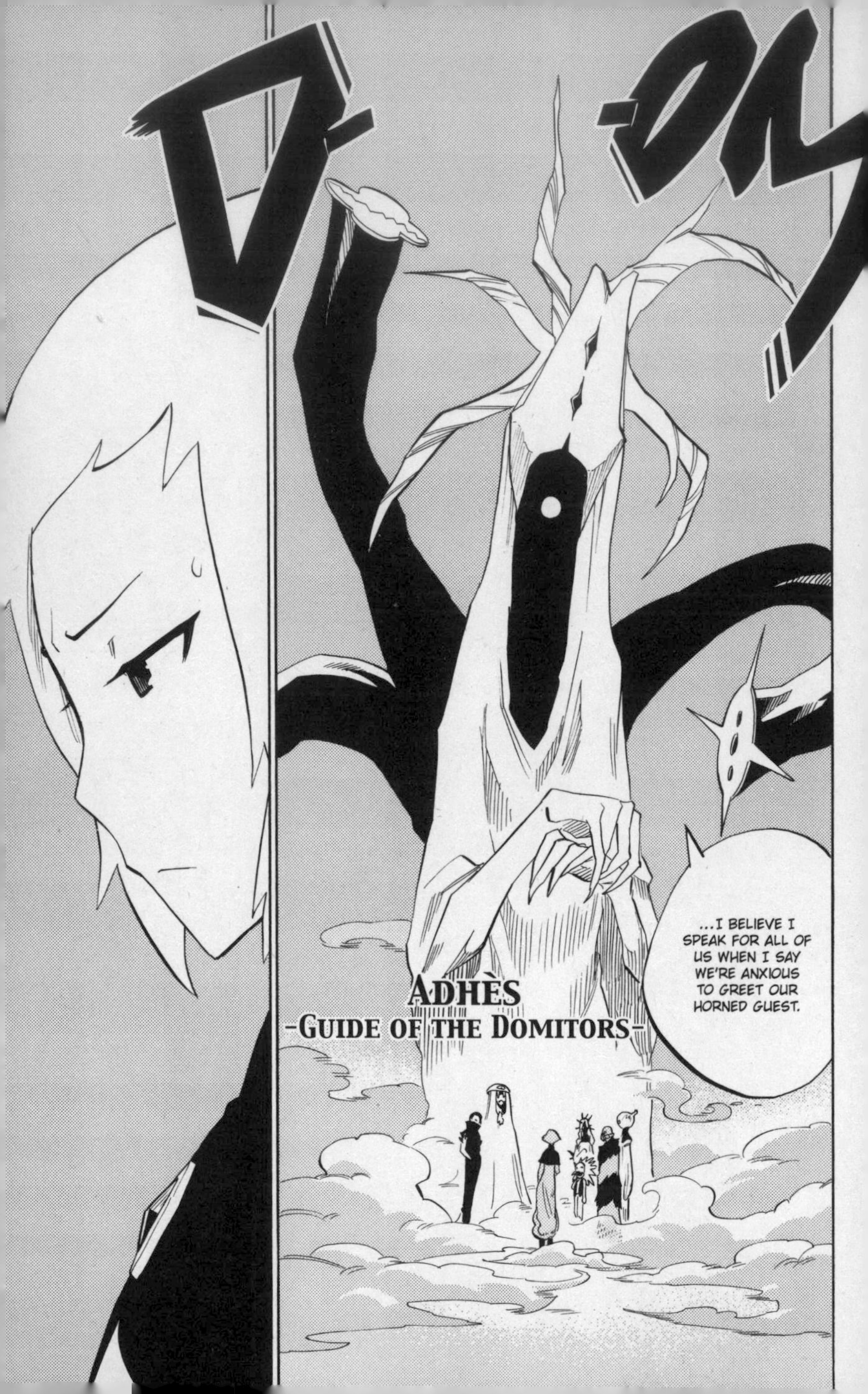
D-DOM
...I BELIEVE I SPEAK FOR ALL OF US WHEN I SAY WE'RE ANXIOUS TO GREET OUR HORNED GUEST.
ADHÈS
-GUIDE OF THE DOMITORS-

TO BE CONTINUED...

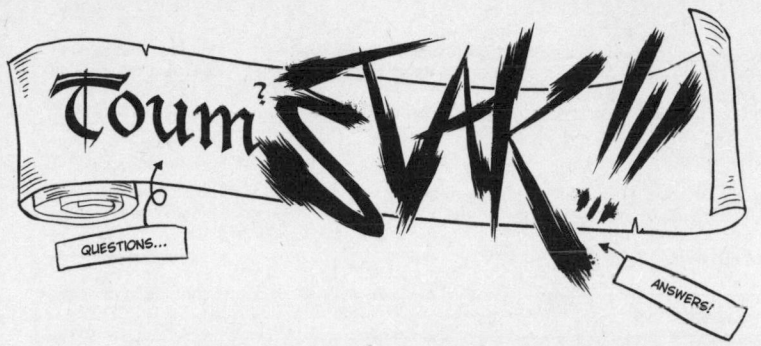

QUESTIONS...

ANSWERS!

Jordi D: Tony, I just discovered *Radiant* and I love it! The world building, the characters, the story, the art... I really hope for you it becomes as successful as *One Piece*. Ocoho's my favorite character. Finally a woman in a shonen manga who has permission to be a powerful warrior with a sense of humor, and above all, who isn't being portrayed as a sex object. And I love that look of hers with her armor, very cool! Do take care of her, please. My question might be a little bit of a delicate subject, but do you think that one day we might see a homosexual protagonist in a shonen manga, someone who is inspiring, and not a slap in the face? Shonen manga aren't exactly well-known for their respectful LGBT characters. All the ones I've seen were insulting stereotypical personas, and only good at further perpetuating ignorance and I'm sure that has something to do with the Japanese culture. The theme of discrimination in your story really touched me. To see how the Infected are treated, how the people hate them and reject them really touched me on a personal level because I myself am gay. I've experienced verbal and psychological aggression and I know that ignorance can push people into saying and/or doing horrible things. So I hope you'll continue to entertain us and let us travel through this magical and wondrous world. Thank you.

Tony Valente: Thank you for your comments on Ocoho! I'll try to stay faithful to those characters! As for the question you asked: yes, it is a subject I'd like to address. Actually, I've wanted to do that since the very start. It's just that I don't want to introduce a cliché character solely to be able to talk about it! I don't want the extent of that character to be mainly defined by him being part of the LGBT community, I'd like so many other aspects to define them... But without dodging the subject either! In short, being able to address the topic without hurting the community concerned is a balance that will require some work to find. It's the same work that I devote to the characters that I create and are gradually making their way to the pages of my series.

....

Gaëlle B.: Hi Tony! First of all, thank you for your manga (I just finished reading volume 10 in 30 seconds, darn!). What I especially like about *Radiant* are the themes that we, as French people, will understand much better in terms of how deep they go as opposed to themes from the Japanese archipelago that don't relate to us as much. (I think there are also the strong female characters that we don't come across very often in the manga format.) So, yeah, here's my question: will you continue to deal with themes that are important to yourself and could potentially resonate with us?

Tony Valente: Actually, that is the reason why I write these things! I just write what I'm interested in, what I like, what worries me. I think that I wouldn't be able to write a story whose sole purpose would be to have an adventure and have fun. Even if I do like fireballs myself...

-Second question: Mr. Boobrie is so small... Is he still a baby?

Now there's an unexpected and yet so pertinent question! And here's a vague and completely meaningless answer, along with some first class deflection and dodging to go with it! There, cheers!

So you're originally from Toulouse, in the southwest of France? That's where I'm from! I'd love to cause some chaos here, so could you please tell me... "Chocolate croissant" or "chocolatine"?

Oh, no, go right ahead, it doesn't bother me at all, because honestly, there's not even a doubt about it, they're "chocolatines." Yeah, no, really.

....

Alban H.: Hello Mr. Valente. Following the release of volume 10, I've got two questions:
-The Commander Inquisitor of the aerial fleet, is that the same man as the one we saw in Konrad of Marbourg's flashback?

Tony Valente: Exactly right! But he's gained status since!

-If Commander Ullmina is Vérone's mother, then why does she not have the title of princess or queen?

Because she's neither! Vérone is, yes, the king's son, but Ullmina is not the king's wife. Yup, sometimes kings step outside the bounds of matrimony...

....

Killian M.: Hello, and congratulations on volume 10 and the adaptation into an animated series. I had a few questions. If what Diabal says is true (and let's hope he survives Piodon), is it possible then that Seth has a second, secret Infection if both his parents were wizards?

Tony Valente: Aaaah! Well, no. I mean, it could have been... But no.

-And Mr. Boobrie, did he appear along with Mélie's Infection or is he just a pet who comes from her clan?

He's a free and autonomous animal. He likes to think that Mélie is his hooman.

-Will we someday see more dryads like Jill's father?

Yeeeees! I'm planning on it! Just not right away...

-And to finish off, I was wondering if you are going to bring back the extras and contests at the end of the manga volumes. And also maybe add a little recap at the start of the volumes now that we've gone past a certain number of volumes?

The extras, yeah, I think I will. As for the recaps, I'd love to. It's been a while and I've been thinking about doing that, actually... But I'm always so busy and then I just don't do it. Every time a volume comes out I think, okay, so for the next one I'll do it! And then another one comes out and I'll think "next one!" and then another one and another one and...

You know how it is...

Please send your questions to: radiant@ankama.com

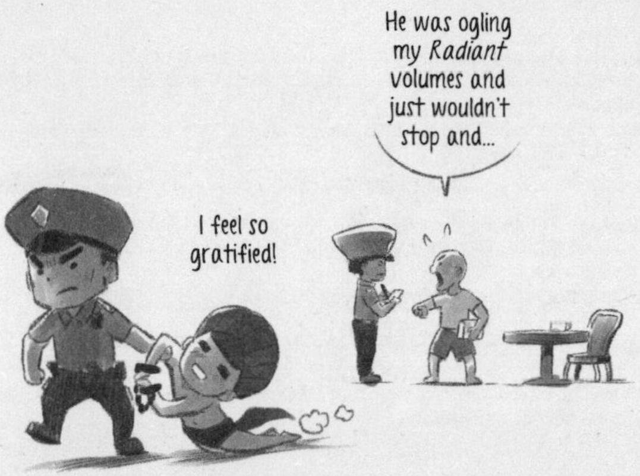
He was ogling my *Radiant* volumes and just wouldn't stop and...
I feel so gratified!

Sometimes I come across people reading *Radiant* on the street, in a library, on the subway...and it's so gratifying!! The other day, I was passing by a café terrace, and *bam*! I see four volumes of *Radiant* laid out on the table. Quadruple-y gratifying.

So that's when I give out a little "Oh!" and the guy, looking at my suspicious face, picks up his volumes and, annoyed, says, "Hey! Don't touch them! These are mine!!" He thought I was going to steal them from him. The fact that he was protecting his *Radiant* volumes like that really sparked a lot of joy in me. Go figure. Quintuple-y gratifying.

If you ever see some guy looking over your shoulder while you're reading this book, please do forgive him... It might just be me. Or not.

—Tony Valente

Tony Valente began working as a comic artist with the series *The Four Princes of Ganahan*, written by Raphael Drommelschlager. He then launched a new three-volume project, *Hana Attori*, after which he produced *S.P.E.E.D. Angels*, a series written by Didier Tarquin and colored by Pop.

In preparation for *Radiant*, he relocated to Canada. Through confronting caribou and grizzlies, he gained the wherewithal to train in obscure manga techniques. Since then, his eating habits have changed, his lifestyle became completely different and even his singing voice has changed a bit!

RADIANT VOL. 12
VIZ MEDIA Manga Edition

STORY AND ART BY **TONY VALENTE**
ASSISTANT ARTIST **TPIU**

Translation/(´・∀・`)ｻﾌﾟ?
Touch-Up Art & Lettering/**Erika Terriquez**
Design/**Julian [JR] Robinson**
Editor/**Gary Leach**

Published by arrangement with MEDIATOON LICENSING/Ankama.
RADIANT T12
© ANKAMA EDITIONS 2019, by Tony Valente
All rights reserved

Printed in the U.S.A.

Published by VIZ Media, LLC
P.O. Box 77010
San Francisco, CA 94107

10 9 8 7 6 5 4 3 2 1
First printing, July 2020

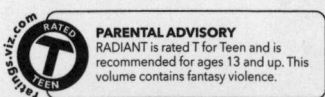

YOU'RE READING THE WRONG WAY

RADIANT reads from right to left, starting in the upper-right corner, meaning that action, sound effects, and word-balloon order are completely reversed from English order.

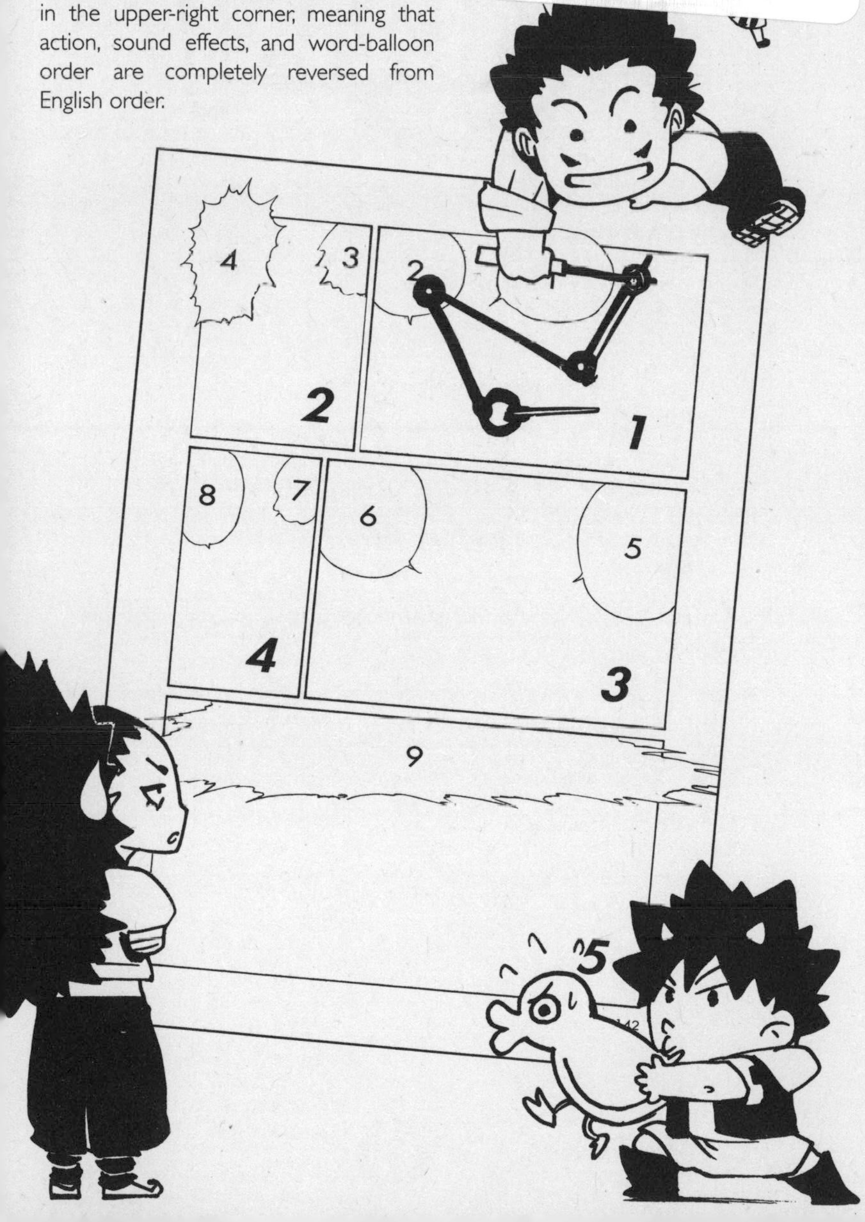

1
2
2
3
4
3
5
6
4
7
8
9
5